Log-Linear
Models for
Event
Histories

Advanced Quantitative Techniques
in the Social Sciences

Introduction to the Series:
Advanced Quantitative Techniques in the Social Sciences

The volumes in the new AQTSS series consider quantitative techniques that have proven to be or that promise to be particularly useful for application in the social sciences. In many cases, these techniques will be advanced, not necessarily because they require complicated mathematics, but because they build on more elementary techniques such as regression or descriptive statistics. As a consequence, we expect our readers to have a more thorough knowledge of modern statistics than is required for the volumes in the QASS series. The AQTSS series is aimed at graduate students in quantitative methods specializations, at statisticians with social science interests, and at quantitative social scientists who want to be informed about modern developments in data analysis.

The AQTSS series aims to be interdisciplinary. We prefer to publish volumes about techniques that can be used, and have been used, in different social disciplines and, in some cases, in the behavioral, medical, or physical sciences. This also is reflected in the composition of our editorial board. The board consists of scientists from many different disciplines, all of whom are involved in creating the Department of Statistics at UCLA.

The series also seeks to be practical. Although a good mathematical background may be essential to understand some aspects of the techniques, we insist on an emphasis on real data, real social science problems, and real analyses. This means that both data structures and computer packages get a great deal of emphasis in the volumes of this series.

Statistics present us with a series of techniques that ransfrm raw data into a form that is easier to understand and to communicste or, to put it differently, that make it easy for the data to tell their story. In order to use the results of a statistical analysis in a responsible way, it is necessary to understand the implementations and the sensitivities of the transformation that are applied. We hope that the volumes in this new series contribute to quantitative social science application that are both persuasive and precise.

Jan de Leeuw, UCLA
Richard Berk, UCLA

For information:

SAGE Publications, Inc.
2455 Teller Road
Thousand Oaks, California 91320
E-mail: order@sagepub.com

SAGE Publications Ltd.
6 Bonhill Street
London EC2A 4PU
United Kingdom

SAGE Publications India Pvt. Ltd.
M-32 Market
Greater Kailash I
New Delhi 110 048 India

Printed in the United States of America

The first edition of this book was published in 1996 by
Tilburg University Press, Tilburg, The Netherlands.

Library of Congress Cataloging-in-Publication Data

Vermunt, Jeroen K.
    Log-linear models for event histories / by Jeroen K. Vermunt.
        p.   cm. — (Advanced quantitative techniques in the social
    sciences; vol. 8)
        Includes bibliographical references (p.   ) and index.
        ISBN 0-7619-0937-0 (cloth)
        1. Log-linear models. 2. Longitudinal method—Statistical
    methods. I. Title. II. Series. III. Series: Advanced
    quantitative techniques in the social sciences; 8.
    QA278.V483 1997
    519.5'35—dc21   97-4805

This book is printed on acid-free paper.

97   98   99   00   01   02   03   10   9   8   7   6   5   4   3   2   1

Acquiring Editor:	C. Deborah Laughton
Editorial Assistant:	Eileen Carr
Production Editor:	Diana E. Axelsen
Typesetter:	Technical Typesetting, Inc.
Print Buyer:	Anna Chin

Log-Linear Models for Event Histories

Jeroen K. Vermunt

Advanced Quantitative Techniques
in the Social Sciences Series

8

SAGE Publications
International Educational and Professional Publisher
Thousand Oaks   London   New Delhi

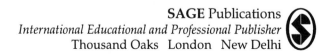

Contents

QA
278
.V483
1997

Series Editor's Introduction

The **Advanced Quantitative Techniques** series has already published a number of books on models and techniques for categorical data analysis. These can all be thought of as extensions of the classical log-linear analysis model studied in great detail by Goodman, Clogg, Haberman, Bishop, Andersen, and many others.

Clogg and Shihadeh studied extensions to ordinal variables, with an emphasis on low-dimensional tables. Heinen compared latent class models and latent trait models with discrete outcomes. The latent variables are used to describe the relationships in data structures which can be quite high-dimensional. In this new volume in the series Vermunt takes the generalizations yet another step further. Categorical data are now studied in time, and a framework is developed which includes event history analysis and log-linear analysis with latent variables, and eventually combines the two.

Social scientists have realized for many years that event history analysis, in which individuals move in time through a finite number of states, is a very useful tool to describe their data. Initially, simple Markov chains were studied by Goodman, Anderson, and Billingsley. These simple models could be studied with multinomial (log-linear) methods, but they were rather limited in the types of data they could handle. In the 1970s, event history analysis got a huge impetus from the work of Hannan, Tuma, Singer, and others, who showed how to deal with continuous time. Unfortunately, much of this work was incomprehensible to practicing social scientists, because a fairly high level of mathematical sophistication is required to deal with continuous-time processes in a rigorous manner.

It took about ten years to translate the theoretical results, which are intimately linked with work of Cox, Aalen and Gill in survival analysis, into practical procedures that appealed to social scientists. Allison, for instance, showed the intimate link with logistic regression. Vermunt discusses event history analysis in a more general framework, and relates it throughout the discussion with log-linear models with or without latent variables. Discussing something which is relatively new and complicated by relating it along the way to things that are more simple and more familiar is a great didactic strategy, and in this book it works really well.

The book is quite comprehensive. There are long introductions to log-linear analysis and to latent variable models, and the appendixes cover computational procedures and available software in great detail. event history analysis is discussed in its basic form in Chapter 4, which extends Chapter 2 on log-linear analysis. Chapter 5 on event history analysis with latent variables and missing data extends Chapter 3 on latent variables and missing data in a similar way. The steps from the simple models to the more complicated ones are clearly described, and thus the reader can start at a relatively low level and proceed slowly to the very general class of models described in later chapters.

One of the major advantages of anchoring event history analysis in log-linear, logit, and latent variable methods is that not much mathematics is required to follow the discussion. Most of the material is written in a language that is by now familiar to many social scientists. Although the book is basically Vermunt's dissertation, unlike most other dissertations that I know of, it could actually be used quite easily as the basis of a graduate course. It is a fine textbook, and at the same time an excellent research monograph. This is a rare combination, but a very valuable one. We hope the group at Tilburg University will produce more examples of this type of book in the future.

JAN DE LEEUW
Professor and Director, Interdivisional Program in Statistics, UCLA

Acknowledgements

Many persons have contributed directly or indirectly to this book. First of all, I would like to thank my dissertation advisors, Jacques Hagenaars and Frans Willekens, as well as Marcel Croon for their critical comments which helped enormously. I would also like to thank Ruud Luijkx, Wicher Bergsma, Ton Heinen, Francesca Bassi, Werner Georg, Rolf Langeheine, and Ulf Böckenholt for the interesting discussions we had on new applications and extensions of log-linear models. These discussions form the basis of many of the ideas presented in this book. Mark Vitullo and Hildegard Penn did an excellent job in editing the text. I am very grateful for the financial support that I received from the Work and Organization Research Centre. And last but not least, I would like to thank my colleagues at the Methodology Department of the Faculty of Social and Behavioral Sciences at Tilburg University for giving me the opportunity to write this thesis.

To Harriet, Lisa,
Kees, Tuur, and Daan

1 Introduction

Since many theories in the social sciences deal with processes of social change, increasing attention is being given to the collection of longitudinal data and to the development of methods for analyzing longitudinal data. This book discusses techniques for analyzing a particular type of longitudinal data: event history data. More precisely, it provides a general framework for dealing with missing data problems in the analysis of event history data. These missing data problems involve unobserved heterogeneity, measurement error, and partial nonresponse. An important characteristic of the approach that is presented is that it is based on using models which were originally developed in the field of categorical data analysis.

In this introductory chapter, attention is given to the difference between event history data and other types of longitudinal data, to methods for analyzing event history data and their relationship with log-linear models, and to the three above-mentioned missing data problems. In addition, an outline of the book is presented.

1

1.1. Types of longitudinal data

Longitudinal data can be classified according to the type of information that it provides about change and, as a result, the type of research
questions that can be answered using it. The term change refers to a
change that occurs in an individual's scores on the variables of interest.
Other terms which can be used interchangeably with change are transition and event.

The least informative type of longitudinal data is *time-series or trend
data*. Time series are obtained by collecting the same type of information at different points in time. But unlike other types of longitudinal
data, there is a different sample of individuals at each point in time.
As a result, there is no information on individual changes, transitions,
or events, but only on net or aggregate changes in the population to be
studied.

Panel data is obtained by investigating the same sample units at different points in time. Panel data, thus, provides information on the values
of the variables of interest at particular points in time. What is observed
is whether the value of a variable on one occasion equals its value on
the previous occasion. If these values are not equal, it is certain that
the individual concerned experienced at least one transition or event.
On the other hand, if the two values are equal, there may or there may
not have occurred events between the two points in time. As a result,
panel data not only provides information on net changes, but also partial
information on gross or individual changes.

Two types of longitudinal data which are more informative than panel
data but still less informative than event history data are *event-count
data* and *event-sequence data* (Tuma and Hannan, 1984:19-20). Event-
count data records the number of changes, transitions, or events that
occur in a particular time interval, while event-sequence data records the
sequence of values of the dependent variable of interest for each sample
member. Event-count data and event-sequence data can, for instance, be
collected by means of a panel design in which the number and sequence
of events between the previous and the current occasion is requested
retrospectively.

Event history data is even more informative since it contains information on the timing of changes, transitions, or events. In other words,
event history data records the number of events, their sequence, and the
time at which they occur. In experimental settings, it is generally possible
to observe the subjects involved in the study continuously, which makes
recording the timing of events a rather straightforward procedure. In

nonexperimental studies, it is more difficult to collect event history data. Sometimes, event history data can be obtained from archives. Another possibility is to gather data on the timing of events retrospectively. The best known method is the life-history calendar which is a one-shot survey in which information on different types of life-course events are collected simultaneously (Freedman et al., 1988). Another method for collecting event history data retrospectively is by means of a panel design in which individuals are questioned about the timing of events which occurred between subsequent occasions.

1.2. Methods for analyzing event history data

The general purpose of the analysis of event history data is to explain why certain individuals are at a higher risk of experiencing the event(s) of interest than others. This can be accomplished by using special types of methods which, depending on the field in which they are applied, are called failure-time models, life-time models, survival models, transition-rate models, response-time models, event history models, duration models, or hazard models. Here, the terms event history model and hazard model are used interchangeably.

In hazard models, the risk of experiencing an event within a short time interval is regressed on a set of covariates. Two special features distinguish hazard models or event history models from other types of regression models: they make it possible to include censored observations in the analysis and to use time-varying explanatory variables. An observation is called censored if the event of interest did not occur before the end of the observation period. Censoring is, in fact, a form of partially missing information: On the one hand, it is known that the event did not occur during a given period of time, but, on the other hand, the time at which the event occurred is unknown. Time-varying covariates are covariates that may change their value during the observation period. The possibility of including covariates which may change their value in the regression model makes it possible to perform a truly dynamic analysis.

Event history models can be classified according to different types of dimensions. The first distinction that can be made is based on the nature of the dependent variable which is being modelled. The dependent variable may be either discrete or continuous. While most of the work which has been done in the field of event history analysis involves models for discrete dependent variables, there are also methods for analyzing changes in continuous dependent variables (Tuma and Hannan, 1984: Part 3; Allison, 1990). This book deals solely with models for discrete dependent variables.

The category of event history models for discrete dependent variables can be subdivided into two subgroups: continuous-time methods and discrete-time methods. As the terms indicate, the time variable is assumed to be continuous in continuous-time methods, while in discrete-time methods it is assumed to be discrete. In other words, the former type of methods assume that events may occur at any point in time, while the latter type of methods assume that changes occur at certain discrete time points. The category of continuous-time methods can be subdivided on the basis of whether the time dependence of the process being studied is parameterized. In parametric models, the time dependence is assumed to have a particular functional form, while in the semi-parametric model proposed by Cox (1972), the time dependence remains unspecified, which means that it is not restricted at all. In discrete-time models, it is possible to restrict the time dependence as in parametric models or to leave it unspecified as in Cox's model. This does not, however, lead to fundamentally different types of models. Therefore, it suffices to distinguish the following three main types of hazard models: parametric continuous-time models, the Cox semi-parametric continuous-time model, and discrete-time models.

The simplest situation in the analysis of event history data is that in which there is only one type of event and each individual can experience only one event, in other words, if there is a single nonrepeatable event. As is demonstrated in Chapter 4, methods for analyzing event history data can easily be adapted to deal with more complex situations, that is, situations in which there are different types of events and in which individuals may experience more than one event.

An important feature in the context of this book is the fact that hazard models are strongly related to log-linear models for frequency tables. Both the piecewise exponential survival model, which is a parametric continuous-time model in which the risk of experiencing an event is assumed to be constant within time intervals, and the Cox semi-parametric model can be shown to be equivalent to log-linear models for the analysis of rates, also known as log-rate models (Holford, 1980; Laird and Oliver, 1981). In addition, it can be demonstrated that the discrete-time logit model, which is the most frequently used discrete-time method, is a log-linear model in the form of the modified path model proposed by Goodman (1973).

1.3. Missing data problems

This book deals with three types of missing data problems that may occur in event history analysis: unobserved heterogeneity, measurement error, and partial nonresponse.

Unobserved heterogeneity means that particular variables which explain individual differences in the risk of experiencing the given event(s) being studied cannot be included as covariates in the hazard model because they are not observed. As is demonstrated in sections 4.6-4.8, unobserved heterogeneity can seriously distort the results of hazard models. It may lead to spurious time dependence, spurious time-covariate interactions, spurious time-varying covariate effects, spurious dependence between different types of events, and spurious dependence between the events experienced by the same observational unit.

Measurement error is another problem that is often conceptualized as a missing data problem. In latent structure models, an individual's true score on a variable which is measured erroneously is treated as a latent or unobserved variable. Measurement error may distort the results obtained from an event history model. Measurement error in the dependent variable generally leads to an overestimation of the amount of change that has occurred since not only true change but also measurement error is contributing to the observed change. Measurement error in the covariates used in an event history model leads to biased parameter estimates.

In the case of unobserved heterogeneity and in the case of measurement error, there are one or more variables which are completely unobserved, in other words, which are missing for all subjects involved in the study. There are, however, also situations in which information on particular variables is *partially missing*, that is, observed for some persons and not observed for others. As was mentioned above, censoring is a form of partially missing data on the dependent variable. Although hazard models are well suited for dealing with censored observations, the results are only valid if the censoring mechanism is independent of the process being studied. There may also be partially missing data in the covariates used in a hazard model. It is well known that excluding the observations with partially missing covariate values from the analysis may lead to biased parameter estimates if the missing data are not missing completely at random.

The best solution to these three missing data problems is to prevent them from occurring, that is, to observe all relevant explanatory variables, to measure all variables without error, and to prevent partially missing variables. If, however, there is missing data, the models which are used to analyze the data have to be adapted to minimize the distortion caused by missing information. In the field of event history modeling, a great deal of work has been done on methods for dealing with unobserved heterogeneity (Vaupel, Manton, and Stallard, 1979; Manton, Vaupel, and Stallard, 1981, 1986; Vaupel and Yashin, 1985; Heckman and Singer, 1982, 1984; Flinn and Heckman, 1982; Trussell and Richards, 1985; Mare, 1994; Guo and Rodriguez, 1994; Yamaguchi, 1986; Clayton and Cuzick, 1985; Heckman and Honore, 1989). In addition, some work has been dedicated to covariates which are measured with error (Gong, Whittemore, and Grosser, 1990) and to covariates which are subject to partial nonresponse (Schluchter and Jackson, 1989; Baker, 1994).

The book presents a general approach to missing data problems in event history analysis which is based on the similarities between log-linear models and event history models. Log-linear models which have been developed for dealing with unobserved heterogeneity, measurement error, and partial nonresponse are used to deal with the same kinds of missing data problems in event history analysis. The general approach incorporates some of the existing approaches as special cases, extends some existing approaches by making it possible to relax some of their basic assumptions, and leads to some new applications, such as event history models with latent or indirectly measured covariates and discrete-time logit models with measurement error in the dependent variable of interest.

The general model consists of two parts: a model for the covariates included in the model and a hazard model for the dependent process which is to be studied. The hazard model may be either a log-rate model or a discrete-time logit model. The model for the covariates is a modified path model proposed by Goodman (1973). It has been shown that it is possible to incorporate latent variables (Hagenaars, 1990) and partially observed variables (Fay, 1986; Baker and Laird, 1988) in a modified path model. Although the approach presented in this book is quite general, it has one important limitation, which results from it being based on the use of log-linear models: the missing information must be in categorical variables. This implies that a non-parametric approach to unobserved heterogeneity is used, that measurement error is dealt with by means of latent class models, and that partially missing information may only occur in the dependent variable and in covariates which are categorical.

1.4. An outline of this book

In addition to this introductory chapter, this book consists of four chapters. Chapter 2 discusses log-linear models. The main purpose of this chapter is to explain log-rate models, modified path models, and methods for obtaining maximum likelihood estimates of the parameters of log-linear models implemented in the ℓ*EM* program (Vermunt, 1993), which, in turn, can be used to estimate the general class of models discussed in this book. Chapter 3 shows how to incorporate variables with missing information in log-linear models. It presents latent class models, modified path models with latent variables, and log-linear models for nonresponse.

Chapter 4 deals with event history models. After the basic concepts and the main types of hazard models are presented, some more advanced topics are discussed, such as censoring, the use of time-varying covariates, models for competing risks, and multivariate hazard models. Chapter 5 presents the general approach for dealing with missing data problems in event history analysis. It shows how to combine the log-linear models with latent variables and partially missing data discussed in Chapter 3 with the log-rate and discrete-time logit models discussed in Chapter 4. In addition, it presents a number of applications of models with unobserved heterogeneity, measurement error in the dependent variable, measurement error in the covariates, partially missing information on the dependent variable, and partially observed covariate values.

2 Log-Linear Analysis

Log-linear analysis has become a widely used method for the analysis of multivariate frequency tables. There are several excellent textbooks which give extensive overviews of categorical data analysis by means of log-linear models (Bishop, Fienberg, and Holland, 1975; Goodman, 1978; Haberman, 1978, 1979; Fienberg, 1980; Agresti, 1990; Hagenaars, 1990). The aim of this chapter is not to provide another overview of the field of log-linear analysis, but to introduce those elements of log-linear modeling that are necessary to understand the main chapters of this book.

Three topics deserve special attention: estimation by means of iterative proportional fitting and uni-dimensional Newton, log-rate models, and log-linear path models. Understanding iterative proportional fitting and uni-dimensional Newton is important because these procedures for obtaining maximum likelihood estimates are implemented in the ℓEM program (Vermunt, 1993), which was used to estimate all models discussed in this book. Log-rate models are important because of their equivalence to piecewise exponential survival models, which are extensively discussed in Chapter 4. Lastly, it is important to thoroughly explain the less known log-linear path model for at least two reasons. First, the discrete-time event history model is a special case of this model. Sec-

8

ond, most of the log-linear models with missing data discussed in the following chapter are log-linear path models.

Some standard topics in log-linear modeling are introduced in the first four sections of this chapter. In sections 2.1, 2.2, 2.3, and 2.4, attention is paid to saturated and non-saturated hierarchical log-linear models, sampling distributions, estimation procedures, and model selection, respectively. Non-hierarchical log-linear models are discussed in section 2.5. Log-rate models or models with a weight vector are presented in section 2.6. Section 2.7 demonstrates how to incorporate non-linear terms in a log-linear model. 'Regression-analytic' variants of the standard log-linear model, i.e., the logit model and the multinomial response model, are presented in section 2.8. The final section deals with a 'path-analytic' causal model for categorical data, Goodman's modified path model (Goodman, 1973).

2.1. Hierarchical log-linear models

2.1.1. Saturated log-linear models

Suppose we have a frequency table formed by three categorical variables which are denoted by A, B, and C, with indices a, b, and c. The number of categories of A, B, and C is denoted by A^*, B^*, and C^*, respectively. Let m_{abc} be the expected frequency for the cell belonging to category a of A, b of B, and c of C. The saturated log-linear model for the three-way table ABC is given by

$$\log m_{abc} = u + u_a^A + u_b^B + u_c^C + u_{ab}^{AB} + u_{ac}^{AC} + u_{bc}^{BC} + u_{abc}^{ABC}. \quad [2.1]$$

The consequence of specifying a linear model for the log of m_{abc} is that a multiplicative model is obtained for m_{abc}, i.e.,[1]

$$m_{abc} = \exp\left(u + u_a^A + u_b^B + u_c^C + u_{ab}^{AB} + u_{ac}^{AC} + u_{bc}^{BC} + u_{abc}^{ABC}\right)$$
$$= \tau \tau_a^A \tau_b^B \tau_c^C \tau_{ab}^{AB} \tau_{ac}^{AC} \tau_{bc}^{BC} \tau_{abc}^{ABC}. \quad [2.2]$$

From Equations 2.1 and 2.2, it can be seen that the saturated model contains all interactions terms among A, B, and C. That is, no a priori

---

[1] It should be noted that the log transformation of m_{abc} is tractable because it restricts the expected frequencies to remain within the admissible range. However, there are also linear models for the analysis of categorical data (Grizzle, Starmer, and Koch, 1969). In addition, models have been proposed which combine linear and log-linear constraints on the expected frequencies (Haber and Brown, 1986; Lang and Agresti, 1994).

restrictions are imposed on the data. However, Equations 2.1 and 2.2 contain too many parameters to be identifiable. Given the values for the expected frequencies m_{abc}, there is not a unique solution for the u and τ parameters. Therefore, constraints must be imposed on the log-linear parameters to make them identifiable. One option is to use ANOVA-like constraints, namely,

$$\sum_a u_a^A = \sum_b u_b^B = \sum_c u_c^C = 0,$$

$$\sum_a u_{ab}^{AB} = \sum_b u_{ab}^{AB} = \sum_a u_{ac}^{AC} = \sum_c u_{ac}^{AC} = \sum_b u_{bc}^{BC} = \sum_c u_{bc}^{BC} = 0,$$

$$\sum_a u_{abc}^{ABC} = \sum_b u_{abc}^{ABC} = \sum_c u_{abc}^{ABC} = 0.$$

This parameterization in which every set of parameters sums to zero over each of its subscripts is called *effect coding*.[2] It is the most often used parameterization in applications of log-linear modeling. In effect coding, the u term denotes the grand mean of $\log m_{abc}$. The one-variable parameters u_a^A, u_b^B, and u_c^C indicate the relative number of cases at the various levels of A, B, and C as deviations from the mean. More precisely, they describe the partial skewness of a variable, that is, the skewness within the combined categories of the other variables. The two-variable interaction terms u_{ab}^{AB}, u_{ac}^{AC}, and u_{bc}^{BC} indicate the strength of the partial association between A and B, A and C, and B and C, respectively. The partial association can be interpreted as the mean association between two variables within the levels of the third variable. And finally, the three-factor interaction parameters u_{abc}^{ABC} indicate how much the conditional two-variable interactions differ from one another within the categories of the third variable. In other words, they describe the size of the discrepancy between the partial and the conditional associations.

Another method to identify the log-linear parameters involves fixing the parameters to zero for one category of A, B, and C, respectively. This parameterization, which is called dummy coding,[3] is often used in regression models with nominal regressors. Although the expected frequencies under both parameterizations are equal, the interpretation of the parameters is rather different. When effect coding is used, the pa-

---

[2] Other terms which are sometimes used for this parameterization are marginal coding and deviation from means parameterization (Willekens, 1994:123).

[3] This parameterization is sometimes also referred to as the partial method or reference cell parameterization (Willekens, 1994:123).

rameters must be interpreted in terms of deviations from the mean, while under dummy coding, they must interpreted in terms of deviations from the reference category (Alba, 1987; Long, 1984).

2.1.2. Non-saturated hierarchical log-linear models

As mentioned above, in a saturated log-linear model, all possible interaction terms are present. In other words, no a priori restrictions are imposed on the model parameters apart from the identifying restrictions. However, in most applications, the aim is to specify and test more parsimonious models, that is, models in which some a priori restrictions are imposed on the parameters. Log-linear models in which the parameters are restricted in some way are called non-saturated models. There are different kinds of restrictions that can be imposed on the log-linear parameters. One particular type of restriction leads to the family of hierarchical log-linear models. Hierarchical log-linear models are models in which the log-linear parameters are fixed to zero in such a way that when a particular interaction effect is included in the model, all lower-order effects containing a subset of the indices of the effect concerned must also be included in the model. For example, when a model contains the two-variable interaction term u_{ab}^{AB}, the one-variable terms u_a^A and u_b^B must be included too. The opposite applies as well. When a particular interaction term is fixed to zero, all higher-order interaction terms containing all its indices must also be fixed to zero. For example, if the partial association between A and B is assumed not to be present, the three-variable interaction u_{abc}^{ABC} must be fixed to zero as well. Applying this latter restriction to Equation 2.1 results in the following hierarchical log-linear model:

$$\log m_{abc} = u + u_a^A + u_b^B + u_c^C + u_{ac}^{AC} + u_{bc}^{BC}.$$

Another example of a hierarchical log-linear model is the independence model

$$\log m_{abc} = u + u_a^A + u_b^B + u_c^C.$$

Hierarchical log-linear models are the most popular log-linear models because, in most applications, it is not meaningful to include higher-order interaction terms without including the lower-order interaction terms concerned (Agresti, 1990:144). Another reason is that it is relatively easy to estimate the parameters of hierarchical log-linear models because of the existence of simple sufficient statistics (Bishop, Fienberg, and Holland, 1975). The estimation of the parameters of hierarchical log-linear models will be discussed in the next subsections.

2.2. Sampling distributions

The above-mentioned log-linear models for the three-way frequency table ABC are population models. However, since generally only a sample of the population is observed, the parameters of a log-linear model that is postulated for the population have to be estimated using the observed cell counts n_{abc}. The parameters of log-linear models are usually estimated by means of the maximum likelihood method (ML). Some alternative methods are weighted least squares (Grizzle, Starmer and Koch (1969), minimum chi-square (Berkson, 1968), and minimum discrimination information (Berkson, 1972; Darroch and Ratcliff, 1972). A common element in these methods is that the unknown parameters are found by maximizing (or minimizing) some criterion or object function. The maximum likelihood method estimates for the expected cell frequencies, $\hat{m}$, and the parameters of a log-linear model are obtained by maximization of the likelihood function. To determine the likelihood function, it is necessary to make assumptions about the sampling distribution of the observed cell counts of a contingency table. In log-linear analysis, usually a Poisson distribution, a multinomial, or a product-multinomial distribution is assumed (Bishop, Fienberg and Holland, 1975:62-64; Agresti, 1990:36-39).

The Poisson sampling scheme assumes each observed cell count, n_{abc}, to be an independent Poisson random variable with one single parameter, the mean m_{abc}. This sampling scheme may be used for counting events which occur independently of each other in time or in space. The probability density function for the observed frequency in cell (a, b, c) is

$$f\left(n_{abc} \mid m_{abc}\right) = \frac{\exp\left(-m_{abc}\right)\left(m_{abc}\right)^{n_{abc}}}{n_{abc}!}.$$

But, in most applications in social science, it may not be appropriate to use a Poisson sampling scheme because under that sampling scheme, the sample size N is assumed to be a Poisson random variable as well. This is generally not a realistic assumption in social research since the sample size is fixed by the sample design. However, given the total sample size N, the n_{abc} no longer have a Poisson distribution but a multinomial distribution with parameters N and π_{abc}, where π_{abc} (m_{abc}/N) denotes the probability of belonging to cell (a, b, c) (Bishop, Fienberg and Holland, 1975:63; Agresti, 1990:37). The multinomial probability density for the observed cells in table ABC is

$$f(n_{abc} | N; \pi_{abc}) = \left(\frac{N!}{\prod_{abc} n_{abc}!} \right) \prod_{abc} (\pi_{abc})^{n_{abc}},$$

where the indices a, b, and c of $\prod$ indicate that the product is over all cell entries.

The multinomial density function can be applied when a simple random sample is taken from a population with fixed N. However, it is also possible to condition on the observed marginal distribution of one or more variables included in the model instead of on the total sample size N. This may be useful when the observed cell counts of table ABC are obtained with a stratified sample. For example, when a simple random sample is taken within levels of A, it may be assumed that the observed frequencies in every stratum come from A^* independent multinomial distributions with parameters N_a ($= \sum_{bc} n_{abc}$) and $\pi_{bc|a}$. This sampling scheme is called independent multinomial sampling or product-multinomial sampling. In this case, the probability density function for the observed frequencies in the cells with $A = a$ is

$$f(n_{abc} | N_a; \pi_{abc}) = \left(\frac{N_a!}{\prod_{bc} n_{abc}!} \right) \prod_{bc} (\pi_{bc|a})^{n_{abc}}.$$

Independent multinomial sampling is especially useful for models in which a distinction is made between dependent and independent variables, such as in logit models and multinomial response models. In such cases, independent binomial or multinomial sampling is assumed for each of the joint categories of the independent variables.

The three sampling schemes discussed above are very strongly related: multinomial sampling is equivalent to Poisson sampling with fixed N, and product-multinomial sampling is equivalent to Poisson sampling with a marginal distribution which has been fixed by the sampling design or by the nature of the model to be estimated. The implication of this equivalence is that in maximum likelihood estimation, a likelihood function based on Poisson sampling may also be used in cases in which multinomial or product-multinomial sampling is assumed. However, when a Poisson likelihood is used instead of a multinomial or a product-multinomial likelihood, the log-linear effects belonging to the fixed margins have to be included in the model. For multinomial sampling, this implies including the u term, the grand mean, in the model.

In the above example of product-multinomial sampling with fixed margins A, u_a^A has to be included. Note that in such situations u and u_a^A are not random but fixed quantities.

2.3. Maximum likelihood estimation

After defining a particular log-linear model, estimates for the model parameters have to be obtained by means of the observed data and the assumptions implied by the model. Here, only maximum likelihood estimation will be used. The likelihood function is the 'probability' function of the data, i.e., the observed frequencies n_{abc}, given the postulated sampling scheme and the values of the (unknown) parameters. Maximum likelihood estimates are those estimated parameter values that maximize the likelihood function, or, in other words, that maximize the 'probability' or the likelihood of occurrence of the observed data.

2.3.1. Sufficient statistic and likelihood equations

In this subsection, it is demonstrated how to obtain maximum likelihood estimates for the expected frequencies for a specific hierarchical log-linear model assuming a Poisson sampling scheme, which is the simplest sampling scheme. Moreover, it can easily be transformed into a multinomial or product-multinomial sampling scheme by including particular effects in the log-linear model. Assuming Poisson distributed data, the kernel of the log-likelihood function is

$$\log \mathcal{L} = \sum_{abc} (n_{abc} \log m_{abc} - m_{abc}), \qquad [2.3]$$

where the expected frequencies m_{abc} are a function of the unknown u parameters. The kernel of the likelihood function is that part of the likelihood function that depends on the parameters to be estimated. Therefore, it is the only part that has to be considered. Moreover, the log-likelihood function is presented instead of the likelihood function, since for most probability functions, including the Poisson and the multinomial, it is simpler to maximize the log-likelihood function than the likelihood function itself. Because the log of the likelihood function is a monotone function of it, this does not make any difference for the estimated parameters values.

Suppose we want to find maximum likelihood estimates for the parameters of the hierarchical log-linear model

$$\log m_{abc} = u + u_a^A + u_b^B + u_c^C + u_{ab}^{AB} + u_{bc}^{BC}. \qquad [2.4]$$

Substitution of Equation 2.4 into Equation 2.3 gives

$$\log \mathcal{L} = \sum_{abc} n_{abc} \left(u + u_a^A + u_b^B + u_c^C + u_{ab}^{AB} + u_{bc}^{BC} \right)$$

$$- \sum_{abc} \exp \left(u + u_a^A + u_b^B + u_c^C + u_{ab}^{AB} + u_{bc}^{BC} \right).$$

By collapsing the cells which contain the same u parameter, the log-likelihood function simplifies to

$$\log \mathcal{L} = n_{+++}u + \sum_a n_{a++}u_a^A + \sum_b n_{+b+}u_b^B + \sum_c n_{++c}u_c^C$$

$$+ \sum_{ab} n_{ab+}u_{ab}^{AB} + \sum_{bc} n_{+bc}u_{bc}^{BC}$$

$$- \sum_{abc} \exp \left(u + u_a^A + u_b^B + u_c^C + u_{ab}^{AB} + u_{bc}^{BC} \right), \qquad [2.5]$$

where a + is used as a subscript to denote that the observed frequencies have to be collapsed over the dimension concerned. It can now be seen that the observed marginals n_{+++}, n_{a++}, n_{+b+}, n_{++c}, n_{ab+}, and n_{+bc} contain all the information needed to estimate the unknown parameters. Because knowledge of the bivariate marginals AB and BC implies knowledge of n_{+++} and of the univariate marginals A, B, and C, n_{ab+} and n_{+bc} are the minimal sufficient statistics for the model given in Equation 2.4. These two marginals AB and BC contain all the information necessary for estimating the log-linear parameters of the model described in Equation 2.4.

In hierarchical log-linear models, the minimal sufficient statistics are always the marginals corresponding to the interaction terms of the highest order. For this reason, hierarchical log-linear models are mostly denoted by their minimal sufficient statistics (Goodman, 1978; Agresti, 1990:166-167; Hagenaars, 1990:50). The model given in Equation 2.4 may then be denoted as $\{AB, BC\}$, the independence model as $\{A, B, C\}$, and the saturated model as $\{ABC\}$.

To obtain maximum likelihood estimates for the model parameters of Equation 2.4, it is necessary to find the parameter values that maximize the log-likelihood function of Equation 2.5. This can be accomplished by differentiating the log-likelihood function with respect to the unknown parameters and setting the result equal to zero. Differentiating the log-likelihood function concerned with respect to the u parameters gives

$$\frac{\partial \log \mathcal{L}}{\partial u} = n_{+++} - \sum_{abc} m_{abc} = n_{+++} - m_{+++} \, ,$$

$$\frac{\partial \log \mathcal{L}}{\partial u_a^A} = n_{a++} - \sum_{bc} m_{abc} = n_{a++} - m_{a++} \, ,$$

$$\frac{\partial \log \mathcal{L}}{\partial u_b^B} = n_{+b+} - \sum_{ac} m_{abc} = n_{+b+} - m_{+b+} \, ,$$

$$\frac{\partial \log \mathcal{L}}{\partial u_c^C} = n_{++c} - \sum_{ab} m_{abc} = n_{++c} - m_{++c} \, ,$$

$$\frac{\partial \log \mathcal{L}}{\partial u_{ab}^{AB}} = n_{ab+} - \sum_{c} m_{abc} = n_{ab+} - m_{ab+} \, ,$$

$$\frac{\partial \log \mathcal{L}}{\partial u_{bc}^{BC}} = n_{+bc} - \sum_{a} m_{abc} = n_{a+c} - m_{a+c} \, .$$

Setting these derivatives to zero yields likelihood equations

$$n_{+++} = \hat{m}_{+++} \, ,$$

$$n_{a++} = \hat{m}_{a++} \, ,$$

$$n_{+b+} = \hat{m}_{+b+} \, ,$$

$$n_{++c} = \hat{m}_{++c} \, ,$$

$$n_{ab+} = \hat{m}_{ab+} \, , \qquad [2.6]$$

$$n_{+bc} = \hat{m}_{+bc} \, , \qquad [2.7]$$

where the $\hat{m}$'s denote estimates for the expected marginal cell count concerned. It can easily be seen that if the last two conditions are fulfilled, the other four are fulfilled as well. Therefore, Equations 2.6 and 2.7 determine the maximum likelihood estimates for the expected frequencies m_{abc} and the corresponding log-linear parameters. In other words, in the maximum likelihood solution, the table containing the estimated expected frequencies has the same marginals AB and BC as the table with the observed frequencies. The same holds for any other hierarchical log-linear model. In hierarchical log-linear models, the minimal sufficient statistics are equal to the marginals which have to be reproduced according to the specified model.

The other two sampling schemes mentioned above lead to the same likelihood equations because the additional conditions are automatically fulfilled. In the case of multinomial sampling, $\sum_{abc} \hat{m}_{abc}$ has to be equal to the total sample size N, or n_{+++}. Moreover, when multinomial sampling is assumed within the categories of A, $\sum_{bc} \hat{m}_{abc}$ has to be equal to n_{a++}. Thus, the inclusion of mean effect u in a log-linear model makes the estimates under a Poisson sampling scheme identical to the ones obtained under a multinomial sampling scheme. Furthermore, the inclusion of effect u_a^A causes Poisson sampling to be identical to independent multinomial sampling within categories of A (Bishop, Fienberg and Holland, 1975; Agresti, 1990).

2.3.2. The iterative proportional fitting algorithm

For some models, there are closed form solutions for the estimated expected frequencies $\hat{m}_{abc}$, that is, the conditions given in the likelihood function can be fulfilled without using an iterative method. Actually, all log-linear model which are decomposable graphical models have closed form solutions for the estimated expected frequencies (Whittaker, 1990: section 10.4; Wermuth and Lauritzen, 1983, 1990). Model $\{AB, BC\}$ is such a model because it implies the conditional independence of A and C given B. The estimated expected frequencies for this model are found by

$$\hat{m}_{abc} = \frac{\hat{m}_{ab+}\hat{m}_{+bc}}{\hat{m}_{+b+}} = \frac{n_{ab+}n_{+bc}}{n_{+b+}} \cdot$$

In the tradition of graphical modeling, where models have to be formulated in terms of conditional independence, it is sometimes also written as

$$\hat{m}_{abc} = n_{ab+}p_{c|b} = Np_{ab+}p_{c|b},$$

where p_{ab+} denotes the observed probability that $A = a$ and $B = b$, and $p_{c|b}$ the observed probability that $C = c$ given $B = b$. The independence model and the saturated model are other examples of models which have closed solutions. In the saturated model, $\hat{m}_{abc} = n_{abc}$.

When no closed form expression exists for $\hat{m}_{abc}$, maximum likelihood estimates for the expected cell counts can be found by means of the iterative proportional fitting algorithm (IPF) (Deming and Stephan, 1940; Fienberg 1970; Darroch and Ratcliff (1972). This a conceptually and computationally simple procedure. Its basic principle is that the marginal constraints from the likelihood equations are satisfied by adjusting the estimated expected frequencies. Often, this has to be done iteratively because there is no guarantee that after fulfilling one set of conditions, the previous restrictions are still satisfied. The iterations continue until convergence is reached, in other words, until the estimated expected frequencies do not change more than an arbitrary small constant. The IPF algorithm can also be applied to models for which closed formed expressions exist. In such cases, the algorithm converges after two iterations when the table which is being analyzed does not consist of more than six variables (Haberman, 1974:197).

Let $\hat{m}_{abc}^{(\nu)}$ denote the estimated expected frequencies after the νth IPF iteration. Before starting the first iteration, arbitrary starting values are needed for the log-linear parameters that are in the model. In most computer programs based on the IPF algorithm, the iterations are started with all the u parameters equal to zero, in other words, with all estimated expected frequencies $\hat{m}_{abc}^{(0)}$ equal to 1. It is important to note that the $\hat{m}_{abc}^{(0)}$ may not implicitly contain parameters that are not included in the model. For the model in Equation 2.4, every IPF iteration consists of the following two steps:

$$\hat{m}_{abc}^{(\nu)'} = \hat{m}_{abc}^{(\nu-1)} \frac{n_{ab+}}{\hat{m}_{ab+}^{(\nu-1)}} \, ,$$

$$\hat{m}_{abc}^{(\nu)} = \hat{m}_{abc}^{(\nu)'} \frac{n_{+bc}}{\hat{m}_{+bc}^{(\nu)'}} \, ,$$

where the $\hat{m}_{abc}^{(\nu)'}$ and $\hat{m}_{abc}^{(\nu)}$ denote the improved estimated expected frequencies after imposing the restrictions of Equations 2.6 and 2.7, respectively.

Obtaining the log-linear parameters If there are no zero-estimated expected frequencies, the log-linear parameters can easily be computed by means of the estimated expected frequencies.[4] When ANOVA-like constraints are imposed on the parameters, that is, when effect coding is

---

[4] It should be noted that if the observed table contains zero cell counts, maximum likelihood estimates for the log-linear parameters may not exist (Haberman, 1974; Agresti, 1990:245). Maximum likelihood estimates do not exist if there are zero counts in the sufficient marginal cells. However, even if all sufficient statistics are positive, maximum likelihood estimates may not exist. A well-known example occurs in the case of the no-three-variable interaction model for a 2-by-2-by-2 table. The parameters of this model cannot be estimated if there is more than one zero observed frequency (Santner and Duffy, 1989).

used to identify the parameters, the log-linear parameters can be computed in two different ways. One method consists of calculating the average of the log of the estimated expected frequencies given the values of the variables appearing in the u parameters concerned and, subsequently, subtracting the lower other effects (Bishop, Fienberg and Holland, 1975:16-17; Hagenaars, 1990:38). In the other method, the parameters are calculated by means of mean removal on the logs of the estimated expected frequencies (Laird and Olivier, 1981). The latter method is explained in more detail in Appendix A.1. The difference between the two methods is that in the former, the lower-order effects are removed after calculating the mean of the log $\hat{m}_{abc}$'s, while in the latter, an effect is directly removed from the estimated expected frequencies, or, in other words, before calculating the next set of parameters. Of course, both methods give identical values for the parameter estimates.[5]

Although the IPF algorithm is very attractive because of its simplicity and its computational efficiency, it has two serious disadvantages. In its simplest form, it can handle only hierarchical log-linear models and it does not supply standard errors for the parameter estimates.

2.4. Model selection

2.4.1. Testing goodness of fit

The goodness of fit of a postulated log-linear model can be assessed by comparing the observed frequencies, n, with the estimated expected frequencies, $\hat{m}$. For this purpose, usually two chi-square statistics are used: the likelihood-ratio statistic and the Pearson statistic. For a three-way table, the Pearson chi-square statistic equals

$$X^2 = \sum_{abc} \frac{(n_{abc} - \hat{m}_{abc})^2}{\hat{m}_{abc}} ,$$

and the likelihood-ratio chi-square statistic is

$$L^2 = 2 \sum_{abc} n_{abc} \log\left(\frac{n_{abc}}{\hat{m}_{abc}}\right) . \qquad [2.8]$$

---

[5] Another method, which is explained in more detail in section 2.6 and in Appendix A.2, is based on using the cumulated multipliers of the IPF iterations rather than the estimated expected frequencies.

The number of degrees of freedom for a particular model is

df = number of cells − number of independent u parameters.

When structural zeros occur in the estimated expected frequencies or when some parameters cannot be estimated as a result of zeros in the sufficient statistics, the calculation of the number of degrees of freedom is a bit more complicated (Clogg and Eliason, 1987). In such cases, df can be obtained by

df = number of non-zero fitted cells

− number of estimable u parameters.

Both chi-square statistics have asymptotic, or large sample, chi-square distributions when the postulated model is true. In the case of small sample sizes and sparse tables, the chi-square approximation will generally be poor (Read and Cressie, 1988; Agresti, 1990:246). Koehler and Larntz (1980) and Koehler (1986) showed that X^2 is valid with smaller sample sizes and sparser tables than L^2. They showed that the distribution of L^2 is usually poor when the sample size divided by the number of cells is less than 5 (Agresti, 1990:246). Therefore, when sparse tables are analyzed, it is best to use both chi-square statistics together. When X^2 and L^2 have almost the same value, it is more likely that both chi-square approximations are good. Otherwise, at least one of the two approximations is poor. Haberman (1978: section 5.3) showed that when tables are sparse, both chi-square approximations are not only poor, but they also have different distributions.[6]

Recently, Read and Cressie (1988) introduced a family of statistics,

$$\frac{2}{\lambda(\lambda+1)} \sum_{abc} n_{abc} \left[\left(\frac{n_{abc}}{\hat{m}_{abc}} \right)^{\lambda} - 1 \right],$$

called power divergence statistics. This is equal to X^2 for $\lambda = 1$ and L^2 as $\lambda \to 0$. Read and Cressie recommended the statistic with $\lambda = 2/3$, which they found less susceptible to effects of sparseness than X^2 and L^2 (Agresti, 1990:249). A simulation study of Collins et al. (1993) showed, however, that in the context of latent class analysis X^2 performs better than both the Read-Cressie and the L^2 statistic.

---

[6] An alternative approach is based on estimating the sampling distributions of the statistics concerned rather than using their asymtotic distributions. This can be done by bootstrap methods (Langeheine, Pannekoek, and Van de Pol, 1996). These computationally intensive methods are becoming more and more applicable as computers become faster.

2.4.2. Comparison of models

The likelihood-ratio chi-square statistic is actually a conditional test for the significance of the difference in the value of the log-likelihood function for two nested models. Two models are nested when the restricted model has to be obtained by only linearly restricting some parameters of the unrestricted model. Thus, the likelihood-ratio statistic can be used to test the significance of the additional free parameters in the unrestricted model, given that the unrestricted model is true in the population. Assuming multinomial sampling, L^2 can be written more generally as

$$L^2_{(r|u)} = \left(-2 \log \mathcal{L}_{(r)}\right) - \left(-2 \log \mathcal{L}_{(u)}\right)$$
$$= 2\, n_{abc} \log \hat{\pi}_{abc(u)} - 2\, n_{abc} \log \hat{\pi}_{abc(r)}$$
$$= 2\, n_{abc} \log \left(\frac{\hat{m}_{abc(u)}}{\hat{m}_{abc(r)}}\right),$$

where the subscript (u) refers to the unrestricted model and the subscript (r) to the restricted model. Note that in Equation 2.8, a particular model is tested against the completely unrestricted model, the saturated model. Therefore, in Equation 2.8, the estimated expected frequency in the numerator is the observed frequency n_{abc}. The $L^2_{(r|u)}$ statistic has a large sample chi-square distribution if the restricted model is approximately true. The approximation of the chi-square distribution may be good for conditional L^2 tests between non-saturated models even if the test against the saturated model is problematic, as in sparse tables (Haberman, 1977, 1978:325). The number of degrees of freedom in conditional tests equals the number of parameters which are fixed in the restricted model compared to the unrestricted model. The $L^2_{(r|u)}$ statistic can also be computed from the unconditional L^2 values of two nested models,

$$L^2_{(r|u)} = L^2_{(r)} - L^2_{(u)},$$

with

$$df_{(r|u)} = df_{(r)} - df_{(u)}.$$

Another approach to model selection is based on information theory.[7] The aim is not to detect the true model but the model that provides the most information about the real world. The best known information criteria are the Akaike information criterion (AIC) (Akaike, 1987) and the Bayesian information criterion (BIC) (Schwarz, 1978; Raftery, 1986, 1993). These two measures, which can be used to compare both nested and non-nested models, are defined as

$$AIC = -2 \log \mathcal{L} + 2 \, npar, \qquad [2.9]$$

$$BIC = -2 \log \mathcal{L} + (\log N) \, npar, \qquad [2.10]$$

where $npar$ denotes the number of unknown parameters. The lower the AIC or BIC, the better a particular model, or the more information it contains. It can be seen that the two information criteria give a different weight to the parsimony of a model. In the context of log-linear modeling, they are most often calculated as

$$AIC^* = L^2 - 2 \, df.$$

$$BIC^* = L^2 - \log N \, df.$$

These are, in fact, conditional information indices which compare the model of interest with the saturated model. For example, AIC^* can also be obtained by subtracting the value of AIC for the saturated model, $-2 \, n_{abc} \log(n_{abc}/N) + 2$(number of cells), from the value of AIC for the model concerned.

For more extended overviews on model testing and model selection in log-linear analysis, see Read and Cressie (1988), Agresti (1990: Chapter 7), and Hagenaars (1990:56-68).

2.5. Non-hierarchical log-linear models

So far, attention has been paid to only one special type of log-linear models, the hierarchical log-linear models. As demonstrated, hierarchical log-linear models are based on one particular type of restriction on the log-linear parameters. But, when the goal is to construct models which are as parsimonious as possible, the use of hierarchical log-linear models

---

[7] An interesting approach which is not discussed here are R-squared measures for categorical data based on different types of definitions of dispersion (Magidson, 1981; Gilula and Haberman, 1994).

is not always appropriate. To be able to impose other kinds of linear restrictions on the parameters, it is necessary to use more general kinds of log-linear models.

As demonstrated in Appendix B, log-linear models can also be defined in a much more general way by viewing them as a special case of the generalized linear models (GLM) (Nelder and Wedderburn, 1972; McCullagh and Nelder, 1983: Chapter 6, 1989). In its most general form, a log-linear model can be defined as

$$\log m_i = \sum_j \beta_j x_{ij}, \qquad [2.11]$$

where i denotes a cell entry, β_j is a particular u term, and x_{ij} is an element of the design matrix.

The design matrix provides us with a very flexible tool for specifying log-linear models with various restrictions on the parameters. Detailed discussions on the use of design matrices in log-linear analysis can be found in, for instance, Evers and Namboodiri (1977), Haberman (1978, 1979), and Rindskopf (1990).

2.5.1. Possible specifications of the design matrix

Suppose we want to specify the design matrix for an *hierarchical log-linear model* of the form $\{AB, BC\}$. Assume that A^*, B^*, and C^*, the number of categories of A, B, and C, are equal to 3, 3, and 4, respectively. Because in that case model $\{AB, BC\}$ has 18 independent parameters to be estimated, the design matrix will consist of 18 columns: 1 column for the mean effect u, 7 ($[A^* - 1] + [B^* - 1] + [C^* - 1]$) columns for the one-variable terms u_a^A, u_b^B, and u_c^C, and 10 ($[A^* - 1] * [B^* - 1] + [B^* - 1] * [C^* - 1]$) columns for the two-variable interaction terms u_{ab}^{AB} and u_{bc}^{BC}. The exact values of the cells of the design matrix, the x_{ij}, depend on the restrictions which are imposed to identify the parameters. Suppose, for instance, that column j refers to the one-variable term u_a^A and that the highest level of A, A^*, is used as the (arbitrary) reference category. In effect coding, the element of the design matrix corresponding to the ith cell, x_{ij}, will equal 1 if $A = a$, -1 if $A = A^*$, and otherwise 0. On the other hand, in dummy coding, x_{ij} would be 1 if $A = a$, and otherwise 0. The columns of the design matrix referring to the two-variable interaction terms can be obtained by multiplying the columns for the one-variable terms for the variables concerned (Evers and Namboodiri, 1977; Haberman, 1978).

The design matrix can also be used to specify all kinds of *non-hierarchical models*. Actually, by means of the design matrix, three kinds of linear restrictions can be imposed on the log-linear parameters: a parameter can be fixed to zero, a parameter can be specified to be equal to another parameter, and a parameter can be specified to be in a fixed ratio to another parameter.

The first kind of restriction, *fixing a parameter to zero*, can be accomplished by simply deleting the column of the design matrix referring to the effect concerned. Note that, in contrast to hierarchical log-linear models, parameters can be fixed to be equal to zero without the necessity of deleting the higher-order effects containing the same indices.

Imposing *equality restrictions* among parameters is likewise very simple. Equality restrictions can be imposed by adding up the columns of the design matrix which belong to the effects which are assumed to be equal. Suppose, for instance, that we want to specify a model with a symmetric association between the variables A and B, each having three categories. This implies that

$$u_{ab}^{AB} = u_{ba}^{AB} .$$

When using effect coding, the design matrix for the unrestricted effect u_{ab}^{AB} contains four columns, one for each of the parameters u_{11}^{AB}, u_{12}^{AB}, u_{21}^{AB}, u_{22}^{AB}. In terms of these four parameters, the symmetric association between A and B implies that u_{12}^{AB} is assumed to be equal to u_{21}^{AB}. This can be accomplished by summing the columns of the design matrix referring to these two effects.[8]

As already mentioned above, parameters can also be restricted to be in a *fixed ratio* to each other. This is especially useful when the variables concerned can be assumed to be measured on a interval level scale, with known scores for the different categories. Suppose, for instance, that we want to restrict the one-variable effect of variable A to be linear. Assume that the categories scores of A, denoted by a, are equidistant, that is, that they take values 1, 2, and 3. Retaining the effect coding scheme, a linear effect of A is obtained by

$$u_a^A = (a - \bar{a})u^A .$$

---

[8] Log-linear models with symmetric interaction terms may be used for various purposes. In longitudinal research, they may be applied to test the assumption of marginal homogeneity (Agresti, 1990:387-388; Hagenaars, 1990:156-162). Other applications of log-linear models with symmetric association parameters are Rasch models for dichotomous (Mellenbergh and Vijn, 1981; Kelderman, 1984) and polytomous items (Agresti, 1993) and for repeated categorical measurements (Conaway, 1989).

Here, $\bar{a}$ denotes the mean of the category scores of A, which in this case is 2. Moreover, u^A denotes the single parameter describing the one-variable term for A. It can be seen that the distance between the u_a^A parameters of adjacent categories of A is u^A. In terms of the design matrix, such a specification implies that instead of including $A^* - 1$ columns for the one-variable term for A, one column with scores $(a - \bar{a})$ has to be included.

These kinds of linear constraints can also be imposed on the bivariate interaction parameters of a log-linear model. The best known examples are linear-by-linear interaction terms (Haberman, 1979: Chapter 6) and row- or column-effect models (Goodman, 1979, 1984; Clogg, 1982; Clogg and Shihadeh, 1994). When specifying a linear-by-linear interaction term, it is assumed that the scores of the categories of both variables are known. Assuming equidistant scores for the categories of the variables A and B and retaining the effect coding scheme, the linear-by-linear interaction between A and B is given by

$$u_{ab}^{AB} = (a - \bar{a})(b - \bar{b})u^{AB}.$$

Using this specification, which is sometimes also called uniform association, the (partial) association between A and B is described by a single parameter instead of using $(A^* - 1)(B^* - 1)$ independent u_{ab}^{AB} parameters. As a result, the design matrix contains only one column for the interaction between A and B consisting of the scores $(a - \bar{a})(b - \bar{b})$.

A row association structure is obtained by assuming the column variable to be linear. When A is the row variable, a row association is defined as

$$u_{ab}^{AB} = (b - \bar{b})u_a^{AB}.$$

Note that for every value of A, there is a u_a^{AB} parameter. Actually, there are $(A^* - 1)$ independent row parameters. Therefore, the design matrix will contain $(A^* - 1)$ columns which are based on the scores $(b - \bar{b})$. The column association model is, in fact, identical to the row association model, only the roles of the column and row variable change.

2.5.2. Estimation

Finding maximum likelihood estimates for the parameters of non-hierarchical log-linear models is a bit more complicated than for the hierarchical log-linear model because the sufficient statistics are no longer equal to particular observed marginals. For GLMs, ML estimates for the model parameters may be obtained with Fisher's scoring algorithm (McCullagh and Nelder, 1983:31-34, 1989). If, as in the application used here, a canonical link is used, the scoring algorithm is equivalent to the *Newton-Raphson algorithm* (Agresti, 1990:114). The Newton-Raphson algorithm for obtaining maximum likelihood estimates for the parameters of the general log-linear model given in Equation 2.11 is explained in Appendix C.1.

The Newton-Raphson algorithm, which is implemented in, among others, the GLIM program and Haberman's FREQ program, has two strong points: it converges in a few iterations and it supplies standard deviations of the parameters as a by-product. However, when a model contains many parameters, the necessary computation and inversion of the Hessian matrix, the matrix of second-order derivatives to all parameters, is very time consuming. Another weak point of the Newton-Raphson algorithm is that it may become unstable when some estimated expected cell counts come in the neighborhood of zero as a result of the fact that a particular log-linear parameter goes to minus infinity.

An alternative to the Newton-Raphson algorithm is the *uni-dimensional Newton algorithm*. It differs from the multi-dimensional Newton algorithm in that it adjusts only one parameter at a time instead of adjusting them all simultaneously. In that sense, it resembles IPF. Instead of using the complete Hessian matrix, the uni-dimensional Newton algorithm uses only the diagonal element belonging to the parameter to be updated (Andersen, 1990; Jensen, Johansen and Lauritzen, 1991).

Goodman (1979) presented a slightly different version of the uni-dimensional Newton algorithm, which he used to estimate the uniform association models and the row and column association models discussed above (see also Clogg 1982). Goodman's algorithm, which is discussed in more detail in Appendix D.1, is also implemented in the ℓEM program (Vermunt, 1993). There it is used to estimate any log-linear model of the general form of Equation 2.11. Experience with the ℓEM program shows that Goodman's algorithm is very stable, even when 'bad' starting values are used, such as starting values of zero for all β parameters.

Generally, the uni-dimensional Newton algorithm needs more iterations to converge than the Newton-Raphson algorithm. But the difference in number of iterations depends greatly on the magnitude of the correlations among the parameters because that is the information which is disregarded by the uni-dimensional Newton algorithm. Experience with ℓEM shows that when the parameters are not too highly correlated, approximately two or three times as many iterations are needed by the uni-dimensional Newton algorithm. But, when the correlations within a particular set of parameters are high, many more iterations may be needed. Because the uni-dimensional Newton algorithm does not require computation and inversion of the complete Hessian matrix, each iteration costs very little computer time, even with many parameters.

In Appendix D.1, it is demonstrated that IPF is a special case of Goodman's version of the uni-dimensional Newton algorithm. Goodman's uni-dimensional Newton algorithm can be seen as a generalization of the IPF algorithm discussed in the context of hierarchical log-linear models. There is also another generalization of IPF, namely, the well known generalized iterative scaling algorithm developed by Darroch and Ratcliff (1972). However, the uni-dimensional Newton algorithm is much more flexible in that it does not force the values of the design matrix to be greater than or equal to zero. Moreover, for most problems, the uni-dimensional Newton algorithm converges in far fewer iterations than the generalized iterative scaling algorithm (Goodman, 1979).

2.6. Log-rate models or log-linear models with a weight vector

The general log-linear model discussed in the previous section can be extended to include an additional component, viz., a weight for each m_i denoted by z_i (Haberman, 1978:43-61; Laird and Olivier, 1981). These weights can be used to specify log-rate models, to perform a weighted analysis, to fix log-linear parameters to a particular value, and to analyze incomplete tables.

The log-linear model with a weight vector is given by

$$\log\left(\frac{m_i}{z_i}\right) = \sum_j \beta_j x_{ij}$$

which can also written as

$$\log m_i = \log z_i + \sum_j \beta_j x_{ij},$$

where the z_i are fixed a priori. Sometimes the vector with elements $\log z_i$ is also called the offset matrix.

The specification of a z_i for every cell of the contingency table can be used for many different purposes. One possible use of a weight vector is for specifying Poisson regression models for the number of events m_i in which one takes into account the population sizes or the length of the observation period. This leads to what is called a *log-rate model*, a model for rates instead of frequency counts (Haberman, 1978; Willekens and Shah, 1983; Clogg and Eliason, 1987). A rate is a count divided by some quantity, generally the size of the population exposed to some risk (Fleiss, 1981). As will be demonstrated in Chapter 4, log-rate models are equivalent to piecewise exponential survival models (Holford, 1976, 1980; Laird and Olivier, 1981).

The weight vector can also be used to correct for the sample design or for selection resulting from nonresponse (Clogg and Eliason, 1987, Agresti, 1990:198). In that case, the z_i must be set equal to the inverse of the sampling weights. The offset matrix may also be used *to incorporate fixed effects* in a log-linear model. This can be accomplished by adding the values of the β parameters which attain fixed values to the corresponding $\log z_i$'s. Lastly, the vector with weights may be used to analyze tables with structural zeros, sometimes also called *incomplete tables* (Fienberg, 1972; Haberman, 1979: Chapter 7). This can be accomplished by setting the z_i's for the cells which are structurally zero equal to zero.

Estimation Log-linear models with a weight vector can be estimated with the same estimation procedures used for the other log-linear models discussed so far. The GLIM program and Haberman's FREQ program, which are both based on the Newton-Raphson algorithm, allow the user to specify an offset matrix, or a weight vector. When using the IPF algorithm or the uni-dimensional Newton algorithm, the only necessary modification is that z_i must be used as the starting value for the estimated expected frequencies instead of starting with all $m_i^{(0)}$ equal to one. It should be noted that when using IPF, the log-linear parameters can no longer be calculated by means of the estimated expected frequencies, but rather they must be calculated by means of m_i/z_i. However, when particular z_i are equal to zero, an alternative procedure implemented in, for instance, the LOGLIN program (Olivier and Neff, 1976) and the ℓEM program (Vermunt, 1993) has to be used. This procedure which is based on using cumulated multipliers rather than estimated expected cell frequencies is discussed in Appendix A.2.

2.7. Models with log-multiplicative effects

Goodman's row-column associations II The log-linear model is one of the GLMs, that is, it is a linear model for the logs of the cell counts in a frequency table. However, extensions of the standard log-linear model have been proposed which imply the inclusion of non-linear terms, the best known example being the log-multiplicative row-column association models, also denoted as RC association models type II, developed by Goodman (1979, 1984) and Clogg (1982) (see also Clogg and Shihadeh, 1994). These row-column association models differ from the association models discussed in section 2.5 in that the row and column scores are not a priori fixed, but are treated as unknown parameters which have to be estimated as well. More precisely, a linear-by-linear interaction is assumed between two variables, given the unknown column and row scores.

Suppose we have a model for a three-way frequency table *ABC* containing log-multiplicative terms for the relationships between *A* and *B* and *B* and *C*. This gives the following log-multiplicative model:

$$\log m_{abc} = u + u_a^A + u_b^B + u_c^C + \mu_a^{AB}\phi^{AB}\mu_b^{AB} + \mu_b^{BC}\phi^{BC}\mu_c^{BC} .[2.12]$$

The ϕ parameters describe the strength of the association between the variables concerned. The μ's are the unknown scores for the categories of the variables concerned. As in standard log-linear models, identifying restrictions have to be imposed on the parameters μ. One possible set of identifying restrictions on the log-multiplicative parameters which was also used by Goodman (1979) is:

$$\sum_a \mu_a^{AB} = \sum_b \mu_b^{AB} = \sum_b \mu_b^{BC} = \sum_c \mu_c^{BC} = 0$$

$$\sum_a \left(\mu_a^{AB}\right)^2 = \sum_b \left(\mu_b^{AB}\right)^2 = \sum_b \left(\mu_b^{BC}\right)^2 = \sum_c \left(\mu_c^{BC}\right)^2 = 1 .$$

This gives row and column scores with a mean of zero and a sum of squares of one. More recently, alternative identifying restrictions have been proposed in which the μ's are weighted, for instance, by the observed margins (Becker and Clogg, 1989; Goodman, 1991).

On the basis of the model described in Equation 2.12, both more restricted models and less restricted models can be obtained. One possible restriction is to assume the row and column scores within a particular partial association to be equal, for instance, μ_a^{AB} equal μ_b^{AB} for all *a* equal to *b* (Goodman, 1979). Of course, this presupposes that the number of rows equals the number of columns. Such a restriction is often used in the analysis of mobility tables (Luijkx, 1994). It is also possible to assume that the scores for a particular variable are equal for different partial associations (Clogg, 1982), for example, $\mu_b^{AB} = \mu_b^{BC}$. Less restricted models may allow for different μ and/or ϕ parameters within the levels of some other variable (Clogg, 1982), for example, different values of μ_a^{AB}, μ_b^{AB}, or ϕ^{AB} within levels of C. To test whether the strength of the association between the variables father's occupation and son's occupation changes linearly with time, Luijkx (1994) specified models in which the ϕ parameters are a linear function of time (see also Wong, 1995).

A general class of log-multiplicative effects As mentioned above, the RC association models assume a linear-by-linear interaction in which the row and column scores are unknown. Xie (1992) demonstrated that the basic principle behind Goodman's RC association models, i.e., linearly restricting log-linear parameters with unknown scores for the linear terms, can be applied to any kind of log-linear parameter. He proposed a general class of log-multiplicative models in which higher-order interaction terms can be specified in a parsimonious way.[9] An example of such a model is

$$\log m_{abc} = u + u_a^A + u_b^B + u_c^C + u_{ab}^{AB} \phi_c^{AB} + u_{ac}^{AC} + u_{bc}^{BC} \, .$$

This model contains, apart from the one and two-variable interaction parameters for A, B, and C, a three-variable interaction term defined by the multiplicative factor ϕ_c^{AB}. As can be seen, this three-variable interaction term has a very specific form. Actually, the interaction term u_{ab}^{AB} is assumed to be equal among levels of C, except for a multiplicative scaling factor. In other words, the structure of the partial association AB is equal among levels of C, but the strength of the partial association AB differs among levels of C. This leads, of course, to a very parsimonious specification of higher-order interaction terms. In this case, only $C^* - 1$ instead of $(A^* - 1)(B^* - 1)(C^* - 1)$ additional parameters are used for the three-variable interaction term.

For the sake of simplicity, the interaction term u_{ab}^{AB} was not restricted. However, using Xie's approach, it is possible to restrict u_{ab}^{AB} as well. Xie (1992) gave examples of a symmetric association, a linear-by-linear association, and different kinds of row and column associations. In its

---

[9] Another type of generalization of the log-multiplicative models discussed above involves describing the (partial) association between two categorical variables by means of several sets of row and column scores (Goodman, 1986; Becker, 1989; Becker and Clogg, 1989; Clogg and Shihadeh, 1994: Chapter 5). These models are called RC(M) models, where the M refers to the dimensionality of the model, that is, to the number of sets of row and column scores that is used. RC(M) modeling is strongly related to correspondence analysis (Goodman, 1986, 1991; Gilula and Haberman, 1988; Van der Heijden, De Falguerolles, and De Leeuw, 1989) and other types of optimal scaling techniques (Van de Geer, 1993).

most general form, the log-multiplicative model proposed by Xie can be written as

$$\log m_i = \sum_k \left[\sum_{j_k} \beta_{j_k} x_{ij_k} \right] \phi_k x_{ik} \, ,$$

where k is the index for the multiplicative terms and j_k is the index for an effect belonging to the kth multiplicative term. Of course, by setting ϕ_k equal to one and also all x_{ik} equal to one, one can specify standard log-linear terms.

Estimation Both the log-multiplicative association models proposed by Goodman (1979) and Clogg (1982) and the log-multiplicative models proposed by Xie can be estimated by means of the ℓEM program (Vermunt, 1993), in which the version of the uni-dimensional Newton algorithm proposed by Goodman (1979) for estimating log-multiplicative models is implemented (see Appendix D.2). As explained in section 2.5, in this procedure, only one parameter is adjusted at a time, treating the other parameters as fixed.

Of course, log-multiplicative models can also be estimated by means of the Newton-Raphson algorithm. In that case, the complete matrix of second partial derivatives has to be computed and inverted every iteration. However, because of the strong dependencies among the parameters appearing in the same interaction term, the Newton-Raphson algorithm may have difficulties converging. This is a well known phenomenon when applying Newton-Raphson to solve non-linear equations. Recently, Haberman (1995) proposed a stabilized Newton-Raphson algorithm for obtaining maximum likelihood estimates in association models which overcomes these convergence problems.

It must be noted that, in contrast to standard log-linear models, the likelihood function for log-multiplicative models often contains local maxima. It is therefore advisable to estimate each model using different sets of starting values. When different sets of starting values yield the same parameter estimates, one can be more certain that the global maximum likelihood solution has been found.

2.8. Logit models and multinomial response models

In the log-linear models discussed so far, the relationships between the categorical variables are modelled without making a priori assumptions about their 'causal' ordering: no distinction is made between dependent and independent variables. However, one is often interested in predicting the value of a categorical response variable by means of explanatory variables. The logit model is such a 'regression analytic' model for a categorical dependent variable. In the standard logit model, a binary dependent variable is related to a set of categorical regressor variables (Goodman, 1972). When the response variable has more than 2 categories, the model is called a multinomial logit model or multinomial response model (Haberman, 1979: Chapter 6; Agresti, 1990: Chapter 9).

Suppose we have a response variable denoted by C and two categorical explanatory variables denoted by A and B. Moreover, assume that both A and B influence C, but that their effect is equal within levels of the other variable. In other words, it is assumed that there is no interaction between A and B with respect to their effect on C. This gives the following logistic model for the conditional probability of C given A and B, $\pi_{c|ab}$:

$$\pi_{c|ab} = \frac{\exp\left(u_c^C + u_{ac}^{AC} + u_{bc}^{BC}\right)}{\sum_c \exp\left(u_c^C + u_{ac}^{AC} + u_{bc}^{BC}\right)}.$$ [2.13]

When the response variable C is dichotomous, the logit can also be written as

$$\log\left(\frac{\pi_{1|ab}}{1 - \pi_{1|ab}}\right) = \log\left(\frac{\pi_{1|ab}}{\pi_{2|ab}}\right)$$
$$= (u_1^C - u_2^C) + (u_{a1}^{AC} - u_{a2}^{AC}) + (u_{b1}^{BC} - u_{b2}^{BC})$$
$$= w + w_a^A + w_b^B.$$

It should be noted that the logistic form of the model guarantees that the probabilities remain in the admissible interval between 0 and 1. Alternative transformations of $\pi_{1|ab}$ which also fulfill this requisite lead to the probit model and the complementary log-log model (McCullagh and Nelder, 1983:75-77, 1989; Willekens, 1994:25-32).[10]

---

[10] In the probit model, the conditional probabilities are transformed using the cumulative normal distribution, while in the complementary log-log model, the transformation of $\pi_{1|ab}$ would be $\log(-\log(1 - \pi_{1|ab}))$.

The logit model written as a log-linear model It has been shown that the logit model given in Equation 2.13 is equivalent to a log-linear model which includes the same u terms as the logit model concerned but also an effect that fixes the marginal distribution of the independent variables (Goodman, 1972, Haberman, 1978, Fienberg, 1980, Agresti, 1990:152-153). More precisely, it can be shown that the likelihood equations based on independent multinomial sampling are equivalent to the likelihood equations based on a Poisson model, given that condition

$$\sum_c m_{abc} = \sum_c n_{abc} \qquad [2.14]$$

is fulfilled. The proof that the product-multinomial likelihood is equivalent to the Poisson likelihood can be found in Appendix E.1.

Including the same parameters as those in the logit model given in Equation 2.13 and ensuring that the condition given in Equation 2.14 is fulfilled leads to the following log-linear model

$$\log m_{abc} = \alpha_{ab}^{AB} + u_c^C + u_{ac}^{AC} + u_{bc}^{BC}, \qquad [2.15]$$

where

$$\alpha_{ab}^{AB} = u + u_a^A + u_b^B + u_{ab}^{AB}.$$

In other words, the logit model of Equation 2.13 is equivalent to log-linear model $\{AB, AC, BC\}$ for the frequency table with observed counts n_{abc}. Note that when using this formulation of a logit model, it does not matter whether the response variables is dichotomous or not. If the response variables are polytomous, a log-linear or logit model of the form given in Equation 2.15 is sometimes also called a multinomial response model (Haberman, 1979: Chapter 6; Agresti, 1990: Chapter 9). According to Haberman (1979), in its most general form, the multinomial response model may be written as

$$\log m_{ik} = \alpha_k + \sum_j \beta_j x_{ijk}, \qquad [2.16]$$

where k is used as the index for the joint distribution of the independent variables and i as an index for the response variable.

Estimation The parameters of the multinomial response model can be estimated using the same algorithms used for the log-linear models discussed in the previous sections, i.e., IPF, Newton-Raphson, and uni-dimensional Newton. However, Haberman (1979) proposed a more efficient version of the Newton-Raphson algorithm for estimating multinomial response models. This is necessary because the number of α_k can become very large. In fact, Haberman's procedure uses a Newton-Raphson cycle to update the β_j parameters, followed by an IPF-like cycle to update the α_k parameters. The Newton-Raphson algorithm for multinomial response models which is implemented in, among others, Haberman's FREQ program and in SPSS can be found in Appendix C.2.

Logistic regression Up to now, the independent variables used in the logit model were assumed to be categorical. However, it is not a problem to generalize the logit model to also allow for continuous regressors. A model of the form given in Equation 2.13 containing continuous regressors gives the well known logistic regression model. But also Haberman's multinomial response model given in Equation 2.16 is equivalent to a multinomial logistic regression model (McFadden, 1974; Agresti, 1990:313), i.e.,

$$\pi_{i|k} = \frac{\exp\left(\sum_j \beta_j x_{ijk}\right)}{\sum_i \exp\left(\sum_j \beta_j x_{ijk}\right)} . \tag{2.17}$$

The index k now denotes a particular observation instead of a cell in the marginal distribution of the independent variables. So, a particular x_{ijk} contains the value of observation k on the independent variable j for response category i. Note that when k is an individual observation, the expected frequency m_{ik} appearing in Equation 2.16 is actually the probability that observation k gives response i, where the α_k parameters guarantee that the estimated response probabilities add up to one for every observation.

The equivalence between logistic regression analysis and logit analysis implies that programs for log-linear analysis which allow specification of a design matrix can also be used to estimate logistic regression models. It must, however, be noted that in that case the statistics L^2 and X^2 are not appropriate for testing fit of models. But, conditional likelihood ratio tests to compare models can still be performed (Haberman, 1974; Agresti, 1990).

2.9. Causal log-linear models

2.9.1. Goodman's modified path models

In the previous section, a 'regression analytic' extension of log-linear analysis, i.e., the logit model, was discussed. This section presents a 'path-analytic' extension of the logit model which was proposed by Goodman (1973). He proposed a log-linear model which takes a priori information on the causal ordering of the variables into account. The model, which he called a modified path analysis approach, consists of specifying a series of logit models for different marginal tables. As will be demonstrated below, this model has some similarities with chain independence graphical models for categorical data (Wermuth and Lauritzen, 1983, 1990).

Specifying a causal order Suppose we want to investigate the causal relationships between six categorical variables denoted by $A, B, C, D, E,$ and F. Figure 2.1 shows the assumed causal ordering of these variables, and the assumed relationships between these variables, where a pointed arrow indicates that variables are directly related to each other, and a 'knot' that there is a higher order interaction. The variables A, B, and C are exogenous variables. This means that neither their mutual causal order nor their mutual relationships are specified. The other variables are endogenous variables, where E is assumed to be posterior to D, and F is assumed to be posterior to E. From Figure 2.1, it can be seen that D is assumed to depend on A and on the interaction of B and C.

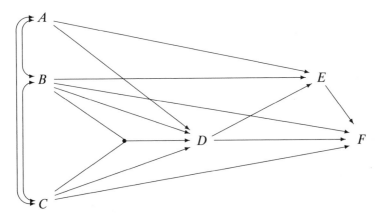

Figure 2.1. Modified path model

Moreover, E is assumed to depend on A, B, and D, and F on B, C, D, and E.

Let π_{abcdef} denote the probability that $A = a$, $B = b$, $C = c$, $D = d$, $E = e$, and $F = f$. the information on the causal ordering of the variables is used to decompose this joint probability into a product of marginal and conditional probabilities (Goodman, 1973, Wermuth and Lauritzen, 1983). In this case, π_{abcdef} can also be written as

$$\pi_{abcdef} = \pi_{abc}\,\pi_{d|abc}\,\pi_{e|abcd}\,\pi_{f|abcde}\,. \qquad [2.18]$$

This is a straightforward way to indicate that the value on a particular variable can only depend on the preceding variables and not on the posterior ones. For instance, E is assumed to depend only on the preceding variables A, B, C, and D, but not on the posterior variable F. Therefore, the probability that $E = e$ depends only on the values of A, B, C, and D, and not on the value of F. Note that this representation can only be used to specify recursive models. Recently, Mare and Winship (1991) presented a possible approach to non-recursive models for categorical data which requires the use of the latent variables techniques discussed in the next chapter.

Decomposing the joint probability π_{abcdef} into a set of marginal and conditional probabilities is only the first step in describing the causal relationships between the variables under study. Generally, the aim of an analysis is to reduce the number of parameters in some way, while the right-hand side of Equation (2.18) contains as many unknown (conditional) probabilities as observed cell frequencies. In other words, the model given in Equation 2.18 is a saturated model in which it is assumed that a particular dependent variable depends on all its posterior variables, including all the higher-order interaction terms. Generally, one is interested in more parsimonious specifications of the conditional probabilities in which it is possible to specify which variables influence each other and which do not.

Simple restrictions on probabilities The simplest way to specify more parsimonious models is to restrict directly the conditional probabilities appearing in Equation 2.18. Suppose that, as depicted in Figure 2.1, E depends on A, B, and D, but not on C. Because in that case $\pi_{e|abcd} = \pi_{e|abd}$, in Equation 2.18, $\pi_{e|abcd}$ can be replaced by $\pi_{e|abd}$. These kinds of restrictions are also applied in, for instance, discrete-time Markov models (Bishop, Fienberg and Holland, 1975: Chapter 7; Van de Pol and Langeheine, 1990). On the basis of the relationships depicted in

Figure 2.1, a more restricted version of the general Equation 2.18 would be

$$\pi_{abcdef} = \pi_{abc} \, \pi_{d|abc} \, \pi_{e|abd} \, \pi_{f|bcde} \, . \qquad [2.19]$$

However, as is shown below, this model is still not completely in agreement with Figure 2.1.

The above-mentioned method of restricting the general model given in Equation 2.18 is similar to the formulation of so-called *chain independence graphical models or block recursive graphical models* (Whittaker, 1990: section 3.6; Wermuth and Lauritzen, 1983, 1990). In a chain independence graph, the variables are grouped in blocks which can be completely ordered. The relationships between variables within one block are assumed to be symmetric, while the relationships between variables belonging to different blocks are assumed to be asymmetric. This is depicted graphically by undirected and direct edges (arrows), respectively. Like any other graphical model, a chain independence graphical model must be completely formulated in terms of conditional independence.

The restrictions which are imposed on conditional probabilities in Equation 2.19 are in agreement with the conditional independence rules of chain independence graphical models. For instance, E is assumed to be independent of C given A, B, and D, whereas the effects of A, B, and D on E are not restricted.

Specifying more restricted models by means of the procedure applied in Equation 2.19 has, however, one important disadvantage. The dependent variable must always be related to the joint independent variable. The variable E, for instance, depends on the joint variable ABD, that is, the variable which is obtained by combining the levels of A of B and D. Therefore, for every combination of A, B, and D, a separate parameter is included to describe the probability that $E = e$. Thus, when a particular variable is thought to influence the dependent variable concerned, all higher-order interactions with the other independent variables are automatically included in the model as well.

Logit parameterization Goodman's modified path analysis approach consists of using a log-linear or logit parameterization of the marginal and conditional probabilities appearing in Equation 2.18 rather than using the simple restrictions described above (Goodman, 1973). Since in these logit models it is possible to exclude certain higher-order interactions, such an approach leads to more parsimonious causal models for categorical data.[11] While only simple hierarchical log-linear models will be here used, the results presented apply to other kinds of log-linear models as well, including the log-multiplicative models discussed in section 2.7.

A system of logit models consistent with the path model depicted in Figure 2.1 leads to the following parameterization of the conditional probabilities appearing in Equation 2.18:

$$
\pi_{abc} = \frac{\exp\left(u_a^A + u_b^B + u_c^C + u_{ab}^{AB} + u_{ac}^{AC} + u_{bc}^{BC} + u_{abc}^{ABC}\right)}{\sum_{abc} \exp\left(u_a^A + u_b^B + u_c^C + u_{ab}^{AB} + u_{ac}^{AC} + u_{bc}^{BC} + u_{abc}^{ABC}\right)},
$$

$$
\pi_{d|abc} = \frac{\exp\left(u_d^D + u_{ad}^{AD} + u_{bd}^{BD} + u_{cd}^{CD} + u_{bcd}^{BCD}\right)}{\sum_{d} \exp\left(u_d^D + u_{ad}^{AD} + u_{bd}^{BD} + u_{cd}^{CD} + u_{bcd}^{BCD}\right)},
$$

$$
\pi_{e|abcd} = \frac{\exp\left(u_e^E + u_{ae}^{AE} + u_{be}^{BE} + u_{de}^{DE}\right)}{\sum_{e} \exp\left(u_e^E + u_{ae}^{AE} + u_{be}^{BE} + u_{de}^{DE}\right)},
$$

$$
\pi_{f|abcde} = \frac{\exp\left(u_f^F + u_{bf}^{BF} + u_{cf}^{CF} + u_{df}^{DF} + u_{ef}^{EF}\right)}{\sum_{f} \exp\left(u_f^F + u_{bf}^{BF} + u_{cf}^{CF} + u_{df}^{DF} + u_{ef}^{EF}\right)}.
$$

It can be seen that the model for the marginal distribution of the exogenous variables A, B, and C is a saturated model since it contains all the interaction terms among A, B, and C. It would also have been possible to specify a non-saturated model for relationships between the exogenous variables. In the next three equations, D, E, and F appear as dependent variables, respectively. Variable D depends on A, B, and C, and there is a three-variable interaction between B, C, and D. Moreover, E depends on A, B, and D, but there are no higher-order interactions between E and the independent variables. And finally, F depends on B, C, D, and E. It is clear that this recursive system of logit equations contains far fewer parameters than the restricted model given in Equation 2.19.

Since specifying a logit model for conditional probabilities is equivalent to specifying a log-linear model for a frequency table in which the marginal distribution of the independent variables is treated as fixed, the logit equations given above can also be written as log-linear models. For instance, the logit model for $\pi_{e|abcd}$ is equivalent to the log-linear logit

---

[11] An alternative approach proposed by Arminger (1996) is based on using probit rather than logit models for the endogenous variables in the path model.

model $\{ABCD, AE, BE, DE\}$ for (marginal) frequency table $ABCDE$, or

$$\log m_{abcde} = \alpha_{abcd}^{ABCD} + u_e^E + u_{ae}^{AE} + u_{be}^{BE} + u_{de}^{DE},$$

where m_{abcde} denotes an expected frequency in marginal table $ABCDE$. Moreover, α_{abcd}^{ABCD} denotes the effect which fixes the marginal distribution of the dependent variables.

Thus, specifying a causal log-linear model for a set of categorical variables can be simply accomplished by specifying separate log-linear models for different marginal tables or subtables. The marginal tables are formed by the variables used in the previous marginal table and the variable which appears as the dependent variable. In this case, log-linear or logit models have to be specified for tables ABC, $ABCD$, $ABCDE$, and $ABCDEF$. Goodman (1973) showed how to specify separate log-linear models for different marginal tables (see also Hagenaars, 1990:75-82). He subsequently showed how to obtain the overall expected frequencies with an equation similar to Equation 2.18. Note that the probabilities in Equation 2.18 can easily be obtained by means of the expected frequencies. For instance,

$$\pi_{e|abcd} = \frac{m_{abcde}}{\sum_e m_{abcde}}. \qquad [2.20]$$

A remark has to be made with respect to marginal tables for which the logit models or the equivalent log-linear models have to be specified given the assumed causal order among the variables. Suppose that, contrary to what is depicted in Figure 2.1, the variables E and F are assumed to be independent of one another given a person's scores on the posterior variables A, B, C, and D. In other words, it is assumed that there is no direct effect of E on F. In that case, the modified path model described above may also be specified in a slightly different manner, that is, it is possible to combine the logit models for D and E into a single modified path step with two dependent variables. This follows from the *collapsibility theorem* (Bishop, Fienberg, and Holland, 1975:47, Agresti, 1990:151-152) which states that if two variables are assumed to be conditionally independent, the sizes of their relationships with the remaining variables may be estimated in the table in which the other conditionally independent variable is included or not. Thus, if two variables are conditionally independent of one another, their relationships with the other variables may be estimated either in the same table or in separate tables.

The possibility of specifying the same model in alternative ways as a result of collapsibility is a feature that will be encountered several times in the next chapter which presents models with latent variables.

Combining the two kinds of restrictions Above, two different ways of restricting the conditional probabilities of a modified path model were presented, viz., assuming that a variable does not depend on one or more of the preceding variables and assuming that particular higher-order interaction terms are zero. But actually, it is simpler and computationally more efficient to combine the two ways of restricting the conditional probabilities because it often reduces the dimensionality of the tables one has to work with. More precisely, the model can be restricted as in Equation 2.19, and then the conditional probabilities appearing in this equation can be restricted via a logit parameterization. This leads to a (small) modification of the procedure proposed by Goodman.

Let us look at the model for dependent variable E. Because E does not depend on C, $\pi_{e|abcd}$ can be replaced by $\pi_{e|abd}$. Therefore, the log-linear restrictions which were imposed on $\pi_{e|abcd}$ can now be imposed directly on $\pi_{e|abd}$, or equivalently, the log-linear model that was specified for marginal table *ABCDE* can now be specified for marginal table *ABDE*. It should be noted that this result also follows from the collapsibility theorem. Since C and E are conditionally independent, the effects of A, B, and D on E may be estimated after collapsing the table over C. Specifying log-linear model $\{ABD, AE, BE, DE\}$ for marginal table *ABDE* gives

$$\log m_{abde} = \alpha_{abd}^{ABD} + u_e^E + u_{ae}^{AE} + u_{be}^{BE} + u_{de}^{DE} ,$$

where m_{abde} denotes an expected frequency in the marginal table *ABDE*. Thus, by imposing restrictions in two steps, the parameters can be estimated in the marginal table which includes only the independent variables which are really used. This two-step procedure may not only reduce the size of a problem, but it also has another important advantage: It prevents fitted zeros when the observed table contains zeros in the fixed margin *ABCD*, but not in the margin *ABD*.

Continuous exogenous variables So far, all variables included in the modified path model were assumed to be categorical, which is in agreement with the way Goodman presented his modified path model. However, it is also possible to include continuous exogenous variables in modified path models. In fact, this extension is analogous to what was discussed in the context of the logit model. When the variables A, B, and C are continuous rather than categorical, and when, as in Figure 2.1, D, E, and F are mutually ordered endogenous variables, a modified path model is obtained:

$$\pi_{def|x_{djk}x_{ejk}x_{fjk}} = \pi_{d|x_{djk}} \, \pi_{e|x_{ejk}d} \, \pi_{f|x_{fjk}de} \, ,$$

where x_{djk}, x_{ejk}, and x_{fjk} denote the observed value of person k on exogenous variable j for $D = d$, $E = e$, and $F = f$, respectively. In this case, the marginal distribution of the exogenous variables cannot be restricted by means of a log-linear model. The conditional probabilities can, of course, be restricted via a general logit model or logistic regression model of the form given in Equation 2.17.

2.9.2. Estimation and testing

Goodman (1973) demonstrated that the maximum likelihood estimates for the log-linear parameters and the expected frequencies in the various submodels of a modified path model can be estimated separately for each submodel. This results from the fact that when the parameters of the various submodels are distinct, the likelihood can be factorized into submodel specific parts which may be maximized separately:

$$
\begin{aligned}
\log \mathcal{L} &= \sum_{abcdef} n_{abcdef} \log \left(\pi_{abcdef} \right) , \\
&= \sum_{abc} n_{abc+++} \log \left(\pi_{abc} \right) + \sum_{abcd} n_{abcd++} \log \left(\pi_{d|abc} \right) \\
&\quad + \sum_{abcde} n_{abcde+} \log \left(\pi_{e|abcd} \right) + \sum_{abcde} n_{abcdef} \log \left(\pi_{f|abcde} \right) .
\end{aligned}
$$

In Appendix E.2 it is shown that the likelihood equation for a parameter of a modified path model is identical to the likelihood equation for a parameter of a logit model which has the same structure as the modified path step concerned.

The factorization of the likelihood makes it possible to estimate the parameters of a modified path model by means of standard programs for log-linear or logit analysis. The ℓEM program (Vermunt, 1993) has extra facilities for defining submodels without actually having to 'input' them. In ℓEM, the model specification consists of defining the subtables and the subtable-specific log-linear models. The log-linear models can be of the form of the general multinomial response model given in Equation

2.16. In addition, log-multiplicative interaction terms can be used in the modified path model. So, in fact, any kind of log-linear model can be specified for each subtable.

Restrictions across modified path steps As previously mentioned, the parameters of the different submodels can be estimated separately as long as they are distinct, but, when equality restrictions are imposed on parameters coming from different submodels, the parameters of the modified path model must be estimated simultaneously. In *ℓEM*, two types of equality restrictions can be imposed on parameters appearing in different modified path steps: Log-linear or logit parameters can be assumed to be equal, and (conditional) probabilities can be assumed to be equal. As demonstrated in Appendix E.3, the likelihood equation for a log-linear parameter appearing in different submodels is simply the sum of the contributions of the submodels concerned.

Equality and fixed-value restrictions on the (conditional) probabilities can be imposed by means of a rather simple procedure proposed by Goodman in the context of latent class analysis (Goodman, 1974b). Van de Pol and Langeheine (1990) demonstrated that Goodman's procedure can be used to constrain any type of conditional probability appearing in (mixed and latent) Markov models. They implemented the algorithm in their PANMARK program (Van de Pol, Langeheine, and De Jong, 1989). This procedure, which is described in Appendix F, consists of replacing the conditional probabilities which are assumed to be equal by their weighted mean. Mooijaart and Van der Heijden (1992) demonstrated, however, that Goodman's algorithm does not always work properly. They proposed estimating latent class models with equality and fixed-value restrictions on the probabilities by adding Lagrange multipliers to the log-likelihood function to be maximized. In *ℓEM*, the same type of solution is implemented for estimating modified path models with these types of constraints on the parameters (see Appendix F).

Testing The factorization of the contribution of the submodels to the log-likelihood function can also be used for testing. Goodman (1973) proposed testing the models separately by means of the likelihood-ratio chi-square statistic. The overall test for the complete model can be obtained by adding up the L^2 values and the degrees of freedom of the separate submodels. This is an important feature if the modified path model is estimated with standard programs for log-linear analysis.

This testing procedure can, however, only be applied when the model is specified in the way Goodman did, that is, when every subtable contains all the variables of the previous subtable and when no restrictions are imposed on the parameters across modified path steps. In other cases, the L^2 for the complete model has to be computed by means of the estimated probabilities $\hat{\pi}_{abcde}$.

2.9.3. Discrete-time Markov models

The modified path model is strongly related to the discrete-time Markov model. Actually, the discrete-time Markov model, which can be used for the analysis of multi-wave panel data, is a special case of the modified path model presented above (Vermunt, Langeheine, and Böckenholt, 1995). This can be demonstrated by means of an example. Suppose that S_l denotes the state occupied at time point l and that s_l denotes a category of S_l. For the sake of simplicity, it will be assumed that there are observations for only four points in time, that is, $1 \leq l \leq 4$. In a first-order Markov model, the state occupied at a $L = l$ is assumed to depend only on the state occupied at $L = l - 1$ (Anderson and Goodman, 1957; Bishop, Fienberg and Holland, 1975:261-267; Markus, 1979), or, in terms of our modified path model,

$$\pi_{s_1 s_2 s_3 s_4} = \pi_{s_1} \, \pi_{s_2|s_1} \, \pi_{s_3|s_2} \, \pi_{s_4|s_3} \, .$$

Especially in Markov models, it is important to be able to restrict the parameters to be equal across modified path steps. The most common set of restrictions,

$$\pi_{s_2|s_1} = \pi_{s_3|s_2} = \pi_{s_4|s_3} ,$$

gives rise to a stationary or time-homogeneous Markov model. These equality restrictions can also be imposed indirectly by restricting the log-linear parameters of different modified path steps to be equal, that is, by parameterizing

$$\pi_{s_l|s_{l-1}} = \frac{\exp\left(u_{s_l}^{S_l} + u_{s_{l-1}s_l}^{S_{l-1}S_l}\right)}{\sum_{s_l} \exp\left(u_{s_l}^{S_l} + u_{s_{l-1}s_l}^{S_{l-1}S_l}\right)} ,$$

and restricting

$$u_{s_2}^{S_2} = u_{s_3}^{S_3} = u_{s_4}^{S_4} ,$$
$$u_{s_1 s_2}^{S_1 S_2} = u_{s_2 s_3}^{S_2 S_3} = u_{s_3 s_4}^{S_3 S_4} \, .$$

Equivalently, higher-order Markov chain models can be specified. The only difference is that in such models, the value of S_l depends not only on S_{l-1}, but also on the state occupied on earlier occasions (Bishop, Fienberg and Holland, 1975:267-270; Van de Pol and Langeheine, 1990).

Covariates In most cases, Markov models are used only for descriptive purposes. However, with the modified path analysis approach, it is easy to incorporate explanatory variables into a Markov model.[12] Suppose, for instance, that one has three explanatory variables denoted by A, B, and C. Given a first-order Markov chain, the following modified path model is obtained:

$$\pi_{abcs_1s_2s_3s_4} = \pi_{abc} \, \pi_{s_1|abc} \, \pi_{s_2|abcs_1} \, \pi_{s_3|abcs_2} \, \pi_{s_4|abcs_3} \, .$$

This is also the way covariates can be incorporated into a Markov model using the PANMARK program (Van der Pol, Langeheine and De Jong, 1989). However, as demonstrated above, when using a modified path model, it is possible to use a logit parameterization for the conditional probabilities appearing in the Markov model with exogenous variables. Together with the possibility to restrict parameters across points in time, this results in rather flexible and parsimonious regression models for the states occupied at different points in time.[13]

Suppose that the variables A and B influence the state occupied at the first point in time, but that there is no three-variable interaction between A, B, and S_1. Furthermore, suppose that B influences the value of S_l and that C influences the size of the association between S_{l-1} and S_l. In other words, S_{l-1}, B, and C have direct effects on S_l, and there is a three-variable interaction between C, S_{l-1}, and S_l. This yields the

---

[12] Diggle, Liang, and Zeger (1994) distinguished three types of regression models for longitudinal data: marginal models, random effects models, and transition models. Markov models, as well as the event history models which are discussed in Chapter 4, belong to the family of transition models. Random effect models can be specified with the latent class models presented in the next chapter. For the estimation of marginal models, however, one needs methods which are outside the scope of this book, such as generalized estimating equations (GEE) (Liang and Zeger, 1986; Lipsitz, Laird, and Harrington, 1991) or the maximum likelihood methods proposed by Lang and Agresti (1994) and Bergsma (1997).

[13] Recently, Gilula and Haberman (1994) proposed a similar approach for analyzing categorical panel data, which they called conditional log-linear models.

following logit models for $\pi_{s_1|abc}$ and $\pi_{s_l|abcs_l}$, respectively:

$$\pi_{s_1|abc} = \frac{\exp\left(u_{s_1}^{S_1} + u_{as_1}^{AS_1} + u_{bs_1}^{BS_1}\right)}{\sum_{s_1} \exp\left(u_{s_1}^{S_1} + u_{as_1}^{AS_1} + u_{bs_1}^{BS_1}\right)},$$

$$\pi_{s_l|abcs_{l-1}} = \frac{\exp\left(u_{s_l}^{S_l} + u_{bs_l}^{BS_l} + u_{cs_l}^{CS_l} + u_{s_{l-1}s_l}^{S_{l-1}S_l} + u_{cs_{l-1}s_l}^{CS_{l-1}S_l}\right)}{\sum_{s_l} \exp\left(u_{s_l}^{S_l} + u_{bs_l}^{BS_l} + u_{cs_l}^{CS_l} + u_{s_{l-1}s_l}^{S_{l-1}S_l} + u_{cs_{l-1}s_l}^{CS_{l-1}S_l}\right)},$$

where $\pi_{s_1|abc}$ may be replaced by $\pi_{s_1|ab}$ and $\pi_{s_l|abcs_{l-1}}$ by $\pi_{s_l|bcs_{l-1}}$. This modified path model can be simplified by assuming the log-linear parameters for the transition probabilities to be time independent or, equivalently, by assuming $\pi_{s_l|bcs_{l-1}}$ does not depend on l. As will be demonstrated in section 4.8, parameterizing the discrete-time Markov model as a modified path model yields a model which is equivalent to a specific type of discrete-time event history model.

3 Log-Linear Analysis With Latent Variables and Missing Data

In the discussion of the various types of log-linear models in the previous chapter, it was implicitly assumed that the values of all variables used in the analysis were observed for all subjects being studied. In social research, however, it is often the case that some variables are completely or partially unobserved. This chapter extends the log-linear models discussed in the previous chapter so that they can be applied even if there are missing data.

Completely unobserved variables occur in *latent structure models*. These are models which can be used to *correct for measurement error* in observed variables (Bartholomew, 1987; Heinen, 1996). The categorical variant of the latent structure models, which was first proposed by Lazarsfeld (1950a, 1950b), is called *latent class analysis*. Latent structure models for data of different measurement levels have in common that they are all based on the assumption of local independence. The manifest variables which are used as indirect measures for the latent variable(s) are assumed to be mutually independent given the score on the latent variable concerned. In a latent class model, the existence of a categorical latent variable is postulated, which accounts for the relationships between a set of categorical manifest, or observed, variables.

The latent class model is a member of the family of *finite mixture models* (Everitt and Hand, 1981; Titterington, Smith, and Makov, 1985). In finite mixtures models, it is assumed that the population being studied is composed of a number of subpopulations which are not observed. In other words, the observed data is a mixture of the data of a finite number of subgroups, but it is not observed which subgroup a particular person belongs to. Furthermore, the parameters of the postulated model within these subpopulations are assumed to differ in some respect. The latent class model is a finite mixture model in which the observed variables are assumed to be mutually independent within subpopulations and to have different marginal distributions among subpopulations. Although only applications in the field of log-linear modeling are presented here, it must be noted that the finite mixture approach is applicable to any type of statistical method.

Several important extensions of Lazarsfeld's latent class model have been proposed, such as models for more than one latent variable (Goodman, 1974a, 1974b; Haberman, 1979:558-560), models with external or explanatory variables (Goodman, 1974a, 1974b; Haberman, 1979:542-544), models for multiple-group analysis (Clogg and Goodman, 1984, 1985, 1986), and models with direct effects among indicators (Hagenaars, 1988). The most extended model is, however, Hagenaars's modified Lisrel model (Hagenaars, 1985, 1990, 1993), in which all of the other latent class models are viewed as special cases. The modified Lisrel model is a log-linear path model in which some of the variables are unobserved. It resembles the well-known LISREL model for continuous data (Jöreskog and Sörbom, 1988) in that a measurement model for the latent variables is specified simultaneously with a structural model for the relationships among the latent variables and the manifest variables used as structural variables (Vermunt, 1994, 1996).

Correcting for measurement error in observed variables is not, however, the only application of log-linear models with latent categorical variables. Another well-known application of such finite mixture models is correction for *unobserved heterogeneity* (Wedel and DeSarbo, 1994, 1995). The term unobserved heterogeneity refers to a 'regression' model in which specific explanatory variables are not observed. By introducing an unobserved regressor, an attempt can be made to eliminate or decrease the bias caused by not observing important regressors given certain appropriate assumptions. Formann (1992) presented a logit model with a latent regressor which was assumed to be independent of the other explanatory variables. He called the model a mixed logistic regression model. Also, a mixed variant of the discrete-time Markov discussed in the previous chapter has been proposed (Poulsen, 1982; Van de Pol and Langeheine, 1990). These 'mixed' models are, likewise, special cases of the modified Lisrel model (Vermunt, 1996).

Apart from measurement error and unobserved heterogeneity, one is often confronted with another kind of missing data problem in social research, the problem of *partially observed variables*. The term partially observed or partially unobserved variable denotes that a variable is not observed for all persons. In survey research, partially observed variables are generally the result of item nonresponse. However, this kind of missing data can also be caused by the data collection design itself: it could be too expensive or impossible to gather all information for all persons.

Fuchs (1982) proposed a method which makes it possible to estimate the parameters of a log-linear model using incomplete data. However, this method is based on the assumption that the mechanism causing the missing data can be ignored when estimating the parameters of interest (Little and Rubin, 1987). More recently, a variant of the log-linear path model has been developed which makes it possible to simultaneously model the mechanism causing the nonresponse and the relationships among the variables of interest (Fay, 1986, 1989; Baker and Laird, 1988; Vermunt, 1988, 1996). Using this approach, it is also possible to estimate parameters within the context of nonignorable response mechanisms.

From a statistical point of view, partially unobserved variables can be handled in the same fashion as completely unobserved covariates. In fact, a partially observed variable is manifest for some individuals and latent for others (Winship and Mare, 1989). Therefore, the same estimation procedures can be used to estimate the parameters of log-linear models with unobserved or with partially observed variables. As will be shown in this chapter, there is no difficulty in dealing with both kinds of missing data simultaneously (Hagenaars, 1985, 1990; Vermunt, 1988, 1994).

The remainder of this chapter consists of two sections, the first of which focusses on log-linear models with latent variables. It deals with the classical and log-linear latent class model, the most important extensions of the standard latent class model, modified Lisrel models, and mixture models for dealing with unobserved heterogeneity. Log-linear models with variables subject to nonresponse are described in section 3.2. Attention is given to the different kinds of response mechanisms and to Fuchs's and Fay's methods for dealing with partially observed variables.

3.1. Latent variables

3.1.1. Latent class analysis

As many concepts in the social sciences are difficult or impossible to measure directly, several directly observable variables, or indicators, are often used as indirect measures of the concept to be measured. The values of the indicators are assumed to be determined only by the unobservable value of the underlying variable of interest and by measurement error. In latent structure models, this principle is implemented statistically by assuming probabilistic relationships between latent and manifest variables and by the assumption of local independence. Local independence means that the indicators are assumed to be independent of each other given a particular value of the unobserved or latent variable; in other words, they are only correlated because of their common cause.

Latent structure models can be classified according to the measurement level of the latent variable(s) and the measurement level of the manifest variables (Bartholomew, 1987; Heinen, 1993:3-10, 1996). In factor analysis, continuous manifest variables are used as indicators of one or more continuous latent variables. In latent trait models, a continuous latent variable is assumed to underlie a set of categorical indicators. Finally, when both the manifest and the latent variables are categorical, a latent class model is obtained. Note that a categorical variable does not need to be a nominal variable; it can also be an ordinal or a discrete interval variable. The latent class model was originally proposed by Lazarsfeld (1950a, 1950b), while its practical applicability is to a large extent the result of the work by Goodman (1974a, 1974b) and Haberman (1979: Chapter 10). Although all variables are treated as nominal variables in the unrestricted latent class model, restricted latent class models have been proposed which make it possible to make a priori assumptions on the order and the distances among the categories of the latent and manifest variables (Rost, 1988; Croon, 1990; Formann, 1992; Heinen, 1996; Vermunt and Georg, 1995).

Unrestricted latent class model The latent class model can be parameterized in two different ways. It is possible to use either the classical parameterization in terms of (conditional) probabilities introduced by Lazarsfeld (Lazarsfeld, 1950a, 1950b; Lazarsfeld and Henry, 1968: Chapter 3), which is also used by Goodman (1974a, 1974b), or the log-linear parameterization introduced mainly by Haberman (1979: Chapter 10).

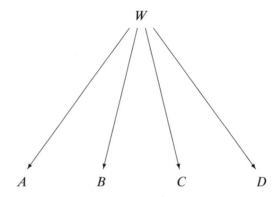

Figure 3.1. Latent class model

Suppose there is, as depicted in Figure 3.1, a latent class model with one latent variable W with index w and 4 indicators A, B, C, and D with indices a, b, c, and d. Moreover, let W^* denote the number of latent classes. The basic equations of the latent class model are

$$\pi_{abcd} = \sum_{w=1}^{W^*} \pi_{wabcd} \, , \qquad [3.1]$$

in which

$$\pi_{wabcd} = \pi_w \pi_{abcd|w} = \pi_w \pi_{a|w} \, \pi_{b|w} \, \pi_{c|w} \, \pi_{d|w} \, . \qquad [3.2]$$

Here, π_{wabcd} denotes the probability of being in cell (w, a, b, c, d) of the joint distribution $WABCD$. Furthermore, π_w is the probability of belonging to latent class w and $\pi_{abcd|w}$ is the probability of having a particular observed response pattern given $W = w$. The other π parameters are conditional response probabilities. For instance, $\pi_{a|w}$ is the probability of being in category a of variable A, given that one belongs to latent class w.

As can be seen from Equation 3.1, the latent class model assumes that the population can be divided into W^* exhaustive and mutually exclusive classes. Therefore, the joint probability of the observed variables can be obtained by summation over the latent dimension. The classical parameterization of the latent class model proposed by Lazarsfeld (1950a, 1950b) is given in Equation 3.2. It can be seen that the observed variables A, B, C, and D are postulated to be mutually independent given a particular score on the latent variable W.

Note that Equation 3.2 is very similar to the modified path models discussed in the previous chapter. Actually, it is a modified path model in which one variable is unobserved. Because the latent class model is completely defined in terms of conditional independence, it is also a graphical model (Wermuth and Lauritzen, 1990).

Haberman (1979: Chapter 10) demonstrated that the unrestricted latent class model given in Equation 3.2 is formally identical to the hierarchical log-linear model {*WA*, *WB*, *WC*, *WD*}, written as

$$\log m_{wabcd} = u + u_w^W + u_a^A + u_b^B + u_c^C + u_d^D + u_{wa}^{WA} + u_{wb}^{WB} + u_{wc}^{WC}$$
$$+ u_{wd}^{WD}, \qquad [3.3]$$

in which $m_{wabcd} = N \pi_{wabcd}$. Equation 3.3 contains, in addition to the overall mean and the one-variable terms, only the two-variable interaction terms between the latent variable W and the manifest variables. As none of the interactions between the manifest variables are included, it can be seen that they are assumed to be conditionally independent of each other.

The relation between the parameters of the two different parameterizations of the latent class model, that is, between the conditional probabilities appearing in Equation 3.2 and the log-linear parameters appearing in Equations 3.3, is (Haberman, 1979:551; Heinen 1993:13-22)

$$\pi_{a|w} = \frac{\exp\left(u_a^A + u_{wa}^{WA}\right)}{\sum_a \exp\left(u_a^A + u_{wa}^{WA}\right)}. \qquad [3.4]$$

It should be noted that this is the same type of logit parameterization of a conditional probability that is used in modified path models. Moreover, since the indicators are assumed to be independent of one another given W, it does not matter whether the relationships between W and the indicators are estimated by specifying a separate logit model for each indicator or by specifying a log-linear model for the full table m_{wabcd}. This follows from the collapsibility theorem (see section 2.9).

Restricted latent class models If it is not necessary to impose further restrictions on the parameters, the two formulations of the latent class model are completely equivalent. However, if the model is restricted in some way, the parameterization choice depends on the type of restrictions that have to be imposed. Because of the possibility of applying a reparameterization, particular kinds of restrictions can be used under both parameterizations though others are specific to one of the two parameterizations.

It should be noted that in writing the latent class model in terms of conditional probabilities in combination with logit models for these conditional probabilities, a combined parameterization is obtained which is similar to the modified path model discussed in the previous chapter. Actually, Formann's linear logistic latent class model combines the two parameterizations discussed above (Formann, 1982, 1992). Formann specified the latent class model in terms of latent and conditional probabilities, for which the probabilities are parameterized as in Equation 3.4. This type of formulation makes it possible to combine restrictions on the probabilities with restrictions on the log-linear, or linear logistic, parameters.

Restrictions which are typical of the classical latent class model are fixed-value and equality restrictions on the latent and conditional response probabilities (Goodman, 1974a, 1974b; Mooijaart and Van der Heijden, 1992). On the other hand, in the log-linear latent class model, it is common to impose linear restrictions on the log-linear parameters, such as equal effects of the latent variable among indicators, linear-by-linear interactions, and row and/or column effects. Besides these more standard restrictions, there are many other types of linear and non-linear restrictions which can be imposed on the probabilities. Croon (1990), for instance, demonstrated the implementation of particular kinds of inequality restrictions on the conditional response probabilities leading to an ordinal latent class model. Moreover, although not yet implemented in the context of latent class analysis, the general model developed by Lang and Agresti (1994) would make it possible to combine a large variety of linear and log-linear restrictions on (sums of) probabilities in latent class models.

Sometimes, it is possible to translate equality restrictions on probabilities into equality restrictions on log-linear parameters. As can be seen from Equation 3.4, for instance, equal conditional response probabilities among indicators can also be obtained by specifying both the one-variable terms for the indicators concerned and their two-variable interaction terms with the latent variable as equal. Equal conditional probabilities are, however, a rather restrictive assumption. Using the log-linear parameterization, it is also possible to impose a weaker type of restriction on the conditional response probabilities, that is, equal strength of association between the latent variable and the various indicators. This can be accomplished by constraining the two-variable interactions appearing in Equation 3.3 to be equal among indicators. Although there is no exact correspondence, the imposition of equality restrictions of this type on the item parameters is similar to the work by Jöreskog (1971) on parallel and tau-equivalent items in the context of factor analysis (see also Mellenbergh, 1994). If the conditional response probabilities are equal among items, the items may be called parallel, while they may be called tau equivalent if only their two-variable interactions with the latent variable are equal.

Another restriction that is often used in classical latent class analysis is the fixing of particular conditional response probabilities to zero. Such a restriction can, among other things, be used to construct latent Guttman scales (Clogg and Sawyer, 1981; Clogg and Goodman, 1986) and to define quasi-latent variables (Hagenaars, 1990:117-119). Fixing a probability to zero is equivalent to setting the log-linear parameters associated with it to minus infinity. This can be accomplished by incorporating structural zero-expected frequencies in the log-linear model (Haberman, 1979:554-556).

Restrictions specific to the log-linear parameterization are linear-by-linear effects and row and/or column effects. These restrictions are useful if either the latent variable or the manifest variables or both can be assumed to be interval-level variables (Heinen, 1996; Rost, 1988). Heinen (1996) demonstrated that when the latent variable is discretized, most latent trait models can be written as latent class models with restrictions on the log-linear parameters. For instance, a discrete variant of the well-known Rasch model for item analysis is obtained by specifying a latent class model with a certain number of latent classes in which the two-variable interaction parameters between the latent variable and the indicators are specified as linear-by-linear and equal among indicators. Within the log-linear modeling framework, it is even possible to specify models with log-multiplicative interaction terms. This option can be used, for instance, to specify a discrete Rasch model with random scores for the categories of the latent variable. Lindsay, Clogg, and Grego (1991) called this model a semi-parametric Rasch model.

3.1.2. Extensions of the standard latent class model

Several important extensions of the standard latent class model have been developed. Some of these are specific for either the classical or the log-linear formulation of the latent class model, while others can be implemented under both parameterizations. Below, the most important extensions developed within the framework of either the classical or the log-linear latent class model are discussed. Moreover, it is demonstrated

that these extended latent class models can also be formulated as modified path models, that is, in terms of conditional probabilities which are
possibly subjected to logit restrictions.

Models with several latent variables Goodman (1974a, 1974b) and
Haberman (1979:558-560) showed how to specify latent class models
with more than one latent variable. This led to a model which is analogous to a factor analytic model with more than one factor. Latent class
models with several latent variables can be specified either by imposing
equality restrictions on the conditional probabilities or by formulating a
log-linear model.

Suppose there is a model with four indicators and two latent variables, in which A and B are indicators of the latent variable W, and
C and D of the latent variable Y. Moreover, assume W and Y are
related to each other. This results in the log-linear latent class model
$\{WY, WA, WB, YC, YD\}$ which is displayed in Figure 3.2, or

$$\log m_{wyabcd} = u + u_w^W + u_y^Y + u_a^A + u_b^B + u_c^C + u_d^D + u_{wy}^{WY} + u_{wa}^{WA}$$
$$+ u_{wb}^{WB} + u_{yc}^{YC} + u_{yd}^{YD} .\qquad [3.5]$$

Just as in the standard latent class model, additional restrictions can
be imposed on the log-linear parameters in this model. Note that it is
not only possible to restrict the item parameters but also the relationships between the latent variables. In a model with three latent variables,
for instance, a no-three-variable interaction model can be specified for
the latent variables. Hagenaars (1986) proposed symmetry and quasi-
symmetry models for the associations between the latent variables.

In terms of conditional probabilities, the latent class model of Equation 3.5 can be written as

$$\pi_{wyabcd} = \pi_{wy}\,\pi_{a|w}\,\pi_{b|w}\,\pi_{c|y}\,\pi_{d|y} .$$

Models with external variables Another extension of the ordinary latent
class model is the incorporation of external variables in the model (Hagenaars, 1985, 1990:113-119, 1993). Since external variables are manifest
variables which are not indicators, the assumption of conditional independence does not need to hold for these variables. Clogg (1981), for
example, applied latent class models with external variables to specify
multiple-indicator multiple-cause models (MIMIC) for categorical data.
These models resemble the well-known MIMIC models for continuous
data presented by Jöreskog and Goldberger (1975).

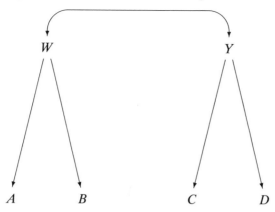

Figure 3.2. Latent class model with 2 latent variables

Clogg (1981) specified the MIMIC model for categorical data using the classical parameterization of the latent class model. However, this parameterization is limited with respect to the models that can be postulated for the relationships among the external variables and the latent variables: Only a saturated model and particular kinds of independence models can be specified for these variables. When using the log-linear parameterization, it is possible to specify any kind of non-saturated model for the relationships among the external and the latent variables.

Suppose there is a MIMIC model with two external variables I and J and one latent variable W with three indicators A, B, and C. Moreover, assume that the external variables influence W and that there is no three-variable interaction among I, J, and W. The MIMIC model concerned, which is depicted in Figure 3.3, is equivalent to log-linear latent class model $\{IJ, IW, JW, WA, WB, WC\}$, or

$$\log m_{wabcij} = u + u_i^I + u_j^J + u_w^W + u_a^A + u_b^B + u_c^C + u_{ij}^{IJ} + u_{iw}^{IW} + u_{jw}^{JW}$$
$$+ u_{wa}^{WA} + u_{wb}^{WB} + u_{wc}^{WC} .$$

In terms of conditional probabilities, it can be written as

$$\pi_{wabcij} = \pi_{ij} \, \pi_{w|ij} \, \pi_{a|w} \, \pi_{b|w} \, \pi_{c|w} ,$$

in which $\pi_{w|ij}$ is restricted by a logit model without a three-variable interaction term. Although above the external variables were assumed to be exogenous variables, it is also possible to use external variables as dependent variables.

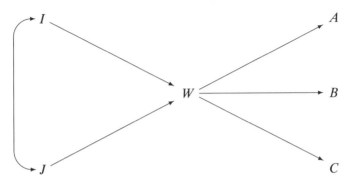

Figure 3.3. Latent class model with external variables

Models for several subpopulations Other extensions are latent class models for several subpopulations which may differ with respect to the latent distribution and the relationships between the latent variables and their indicators (Hagenaars, 1990:127-135). This is comparable to simultaneous factor analysis in several populations (Jöreskog, 1971; Sörbom, 1974). Clogg and Goodman (1984, 1985) presented what they called a simultaneous latent structure model using the classic parameterization of the latent class model. McCutcheon (1987) applied this model to compare latent distributions at different points in time.

Simultaneous latent class analysis involves incorporating a group variable in the model. This group variable may influence the latent distribution and the conditional response probabilities. If G denotes the group variable in a latent class model with latent variable W and indicators A, B, and C, the multi-group latent class model can be written as

$$\pi_{wabcg} = \pi_g \ \pi_{w|g} \ \pi_{a|wg} \ \pi_{b|wg} \ \pi_{c|wg} \ .$$

Note that this unrestricted multiple-group model is equivalent to log-linear model $\{GWA, GWB, GWC\}$. A specification of this kind implies that the latent distribution, the distributions of the indicators, and the relationships between the latent variable and the indicators are all assumed to be different among subpopulations.

However, often one wants to impose restrictions on the parameters across groups. An example of a restricted model is the log-linear model $\{GW, WA, WB, WC, GA, GB, GC\}$. In this model, it is assumed that the latent and manifest distributions differ among groups, but that the strengths of the relationships between the latent variable and the indicators are the same for all of the subpopulations. An even more restrictive model is {*GW, WA, WB, WC*}. Here, the measurement part of the model is assumed to be equal for all subgroups. In terms of conditional probabilities, this model can also be written as

$$\pi_{wabcg} = \pi_g \, \pi_{w|g} \, \pi_{a|w} \, \pi_{b|w} \, \pi_{c|w} \, .$$

Actually, this model tests the assumption of invariance of the latent construct (Jöreskog, 1971), which is a vital test if the aim is to compare the latent distributions of different groups. Latent distributions can only be compared when the latent variable has the same meaning for all subpopulations, which often implies that one wants the relationships between the latent variable and the items to be equal among subgroups.

Local dependence models The log-linear latent class model can also be used to specify models in which particular indicators are related to one another. Hagenaars (1988) demonstrated how to specify these so-called local dependence models. Figure 3.4 shows an example of a local dependence model, i.e., model {*WA, WB, WC, WD, CD*}. In this model with one latent variable and four indicators, there is a direct association between the indicators *C* and *D*. In terms of conditional probabilities, the model can be written as

$$\pi_{wabcd} = \pi_w \, \pi_{a|w} \, \pi_{b|w} \, \pi_{cd|w} \, , \qquad\qquad [3.6]$$

where $\pi_{cd|w}$ is restricted by means of a no-three-variable interaction log-linear model. These local dependence models are analogous to factor analytic models with correlated error terms (Sörbom, 1975).

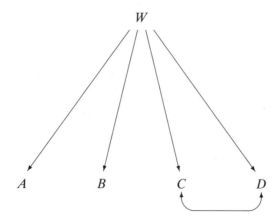

Figure 3.4. Local dependence model

3.1.3. Causal log-linear models with latent variables

Some extensions of the standard latent class model were discussed in the previous subsection. A limitation of these extensions is that they were all developed within the framework of either the classical or the log-linear latent class model. Therefore, it is not always possible to postulate the desired a priori causal order among the variables incorporated in the model. But, as was demonstrated, all these extended latent class models can be written as modified path models in which one or more variables are not observed. This subsection presents the general formulation of the modified path model with latent variables which was proposed by Hagenaars (1985, 1990:135-142, 1993). Because of the analogy with the LISREL model for continuous variables (Jöreskog and Sörbom, 1988), Hagenaars called it a modified Lisrel approach.[1]

Suppose we want to investigate the causal relationships between six categorical variables denoted by E, F, G, H, W, and Y, where W and Y are latent variables. Figure 3.5 shows the assumed causal order and the assumed direct relations of the variables. It can be seen that the variables E, F, and G are exogenous variables. The others are endogenous, where H is assumed to be posterior to W, and Y is assumed to be posterior to H. Moreover, A and B serve as indicators for the latent variable W, and C and D serve as indicators for Y.

The probability of belonging to cell $(e, f, g, w, h, y, a, b, c, d)$ of the joint distribution of all the variables included in the model is denoted as $\pi_{efgwhyabcd}$. As demonstrated in section 2.9, the a priori information on the causal order of the variables can be used to decompose $\pi_{efgwhyabcd}$ as follows:

$$\pi_{efgwhyabcd} = \pi_{efg} \, \pi_{w|efg} \, \pi_{h|efgw} \, \pi_{y|efgwh} \, \pi_{abcd|wy} \, . \qquad [3.7]$$

The only difference between a modified path model containing only observed variables and the modified Lisrel model described in Equation 3.7 is that the latter contains an additional component in which the relationships between the latent variables and their indicators are specified (Hagenaars, 1993; Vermunt, 1994, 1996), in this case $\pi_{abcd|wy}$. This part will be called the measurement part of the model, while the other part will be called the structural part of the model. On the basis of the relationships between the variables depicted in Figure 3.5, the model

---

[1] Another Lisrel-like approach to ordinal categorical data which is more similar to the standard LISREL model is the model proposed by Muthén (1984).

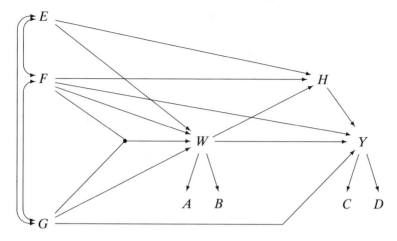

Figure 3.5. Modified Lisrel model

represented in Equation 3.7 can be written in a more restricted form as

$$\pi_{efgwhyabcd} = \pi_{efg}\,\pi_{w|efg}\,\pi_{h|efw}\,\pi_{y|fgwh}\,\pi_{a|w}\,\pi_{b|w}\,\pi_{c|y}\,\pi_{d|y}\,. \qquad [3.8]$$

As in a modified path model containing only observed variables, the probabilities appearing in Equation 3.8 can be restricted further by means of a logit parameterization or by the equivalent log-linear parameterization proposed by Goodman (1973). For instance, in accordance with the relationships depicted in Figure 3.5, $\pi_{w|efg}$ has to be restricted as follows:

$$\pi_{w|efg} = \frac{\exp\left(u_w^W + u_{we}^{WE} + u_{wf}^{WF} + u_{wg}^{WG} + u_{wfg}^{WFG}\right)}{\sum_w \exp\left(u_w^W + u_{we}^{WE} + u_{wf}^{WF} + u_{wg}^{WG} + u_{wfg}^{WFG}\right)},$$

or equivalently, by means of log-linear model

$$\log m_{efgw} = \alpha_{efg} + u_w^W + u_{we}^{WE} + u_{wf}^{WF} + u_{wg}^{WG} + u_{wfg}^{WFG}\,.$$

This model contains direct effects of E and F and G on W, where there is an interaction between F and G with respect to their effects on W.

Some other special cases As was shown in the previous subsection, all extensions which have been proposed for the standard latent class model are special cases of the modified Lisrel model. There are, however, other models which are special cases of the modified Lisrel model.

Hagenaars (1988) specified a *local dependence model* in which he assumed the relationships between indicators to be asymmetrical. Suppose we want to specify a local dependence model like the one depicted in Figure 3.4, but now with a direct effect of C on D instead of a symmetrical relationship. Such a model is equivalent to a modified path model of the form

$$\pi_{wabcd} = \pi_w \; \pi_{a|w} \; \pi_{b|w} \; \pi_{c|w} \; \pi_{d|wc} \,,$$

where $\pi_{d|wc}$ is restricted by a no-three-variable interaction model. Although in this case the model with an asymmetrical direct relationship between indicators gives the same model fit as the symmetrical specification used in Equation 3.6, this is not always the case. Moreover, even though the model fit is the same, the estimated effect of W on C will be different in the two specifications.

Another special case of the modified Lisrel model is the *latent budget model* which was proposed by Van der Heijden, Mooijaart, and De Leeuw (1992). A latent budget model is a kind of MIMIC model in which one set of variables is used as a joint explanatory variable and another set of variables is used as a joint response variable or observed budget. When A denotes the joint explanatory variable, B, the observed budget, and W, the latent budget, the latent budget model is given by

$$\pi_{awb} = \pi_a \; \pi_{w|a} \; \pi_{b|w} \,,$$

where the marginal distribution of A, π_a, is not restricted, and where $\pi_{w|a}$ and $\pi_{b|w}$ can be restricted via fixed-value or equality restrictions on the conditional probabilities or via a logit parameterization.

In the previous chapter, it was shown that the discrete-time Markov model is a special case of the modified path model. Therefore, it is not surprising that the *discrete-time latent Markov model* is a special case of the modified Lisrel model. The discrete-time latent Markov model was originally proposed by Wiggins (1955, 1973), while more recently Poulsen (1982), Van de Pol and De Leeuw (1986), Van de Pol and Langeheine (1990), and Collins and Wugalter (1992) contributed to the practical applicability of the latent Markov model. Suppose that S_l denotes the observed state at time point l and that s_l denotes a category of S_l. Moreover, let Φ_l denote the true state at time point l with values ϕ_l. For the sake of simplicity, it will be assumed that there are observations for only 3 points in time, $1 \leq l \leq 3$. In that case, a first-order latent Markov model can be represented as follows:

$$\pi_{s_1 s_2 s_3 \phi_1 \phi_2 \phi_3} = \pi_{\phi_1} \, \pi_{\phi_2|\phi_1} \, \pi_{\phi_3|\phi_2} \, \pi_{s_1|\phi_1} \, \pi_{s_2|\phi_2} \, \pi_{s_3|\phi_3} \, ,$$

where some restrictions have to be imposed on either the transition probabilities $\pi_{\phi_l|\phi_{l-1}}$ or the conditional response probabilities $\pi_{s_l|\phi_l}$ to make the model identifiable (Van de Pol and Langeheine, 1990). Explanatory variables can be incorporated in the model in the same way as in manifest Markov models (Vermunt and Georg, 1995; Vermunt, Langeheine, and Böckenholt, 1995).

As in modified path models, every conditional probability in modified Lisrel models may be parameterized by means of a multinomial logit model of the general form

$$\pi_{i|k} = \frac{\exp \left(\sum_j \beta_j x_{ijk} \right)}{\sum_i \exp \left(\sum_j \beta_j x_{ijk} \right)} , \qquad [3.9]$$

where i denotes a level of the response variable, k, a level of the joint explanatory variable, and j, a particular effect. This implies that, as was demonstrated for modified path models, modified Lisrel models can also be used with continuous exogenous variables. Dayton and Macready (1988) and Van der Heijden and Dessens (1994) proposed a *latent class model with continuous covariates*. In their model, the latent proportions are regressed on one or more continuous explanatory variables using a logistic regression model. Assuming that the latent variable W has 3 indicators A, B, and C, in our notation, such a model can be written as

$$\pi_{abc|w|k} = \pi_{w|x_{wjk}} \, \pi_{a|wx_{ajk}} \, \pi_{b|wx_{bjk}} \, \pi_{c|wx_{cjk}} \, ,$$

where x_{wjk}, x_{ajk}, x_{bjk}, and x_{cjk} denote the observed value for person k on the exogenous variable j for $W = w$, $A = a$, $B = b$, and $C = c$, respectively. These conditional probabilities can, of course, be restricted using the multinomial logit model or the logistic regression model given in Equation 3.9. Note that this modified path model with a latent variable is, in fact, more general than the model proposed by Dayton and Macready because the conditional response probabilities may also depend on the continuous covariates.

3.1.4. Unobserved heterogeneity

Above, one particular application of log-linear models with latent variables models was discussed, i.e., correcting for measurement error in observed variables. However, log-linear models with latent variables can also be used to correct for unobserved heterogeneity. The term unobserved heterogeneity is generally used in the context of regression models.[2] It means that particular variables that influence the dependent variable are not measured and can therefore not be used as covariates in the regression model (Heckman and Singer, 1982, 1984). One possible solution in such situations is to include in the regression model a latent unobserved covariate which is assumed to capture (part of) the unobserved causes of the phenomenon under study (Wedel and DeSarbo, 1994, 1995).

From a technical point of view, the main difference between the latent class models discussed in the previous subsections and the finite mixture models which are used to correct for unobserved heterogeneity is that in the latter, the latent variable incorporated in the model does not have indicators. Since this makes the models more difficult to identify, models with unobserved heterogeneity will generally be rather restrictive. Moreover, the results obtained from mixture models may be sensitive to the choice of the identifying restrictions.

Follman and Lambert (1989) and Formann (1992) proposed a logit model with a non-parametric unobserved heterogeneity component. Formann called this model a *mixed logistic regression model*. In this model, the existence of a categorical latent variable is assumed which may influence not only the dependent variable but also the effect of the other independent variables on the dependent variable. An important assumption of the model is that the mixture distribution is independent of the other explanatory variables.[3]

Suppose we want to explain C using the observed variables A and B and the unobserved variable W as regressors. In that case, the mixed logit model is given by

$$\pi_{wabc} = \pi_w \, \pi_{ab} \, \pi_{c|abw} \,, \qquad [3.10]$$

---

[2] Other terms that are sometimes used to describe this phenomenon are omitted variable bias (Chamberlain, 1985) and overdispersion (MCCullagh and Nelder, 1983).

[3] These models are sometimes also called random-effects logistic regression models (Willekens, 1994). The approach that is used here is a non-parametric random-effects approach because the distribution of the latent variable which is included in the regression model is not parameterized. Sections 4.8 and 5.2 explain the different ways of handling unobserved heterogeneity in the context of event history analysis in more detail.

where the probability $\pi_{c|abw}$ has to be restricted in some way because, otherwise, the model is not identified. One possibility is to postulate a logit model in which all regressors influence C through the two-variable effects, but in which all higher-order interaction terms are absent.

Another model for categorical data in which a latent variable is used to correct for unobserved heterogeneity is the *discrete-time mixed Markov model* (Poulsen, 1982, Langeheine and Van de Pol, 1990, 1994). In this model, it is assumed that the observed transition probabilities are actually a mixture of the transition probabilities of several unobserved groups. This is equivalent to assuming that there is an unobserved variable which influences the transition probabilities. The mixed Markov model can be identified without further restrictions when a first-order Markov model is postulated within the unobserved subgroups. Suppose that S_l denotes the state occupied at time point l, that s_l denotes a category of S_l, and that $1 \leq l \leq 4$. Assuming that W is the latent variable, the mixed Markov can be written as

$$\pi_{ws_1s_2s_3s_4} = \pi_w \, \pi_{s_1|w} \, \pi_{s_2|ws_1} \, \pi_{s_3|ws_2} \, \pi_{s_4|ws_3} \, . \tag{3.11}$$

It should be noted that the well-known mover-stayer model (Goodman, 1961) is a special case of the mixed Markov model. It is obtained by restricting the probabilities $\pi_{s_l|ws_{l-1}}$ to be equal to zero if $S_l \neq S_{l-1}$ for one latent class.

Van de Pol and Langeheine (1990) extended the mixed Markov by incorporating observed covariates. Moreover, they combined the mixed Markov model and the latent Markov model into one general model which they called the mixed Markov latent class model.

From Equations 3.10 and 3.11, it can easily be seen that both the mixed logistic regression model and the mixed Markov model are also special cases of the modified Lisrel model. The same applies to Van de Pol and Langeheine's extensions of the mixed Markov model. Other examples of mixture models that can be dealt with within the context of modified path analysis with latent variables are the mixed Rasch model proposed by Rost (1990) and models for analyzing ranking data (Croon, 1989; Croon and Luijkx, 1993; Böckenholt, 1996) and other types of choice data (Kamakura, Wedel, and Agrawal, 1992).

3.1.5. Estimation and testing

Obtaining maximum likelihood estimates of the parameters of latent class models, log-linear models with latent variables, and modified Lisrel models is a bit more complicated than for log-linear models in which all variables are observed. Several estimation methods can be used to estimate the parameters of the models discussed in the previous subsections. The best known methods are the Newton-Raphson algorithm, including variants such as Fisher's scoring algorithm and other quasi-Newton algorithms, and the Expectation-Maximization (EM) algorithm. Lazarsfeld and Henry (1968:101-105) have already demonstrated how to apply Fisher's scoring method to estimate latent class models, while Goodman (1974a, 1974b) was the first to use the EM algorithm for estimating latent class models.

Computer programs Fisher's scoring algorithm is implemented in the LAT program which was developed by Haberman (1979: Appendix A.2), while Haberman's NEWTON program is based on the Newton-Raphson algorithm (Haberman, 1988). These programs were developed to estimate latent class models using a log-linear parameterization. Mare and Winship (1989) showed that with a complicated reparameterization, it is also possible to estimate modified path models by means of NEWTON. The other widely available programs for latent class analysis are all based on the EM algorithm. Clogg's MLLSA program can be used to estimate the classical latent class model, including some of its extensions discussed above (Clogg, 1977). Hagenaars and Luijkx' LCAG program can be used to estimate classical latent class models and modified Lisrel models with hierarchical log-linear models (Hagenaars and Luijkx, 1990). The DILTRAN program can be used to estimate latent class models with different types of linear restrictions on the log-linear parameters or, more precisely, discrete latent trait models (Heinen and Vermaseren, 1992). The PANMARK program was especially developed for estimating latent and mixed Markov models, but it can also be used to estimate classical latent class models (Van de Pol, Langeheine and De Jong, 1989).

The *ℓEM* program is the most general program for estimating log-linear models with latent variables (Vermunt, 1993) since it combines all the features of the above-mentioned programs. It can be used to estimate modified Lisrel models which, as was shown in the previous section, are the most general models of which all other models are special cases. By means of *ℓEM*, equality, fixed-value, and particular kinds of inequality restrictions can be imposed on the (conditional) probabilities appearing in a modified path model with latent variables. In addition, a general multinomial logit parameterization of the conditional probabilities can be used in which log-multiplicative effects can be included. It is also possible to use cumulative link functions leading to models for ordinal dependent variables, that is, cumulative logit, probit, complementary log-log, and log-log models.

Newton-Raphson and Fisher's scoring   The Newton-Raphson algorithm and Fisher's scoring algorithm are strongly related gradient search methods. The difference between them is that Fisher's scoring algorithm uses the expected information matrix, or Fisher's information matrix, while Newton-Raphson uses the observed information matrix to determine the optimal step size to improve the parameter estimates. When all variables of a log-linear model are observed, the procedures are equivalent because, in that case, the observed and the expected information matrix are identical (Agresti, 1990:114; Heinen, 1993:287). The main advantage of using Fisher's scoring algorithm rather than Newton-Raphson to estimate the parameters of models with latent variables is that the expected information matrix can be obtained from the first-order derivatives of the log-likelihood function. Therefore, it is no longer necessary to compute the second-order derivatives. Appendix G explains how to obtain the expected information matrix for modified path models with latent variables. It must be noted that this version of Fisher's scoring algorithm for estimating modified path models with latent variables has not yet been implemented in a computer program.

The main advantage of using Newton Raphson or Fisher's scoring in comparison with the EM algorithm is that they converge very fast when the model does not contain too many parameters, and, moreover, they provide standard deviations of the parameter estimates as a by-product. A major disadvantage is that they need starting values which are close to the final solution to converge to the maximum likelihood solution (Hagenaars, 1988; Heinen, 1993:65). Therefore, Haberman (1988) proposed a so-called stabilized Newton-Raphson algorithm, which he implemented in his NEWTON program (Haberman, 1988). Although in most kinds of latent class models this algorithm performs better, in particular types of restricted latent class models, convergence is still problematic (Heinen, 1993:65). Another disadvantage of the Newton algorithms is that when a model contains many parameters, they may become very time consuming because of the necessity to compute and to invert the Hessian matrix or the expected information matrix at every iteration. And finally, numerical problems may occur when some estimated cell counts go to zero, that is, when some log-linear parameters go to minus infinity.

The EM algorithm   The EM algorithm appears to be a good alternative (Dempster, Laird, and Rubin, 1977). The main advantage of the EM algorithm compared with the Newton methods is that it does converge to at least a local maximum under relatively weak conditions, even with bad starting values (Wu, 1983). Generally, random starting values are good enough. Furthermore, the EM algorithm is both conceptually and computationally very simple. The main disadvantages are that it may need many iterations to converge and that it does not give estimates of the standard deviations of the parameter estimates. However, since every EM iteration is performed relatively fast, it is not problematic that many more iterations are needed than with the Newton methods. Moreover, standard errors for the parameter estimates can be computed afterwards, for instance, by computing the inverse of the expected information matrix. The ideal algorithm would be a composite algorithm which starts with a number of EM iterations and which, when it is close enough to the final solution, at which point the EM becomes slow and Newton methods become more stable, switches to one of the Newton algorithms (Titterington, Smith, and Makov, 1985; Guo and Rodriguez, 1992).[4]

The EM algorithm is a general iterative estimation procedure which can be used when there are missing data (Dempster, Laird, and Rubin, 1979). In log-linear models with latent variables, the scores on the latent variables are missing. Each EM iteration consists of two steps. The E(xpectation) step involves computing the expected complete data, given the observed data and the 'current' parameter estimates. In the M(aximization) step, the complete data likelihood function is maximized. This implies computing updated estimates of the model parameters as if there were no missing data. These EM iterations continue until convergence is reached.

Suppose one wants to obtain maximum likelihood estimates for the model parameters of the modified Lisrel model presented in Equations 3.7 and 3.8. Assuming multinomial sampling, this involves maximizing the following incomplete data log-likelihood function

$$\log \mathcal{L}_{(\pi)} = \sum_{efghabcd} n_{efghabcd} \log \sum_{wy} \hat{\pi}_{efgwhyabcd} . \qquad [3.12]$$

Here, $\hat{\pi}_{efgwhyabcd}$ denotes the estimated probability of belonging to cell $(e, f, g, w, h, y, a, b, c, d)$ in joint distribution of the observed and unobserved variables. Note that in Equation 3.12, the estimated probabilities

---

[4] In the ℓ_{EM} program (Vermunt, 1993), standard errors of the log-linear parameters are based on a numerical approximation of the observed information matrix (see Appendix G). In addition, it is possible to switch to the Newton-Raphson, Broyden-Fletcher-Goldfarb-Shanno (BFGS), or Levenberg-Maquardt method after some EM iterations. For an extended discussion of these algorithms see Press et al. (1986).

are collapsed over the dimensions that are missing, i.e., the dimensions pertaining to the latent variables W and Y.

In the *E step* of the EM algorithm, the expectation of the complete data log-likelihood, given the incompletely observed data and the 'current' parameter estimates is computed, i.e.,

$$\log \mathcal{L}^*_{(\pi)} = \sum_{efgwhyabcd} \hat{n}_{efgwhyabcd} \log \hat{\pi}_{efgwhyabcd} \, .$$

This log-likelihood function is sometimes also called the complete data likelihood. In this equation, $\hat{n}_{efgwhyabcd}$ denotes an estimated cell count in the frequency table including the latent dimensions. Thus, the E step involves computing estimates for the unobserved frequencies of the table including the latent dimensions, i.e.,

$$\hat{n}_{efgwhyabcd} = n_{efghabcd} \, \hat{\pi}_{wy|efghabcd} \, , \qquad [3.13]$$

in which $\hat{\pi}_{wy|efghabcd}$ is the estimated probability that $W = w$ and $Y = y$, given $A = a$, $B = b$, $C = c$, $D = d$, $E = e$, $F = f$, and $G = g$, in other words, the probability of the missing data given the observed data, evaluated using the estimated probabilities resulting from the previous EM iteration. The quantity $\hat{\pi}_{wy|efghabcd}$ is sometimes also called the posterior probability.

In the *M step*, the complete data log-likelihood function given in Equation 3.13 is maximized to obtain improved parameter estimates, or equivalently, improved estimated probabilities $\hat{\pi}_{efgwhyabcd}$. In fact, the model parameters are updated using the $\hat{n}_{efgwhyabcd}$'s as if they were observed cell counts. For that purpose, the estimation procedures are the same as those used in the case of log-linear models without missing data. In the M of the EM algorithm as implemented in the *ℓEM* program (Vermunt, 1993), it is possible to use IPF, uni-dimensional Newton, and the methods proposed by Goodman (1974b) to estimate unrestricted and restricted conditional probabilities. For more information about these estimation procedures, see the subsections on IPF and uni-dimensional Newton in Chapter 2 and the Appendices E and F.

The new estimates for the estimated probabilities $\hat{\pi}_{efgwhyabcd}$ are again used in a new E step to obtain new estimates for the frequencies in the complete table. The EM iterations continue until convergence is reached, for instance, until the log-likelihood function given in Equation 3.12 increases less than a specified minimum value or until the parameters no longer change significantly.

It has been proven that the EM algorithm converges to a local maximum under rather weak conditions (Wu, 1983). However, there is no guarantee that the global maximum of the likelihood function will actually be found. Therefore, it is recommended that the model of interest be estimated using different sets of starting values (Hagenaars, 1990:112; Formann, 1992). When all runs lead to the same value of the likelihood function, it is more certain that the global maximum has been found. On the other hand, if different solutions are found using different sets of starting values, the solution with the highest likelihood value is to be preferred. But, as with any kind of model which is known to have local maxima, one can never be completely sure that the global maximum of the likelihood function has been found.

Modifications of EM The algorithm used in *ℓEM* is a modified version of the true EM algorithm because the M step consists of only one iteration. Generally, therefore, the complete data likelihood is not maximized but only improved within a particular M step. This is a special case of the GEM algorithm which states that every increase in the complete data likelihood also leads to an increase of the incomplete data likelihood that actually has to be maximized (Dempster, Laird, and Rubin, 1977; Little and Rubin, 1987). Rai and Matthews (1993) called this version of the EM algorithm the EM1 algorithm.

The algorithm which is used in *ℓEM* is also a special case of the ECM algorithm (Meng and Rubin, 1993), in which the M step is replaced by a conditional maximization (CM) step. Conditional maximization means that instead of improving all the parameters simultaneously, subsets of parameters are updated fixing the others at their previous values. This is exactly what is done using IPF and the uni-dimensional Newton algorithm. Meng and Rubin (1993) state that such simple and stable linear convergence methods are often more suitable for the M (or CM) step of the EM (or ECM) algorithm than superlinear converging but less stable algorithms as Newton-Raphson.

In most situations, this GEM, EM1 or ECM algorithm converges in about the same number of (EM) iterations as the true EM algorithm. This means that when the M step needs more than one (M) iteration to converge, the modified EM algorithm is faster than the true EM algorithm. However, experience with *ℓEM* has shown that sometimes it is more efficient to perform more than one M iteration. This is true in models in which the uni-dimensional Newton algorithm takes numerous iterations in order to converge. As was mentioned in the previous chapter, if the parameters are highly correlated, this algorithm requires a large number of iterations in order to converge. In such cases, it may be more efficient to perform, for instance, five M iterations when using *ℓEM*, especially if the M step is faster than the E step.

Identifiability It is well known that the parameters in models with latent variables cannot always be uniquely determined. Of course, as in log-linear models without latent variables, it is necessary that the number of independent parameters does not exceed the number of observed frequencies. In models with latent variables this is not a sufficient condition for identifiability. According to Goodman (1974b), a sufficient condition for local identifiability is that the information matrix is positive definite (see Appendix G). Therefore, when using Fisher's scoring method or Newton-Raphson to estimate the parameters of a log-linear model with latent variables, the identifiability of a model is automatically checked. Some programs which are based on the EM algorithm, such as PAN-MARK (Van de Pol, Langeheine, and De Jong, 1988) MLLSA (Clogg, 1977), and *ℓEM*, also make it possible to check the identification of the parameters. Another way of checking identifiability when using the EM algorithm is to estimate the given model using different sets of starting values. If different sets of starting values result in the same value for the log-likelihood function but different parameter estimates, the model is not identifiable (Hagenaars, 1990:112).

Testing Log-linear models with latent variables can be tested in the same fashion as the log-linear models discussed in the previous chapter. Both the likelihood-ratio chi-square statistic L^2 and the Pearson chi-square statistic X^2 may be used to compare the observed frequencies with the estimates of the expected manifest frequencies. The estimated expected frequencies $\hat{m}_{efgwhyabcd}$ can be obtained by multiplying the estimated probabilities $\hat{\pi}_{efgwhyabcd}$ by the sample size N. The likelihood-ratio chi-square statistic can be obtained by

$$L^2 = 2 \sum_{efghabcd} n_{efghabcd} \log \frac{n_{efghabcd}}{\sum_{wy} \hat{m}_{efgwhyabcd}}.$$

Note that the $\hat{m}_{efgwhyabcd}$ have to be collapsed over the latent dimensions to obtain the estimated expected frequencies in the observed table *EFGHABCD*.

As in the case of log-linear models without latent variables, conditional tests may be used to compare nested models. However, it should be noted that although latent class models with different numbers of latent classes are nested, they cannot be tested against each other using conditional L^2 tests. The reason for this is that the more parsimonious model, the model with fewer latent classes, can only be expressed as a restricted version of the less parsimonious model by fixing one or more latent proportions to zero. The asymptotic theory no longer holds because these latent proportions are on the boundary of the parameter space (Titterington, Smith, and Makov, 1985; Formann, 1992).[5] Everitt (1988) examined the distribution of the conditional L^2 statistic for pairs of nested latent class models and found that L^2 was not distributed as χ^2. The use of the *AIC* and *BIC* information criteria does not resolve the testing problem because they rely on the same regularity conditions as the chi-square statistics (Heinen, 1993:73).

3.2. Nonresponse

The previous section discussed one type of missing data problem in log-linear analysis, that is, how to formulate models when one or more variables are completely unobserved. In this section, attention is given to another type of missing data problem. Log-linear models are presented which can be used when the scores on particular variables are partially missing.

In most studies, the values of one or more variables are missing for subsets of the original sample. It is common practice in such cases to use only the complete observations in the analysis. This leads to less powerful statistical tests and, if the nonresponse is selective, to biased parameter estimates. However, methods have been developed which can also make use of partially observed information in fitting log-linear models. These methods are analogous to methods developed to deal with partially observed continuous data (Marini, Olsen, and Rubin, 1979; Allison, 1987; Muthén, Kaplan, and Hollis, 1987).

Suppose there is a four-way contingency table composed of the variables A, B, C, and D, for which the values of C, D, or both are missing for a part of the sample. On the basis of the nonresponse patterns, it is possible to divide the observations into four subgroups. Subgroup AB consists of the subjects for which only the values of A and B are known; for subgroup ABC, only A, B, and C are observed; for subgroup ABD, C is missing; and finally, for subgroup $ABCD$, all variables are observed.

---

[5] It should be noted that this does not only hold for the latent proportions, but for any probability appearing in the models discussed so far. It is never allowed to use a conditional L^2 test to investigate whether a probability equals zero.

The observed frequencies for these four subgroups will be denoted as n_{ab}, n_{abc}, n_{abd}, and n_{abcd}, respectively. The sizes of the subgroups will be denoted as N^{AB}, N^{ABC}, N^{ABD}, and N^{ABCD}, respectively.

3.2.1. Assumptions about the response mechanism

Different kinds of assumptions can be made with regard to the mechanism causing the missing data. Generally, three basic types of mechanisms are distinguished: *missing completely at random* (MCAR), *missing at random* (MAR), and *not missing at random* (NMAR) (Rubin, 1976; Little, 1982; Little and Rubin, 1987). MCAR means that the nonresponse is independent of the variables included in the analysis. In other words, when the missing data is MCAR, the probability of having a particular pattern of nonresponse is assumed to be equal for each cell of the 'hypothetical' complete table. The much less restrictive MAR assumption implies that the probability of having a particular pattern of nonresponse depends only on the observed variables in the nonresponse pattern or subgroup concerned. For example, MAR means that for a given individual who only has a missing value on D (subgroup ABC), the probability of nonresponse on D may depend on A, B, and C, but not on D. For an individual who has missing values on both C and D (subgroup AB), the probability of not observing C and D may only depend on A and B. If the missing data are not MAR or MCAR, they are NMAR. This occurs when the probability of having a particular pattern of nonresponse depends on the variables with missing values in the nonresponse pattern concerned. For example, the response mechanism is MCAR if for subgroup ABC the probability of nonresponse on D also depends on D, or if for subgroup AB the probability of nonresponse on both C and D also depends on C, D, or both.

Besides the distinction between MCAR, MAR, and NMAR response mechanisms, there is another strongly related distinction when dealing with partially observed data, that is, whether the missing data mechanism is *ignorable* or *nonignorable* for likelihood-based inference. According to Rubin (1976), the missing data mechanism is ignorable for likelihood-based inference if two conditions are fulfilled, namely, if the missing data are MAR and if the parameters of the structural model[6] and the parameters associated with the response mechanism are distinct

---

[6] The term structural model is used to denote the model for the variables which relationships we are interested in. In the context of this section, the structural model will be a (causal) log-linear model.

(see also Little, 1982, and Little and Rubin, 1987). The condition that the two sets of parameters must be distinct means that no restrictions may be imposed between the parameters of the structural model and the parameters describing the response mechanism. As is demonstrated below, this condition is almost always fulfilled. Therefore, for practical applications, ignorability can be equated to MAR.

The consequence of ignorability is that the parameter estimates are identical regardless of the precise ignorable mechanism causing the missing data, and that, therefore, the response mechanism can be ignored when estimating the structural parameters. This is possible because in that case, the likelihood can be factored into a part containing the structural parameters and a part containing the information on the missing data mechanism. On the other hand, such a factorization is impossible when the response mechanism is NMAR or when the two sets of parameters are not distinct, and, therefore, the response mechanism is nonignorable.

Assuming a multinomial sampling scheme for the same variables and subgroups as above, estimation of a log-linear model with partially observed data involves maximizing the following incomplete data likelihood

$$
\begin{aligned}
\log \mathcal{L}_{(\pi,\theta)} = &\sum_{abcd} n_{abcd} \log \pi_{abcd}\, \theta_{ABCD|abcd} \\
&+ \sum_{abc} n_{abc} \log \sum_{d} \pi_{abcd}\, \theta_{ABC|abcd} \\
&+ \sum_{abd} n_{abd} \log \sum_{c} \pi_{abcd}\, \theta_{ABD|abcd} \\
&+ \sum_{ab} n_{ab} \log \sum_{cd} \pi_{abcd}\, \theta_{AB|abcd} \,,
\end{aligned}
$$

where

$$
\theta_{ABCD|abcd} + \theta_{ABC|abcd} + \theta_{ABD|abcd} + \theta_{AB|abcd} = 1 \,.
$$

Here, $\theta_{ABC|abcd}$, $\theta_{ABC|abcd}$, $\theta_{ABD|abcd}$, and $\theta_{AB|abcd}$ denote the conditional probability of belonging to subgroup $ABCD$, ABC, ADC, and AB, respectively, given that $A = a$, $B = b$, $C = c$, and $D = d$. The θ's, or the response probabilities, contain the parameters associated with the response mechanism. The missing data are MAR if the θ's are independent of the missing variables in the subgroup concerned, that is, if

$$
\theta_{ABC|abcd} = \theta_{ABC|abc} \,, \tag{3.14}
$$

$$\theta_{ABD|abcd} = \theta_{ABD|abd}\,, \qquad\qquad\qquad [3.15]$$

$$\theta_{AB|abcd} = \theta_{AB|ab}\,, \qquad\qquad\qquad [3.16]$$

$$\theta_{ABCD|abcd} = 1 - \theta_{ABC|abc} - \theta_{ABD|abd} - \theta_{AB|ab}\,. \qquad [3.17]$$

In that case, the likelihood function can be factored into a component which depends solely on the log-linear parameters and a component which depends solely on the response mechanism:

$$\log \mathcal{L}_{(\pi,\theta)} = \log \mathcal{L}_{(\pi)} + \log \mathcal{L}_{(\theta)}\,,$$

where

$$\log \mathcal{L}_{(\pi)} = \sum_{abcd} n_{abcd} \log \pi_{abcd} + \sum_{abc} n_{abc} \log \sum_{d} \pi_{abcd}$$
$$+ \sum_{abd} n_{abd} \log \sum_{c} \pi_{abcd} + \sum_{ab} n_{ab} \log \sum_{cd} \pi_{abcd}\,,$$

and

$$\log \mathcal{L}_{(\theta)} = \sum_{abcd} n_{abcd} \log \theta_{ABCD|abcd} + \sum_{abc} n_{abc} \log \theta_{ABC|abc}$$
$$+ \sum_{abd} n_{abd} \log \theta_{ABD|abd} + \sum_{ab} n_{ab} \log \theta_{AB|ab}\,.$$

If, in addition, no restrictions are imposed across the parameters determining the θ's and the parameters determining the π's, the two parts may be maximized separately. This means that the structural parameters can be estimated without estimating the parameters of the response mechanism. For this reason, the response mechanism is called ignorable for likelihood-based inference.

The constraints imposed on the θ's in Equations 3.14-3.17 to make the response mechanism ignorable are the least restrictive ones. There are as many free θ's as observed frequencies in the subgroups with partially observed data. Actually, a 'saturated' MAR model is assumed for the response mechanism. In other words, it is a model which uses all the additional degrees of freedom obtained by using the partially observed data. Of course, it is also possible to impose more restrictive constraints on the θ's. Assuming the θ's to be equal for every value of *A, B, C*, and *D*, for instance, provides MCAR missing data. There are several 'non-saturated' MAR models which are less restrictive than the MCAR model but more restrictive than the 'saturated' MAR model. All of these MAR models lead to the same parameter estimates for the structural model.

3.2.2. Fuchs's approach

Extending earlier work by Chen and Fienberg (1974), Hocking and Oxspring (1971, 1974), and Chen (1979) on the treatment of missing data in the analysis of categorical data, Fuchs (1982) demonstrated how to estimate the parameters of a log-linear model by means of the EM algorithm in cases in which the nonresponse is ignorable (Dempster, Laird, and Rubin, 1977). As always, the E step of the EM algorithm involves computing the conditional expected complete data likelihood. Because of the ignorability of the response mechanism, only the part depending on the log-linear parameters needs to be considered, or

$$\log \mathcal{L}^*_{(\pi)} = \sum_{abcd} \hat{n}_{abcd} \log \hat{\pi}_{abcd} \, .$$

This involves obtaining estimates for the frequencies in the complete table $ABCD$ by

$$\hat{n}_{abcd} = n_{abcd} + n_{abc} \, \hat{\pi}_{d|abc} + n_{abd} \, \hat{\pi}_{c|abd} + n_{ab} \, \hat{\pi}_{cd|ab} \, .$$

In the M step, improved estimates for the probabilities $\hat{\pi}_{abcd}$ are obtained by maximizing the complete data likelihood using $\hat{n}_{abcd}$ as if you were dealing with observed frequencies.

It should be noted that when applying the above-mentioned procedure, caution should be exercised if there are observed zeros in the sufficient statistics for the subgroup for which all variables are observed. In such cases, the starting values may determine the final estimates of particular parameters (Fuchs, 1982).

To test the fit of a postulated log-linear model, Fuchs proposed obtaining the θ's as follows:

$$\theta_{ABCD} = N^{ABCD}/N \, ,$$

$$\theta_{ABC} = N^{ABC}/N \, ,$$

$$\theta_{ABD} = N^{ABD}/N \, ,$$

$$\theta_{AB} = N^{AB}/N$$

which is, in fact, equivalent to assuming that the missing data is MCAR. This leads to the following likelihood chi-square statistic,

$$L^2 = 2 \sum_{abcd} n_{abcd} \log \frac{n_{abcd}}{\hat{m}_{abcd} \, \theta_{ABCD}} + 2 \sum_{abc} n_{abc} \log \frac{n_{abc}}{\sum_d \hat{m}_{abcd} \, \theta_{ABC}}$$

$$+ 2 \sum_{abd} n_{abd} \log \frac{n_{abd}}{\sum_c \hat{m}_{abcd} \, \theta_{ABD}} + 2 \sum_{ab} n_{ab} \log \frac{n_{ab}}{\sum_{cd} \hat{m}_{abcd} \, \theta_{AB}} \, .$$

It can be seen that the estimated expected frequencies for the complete table, $\hat{m}_{abcd}$, are proportionally divided over the subgroups. Since this amounts to assuming that the missing data are MCAR, this L^2 statistic simultaneously tests the fit of the postulated log-linear model and the validity of the MCAR assumption. This is, however, not a problem because the fit of the log-linear model of interest can be tested indirectly by means of a conditional L^2 test. For that purpose, the saturated model, model $\{ABCD\}$, has to be estimated. Since the saturated model itself fits perfectly, the L^2 that is obtained for this log-linear model only tests the validity of the MCAR assumption. By subtracting the L^2 value of the saturated log-linear model from the L^2 value of the model of interest, one obtains a test for the model of interest. This is a test under the weakest ignorable type of missing data, that is, MAR nonresponse.

3.2.3. Fay's approach

Sometimes one is interested in testing assumptions about the ignorable response mechanism itself. Also, it is possible that one wants to specify a nonignorable response mechanism. In such cases, the method proposed by Fuchs is not appropriate. Chen and Fienberg (1974) proposed a method for relaxing the MCAR assumption by simultaneously modeling and testing the log-linear model for the variables of interest and the response model. They demonstrated how to estimate the θ parameters under different types of ignorable response mechanisms. Nordheim (1984) considered nonignorable response mechanisms, or NMAR missing data, for a partially observed binary response variable. By fixing the θ's to particular values, he evaluated the sensitivity of the parameters of the structural model to the assumptions about the response mechanism.

Causal models for nonresponse using indicator variables Little (1985), Fay (1986), and Baker and Laird (1988) presented methods based on defining response indicators for the variables which are partially observed. Using these methods, it is possible to specify either ignorable or nonignorable response mechanisms. Little (1985) used hierarchical log-linear models for the joint distribution of two ordinary variables and two response indicators (see also Winship and Mare, 1989). Fay (1986) and Baker and Laird (1988) used recursive causal log-linear models, or modified path models, in which the response indicators are treated as dependent variables. Below, the procedure which was proposed independently by Fay and by Baker and Laird is presented using the same example as above.

Let R and S denote two response indicators, in which R indicates whether C is observed or not observed and S indicates whether D is observed or not observed. If variable C is observed, R takes the value 1, otherwise R takes the value 2. If variable D is observed, S equals 1, and if D is missing, S equals 2. It is clear that the different subgroups can be identified by the levels of R and S. If a given individual has $R = 1$ and $S = 2$, then C is observed and D is missing, which means that individual belongs to subgroup ABC.

The procedure proposed by Fay (1986, 1989) consists of using these response indicators together which the other variables in a modified path model. More precisely, a log-linear path model is used to specify both a model for the structural variables and a model for the response mechanism. According to Fay, the response indicators may never appear as independent variables in a logit equation in which a structural variable or a research variable is explained. This can easily be accomplished by specifying the model for the structural variables in the first modified path steps and the response model in the last steps. The modified path model for the joint distribution of the structural variables A, B, C, and D, and the response indicators R and S could, for instance, be

$$\pi_{abcdrs} = \pi_{abcd}\, \pi_{rs|abcd}\,, \qquad [3.18]$$

where $\pi_{rs|abcd}$ denotes the probability that $R = r$ and $S = s$, given an individual's scores on A, B, C, and D. In fact, these π's have the same meaning as the θ's. Note that it is also possible to split $\pi_{rs|abcd}$ into two separate modified path steps: $\pi_{r|abcd}$ and $\pi_{s|abcdr}$. This is necessary if R and S are time ordered, for instance, if R and S indicate whether a respondent participated in the first or the second wave of a panel study, respectively. Of course, the structural model may also be in the form of a modified path model.

The conditional probability $\pi_{rs|abcd}$ may be restricted by means of a logit model. Suppose that the probability of responding on C (the score on R) depends on D and that the probability of responding on D (the score on S) depends on C. Moreover, as in the case of MCAR nonresponse, assume that R and S are related. This leads to the following logit model for the joint distribution of R and S

$$\pi_{rs|abcd} = \pi_{rs|cd} = \frac{\exp\left(u_r^R + u_s^S + u_{rs}^{RS} + u_{rd}^{RD} + u_{sc}^{SC}\right)}{\sum_{rs} \exp\left(u_r^R + u_s^S + u_{rs}^{RS} + u_{rd}^{RD} + u_{sc}^{SC}\right)}. \qquad [3.19]$$

It can be seen that the dependence of R on D and of S on C involves including the interaction terms u_{rd}^{RD} and u_{sc}^{SC} in the model for the response mechanism. Note that the inclusion of the interaction term u_{rs}^{RS} in the response model fixes the margin RS, or equivalently, the sizes of the subgroups.

Ignorable versus nonignorable response mechanisms It should be noted that there is not always a simple one-to-one correspondence between the log-linear models for the response mechanism and the classification of types of missing data discussed above. For instance, in the case of the log-linear model for nonresponse specified in Equation 3.19 one would perhaps expect that the missing data are assumed to be MAR, which would imply that the response mechanism is ignorable, since the variables with missing data do not influence their own response indicators. Nonetheless, the missing data are assumed to be NMAR. This can be seen by writing down the response probabilities for the different values of R and S in the terms of log-linear parameters, i.e.,

$$\theta_{ABCD|abcd} = \pi_{11|cd} = \frac{\exp\left(u_1^R + u_1^S + u_{11}^{RS} + u_{1d}^{RD} + u_{1c}^{SC}\right)}{\sum_{rs} \exp\left(u_r^R + u_s^S + u_{rs}^{RS} + u_{rd}^{RD} + u_{sc}^{SC}\right)},$$

$$\theta_{ABC|abcd} = \pi_{12|cd} = \frac{\exp\left(u_1^R + u_2^S + u_{12}^{RS} + u_{1d}^{RD} + u_{2c}^{SC}\right)}{\sum_{rs} \exp\left(u_r^R + u_s^S + u_{rs}^{RS} + u_{rd}^{RD} + u_{sc}^{SC}\right)},$$

$$\theta_{ABD|abcd} = \pi_{21|cd} = \frac{\exp\left(u_2^R + u_1^S + u_{21}^{RS} + u_{2d}^{RD} + u_{1c}^{SC}\right)}{\sum_{rs} \exp\left(u_r^R + u_s^S + u_{rs}^{RS} + u_{rd}^{RD} + u_{sc}^{SC}\right)},$$

$$\theta_{AB|abcd} = \pi_{22|cd} = \frac{\exp\left(u_2^R + u_2^S + u_{22}^{RS} + u_{2d}^{RD} + u_{2c}^{SC}\right)}{\sum_{rs} \exp\left(u_r^R + u_s^S + u_{rs}^{RS} + u_{rd}^{RD} + u_{sc}^{SC}\right)}.$$

Because of the appearance of the parameter u_{rd}^{RD} in its logit expression, $\theta_{ABC|abcd}$ is not independent of the value of D. The same argument applies to $\theta_{ABD|abcd}$ and $\theta_{AB|abcd}$ which both depend on C and D as well. Actually, all the response probabilities are influenced by both C and D because the response probabilities must sum to unity within every level of the joint variable CD, which is accomplished by the scaling factor appearing in the denominator of the logit equations. As a result, the missing data are NMAR. This phenomenon, which is also mentioned by Winship and Mare (1989), occurs because the response probabilities depend on variables with missing data. Even if the variables C and D do not have a direct effect on their own response indicators, the parameter estimates for the structural model differ from the estimates under an ignorable response model. This means that the response mechanism is nonignorable. So, it is necessary to be cautious when labeling log-linear response models as MAR or ignorable. These terms refer only to the fact that the response mechanism can be ignored for likelihood based inference about the structural parameters, and, consequently, they do not always have the expected substantive meaning.

The most restrictive ignorable response mechanism is obtained when the log-linear response model does not incorporate interaction effects between the structural variables and the response indicators, that is, when the data are postulated to be MCAR. In the example, this would imply that $\pi_{rs|abcd} = \pi_{rs}$. On the other hand, the least restrictive mechanism which is still ignorable is obtained when the response indicators depend on all variables which are observed for all persons, including all their higher order interaction terms. In this case, the most extended ignorable log-linear response model is obtained by assuming that $\pi_{rs|abcd} = \pi_{rs|ab}$, which is equivalent to a 'non-saturated' MAR mechanism. A 'saturated' MAR model cannot be specified with a log-linear model for $\pi_{rs|abcd}$. Such a model can only be obtained by imposing the restrictions described in Equations 3.14-3.17 directly on the response probabilities.

Monotone patterns of nonresponse When the nonresponse follows a monotone pattern, is it possible to formulate a log-linear path model for the response mechanism which is equivalent to a 'saturated' MAR model, or, in other words, a response model which uses all the additional degrees of freedom obtained by using the partially observed data. A monotone pattern of nonresponse means that the variables can be ordered in such a way that a missing score on one particular variable implies having missing scores on all subsequent variables too. Such patterns of nonresponse occur often in social research, especially in panel studies, where nonresponse at one point in time often implies nonresponse at the next points in time.

Suppose we have data from a panel study in which A, B, C, and D are measurements of the same variable at four points in time. Moreover, assume that there are four subgroups: A, AB, ABC, and $ABCD$. Subgroup A only participated on the first occasion, subgroup AB on the first and the second occasion, subgroup ABC on the first three occasions, and subgroup $ABCD$ on all four occasions. This yields a monotone or nested missing data pattern since if B is missing, C and D are missing as well, and if C is missing, D is missing as well. Let R, S, and T be the response indicators for B, C, and D, respectively. In this case, a 'saturated' MAR model is obtained when

$$\pi_{rst|abcd} = \pi_{r|a} \, \pi_{s|abr} \, \pi_{t|abcrs} \, .$$

As a result of the monotone pattern of the missing data, certain probabilities are structurally equal to one. More precisely, if $R = 2$, $S = 2$ as well, and if $S = 2$, $T = 2$ too. Therefore, $\pi^S_{2|ab2} = 1$ and $\pi^T_{2|ab12} = \pi^T_{2|ab22} = 1$. Using this additional information, the θ's are given by

$$\theta_{ABCD|abcd} = \pi_{111|abcd} = \pi^R_{1|a} \, \pi^S_{1|ab1} \, \pi^T_{1|abc11} \, ,$$

$$\theta_{ABC|abcd} = \pi_{112|abcd} = \pi^R_{1|a} \, \pi^S_{1|ab1} \, \pi^T_{2|abc11} \, ,$$

$$\theta_{AB|abcd} = \pi_{122|abcd} = \pi^R_{1|a} \, \pi^S_{2|ab1} \, ,$$

$$\theta_{A|abcd} = \pi_{222|abcd} = \pi^R_{2|a} \, .$$

It can easily be seen that the missing data are MAR, since the probability of belonging to a particular subgroup depends only on the observed variables in the subgroup concerned.

Estimation via the EM algorithm Let us return to the model represented in Equations 3.18 and 3.19. Maximum likelihood estimation of the parameters of this model involves maximizing the following incomplete data log-likelihood function,

$$\log \mathcal{L}_{(\pi)} = \sum_{abcd} n_{abcd} \log \pi_{abcd} \pi_{11|abcd} + \sum_{abc} n_{abc} \log \sum_d \pi_{abcd} \pi_{12|abcd}$$

$$+ \sum_{abd} n_{abd} \log \sum_c \pi_{abcd} \pi_{21|abcd} + \sum_{ab} n_{ab} \log \sum_{cd} \pi_{abcd} \pi_{22|abcd} \, .$$

The simultaneous estimation of the model for the relationships between A, B, C, and D and the model for the response mechanism can be accomplished via the EM algorithm. In the E step, the conditional expectation of the complete data, that is, the unobserved frequencies $\hat{n}_{abcdrs}$, have to be computed by means of

$$\hat{n}_{abcd11} = n_{abcd} \, ,$$

$$\hat{n}_{abcd12} = n_{abc} \, \hat{\pi}_{d|abc12} \, ,$$

$$\hat{n}_{abcd21} = n_{abd} \, \hat{\pi}_{c|abd21} \, ,$$

$$\hat{n}_{abcd22} = n_{ab} \, \hat{\pi}_{cd|ab22} \, .$$

Note that unlike the E step for models with latent variables (see Equation 3.13), here the posterior probabilities are subgroup specific because each subgroup has different missing data to be estimated.

In the M step, improved estimates for the parameters of the modified path model are obtained by maximizing the complete data log-likelihood

$$\log \mathcal{L}^*_{(\pi)} = \sum_{abcdrs} \hat{n}_{abcdrs} \log \pi_{abcd} \, \pi_{rs|abcd} \, .$$

Testing The model can be tested by means of the likelihood-ratio statistic

$$L^2 = 2 \sum_{abcd} n_{abcd} \log \left(\frac{n_{abcd}}{\hat{m}_{abcd11}} \right) + 2 \sum_{abc} n_{abc} \log \left(\frac{n_{abc}}{\sum_d \hat{m}_{abcd12}} \right)$$
$$+ 2 \sum_{abd} n_{abd} \log \left(\frac{n_{abd}}{\sum_c \hat{m}_{abcd21}} \right) + 2 \sum_{ab} n_{ab} \log \left(\frac{n_{ab}}{\sum_{cd} \hat{m}_{abcd22}} \right) \, .$$

This is a simultaneous test for the structural model and the response model. The assumptions regarding the response mechanism and the structural model can be tested separately by means of conditional tests. The number of degrees of freedom is

$$df = \text{number of cells} - \text{number of independent } u \text{ parameters} \, ,$$

where the number of cells is the sum of the number of cells of all subgroups, and the number of independent u parameters is the sum of the number of independent parameters of the structural model and the response model.

Latent variables and nonresponse As demonstrated by Hagenaars (1985, 1990:257), Fuchs's method can also be used to deal with nonresponse in latent class models and other types of log-linear models with latent variables. In that case, there is a double missing data problem, namely: partially unobserved and completely unobserved variables. The same kind of solution was used by Vermunt (1988, 1994, 1996) to make Fay's method applicable to log-linear path models with latent variables (see also Hagenaars, 1990:260).

Suppose we want to estimate a model which apart from the completely and partially observed variables A, B, C, and D contains the latent variables W and Y. In that case, the E step of the EM algorithm changes into

$$\hat{n}_{wyabcd11} = n_{abcd}\,\hat{\pi}_{wy|abcd11}\,,$$

$$\hat{n}_{wyabcd12} = n_{abc}\,\hat{\pi}_{wyd|abc12}\,,$$

$$\hat{n}_{wyabcd21} = n_{abd}\,\hat{\pi}_{wyc|abd21}\,,$$

$$\hat{n}_{wyabcd22} = n_{ab}\,\hat{\pi}_{wycd|ab22}\,.$$

Note that for each subgroup, both the values of the missing variables and the values of the latent variable are estimated. The M step proceeds in the same way as discussed above.

Computer programs Several programs have been developed which can be used to estimate log-linear models with partially observed variables. In the LCAG program (Hagenaars and Luijkx, 1990), the method developed by Fuchs is implemented, including Hagenaars's extension for models with latent variables. Although it is rather complicated, LCAG can also be used to specify models with response indicators (Vermunt, 1988). In the *ℓEM* program (Vermunt, 1993), Fay's method is the standard way to treat partially observed data. Moreover, models which contain both partially and completely unobserved variables can be handled by the extension of Fay's method presented above. In addition, Haberman's NEWTON program, which uses a Newton algorithm instead of EM, can be used to estimate models with partially observed data (Haberman, 1988).

4 Event History Analysis

The main characteristic of event history data is that it provides information on the times at which individual transitions between a number of discrete states occurred. Because of the growing availability of event history data, techniques for analyzing this kind of data are becoming increasingly popular in the social sciences. There are many textbooks which describe the fundamentals of this type of model (Kalbfleisch and Prentice, 1980; Cox and Oakes, 1984; Lawless, 1982; Tuma and Hannan, 1984; Blossfeld, Hamerle, and Mayer, 1989; Lancaster, 1990; Yamaguchi, 1991; Courgeau and Lelièvre, 1992; Blossfeld and Rohwer, 1995). The aim of this chapter is to give an overview of event history models, to investigate the relationship between event history models and the log-linear models discussed in Chapter 2, and to discuss all kinds of problems associated with the analysis of event history data.

The first section discusses the characteristics of event history data and explains the necessity of special techniques for analyzing this kind of data. Section 4.2 deals with the basic statistical concepts. Models for the analysis of event history data, or hazard models, are introduced in section 4.3. After discussing the choice of the dependent variable and presenting a classification of hazard models, attention is given to the three main types of hazard models: parametric models, Cox's semi-parametric model, and discrete-time models.

Section 4.4 discusses the relationship between event history models and the log-linear models presented in Chapter 2. More precisely, it shows that particular kinds of event history models are equivalent to the log-rate model which was presented in section 2.6.

While sections 4.3 and 4.4 deal strictly with the simplest kinds of hazard models, that is, models for a single non-repeatable event with time-constant covariates, the last four sections of this chapter illustrate how the main principles of hazard modeling can be generalized to more complex situations. Furthermore, a number of problems associated with the analysis of event history data are discussed, some of which can be solved by means of the event history models with latent variables and missing data which are discussed in the next chapter.

Section 4.5 discusses the issue of censoring. Censoring is a form of missing data which is inherent to event history data. Section 4.6 deals with the potentials and pitfalls of dynamic modeling. Event history models are dynamic models because of the possibility of regressing the hazard rate on different kinds of time variables, on time-varying covariates, and on interactions between time and covariates. It is shown that the problems of selection bias, unobserved heterogeneity, and reverse causation can hamper the causal interpretation of effects.

Section 4.7 presents models which can be used when there are different types of events. These models are often called competing risks models. The most general class of event history models, i.e., multivariate hazard models, are presented in section 4.8. Included in the family of multivariate hazard models are models for repeatable events, multiple-state models, models for clustered observations, and models for different types of life-course events. Special attention is given to the relationship between discrete-time multiple-state models and the modified path models discussed in Chapter 2, and to the problem of dependence among events.

It should be noted that in this chapter it is assumed that all covariates are fully observed. Event history models with partially or totally missing covariates are presented in Chapter 5. However, when discussing particular problems associated with event history modeling, the use of models with unobserved variables are sometimes mentioned as a possible solution.

4.1. Why event history analysis?

In order to understand the nature of event history data and the purpose of event history analysis, it is important to understand the following four elementary concepts: state, event, duration, and risk period (Yamaguchi, 1991:1-3). These concepts are illustrated below using an example from the analyses of marital histories.

The first step in the analysis of event histories is to define the relevant *states* which are distinguished. The states are the categories of the 'dependent' variable the dynamics of which we want to explain. At every particular point in time, each person occupies exactly one state. In the analysis of marital histories, four states are generally distinguished: never married, married, divorced, and widow(er). The set of possible states is sometimes also called the state space (Tuma and Hannan, 1984:45).

An *event* is a transition from one state to another, that is, from an origin state to a destination state. In this context, a possible event is 'first marriage', which can be defined as the transition from the origin state, never married, to the destination state, married. Other possible events are: a divorce, becoming a widow(er), and a non-first marriage. It is important to note that the states which are distinguished determine the definition of possible events. If only the states married and not married were distinguished, none of the above-mentioned events could have been defined. In that case, the only events that could be defined would be marriage and marriage dissolution.

Another important concept is the *risk period*. Clearly, not all persons can experience each of the events under study at every point in time. To be able to experience a particular event, one must occupy the origin state defining the event, that is, one must be at risk of the event concerned. The period that someone is at risk of a particular event, or exposed to a particular risk, is called the risk period. For example, someone can only experience a divorce when he or she is married. Thus, only married persons are at risk of a divorce. Furthermore, the risk period(s) for a divorce are the period(s) that a subject is married. A strongly related concept is the *risk set*. The risk set at a particular point in time is formed by all subjects who are at risk of experiencing the event concerned at that point in time.

Using these concepts, event history analysis can be defined as the analysis of the *duration of the nonoccurrence of an event*[1] during the risk period (Yamaguchi, 1991:3). When the event of interest is 'first marriage', the analysis concerns the duration of nonoccurrence of a first marriage, in other words, the time that individuals remained in the state of never being married. In practice, as will be demonstrated in section 4.3, the

---

[1] Other terms which are used instead of duration are waiting time, sojourn time, and failure time.

dependent variable in event history models is not duration or time itself but a rate. Therefore, event history analysis can also be defined as the analysis of rates of occurrence of the event during the risk period. In the first marriage example, an event history model concerns a person's marriage rate during the period that he/she is in the state of never having been married.[2]

Why is it necessary to use a special type of technique for analyzing event history data? Why is it impossible to relate the incidence of an event within the period of the study to a set of covariates simply by means of, for instance, a logit model, in which the binary dependent variable indicates whether a particular event occurred within the observation period or not? This is, in fact, what is generally done in the analysis of categorical data collected by means of a two-wave panel. If using such a logit modeling approach were a good strategy, it would not be necessary to use special types of methods for analyzing event history data. However, as will be demonstrated below, such an approach has some significant drawbacks.

Suppose there are data on intra-firm job changes of the employees working at company 'C' which have to be used to explain individual differences with regards to the timing of the first promotion. In other words, the aim of the study is to explain why certain individuals in company 'C' remained in their first job longer than others. A single binary dependent variable could be defined indicating whether a given individual received a promotion within, for instance, the first five years after gaining employment in the company concerned. This dependent variable could be related to a set of covariates, such as age, work experience, job level, educational level, family characteristics, and work-related attitudes by means of a logit model.

Although such a simple logit approach can be quite valuable, it has four important drawbacks (Yamaguchi, 1991:9). All of them result from the fact that the choice of the period in which the event may have occurred or not is arbitrary. The first problem is that it leads to a severe loss of information since the information on the timing of a promotion within the five-year period, on the promotions that occur after the five-year period, and on the duration of the nonoccurrence of promotions after the five-year period is not used.

---

[2] While the aim of event history analysis is explaining the occurrence of events, recently, Allison (1994) proposed methods for estimating the effects of events.

The second problem of the approach with a single binary dependent variable is that it does not allow the covariate effects to vary with time; in other words, it cannot contain covariate-time interactions. Suppose that the effect of the variable educational level changes with time, or more precisely, that highly-educated employees have a higher probability of being promoted in the first three years that they work at company 'C', while less educated individuals have a higher probability after three years. In that case, the results will heavily depend on the choice of the length of the time interval. If a short time interval is used, a strong positive effect of the educational level will be found, while longer intervals will lead to a smaller positive effect or perhaps even to a negative effect of the same explanatory variable.

The third disadvantage to the logit approach is that it cannot deal with time-varying covariates. An example of a covariate that can change its value during the five-year period is the number of children that someone has. It may be of interest to test whether the number of children a woman has influences the probability of getting promoted. It is clear that in a real dynamic analysis, it must be possible to use covariates which change their value over time.

The last problem of the simple logit model is that is cannot deal with observations which are censored within the five-year period. In this case, there may be two types of censored observations: individuals who leave before working five years at the company concerned and before getting a first promotion, and individuals who had worked less than five years at company 'C' and had not yet been promoted at the time that the data were collected. These two types of observations have in common that they provide the information that the event of interest did not occur during a given period of time, but they do not provide information on whether the event does occur during the remaining part of the five-year period. Actually, censoring is a form of partially missing data. When using the logit approach, it is not clear what should be done with such censored observations. Ignoring the censored observations implies that the information on non-promotion during a given period of time is not used. On the other hand, incorporating the censored observations in the analysis as observations on individuals that did not experience an event adds information, namely, that they would not have experienced an event if they had worked for at least five years at company 'C'.

Clearly, special techniques are needed which overcome these disadvantages of the simple logit approach discussed above and which fully use the richness of event history data. Before presenting these models, some basic concepts have to be introduced.

4.2. Basic statistical concepts

The manner in which the basic statistical concepts of event history models are defined depends on whether the time variable T, indicating the duration of nonoccurrence of an event, is assumed to be continuous or discrete. Of course, it seems logical to assume T to be a continuous variable. However, in many situations this assumption is not realistic for two reasons. Firstly, in many cases, T is not measured accurately enough to be treated as strictly continuous. An example of this is measuring the duration variable age of the mother in completed years instead of months or days in a study on the timing of the first birth. This will result in many women having the same score on T, which is sometimes also called grouped 'survival' times.

Secondly, the events of interest can sometimes only occur at particular points in time. Such an intrinsically discrete T occurs, for example, in studies on voting behavior. Since elections take place at particular points in time, changes in voting behavior can only occur at particular points in time. Therefore, when analyzing individual changes in voting behavior, the time variable must be treated as a discrete variable. However, if we want to explain changes in political preference rather than in voting behavior, we again have a continuous time variable since political preference may change at any point in time.

4.2.1. Continuous time

Suppose T is a continuous non-negative random variable indicating the duration of nonoccurrence of the event under study, in other words, the time that the event under study occurred. Let $f(t)$ be the probability density function of T, and $F(t)$ the distribution function of T. As always, the following relationships exist between these two quantities,

$$f(t) = \lim_{\Delta t \to 0} \frac{P(t \leq T < t + \Delta t)}{\Delta t} = \frac{\partial F(t)}{\partial t},$$

$$F(t) = P(T \leq t) = \int_0^t f(u)d(u).$$

The survival probability or survival function, indicating the probability of nonoccurrence of an event until time t, is defined as

$$S(t) = 1 - F(t) = P(T \geq t) = \int_t^\infty f(u)d(u).$$

Another important concept is the hazard rate or hazard function, $h(t)$, expressing the instantaneous risk of experiencing an event at $T = t$, given that the event did not occur before t. The hazard rate is defined as

$$h(t) = \lim_{\Delta t \to 0} \frac{P(t \leq T < t + \Delta t | T \geq t)}{\Delta t} = \frac{f(t)}{S(t)}, \qquad [4.1]$$

in which $P(t \leq T < t + \Delta t | T \geq t)$ indicates the probability that the event will occur during $[t \leq T < t + \Delta t]$, given that the event did not occur before t. The hazard rate is equal to the unconditional instantaneous probability of having an event at $T = t$, $f(t)$, divided by the probability of not having an event before $T = t$, $S(t)$. It should be noted that the hazard rate itself cannot be interpreted as a conditional probability. Although its value is always non-negative, it can take values greater than one. However, for small Δt, the quantity $h(t)\Delta t$ can be interpreted as the approximate conditional probability that the event will occur between t and $t + \Delta t$.

Because the functions $f(t)$, $F(t)$, $S(t)$, and $h(t)$ give mathematically equivalent specifications of the distributions of T, it is possible to express both $S(t)$ and $f(t)$ in terms of $h(t)$. Since $f(t) = -\partial S(t)/\partial t$, Equation 4.1 implies that

$$h(t) = \frac{-\partial \log S(t)}{\partial t}.$$

By integrating and using $S(0) = 1$, that is, no individual experienced an event before $T = 0$, the important relationship

$$S(t) = \exp\left(-\int_0^t h(u)d(u)\right), \qquad [4.2]$$

is obtained. From Equations 4.1 and 4.2, it can be seen that the density $f(t)$ can also be written as a function of the hazard rate:

$$f(t) = h(t)S(t) = h(t)\exp\left(-\int_0^t h(u)d(u)\right). \qquad [4.3]$$

Thus, both the survival function and the density function of T can be written in terms of the hazard function.

4.2.2. Discrete time

Suppose T is a discrete random variable indicating the time of occurrence of an event, and t_l is the lth discrete time point, where $0 < t_1 < t_2 < \ldots < t_{L^*}$, with L^* indicating the total number of time points. If the event occurs at t_l, this means that the event did not occur before t_l, in other words, that the duration of nonoccurrence of an event equals t_{l-1}. It should be noted that this is slightly different from the continuous-time situation in which T indicates both the time that an event occurs and the duration of nonoccurrence of an event.

The probability of experiencing an event at $T = t_l$ is given as

$$f(t_l) = P(T = t_l).$$

The survivor function, which indicates the probability of having an event neither before nor at $T = t_l$,[3] is

$$S(t_l) = P(T > t_l) = \sum_{k=l+1}^{L^*} f(t_k).$$

An important quantity in the discrete-time situation is the conditional probability that the event occurs at $T = t_l$, given that the event did not occur prior to $T = t_l$. It is defined as

$$\lambda(t_l) = P(T = t_l | T \geq t_l) = \frac{f(t_l)}{S(t_{l-1})}.$$

Similar to the way $f(t)$ and $S(t)$ are expressed in terms of $h(t)$ in continuous time, $f(t_l)$ and $S(t_l)$ can be expressed in terms of $\lambda(t_l)$. Since $f(t_l) = S(t_{l-1}) - S(t_l)$,

$$\lambda(t_l) = \frac{S(t_{l-1}) - S(t_l)}{S(t_{l-1})} = 1 - \frac{S(t_l)}{S(t_{l-1})}. \qquad [4.4]$$

---

[3] It should be noted that some authors define the survival probability in discrete-time situations as the probability of not having an event before t_l: $S(t_l) = P(T \geq t_l)$.

Rearrangement of this equation results in

$$S(t_l) = S(t_{l-1})[1 - \lambda(t_l)] .$$

Once again, using $S(0) = 1$ leads to the following expressions for $S(t_l)$ and $f(t_l)$:

$$S(t_l) = \prod_{k=1}^{l} [1 - \lambda(t_k)] ,$$ [4.5]

$$f(t_l) = \lambda(t_l)S(t_{l-1}) = \lambda(t_l) \prod_{k=1}^{l-1} [1 - \lambda(t_k)] .$$ [4.6]

Because $\lambda(t_l)$ is defined in much the same way as the continuous-time hazard rate $h(t)$, it is sometimes called a hazard rate (Yamaguchi, 1990:17; Blossfeld, Hamerle, and Mayer, 1989:106). This is, however, not completely correct since a hazard rate is an instantaneous (conditional) probability, and therefore a continuous-time quantity. Nevertheless, it is possible to calculate the hazard rate $h(t)$ from $\lambda(t_l)$ and vice versa. As can be seen from Equation 4.4, the conditional probability of experiencing an event at t_l equals one minus the probability of surviving between t_{l-1} and t_l. Using $h(t)$, this can also be expressed as follows:

$$\lambda(t_l) = 1 - \exp\left(-\int_{t_{l-1}}^{t_l} h(u)d(u)\right) .$$ [4.7]

If the hazard rate is assumed to be constant in time interval t_l and if the length of time interval t_l is 1, the expression in Equation 4.7 can be simplified to

$$\lambda(t_l) = 1 - \exp(-h(t_l)) .$$

This gives the following hazard rate in time interval t_l:

$$h(t_l) = -\log(1 - \lambda(t_l))$$ [4.8]

The quantity $h(t_l)$ could be called a discrete-time hazard rate, or an approximation of the hazard rate in the lth discrete time interval. Note that the relationship between $h(t)$ and $\lambda(t_l)$ as expressed in Equation

4.7 is only meaningful if the event can occur at any point in time, that is, if time is a continuous variable which is measured discretely.

4.3. Hazard rate models

4.3.1. The form of the dependent variable

As defined above, the duration of nonoccurrence of the event under study in an event history model is related to a set of covariates. However, to be able to formulate a regression analytic model for event history data, it first has to be decided which is the best form of the dependent variable. There are at least four candidates for this purpose, namely, duration or time (T), the density of T ($f(t)$ or $f(t_l)$), the survival function ($S(t)$ or $S(t_l)$), and the hazard rate ($h(t)$) or, in discrete time, the conditional probability $\lambda(t_l)$. It is clear that the best candidate is the one which overcomes all the problems associated with the simple logit approach discussed in section 4.1. This means that an event history model must make it possible to

1. use all the information on the duration of the nonoccurrence of an event,
2. specify time dependent effects of covariates (covariate-time inter-actions),
3. use time-varying covariates,
4. use censored observations.

The simplest solution seems to be to use T or some transformation of T, such as $\log T$, as the dependent variable in an ordinary regression model. Models in which $\log T$ is linearly regressed on a set of covariates are known as accelerated failure-time models (Cox and Oakes, 1984: section 6.3; Lancaster, 1990:40). Accelerated failure-time models use all the information on the duration of nonoccurrence of an event. More-over, censored observations can be dealt with by estimating the models using maximum likelihood with missing data. In accelerated failure-time models, it is, however, not possible to let the effects of covariates change with time nor to use time-varying covariates.

As was demonstrated in the previous section, the remaining candidates give equivalent descriptions of the information on the duration of nonoccurrence of an event. Like T or $\log T$, the density function, the survival function, and the hazard rate fulfill the first and last requisite. As in accelerated failure-time models, the censoring problem is solved by using maximum likelihood methods for obtaining estimates of the model parameters. With respect to the second and third requisite, that is, with respect to the dynamic character of event history analysis, the most natural dependent variable seems to be the hazard rate. Modeling the hazard rate is a logical dynamic extension of the simple logit approach presented above in which the probability of occurrence of an event in a period of five years was modelled. By modeling the hazard rate, it becomes possible to regress it both on covariates and on time. When time is entered as an independent variable in the model, it is a rather straightforward procedure to include time-covariate interactions, that is, to allow the covariate effects to be time dependent. Moreover, the hazard rate at $T = t$ can be related to the covariate values at $T = t$, which means that the covariates may be time-varying.

Besides the hazard rate, $f(t)$ and $S(t)$ can also be used as dependent variables in an event history model. However, contrary to the hazard rate, it is prohibitively complicated to take the dynamic character of the process under study into account when modeling either the unconditional (instantaneous) probability of experiencing an event at $T = t$ or the survival probability. As was mentioned above, the hazard rate at $T = t$ depends only on the conditions at $T = t$, that is, on the covariate effects and covariate values at $T = t$. On the other hand, both $S(t)$ and $f(t)$ depend on the circumstances encountered between $T = 0$ to $T = t$ or, more precisely, on the covariate effects and covariate values on the hazard rates between $T = 0$ and $T = t$. This can be seen in Equations 4.2 and 4.3, which describe the relationships between the survival, density, and hazard function.

Because of the necessity of cumulating the covariate effects between $T = 0$ and $T = t$ if the covariate effects change with time or if there are time-varying covariates, it is, compared to $h(t)$, relatively difficult to regress $S(t)$ or $f(t)$ on a set of covariates. It is for this reason that the hazard rate is generally used as the dependent variable in event history models. Sometimes, $S(t)$ is used for this purpose when there are only time-constant covariates which effects do not change with time. The same arguments in favor of using $h(t)$ as the dependent variable in the continuous-time case do also apply for $\lambda(t_l)$ in the discrete-time case.

Here, attention is focussed solely on event history models in which $h(t)$ or $\lambda(t_l)$ is used as the dependent variable. These regression models are also called hazard rate models or simply hazard models.[4]

---

[4] It should be noted that the term hazard model is not always correct in discrete-time situations because there we often model the conditional probability $\lambda(t_l)$ instead of the hazard rate.

4.3.2. Types of hazard models

The classification which is used in most textbook on hazard modeling is the distinction between *parametric models, Cox's semi-parametric model, and discrete-time models* (see, for example, Kalbfleisch and Prentice, 1980; Blossfeld, Hamerle, and Mayer, 1989; Yamaguchi, 1991). Parametric models and Cox's semi-parametric model are used for continuous-time event history data.

The two continuous-time methods differ from each other with respect to the treatment of the time dependence of the hazard rate. In parametric models, the time dependence is assumed to have some known functional form. Well-known parametric models are the exponential model, the Weibull model, the Gompertz model, and the log-logistic model (Lawless, 1982; Blossfeld, Hamerle, and Mayer, 1989:50-55). On the other hand, if the time dependence is not parameterized, i.e., if no model is specified for the time dependence, a semi-parametric hazard model is obtained. Because the semi-parametric hazard model was first proposed by Cox (1972), it is often called the Cox semi-parametric hazard model or the Cox proportional hazard model; the meaning of the term proportional will be explained below.

The distinction between parametric and semi-parametric models is not as relevant when dealing with discrete-time models. The reason for this is that both the parametric and semi-parametric models can be specified with the same discrete-time methods. More precisely, by specifying one time parameter for every discrete time point, a model is obtained that is similar to the semi-parametric hazard model, while more parsimonious specifications of the time dependence, such as polynomials, lead to models similar to the parametric hazard models (Allison, 1982; Yamaguchi, 1991:17).

Another related approach to the analysis of event history data is the use of non-parametric methods. These methods, such as demographic life-table methods (Elandt-Johnson and Jonhson, 1980; Namboodiri and Suchindran, 1987) and Kaplan-Meier's (1958) product-limit estimates for the hazard rates, have in common that the dependence of the hazard rate on covariates is not parameterized. In that sense, they are not real models but tools for the description of event history data. Since these methods fall outside the scope of this book, they will not be discussed in further detail.

Two special families In addition to the three above-mentioned types of hazard models, two special families can be distinguished: *proportional hazard models* and *log-linear hazard models* (Lancaster 1990:42-43).

Let $h(t|\mathbf{x})$ be the hazard rate at $T = t$ for an individual with covariate vector $\mathbf{x}$. When all regressors are time-invariant, a model of the form

$$h(t|\mathbf{x}) = k_1(t)k_2(\mathbf{x}),$$ [4.9]

in which $k_1(t)$ and $k_2(\mathbf{x})$ are the same functions for all individuals is called a proportional hazard model. The reason for this is that the hazard rates for two persons with regressor vectors $\mathbf{x_1}$ and $\mathbf{x_2}$ are in the same ratio, $k_2(\mathbf{x_1})/k_2(\mathbf{x_2})$, for all t. Proportional hazard models can be defined as models in which the effect of T and the total effect of $\mathbf{X}$ on the hazard rate are multiplicative and in which there are no interaction effects between T and $\mathbf{X}$.

The concept of proportional hazard rates is especially relevant for Cox's semi-parametric model. The development of this model is based on the feature that if the hazard rate can be assumed to be proportional, a large simplification of inference in event history models is achieved. More precisely, the proportionality assumption makes it possible to estimate the unknown parameters of $k_2(\mathbf{x})$ without the necessity of specifying $k_1(t)$.

Although Cox's regression model is the best-known proportional hazard model, some of the parametric hazard models also lead to proportional hazard rates. Parametric models in which the effect of T and $\mathbf{X}$ is multiplicative, such as the Weibull model, are proportional hazard models if the effect of T is assumed to be the same for all values of $\mathbf{X}$. As the time variable is treated in the same way as any other time-varying covariate in discrete-time models, it depends on the inclusion of interaction terms between T and $\mathbf{X}$ whether a particular discrete-time model is a proportional hazard model or not.

Another special family of hazard models include the log-linear type. They have the form

$$\log h(t|\mathbf{x}) = \sum_{j=1}^{J} \beta_j k_j[t, \mathbf{x}(t)].$$ [4.10]

Here, $k_j[t, \mathbf{x}(t)]$ denotes some known function either of T or of the time-varying or time-constant covariates $\mathbf{X}(t)$. The β_js are the log-linear parameters which can be effects of T, $\mathbf{X}$, or both. Thus, a hazard rate model is called log-linear if the log of the hazard rate is a linear function of time effects and covariate effects.

It should be noted that these two special families are not exclusive categories. A proportional hazard model may also be a log-linear hazard model, namely, if $k_2(\mathbf{x}) = \exp(\sum_j \beta_j x)$. On the other hand, if there are no time-covariate interaction effects, a log-linear hazard model will also be a proportional hazard model.

Some parametric models, such as the exponential, the piecewise exponential, and the Weibull models, are log-linear or can be reparameterized to be log-linear. Cox's regression model is, likewise, log-linear. In discrete-time methods, either a log-linear specification for the hazard rate or a logit specification for the conditional probability of experiencing an event at a particular point in time is used. While the concept of proportional hazard rates was especially relevant for the development of Cox's semi-parametric model, the special family of log-linear hazard models is particularly relevant in the context of this book because it deals with event history analysis by means of log-linear analysis techniques. As will be demonstrated in section 4.4, log-linear hazard models are, to a great degree, related to the standard log-linear models which were discussed in Chapter 2.

In summary, three fundamentally different types of hazard models were distinguished: parametric hazard models, Cox's semi-parametric proportional hazard model, and discrete-time models. These models will be presented in the next subsections. It was also shown that two special families can be distinguished which contain models belonging to these three main types.

4.3.3. Parametric hazard models

Let $h(t|\mathbf{x})$ be the value of the hazard rate at $T = t$ for an individual with covariate values $\mathbf{x}$. As mentioned above, parametric hazard models assume a particular functional form for the relationship between T and the value of the hazard rate. There are many parametric models, such as exponential, piecewise exponential, Weibull, Gompertz-Makeham, log-logistic, log-normal, gamma, and inverse Gaussian models, the names of which refer to the functional form which is chosen for one of the basic functions $h(t)$, $f(t)$ or $F(t)$. In most textbooks on hazard models, a great deal of attention is given to parametric hazard models (Elandt-Johnson and Johnson, 1980; Kalbfleisch and Prentice, 1980; Cox and Oakes, 1984; Lawless, 1982; Blossfeld, Hamerle, and Mayer, 1989; Lancaster, 1990). Here, a few of the best known parametric models are presented to illustrate the main principles underlying parametric methods, and to show some of the parameterizations which belong to the special families of proportional hazard and log-linear hazard models. For the simplicity of exposition, it will be assumed that the covariates are time-invariant. In section 4.6, it will be demonstrated how to apply the hazard models which are presented below when some of the covariates are time-varying.

The *exponential* survival model is the simplest parametric hazard model. It assumes exponential survival, or a time-constant hazard rate, i.e.,

$$h(t|\mathbf{x}) = \exp\left(\sum_{j=0}^{J} \beta_j x_{ij}\right).$$

Here, β_j is an unknown parameter and x_{ij} is the value of covariate j for subject i. Thus, the hazard rate depends only on the values of the covariates $\mathbf{X}$. Note that β_0 is the intercept which implies that x_{i0} must be one for all persons.

One possible extension of the rather restrictive exponential survival model leads to the *piecewise exponential* survival model, in which the hazard rate is assumed to be constant within time periods. In other words, the hazard rate is a step function of T. Suppose the time axis is split into L^* time periods with upper limits t_l, such that $0 < t_1 < t_2 \ldots < t_{L^*}$. Moreover, let d_l denote one of the L^* indicator variables taking the value 1 if $t_{l-1} < t \leq t_l$, and otherwise the value 0. This gives the following hazard model:

$$h(t|\mathbf{x}) = \exp\left(\sum_{j=1}^{J} \beta_j x_{ij} + \sum_{l=1}^{L^*} \alpha_l d_l\right). \tag{4.11}$$

Note that the intercept β_0 is not included in the model in order to identify all α_l parameters. As a result, the α_l parameters can be interpreted as the log hazard rate of an individual for which all covariates are equal to zero. When the number of time intervals increases, it makes less sense to treat this model as parametric (Lancaster, 1990:43). As will be demonstrated in section 4.4, when the number of time intervals equals the number of distinct times that events occur, a piecewise exponential survival model is equivalent to a semi-parametric hazard model.

Another popular extension of the exponential model is the *Weibull* model, which describes the monotonous time dependence of the hazard rate by means of one additional parameter. It parameterizes the hazard rate as

$$h(t|\mathbf{x}) = \exp\left(\sum_{j=0}^{J} \beta_j x_{ij}\right) \alpha t^{\alpha-1},$$

for $\alpha > 0$. Sometimes it is reparameterized as

$$h(t|\mathbf{x}) = \exp\left(\sum_{j=0}^{J} \beta'_j x_{ij} + \alpha' \log t\right),$$

in which $\alpha' = \alpha - 1$, $\beta'_0 = \ln \alpha + \beta_0$, and, for $j = 1$ to J, $\beta'_j = \beta_j$. As is shown in the last equation, the hazard rate depends on T in the Weibull model, or equivalently, the log hazard rate on log T. If α equals 1, the Weibull model becomes an exponential model. Values for α smaller than 1 indicate that the hazard rate declines as T increases, while values larger than 1 indicate that the hazard rate increases as T increases.

In the *Gompertz-Makeham* model, the hazard rate is given as

$$h(t|\mathbf{x}) = \alpha_1 + \exp\left(\sum_{j=0}^{J} \beta_j x_{ij} + \alpha_2 t\right),$$

with $\alpha_1 \geq 0$. The difference with the Weibull model is that the log hazard rate depends on T instead of log T. The α_1 parameter denotes a lower boundary of the hazard rate. By fixing $\alpha_1 = 0$, a simpler model is obtained which is called the *Gompertz* model, in which the log of the hazard rate is simply a linear function T.

A possible extension of the Gompertz model is a model in which the time dependence of the hazard rate is parameterized by a higher order *polynomial* function of T. Such models can be used when there is a non-monotonous time dependence of the hazard rate. A polynomial model of degree K is

$$h(t|\mathbf{x}) = \exp\left(\sum_{j=0}^{J} \beta_j x_{ij} + \sum_{k=1}^{K} \alpha_k t^k\right),$$

in which the α_k's are the parameters associated with the time dependence of the hazard rate. Instead of T, it also possible to use a polynomial function of $\ln T$ (Clayton, 1983). In that case, an extension of the Weibull model is obtained.

It can be seen that all parametric hazard models presented so far, except for the Gompertz-Makeham model, are both proportional and log-linear hazard models. They are proportional because the total effect of the covariates influences the hazard rate multiplicatively and, moreover, there are no time-covariate interaction effects. Note that the proportionality assumption can be relaxed by allowing the α parameters to depend on the values of particular covariates. The models are log-linear because the log of the hazard rate is a linear function of time effects and covariate effects.

An example of a hazard model which is neither proportional nor log-linear is the *log-logistic* model. This is defined as

$$h(t|\mathbf{x}) = \frac{\alpha \left[\exp\left(\sum_0^J \beta_j x_{ij}\right)\right]^\alpha t^{\alpha-1}}{1 + \left[\exp\left(\sum_0^J \beta_j x_{ij}\right) t\right]^\alpha},$$

for $\alpha > 0$. The log-logistic function can be used to describe non-monotonous hazard rates, or more precisely, hazard rates that first increase then subsequently decrease with time. The model is nonproportional because the size of the hazard rate does not simply result from a multiplication of the total covariate effect and the time effect.[5] It is likewise not log-linear because the log of the hazard rate is not a simple linear function of time and covariate effects.

Estimation The parameters of parametric hazard models are generally estimated by means of the maximum likelihood method. Let t_i be either the time that individual i experienced an event or the time that individual i was censored, that is, either individual i's survival or censoring time. Let δ_i be a censoring indicator taking the value 0 if case i is censored and the value 1 if case i experienced an event. When the censoring mechanism can be assumed to be independent (Lagakos, 1979; Kalbfleisch and Prentice, 1980:119-122), in other words, when the missing data can be assumed to be ignorable for likelihood-based inference, the likelihood function to be maximized can be written as

$$\mathcal{L} = \prod_{i=1}^N f(t_i|\mathbf{x}_i)^{\delta_i} S(t_i|\mathbf{x}_i)^{1-\delta_i} = \prod_{i=1}^N h(t_i|\mathbf{x}_i)^{\delta_i} S(t_i|\mathbf{x}_i)$$

$$= \prod_{i=1}^N h(t_i|\mathbf{x}_i)^{\delta_i} \exp\left(-\int_0^{t_i} h(u|\mathbf{x}_i)du\right), \qquad [4.12]$$

In section 4.5, which deals with censoring, it will be explained under which conditions this likelihood function is correct. When these conditions are fulfilled, the contribution to the likelihood function of a person who experienced an event is $f(t_i|\mathbf{x}_i)$. Since only information on survival

---

[5] Recently, Brüderl and Diekman proposed several generalizations of the log-logistic model, one of which yields proportional hazard rates.

until t_i is available for censored observations, their contribution to the likelihood function is $S(t_i|\mathbf{x}_i)$.

For most parametric models, there is a tractable expression for the survival function appearing in the likelihood function. With regard to the models presented above, numerical integration in order to compute the likelihood equations is only necessary for the polynomial model (Rohwer, 1993). The likelihood equations can be solved by the Newton-Raphson algorithm or one of its variants (Petersen, 1986). In the case of log-linear hazard models, it is also possible to use a simpler conditional maximization method which is discussed in section 4.4 (Aitkin and Clayton, 1980).

The parametric models discussed above can be estimated by means of standard programs for event history analysis. The best known program is Tuma's RATE program (Tuma, 1979). Recently, Rohwer (1993) introduced his TDA program which at this moment is probably the most complete for estimating parametric hazard models. In a series of working papers accompanying the TDA program, Rohwer gave an excellent overview of the different parametric models and of the technical details on obtaining maximum likelihood estimates of their parameters by means of the Newton-Raphson algorithm. Using either RATE or TDA, it is possible to specify models in which the duration parameters (the α's) depend on the covariate values.

4.3.4. Cox's semi-parametric hazard model

The use of the parametric models discussed above requires that the distributional form of T is known. However, in many situations, there is no a priori information on the time dependence of the process under study. That is the main reason that Cox's semi-parametric hazard model, which does not parameterize the time dependence of the process, is so popular in many research fields. More precisely, it involves an unspecified function of T in the form of an arbitrary baseline hazard function. The relationship between the covariates and the hazard rate is parameterized using a log-linear model, which leads to

$$h(t|\mathbf{x}) = h_0(t) \exp\left(\sum_{j=1}^{J} \beta_j x_{ij}\right), \qquad [4.13]$$

in which $h_0(t)$ is the unspecified baseline function. Note that the effect of T, $h_0(t)$, is not allowed to depend on the covariate values as a result of the proportionality assumption. Although the model represented in

Equation 4.13 seems to be very simple, the main problem associated with it is how to estimate the β parameters without the necessity of specifying $h_0(t)$. Cox (1972, 1975) proposed solving this problem by means of what he called partial likelihood estimation.[6]

Estimation Assume that all events occur at distinct times, in other words, that there are no tied durations.[7] To compute the partial likelihood function, the observations must be ordered on the basis of the length of the duration t_i, that is, $t_1 < t_2 < t_3 \ldots < t_N$. The partial likelihood function is formulated as

$$\mathcal{L}_{PL} = \prod_{i=1}^{N} \left[\frac{h(t_i|\mathbf{x}_i)}{\sum_{k=i}^{N} h(t_i|\mathbf{x}_k)} \right]^{\delta_i} = \prod_{i=1}^{N} \left[\frac{h_0(t_i)\exp\left(\sum_j \beta_j x_{ij}\right)}{\sum_{k=i}^{N} h_0(t_i)\exp\left(\sum_j \beta_j x_{kj}\right)} \right]^{\delta_i}$$

$$= \prod_{i=1}^{N} \left[\frac{\exp\left(\sum_j \beta_j x_{ij}\right)}{\sum_{k=i}^{N} \exp\left(\sum_j \beta_j x_{kj}\right)} \right]^{\delta_i}, \qquad [4.14]$$

in which $h(t_i|\mathbf{x}_k)$ is the hazard rate for subject k at $T = t_i$, t_i is either the survival or censoring time of subject i, and δ_i is a censoring indicator.

The partial likelihood is a product of conditional probabilities. Given that an event occurred at t_i, the ith conditional probability represents the likelihood that the event will occur for the particular subject who actually had the event at $T = t_i$ rather than for any other subject who was at risk $T = t_i$ (Yamaguchi, 1991:106). Note that the individuals who are at risk at t_i are those with a survival or censoring time which is greater than or equal to t_i. Since the partial likelihood is affected only by the relative order of durations, information about the exact time that the events and censorings occur is lost. It can be seen that the unspecified baseline hazard $h_0(t)$ cancels out from the partial likelihood function described in Equation 4.14.

---

[6] The procedure is called partial likelihood because some information in the data is not used for parameter estimation. More precisely, only the order in which events occur is used, which means that the length of the time intervals between events is disregarded (Cox and Oakes, 1984: section 8.4).

[7] Two durations are called tied if the two people concerned experienced the event of interest at the same point in time. Ties are problematic in the partial likelihood method because it is based on the observed order between events and the order between tied observations cannot be determined. Note that if T is strictly continuous, ties cannot occur.

By maximizing the partial likelihood as if it were an ordinary likelihood function, maximum partial likelihood estimates for the β parameters are obtained without the necessity of estimating the unspecified baseline hazard function. Although particular information is lost when using this method, it has been proven that it has all the essential properties, such as consistency and asymptotic normality, under quite broad conditions (Tsiatis, 1981; Andersen and Gill, 1982).

By using only the order in which the events occurred and by assuming the hazard rate to be proportional, the partial likelihood provides a simple estimation procedure for the covariate effects without the necessity of specifying the time dependence of the hazard rate. The semi-parametric hazard model does, however, have two weak points: the proportionality assumption is unrealistic in most applications and the non-availability of time effects is problematic if one is interested in the duration dependence of the hazard rate. A simple solution for these two problems is the inclusion of a time-varying covariate indicating time or duration in the model (Cox and Oakes, 1984:73; Yamaguchi, 1991:107-108). The time dependence of the hazard rate can be detected by estimating the effect of this time-varying covariate on the hazard rate. The proportionality assumption can be relaxed by specifying models with interactions between 'time' and other covariates.

Because time changes continuously, in practice, time can only be used as a time-varying covariate if it is treated as discrete. This means that if time is included as a covariate in a semi-parametric hazard model, a model is obtained that is very similar to both the piecewise exponential survival model described in Equation 4.11, in which the hazard rate is assumed to be constant within time intervals (see also section 4.4), and the discrete-time methods which are presented in the next section.

Ties Above, the possibility that two persons have the same survival times, or in other words, that there are ties in the data, was disregarded. However, since duration is always measured discretely, in practice, equal durations frequently occur. Several modifications of the partial likelihood method have been proposed to deal with ties. The solution proposed by Peto (1972) and Breslow (1974) on somewhat different grounds is the one which is used most often. In the case of ties, the data must be ordered such that $t_1 \leq t_2 \leq t_3 \ldots \leq t_N$. Because some t_i are equal, the summation over the risk set in the denominator of Equation 4.14 has to be changed. Instead of starting from $k = i$, it must start from the smallest k for which $t_k = t_i$: Everyone with either the same or a greater value of T than i belongs to the risk set at $T = t_i$. This principle can be formulated in several equivalent fashions, such as

$$\mathcal{L}_{PL} = \prod_{i=1}^{N} \left[\frac{\exp\left(\sum_j \beta_j x_{ij}\right)}{\sum_{k \in (t_k \geq t_i)} \exp\left(\sum_j \beta_j x_{kj}\right)} \right]^{\delta_i}, \qquad [4.15]$$

or

$$\mathcal{L}_{PL} = \prod_{i^*=1}^{N^*} \frac{\exp\left(\sum_j \beta_j s_{i^* j}\right)}{\left[\sum_{k \in (t_k \geq t_{i^*})} \exp\left(\sum_j \beta_j x_{kj}\right)\right]^{n_{i^*}}}. \qquad [4.16]$$

Compared to Equation 4.14, in the first expression (4.15), only the index of the summation in the denominator is changed to include all cases in the risk set for which $t_k \geq t_i$. The second, somewhat more complicated expression (4.16) is the one which is used most often. There, N^* denotes the number of distinct times at which one or more events occurred, t_i^* a particular time at which one or more events occurred, $s_{i^* j}$ is the sum of the values of the jth covariate for all individuals who experience an event at $T = t_{i^*}$, and finally, n_{i^*} is the number of events at $T = t_{i^*}$.

In section 4.4, the solution for ties as proposed by Breslow (1974) is discussed in more detail. The resulting proportional hazard model is shown to be equivalent to a proportional piecewise exponential survival model with as many time categories as different observed times at which events occurred.

4.3.5. Discrete-time models

When the time variable is measured rather crudely, which leads to many ties in the data, or when the process under study is intrinsically discrete, it is more appropriate to use one of the discrete-time event history models.[8] These models involve regressing the conditional probability of occurrence of an event in the lth time interval, given that the event did not occur before this period, denoted by $\lambda(t_l)$, on a set of covariates. It must be noted that when these probabilities are relatively small for all values of T and X, the parameters of discrete-time models and continuous-time models are very similar. The reason for this is that the hazard rate $h(t)$ and $\lambda(t_l)$ have almost the same value if the

---

[8] For applications of discrete-time event history models in situations in which the time dimensions is intrinsically discrete see, for example, Mare (1994) and Van Rees and Vermunt (1996).

hazard rate is small. On the basis of the relationship between $h(t)$ and $\lambda(t_l)$ given in Equation 4.8, it can be seen that values of .1, .2, and .5 for $\lambda(t_l)$ correspond with values of .105, .223, and .693 for $h(t)$. This means that if all $\lambda(t_l)$ are smaller than .1, discrete-time methods provide good approximations of continuous-time methods.

There are several ways to parameterize the dependence of the conditional probability of experiencing an event on time and on covariates. The most popular choice is the logistic regression function (Cox, 1972; Myers, Hankley, and Mantel, 1973; Brown 1975; Thompson 1977; Allison, 1982)

$$\lambda(t_l|\mathbf{x}) = \frac{\exp\left(\alpha_l + \sum_j \beta_j x_{ij}\right)}{1 + \exp\left(\alpha_l + \sum_j \beta_j x_{ij}\right)},$$

which leads to the well-known discrete-time logit model

$$\log\left[\frac{\lambda(t_l|\mathbf{x})}{1 - \lambda(t_l|\mathbf{x})}\right] = \alpha_l + \sum_j \beta_j x_{ij}.$$

Although the logistic regression model is a somewhat arbitrary choice, it has several advantages: It constrains $\lambda(t_l|\mathbf{x})$ to between 0 and 1, and it is computationally convenient because of the existence of sufficient statistics.

On the other hand, as is demonstrated below, if one assumes that the data are generated by a continuous-time proportional hazard model, it is preferable to use the complementary log-log transformation for $\lambda(t_l)$ (Allison, 1982). It can be derived from Equation 4.7, that the conditional probability of experiencing an event in t_l can be written in terms of the hazard rate as

$$\lambda(t_l|\mathbf{x}) = 1 - \exp\left(-\int_{t_{l-1}}^{t_l} h(u|\mathbf{x})d(u)\right).$$

If there is no information on the variation of the hazard rate within the time intervals, it seems reasonable to assume that the hazard rate is constant within each interval t_l, or that

$$\lambda(t_l|\mathbf{x}) = 1 - \exp\left(-h(t_l|\mathbf{x})\Delta t_l\right), \qquad [4.17]$$

in which Δt_l denotes the length of the lth time interval. This amounts to assuming exponential survival within every particular time interval.

Suppose the following log-linear and proportional hazard model is postulated:

$$h(t_l|\mathbf{x})\Delta t_l = \exp\left(\alpha_l + \sum_j \beta_j x_{ij}\right) . \qquad [4.18]$$

Substitution of Equation 4.18 into Equation 4.17 yields

$$\lambda(t_l|\mathbf{x}) = 1 - \exp\left[-\exp\left(\alpha_l + \sum_j \beta_j x_{ij}\right)\right] .$$

Rearrangement of this equation yields what is known as the complementary log-log transformation of the conditional probability of experiencing an event at t_l,

$$\log\left[-\log\left(1 - \lambda(t_l|\mathbf{x})\right)\right] = \alpha_l + \sum_j \beta_j x_{ij} .$$

The β parameters can now be interpreted as the covariate effects on the hazard rate under the assumption that $h(t_l)$ is constant within each of the L^* time intervals. Since $h(t_l|\mathbf{x})\Delta t_l$ appears at the left-hand side of Equation 4.18 instead of $h(t_l|\mathbf{x})$, the estimates for the baseline hazard rates or the time parameters must be corrected for the interval lengths Δt_l. The correct time parameter for the lth time interval equals $\alpha_l - \ln(\Delta t_l)$.

If the model is a proportional hazard model, that is, if there are no time-covariate interactions, the β parameters of a complementary log-log model are not sensitive to the choice of the interval lengths since Δt_l is completely absorbed into α_l. This is the main advantage of this approach compared to the discrete-time logit model, which is not only sensitive to the choice of the length of the intervals, but also requires that the intervals be of equal length (Allison, 1982). The reason for this is that the interval length influences the probability that an event will occur in the interval concerned, and therefore also the logit of $\lambda(t_l)$. Although the complementary log-log model can handle unequal interval lengths in proportional hazard models with one parameter for each time interval, unequal time intervals are problematic when the time dependence is parameterized or when the model is nonproportional (Allison, 1982). Thus, as long as the duration parameters are treated as nuisance parameters, as in a Cox regression model, unequal interval lengths are allowed. If, however, the time dependence itself becomes the object of study, the time intervals must be of equal length.

Estimation Cox (1972) proposed a partial likelihood estimator for the discrete-time logit model which is analogous to the partial likelihood estimator for continuous-time data (see Equation 4.14). However, discrete-time models are generally estimated by means of maximum likelihood methods (Allison, 1982). From Equations 4.5 and 4.6, it is known that

$$f(t_l|\mathbf{x}) = \lambda(t_l|\mathbf{x}) \prod_{k=1}^{l-1} [1 - \lambda(t_k|\mathbf{x})] = \frac{\lambda(t_l|\mathbf{x})}{1 - \lambda(t_l|\mathbf{x})} \prod_{k=1}^{l} [1 - \lambda(t_k|\mathbf{x})] \,,$$

$$S(t_l|\mathbf{x}) = \prod_{k=1}^{l} [1 - \lambda(t_k|\mathbf{x})] \,.$$

Just as in continuous-time models, $f(t_l|\mathbf{x})$ is the contribution to the likelihood function for an individual who experienced an event and $S(t_l|\mathbf{x})$ for an individual who was censored. Let N denote the sample size, and let l_i denote the time interval in which the ith person experienced an event or was censored. In that case, the likelihood function can be written as

$$\mathscr{L} = \prod_{i=1}^{N} \left[\left(\frac{\lambda(t_{l_i}|\mathbf{x}_i)}{1 - \lambda(t_{l_i}|\mathbf{x}_i)} \right)^{\delta_i} \prod_{k=1}^{l_i} (1 - \lambda(t_k|\mathbf{x}_i)) \right] \,.$$

Let $\mathbf{y}_i$ be a vector of l_i indicator variables taking the value 1 if person i experienced an event in $T = t_l$, and otherwise taking the value 0. In fact, the first $l_i - 1$ elements of $\mathbf{y}_i$ are zero and the last one is equal to the censoring indicator δ_i. Using this vector $\mathbf{y}_i$ instead of δ_i, the likelihood function becomes

$$\mathscr{L} = \prod_{i=1}^{N} \prod_{k=1}^{l_i} \left[\left(\frac{\lambda(t_k|\mathbf{x}_i)}{1 - \lambda(t_k|\mathbf{x}_i)} \right)^{y_{ik}} (1 - \lambda(t_k|\mathbf{x}_i)) \right] \,.$$

This is, actually, the likelihood function for regression models for binary response variables (Brown, 1975; Allison, 1982). The only difference is that there is not one observation per individual but l_i observations per individual, that is, one observation for each time interval in which the individual concerned belongs to the risk set. Therefore, discrete-time logit models can be estimated by means of standard software for logistic regression analysis. The input should not consist of one record per individual but one record for every period that an individual belongs to the risk set. These records are sometimes called person-period records. When all covariates are categorical, discrete-time logit models can also be estimated using standard log-linear analysis programs, such as ECTA (Fay and Goodman, 1975), FREQ (Haberman, 1988), GLIM (Baker and Nelder, 1978), and *ℓEM* (Vermunt, 1993). In *ℓEM*, a special option is implemented which makes it possible to use person or episode records as input instead of person-period records. The program generates the contingency table which is used to obtain the parameter estimates. The complementary log-log model can be estimated by means of GLIM (Baker and Nelder, 1978).

4.4. Event history analysis using log-linear models

Particular parametric hazard models as well as Cox's semi-parametric hazard model are based on a log-linear parameterization of the time and covariate dependence of the hazard rate. This section discusses the relationship between the log-linear models for frequency tables discussed in Chapter 2 and log-linear hazard models. It is shown that log-linear hazard models can also be written as ordinary log-linear models.

The piecewise exponential survival model (see Equation 4.11) is one of the hazard models which belongs to the log-linear family. In this continuous-time hazard model, the hazard rate is assumed to be constant within time intervals. Holford (1980) demonstrated that the likelihood function for a piecewise exponential survival model is proportional to both a Poisson and a multinomial likelihood function. The consequence is that when all covariates are categorical, the same estimation and testing procedures can be used as in log-linear models for contingency tables or, more precisely, as in log-rate models (see section 2.6) (Holford, 1976, 1980; Laird and Olivier, 1981). Laird and Olivier (1981) demonstrated how to apply the log-rate model using grouped event history data. Thus, log-rate models, like the discrete-time methods discussed above, can be used to approximate the results of continuous-time models.

In addition to the piecewise exponential survival model, Cox's semi-parametric model (see Equation 4.13) can also be written as an ordinary log-linear model. Holford (1976) demonstrated that Breslow's maximum likelihood procedure for Cox's model (Breslow, 1972, 1974) is equivalent to a piecewise exponential survival model with as many time categories as distinct observed times at which events occur. Laird and Olivier (1981) and Whitehead (1980) showed how to estimate Cox's semi-parametric hazard model using standard log-linear analysis programs.

Aitkin and Clayton (1980) and Clayton and Cuzick (1985) demonstrated how to estimate a general class of log-linear hazard models by a two-step conditional-maximization procedure which they implemented in GLIM (Baker and Nelder, 1978). This conditional maximization procedure makes use of the fact that, given the values of the parameters describing the duration dependence of the hazard rate, the likelihood function for any log-linear hazard model is equivalent to the Poisson likelihood function.

Below, piecewise exponential survival models, Breslow's maximum likelihood approach to Cox's semi-parametric model, and the estimation of a general class of log-linear hazard models by means of log-linear Poisson models are discussed.

4.4.1. Piecewise exponential survival models

The piecewise exponential survival model, or piecewise constant hazard model, described in Equation 4.11 can also be written down using the notation introduced in Chapter 2. Let Z denote the time variable, z a particular value of Z, and Z^* the number of categories of Z. The starting and end points of the Z^* time intervals are $(0, t_1], (t_1, t_2], \ldots, (t_{Z^*-1}, \infty]$, in which the round brackets '(' express that the starting points are excluded from the intervals and the square brackets ']' express that the end points are included. The end point of the last interval may also be assumed to be equal to the longest observed duration or the longest duration to be used in the analysis instead of ∞.

Suppose there is a hazard model with 2 categorical covariates A and B. Let h_{abz} denote the constant hazard rate in the zth time interval for an individual with $A = a$ and $B = b$. The saturated log-linear model for the hazard rate h_{abz}, or the saturated piecewise exponential survival model, is

$$\log h_{abz} = u + u_a^A + u_b^B + u_z^Z + u_{ab}^{AB} + u_{az}^{AZ} + u_{bz}^{BZ} + u_{abz}^{ABZ}, \quad [4.19]$$

in which the u terms are log-linear parameters which are constrained by means of ANOVA-like restrictions. A proportional variant of the piecewise exponential survival model is obtained by assuming the two-variable and higher-variable interaction terms involving Z to be equal to zero, i.e.,

$$\log h_{abz} = u + u_a^A + u_b^B + u_z^Z + u_{ab}^{AB}. \quad [4.20]$$

As demonstrated in the previous section (see Equation 4.12), maximum likelihood estimates for the parameters of parametric continuous-time models can be obtained by maximizing

$$\mathcal{L} = \prod_{i=1}^{N} h(t_i|\mathbf{x}_i)^{\delta_i} \exp\left(-\int_0^{t_i} h(u|\mathbf{x}_i)du\right).$$

If the hazard rate is constant within each of the Z^* time intervals, the likelihood function can also be written as

$$\mathcal{L} = \prod_{i=1}^{N} \prod_{z=1}^{Z^*} h(z|\mathbf{x}_i)^{\delta_{iz}} \exp\left(-h(z|\mathbf{x}_i)e_{iz}\right),$$

in which e_{iz} denotes the total time that individual i belongs to the risk set in time interval z. It is also called the exposure time. Generally, e_{iz} is equal to $t_z - t_{z-1}$ for the time intervals before individual i experienced an event or was censored, equal to $t_i - t_{z-1}$ for the time interval in which an event or censoring occurred, and equal to zero for the other time intervals. Furthermore, δ_{iz} is an indicator variable taking the value 1 if person i experienced an event in time interval z, and otherwise 0.

Since A, B, and Z are categorical variables, the number of events and the total exposure times can be represented in a cross-tabulation. Let n_{abz} denote the number of events and E_{abz} the total exposure time in time interval z for $A = a$ and $B = b$. The tables with observed numbers of events n_{abz} and with the total exposure times E_{abz} are generally called the occurrence matrix and the exposure matrix. They are obtained by

$$n_{abz} = \sum_{i=1}^{N} \delta_{iz} \gamma_{iab}$$

$$E_{abz} = \sum_{i=1}^{N} e_{iz} \gamma_{iab}$$

in which γ_{iab} is an indicator variable taking the value 1 if person i has $A = a$ and $B = b$, and otherwise 0. When cross-tabulated events and exposure times are used rather than the individual data, the likelihood function for a piecewise exponential survival model with covariates A and B can be written as

$$\mathcal{L} = \prod_{abz} h_{abz}^{n_{abz}} \exp\left(-h_{abz}E_{abz}\right). \qquad [4.21]$$

As will be demonstrated below, this likelihood function (4.21) is proportional to a Poisson likelihood function.

Suppose there is a frequency table for the variables A, B, and Z with observed cell counts n_{abz} which, conditional on E_{abz}, are Poisson distributed with means m_{abz}. In other words, there is a Poisson model for the rates m_{abz}/E_{abz}, which is a log-rate model as discussed in section 2.6. Under the Poisson sampling scheme, the likelihood function is proportional to

$$\mathcal{L}_p = \prod_{abz} m_{abz}^{n_{abz}} \exp(-m_{abz})$$

$$= \prod_{abz} (h_{abz} E_{abz})^{n_{abz}} \exp(-h_{abz} E_{abz}) ,$$

in which h_{abz} denotes the Poisson rate m_{abz}/E_{abz}. It can now be seen that the likelihood function for the observed Poisson counts n_{abz} given E_{abz} is proportional to the likelihood function described in Equation 4.21, i.e.,

$$\mathcal{L}_p = \mathcal{L} \prod_{abz} E_{abz}^{n_{abz}} .$$

Since $E_{abz}^{n_{abz}}$ is a constant that does not depend on the unknown parameters which are to be estimated, piecewise exponential survival models with categorical covariates can be estimated with the same estimation methods as are used for the log-rate models discussed in section 2.6. Moreover, piecewise exponential survival models can be written as log-rate models. For instance, the proportional piecewise constant hazard model described in Equation 4.20 can also be formulated as

$$\log\left(\frac{m_{abz}}{E_{abz}}\right) = u + u_a^A + u_b^B + u_z^Z + u_{ab}^{AB} ,$$

or

$$\log m_{abz} = \log E_{abz} + u + u_a^A + u_b^B + u_z^Z + u_{ab}^{AB} , \qquad [4.22]$$

where m_{abz} is the expected number of events in time interval z among persons with $A = a$ and $B = b$. From Equation 4.22, it can easily be seen that the piecewise exponential survival model is equivalent to the log-rate model discussed in section 2.6. As in a log-rate model, the log of the expected cell frequency is a linear function of a cell-specific constant and a set of log-linear parameters.

Grouped duration data The log-rate model can also be used with grouped duration data, which occur when there is only information on the discrete time interval in which events and censorings occurred, in other words, when the exact value of t_i is not known, but only that $t_{z-1} < t_i < t_z$. This implies that there is no exact information on the length of the individual exposure times in the interval in which censoring or an event occurs. This makes it necessary to approximate a person's exposure time in this interval. Generally, it is assumed that on average censorings and events occur in the middle of the time interval concerned (Laird and Olivier, 1981; Yamaguchi, 1991:81 ; Xie, 1994). Thus, the only modification that is necessary in situations in which the observed durations are grouped is that when computing the exposure matrix E for the interval in which an event or censoring occurred, e_{iz} is not equal to $t_i - t_{z-1}$, but equal to $(t_z - t_{z-1})/2$.

This simple approximation procedure amounts to assuming that both events and censorings are uniformly distributed within the discrete time interval in which they occur. It is equivalent to assuming linear survival within time intervals for events, which is not completely in accordance with the postulated piecewise exponential survival model. However, if the hazard rates are not too high, the resulting bias will be small.[9] Of course, when there is additional information on the timing of events and censorings within particular time intervals, this information can be used to get better approximations of the true exposure times (Yamaguchi, 1991:84).

As mentioned in the previous section, discrete-time logit models and discrete-time complementary log-log models can also be used to approximate continuous-time hazard models when there are grouped duration data. However, the logit specification is an arbitrary one which, moreover, is sensitive to the choice of the length of the time intervals. The

---

[9] Suppose that we know that the event of interest occurred in a time interval of length Δ_z and that $h(t_z)$ is the size of the constant hazard rate in this interval. In that case, the mean fraction of Δ_z that an individual is exposed to the event of interest equals $1 + 1/(\Delta_z h(t_z)) - 1/[1 - \exp(-\Delta_z h(t_z))]$ (Chiang, 1984:139; Willekens, 1990). This quantity is close to .5 for almost all relevant values of $h(t_z)$ and Δ_z. For instance, if $\Delta_z = 1$, it ranges from .492 when $h(t_z) = .1$ to .459 when $h(t_z) = .5$. Therefore, Petersen (1991) concluded with respect to the approximation of exposure times: 'Thus, a good rule of thumb is to assign the duration that lies at the midpoint of the window within which the true duration lies.'

complementary log-log transformation approximates the continuous-time proportional hazard model in that it assumes exponential survival within time categories, and the occurrence of censorings at the end of the time intervals. However, unequal time intervals are problematic when the time dependence is restricted in some way or when the hazard rate is assumed to be nonproportional. The main advantage of the log-rate model compared to the complementary log-log model is that unequal time intervals are never problematic. Another advantage is that log-rate models can be estimated using widely available programs for log-linear analysis.

Non-hierarchical models Until now, only hierarchical log-rate models have been given consideration. However, by using a more general formulation, it is also possible to specify non-hierarchical models. In its most general form, the log-rate model can be written as

$$\log m_{iz} = \log E_{iz} + \sum_j \beta_j x_{izj}, \qquad [4.23]$$

in which x_{izj} denotes an element of the design matrix and β_j a particular log-linear parameter. The index i refers to a category of the joint variable formed by all the independent variables, and z to a category of the time variable. From the appearance of the index z in x_{izj}, it follows that the design matrix also includes the time variable and that covariate effects may be time dependent.

Perhaps the most interesting kinds of restrictions that can be imposed with the design matrix appearing in the general model given in Equation 4.23 are restrictions on the time parameters. Yamaguchi (1991:75-77) proposed approximating the Gompertz and Weibull models by means of a step-functional characterization of t and $\ln(t)$. Suppose that the first parameter in Equation 4.23, β_1, is the intercept and that the second parameter, β_2, is the restricted time effect. Furthermore, let $\bar{z}$ denote the middle of the zth time interval, $\bar{z} = (t_{z-1} + t_z)/2$. An approximation of the Gompertz model is obtained by specifying the elements x_{iz2} of the design matrix to be equal to $\bar{z}$. In a Weibull model, we would replace $\bar{z}$ by $\log \bar{z}$. It is also possible to use higher-order polynomials of $\bar{z}$ or $(\log \bar{z})$ to describe the time dependence of the hazard rate. Moreover, these restricted time effects can also be used in time-covariate interaction terms.

Recently, Xie (1994) presented another parsimonious method of specifying time-covariate interactions in log-rate models. He proposed using a log-multiplicative parameterization of time-covariate interaction terms.

In fact, it is an application of the row and column effects model type II discussed in section 2.7 (Goodman, 1979; Clogg, 1982).

Contrary to what is stated by Holford (1980) and Laird and Olivier (1981), log-rate models can also be used when particular covariates are continuous. In the same fashion that a logistic regression model is obtained from a logit model by including continuous covariates (see section 2.8), the log-rate model given in Equation 4.23 can be used with continuous covariates. In that case, individual data have to be analyzed instead of cross-tabulated data, which implies that the index i appearing in Equation 4.23 denotes a particular observation rather than a level of the joint independent variables, which also means that $E_{iz} = e_{iz}$ and $n_{iz} = \delta_{iz}$.

Testing In addition to the estimation procedures available for log-linear modeling, the testing procedures can also be used in log-rate models. The estimated expected number of events, m_{abz}, can be compared with the observed number of events, n_{abz}, using either the Pearson's chi-squared statistic or the likelihood-ratio chi-squared statistic (see section 2.4). As in logistic regression models, the fit of hazard models with continuous covariates cannot be tested because of sparseness of the 'table' which is analyzed. Nevertheless, it is possible to test the significance of particular effects by means of conditional likelihood-ratio chi-squared tests (see section 2.4).

Computer programs Hierarchical log-rate models, such as the one represented in Equation 4.22, can be estimated using log-linear analysis programs which are based on the IPF algorithm. However, the program must calculate the parameters using mean removal on the cumulated multipliers of the IPF cycles in order to get correct parameter estimates (see Appendix A.1). The LOGLIN (Olivier and Neff, 1976) and *ℓEM* (Vermunt, 1993) programs use this procedure. Log-rate models of the general form described in Equation 4.23 can be estimated using programs for log-linear analysis which use a Newton algorithm, such as FREQ (Haberman, 1979) and SPSS Log-linear. In *ℓEM*, such models are estimated by means of the uni-dimensional Newton algorithm. A special feature of *ℓEM* is that, as opposed to standard programs for log-linear analysis, the user does not need to supply the occurrence and exposure matrices as input since these are generated by the program itself, where the exposure time within the time interval in which censorings or events occur can be specified by the user. Moreover, it is possible within *ℓEM* to estimate models which contain the log-multiplicative interaction terms proposed by Xie (1994).

4.4.2. Estimation of Cox's semi-parametric model

Breslow (1972, 1974) proposed estimating the β parameters and the baseline hazard rate $h_0(t)$ of the Cox semi-parametric model (see Equation 4.13) simultaneously by means of maximum likelihood. Holford (1976) and Laird and Olivier (1981) demonstrated that Breslow's approach was a special case of the piecewise exponential survival model, that is, a proportional model with as many time intervals as distinct observed times at which events occurred.

Breslow's approach is as follows. First, as in the partial likelihood approach, the N cases must be ordered according to their observed durations t_i. Then, the time axis has to be divided into Z^* intervals, where Z^* equals the number of distinct times that events occurred. The end points of the time intervals, denoted by t_z, correspond with the durations at which events occur. Each censoring is assumed to have occurred at the nearest preceding event and the hazard rate is assumed to be constant within time intervals just as it would be in a piecewise exponential survival model. An equivalent approach is to assume the hazard rate to be zero everywhere except at the observed times at which events occur (Cox, 1972; Holford, 1976; Laird and Olivier, 1981). The latter approach does not require shifting the censored observation to the nearest previous event.

Suppose there is a semi-parametric hazard model, or equivalently, a piecewise exponential survival model of the form

$$h(z|\mathbf{x}) = h_0(z) \exp \left(\sum_{j=1}^{J} \beta_j x_{ij} \right), \qquad [4.24]$$

in which $h_0(z)$ denotes the baseline hazard rate in time interval z. Note that the hazard rate is assumed to be proportional since the model does not contain interactions between the covariates and time.

The likelihood function for the model described in Equation 4.24 can be obtained by substituting $h(z|\mathbf{x})$ into Equation 4.21, i.e.,

$$\mathscr{L} = \prod_{i=1}^{N} \prod_{z=1}^{Z^*} h(z|\mathbf{x}_i)^{\delta_{iz}} \exp\left(-h(z|\mathbf{x}_i)e_{iz}\right)$$

$$= \prod_{i=1}^{N} \prod_{z=1}^{Z^*} \left\{ \left[h_0(z) \exp \left(\sum_j \beta_j x_{ij} \right) \right] \right\}^{\delta_{iz}}$$

$$\exp\left[h_0(z)\exp\left(\sum_j \beta_j x_{ij}\right)e_{iz}\right]\right\},\qquad\qquad [4.25]$$

in which e_{iz} equals $t_z - t_{z-1}$ if subject i neither experienced an event nor was censored before t_z, in other words, if subject i belongs to the risk set at $Z = z$. Setting the first order derivatives of the log likelihood with respect to $h_0(z)$ equal to zero yields the following maximum likelihood estimate for $h_0(z)$:

$$h_0(z) = \frac{\sum_{i=1}^N \delta_{iz}}{\sum_{i=1}^N \exp\left(\sum_j \beta_j x_{ij}\right)e_{iz}}.\qquad\qquad [4.26]$$

Substitution of this estimate of $h_0(z)$ into Equation 4.25 yields

$$\mathcal{L} = \prod_{i=1}^N \prod_{z=1}^{Z^*} \left(\sum_{i=1}^N \delta_{iz}\right)^{\delta_{iz}} \exp\left(\sum_{i=1}^N \delta_{iz}\right) \left[\frac{\exp\left(\sum_j \beta_j x_{ij}\right)}{\sum_{i=1}^N \exp\left(\sum_j \beta_j x_{ij}\right)e_{iz}}\right]^{\delta_{iz}}.$$

As only one δ_{iz} is 1 for each i, the product over z is redundant. Because $e_{iz} = 0$ for all persons who are not at risk, the sum over i in the denominator consists of the persons at risk at $Z = z$. Note that e_{iz} takes the same value for every person at risk, $t_z - t_{z-1}$. This leads to the following simplification:

$$\mathcal{L} = \prod_{i=1}^N \left[\frac{\exp\left(\sum_j \beta_j x_{ij}\right)}{\sum_{k\in(t_k\geq t_i)} \exp\left(\sum_j \beta_j x_{kj}\right)}\right]^{\delta_i} C,\qquad\qquad [4.27]$$

where

$$C = \prod_{i=1}^N \prod_{z=1}^{Z^*} \left(\sum_{i=1}^N \delta_{iz}\right)^{\delta_{iz}} \exp\left(\sum_{i=1}^N \delta_{iz}\right)\left(\frac{1}{t_z - t_{z-1}}\right)^{\delta_{iz}}.$$

It can be seen that, with the exception of the constant C, Equation 4.27 is equivalent to both Equation 4.14 and Equation 4.15. This implies that if the data contains no ties, a proportional piecewise exponential survival model in which the end points of the time intervals are defined by the event times and in which the censorings are assumed to occur at the nearest preceding event time is equivalent to Cox's semi-parametric model. If the data contains ties, the maximum likelihood approach leads to the solution for ties proposed by Breslow (1972, 1974), which is described in Equation 4.15.

The consequence of the equivalence with the exponential survival model, and therefore with the log-rate model, is that Cox's semi-parametric model can be estimated using standard programs for log-linear analysis. Whitehead (1980), for instance, showed how to estimate the Cox model with the GLIM program using a log-linear Poisson model.

4.4.3. Estimating log-linear hazard models with log-linear Poisson models

Above, it was demonstrated that both the piecewise exponential survival model and the Cox model can be estimated by means of log-linear analysis techniques. Aitkin and Clayton (1980) proposed estimating the parameters of a general class of continuous-time log-linear hazard models using the equivalence between the Poisson likelihood and the likelihood for log-linear hazard rate models.

Let $h(t)$ denote the baseline hazard and $H(t)$ denote the cumulative baseline hazard, $\int_0^t h(u)d(u)$, belonging to a particular parametric hazard model. If the hazard model is log-linear, the likelihood function can be written down as

$$\mathscr{L} = \prod_{i=1}^{N} \left[h(t) \exp\left(\sum_j \beta_j x_{ij}\right) \right]^{\delta_i} \exp\left[-H(t_i) \exp\left(\sum_j \beta_j x_{ij}\right) \right]$$

$$= \prod_{i=1}^{N} \left[m_i^{\delta_i} \exp\left(-m_i\right) \right] [h(t_i)/H(t_i)]^{\delta_i} ,$$

in which

$$m_i = H(t_i) \exp\left(\sum_j \beta_j x_{ij}\right) .$$

The first term in the likelihood function, $m_i^{\delta_i} \exp\left(-m_i\right)$, is equivalent to the kernel of the likelihood function for N independent Poisson variates δ_i with means m_i. The second term does not contain β parameters. It depends only on the α parameters associated with the duration dependence of the process.

Aitkin and Clayton (1980) proposed estimating the α and β parameters by means of a simple two-step conditional maximization method. First, the β parameters can be estimated using the log-linear Poisson, or log-rate, model given the current estimates for the unknown parameters determining $H(t_i)$, i.e.,

$$\log m_i = \log H(t_i) + \sum_j \beta_j x_{ij}, \qquad [4.28]$$

in which $H(t_i)$ is treated as a weight vector, or in the GLIM terminology used by the authors, $\log H(t_i)$ is an offset. In the second step, new estimates for the α parameters must be obtained. Of course, the exact relationship between $H(t)$ and α depends on the parametric model that is chosen (see below). This two step algorithm continues until convergence is reached.

Although the hazard rate is assumed to be proportional in the model given in Equation 4.28, it is also possible to make the α parameters dependent on covariate values. However, then $h(t_i)$ and $H(t_i)$ are subgroup specific. If y is used as an index for the variable interacting with the time dependence, $h(t_i)$ and $H(t_i)$ have to be replaced by $h_y(t_i)$ and $H_y(t_i)$ in all of the given formulas.

The simplest log-linear hazard model is the exponential model in which the cumulated baseline hazard, $H(t)$, equals t. As a result, the estimates for the β parameters can be obtained by using $\log t_i$ as a fixed effect in a log-linear model in which the censoring indicator δ_i is treated as an observed Poisson count. The second step is not necessary because the second part of the likelihood function presented above does not contain unknown parameters. More precisely, it equals $1/t_i$.

As $h(t) = \alpha t^{\alpha-1}$ and $H(t) = t^\alpha$ in Weibull models, $\alpha \log t$ must be used as an offset when obtaining new β_j's in the first step of a particular iteration. In the second step, a new α is obtained by

$$\alpha = \frac{N}{\sum_{i=1}^{N} (m_i - \delta_i) \log t_i}.$$

Although the expressions for $H(t_i)$ and the α parameters may become more complicated, the same principles apply to any parametric hazard model which belongs to the log-linear family.

Clayton and Cuzick (1985) demonstrated that a similar two step maximization method can be used to obtain maximum likelihood estimates for the parameters of Cox's semi-parametric proportional hazard model. Suppose that there are N^* distinct times that events occur, which are denoted by t_{i^*}. As demonstrated above, the maximum likelihood estimates for the baseline hazard parameters can be obtained using Equation 4.26.

If, as Cox did, it is assumed that the hazard rate is zero everywhere except where an event occurs, the formula for the baseline parameters can be simplified to

$$h_0(t_{i*}) = \frac{n_{i*}}{\sum_{t_k \geq t_{i*}} \exp\left(\sum_j \beta_j x_{ij}\right)}, \qquad [4.29]$$

in which n_{i*} indicates the number of events in t_{i*}. The cumulated hazard function for person k with observed survival time t_k, $H(t_k)$, equals $\sum_{t_{i*} \leq t_k} h_0(t_{i*})$. Again, the algorithm consists of two conditional maximization steps. First, new estimates of the β parameters are obtained by means of a log-linear Poisson model for the censoring indicator δ_k in which $\log H(t_k)$ is used as a fixed effect. In the second step, new $h_0(t_{i*})$ are calculated by means of Equation 4.29. These quantities are used to obtain a new $H(t_k)$ for each person. Contrary to the procedure presented above, Clayton and Cuzick (1985) called this two step procedure an EM algorithm, in which the computation of $h_0(t_{i*})$ and $H(t_k)$ form the E step. The reason for this is that the cumulated hazard rate $H(t_k)$ can be seen as an unobservable quantity in the semi-parametric hazard model.

4.5. Censoring

Event history techniques are used to explain individual differences in the duration of nonoccurrence of a particular event. For that purpose, it is necessary that there be, in addition to information on the covariates determining the process under study, information on the calendar time of entry into the risk set (τ_b) and on the calendar time of occurrence of the event (τ_e). The duration of nonoccurrence of an event, T, is defined as $\tau_e - \tau_b$. It often occurs that information is missing on τ_b, τ_e, or both for some of the subjects involved in the study. This means that T is also unknown. Observations with this type of missing data are called censored observations. One of the strong points of hazard models is that they can deal with several kinds of censored observations. As in the log-linear models for nonresponse discussed in Chapter 3, hazard models make it possible to include particular types of partially observed data in the analysis under certain plausible assumptions.

It is possible to illustrate the different kinds of (missing) observations that can occur by giving a hypothetical example. Suppose the aim of a study is to explain the duration preceding the first promotion of employees of a particular company. For that purpose, data are collected from

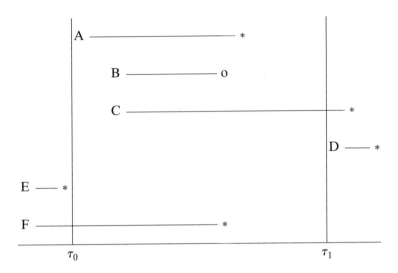

Figure 4.1. Six different types of observations

τ_0 to τ_1, in which τ again denotes calendar time. The period from τ_0 to τ_1 is called the observation period. Figure 4.1 depicts six different types of observations. A solid line indicates the risk period, an '*' at the right hand side of a line indicates that risk period ended because of the occurrence of the event under study, and an 'o' indicates that a person has been removed from the risk set as a result of the occurrence of an event other than the event of interest.

Person A started working at the company after τ_0 and experienced the event, the first promotion, before τ_1. Therefore, the complete duration of nonoccurrence of the event of interest is known for observation A. Observations B and C are examples of right-censored cases. It is known for observations B and C when they entered into the risk set, but it is not known when they will experience their first promotion. Although both cases are right-censored, their censoring has different causes. Observation C is censored because the observation period ended, while observation B is censored as a result of the occurrence of another event which removed it from the risk set, for example, a voluntary job change to another employer. Case D is (fully) right-censored, since neither the time of entry into the risk set nor the time of occurrence of an event is known. This case represents a future employee of the company. Case E is an individual who was given his first promotion before the start of the observation period. It is a (fully) left-censored case. Like case D, both the time of entry into the risk set and the time of experiencing an event are unknown. Finally, case F is a left-censored observation. It represents an individual who started working at the company before τ_0 and who experienced an event during the observation period. Since the time of entry into the risk set is unknown, it is also unknown how long it took for an event to occur. It must be noted that for cases like F, information on the time of entry into the risk set is sometimes collected retrospectively.

Hazard models can deal with right-censored observations under quite mild conditions. Left censoring is a more complicated matter. However, when τ_b is known, there is a simple solution for left censoring which is comparable to the way in which right-censored observations are dealt with. It is important that the procedures which are used for handling right- and left-censored observations satisfy two conditions: they must use as much of the available information as possible, and they must prevent sample selection bias as much as possible. Selection bias means that individuals with certain values of the dependent variable, in this case the duration of nonoccurrence of an event, have a higher or lower probability of being included in the sample than other persons.

4.5.1. Right censoring

There are at least three possible approaches to right censoring problem (Tuma and Hannan, 1984:119): 1] ignoring censored observations and analyzing only the cases who experienced an event; 2] treating censored observations as though events occurred at the censoring times; 3] using methods of estimation that make use of the partially observed information while making certain assumptions with regards to censoring mechanism which are analogous to response mechanisms.

The first solution may lead to a considerable loss of information, since it neglects the information that a particular person did not experience an event during a particular period. Moreover, deleting the censored observation from the analysis may lead to sample selection bias, because censored observations generally have longer durations than noncensored observations. In other words, the hazard rate for censored cases during the risk period will be lower than the hazard rate for noncensored cases. Thus, by deleting the censored cases, the estimated hazard rates for groups with large numbers of censored cases will be biased upwards.

The second solution, in which the times at which the event of interest occurred are treated as censoring times is even worse because nonexistent or wrong information is added to the data. Therefore, recoding non-events as events will generally make the results of the analysis meaningless.

The best way to deal with right-censored cases is to use estimation methods which use this type of partially observed data under certain plausible assumptions. As is shown below, it is relatively easy to use right-censored observations for parameter estimation as long as the missing data mechanism can be assumed to be ignorable for likelihood-based inference (see also section 3.2).

Censoring mechanisms In the fields of engineering, medicine, and the biological sciences, a great deal of attention has been given to right censoring (Kalbfleisch and Prentice, 1980:39-41; Lawless, 1982). In these fields, hazard models are often used to analyze data collected by means of experimental designs. Experimental studies in which, for instance, a new type of apparatus or a new lung cancer medication are tested, generally prevent the occurrence of left-censored data, but right-censored data are unavoidable for two reasons. First, the experiment is generally ended before all of the apparatus fail or all of the subjects die. Second, other events may occur which remove machines or persons from the risk set. A machine may fail as a result of another cause than the one of interest, and an individual's cause of death may not be lung cancer.

If there are right-censored observations, it is relatively easy to derive the likelihood function if, at each t given the covariate values $\mathbf{x}$, the censoring rate is independent of the rate of occurrence of the event under study, in other words, if individuals are not censored because they appear to have high or low risks of experiencing an event. Actually, this is analogous to assuming MAR (missing at random) nonresponse in a panel study with a monotonous missing data pattern. In the context of panel analysis, nonresponse is said to be MAR if, for someone who responded at $T = t - 1$, the probability of nonresponse at $T = t$ is independent of the values of the variables at $T = t$, though it may depend on the values of the variables before $T = t$ (see section 3.2). The same formulation can be applied to right censoring, which is, likewise, a monotonous missing data pattern. The data are MAR if, for someone who is at risk at $T = t$, the probability of censoring in the interval $[t, t + \Delta t]$ is independent of the state occupied at $t + \Delta t$, given the observed covariate values. Since the state occupied at $t + \Delta t$ is determined by the hazard rate at $T = t$ for someone who is at risk at $T = t$, it can also be said that the censoring rate must be conditionally independent of the hazard rate. In the biometrical literature, this form of censoring is most often referred to as independent right censoring (Kalbfleisch and Prentice, 1980:120) or non-informative right censoring (Lagakos, 1979).

In experimental settings, conditional independence between the hazard rate and the censoring rate is usually fulfilled. Two well-known special cases of independent censoring which often occur in experimental studies are Type I censoring and Type II censoring (Kalbfleisch and Prentice, 1980:39-41; Lawless, 1982). Type I occurs when a study is stopped after a fixed time period, while Type II entails that a study continues until a particular number of events have occurred. In both cases, all censored observations are censored at the same value of T. It is clear that in neither of these cases is the censoring rate related to the hazard rate of the event under study since all persons at risk have the same probability of being censored, that is, a probability of zero before the point in time that censoring occurs and a probability of one at the point in time that censoring occurs. However, one cannot be sure that the censoring mechanism is independent of the process under study if observations are censored as a result of other kinds of events, such as other causes of failure or other causes of death.

The mechanism causing the censoring of observation C in Figure 4.1 is very similar to Type I censoring since observation C is censored as a result of the cessation of the observation period. However, contrary to the experimental context on which Type I censoring is based, observations like C enter into the risk set at the different points in calendar time (τ_b) in a survey context. As a result, both the duration in which censoring occurs ($t = \tau_1 - \tau_b$) and the censoring rate will depend on τ_b. More precisely, there is, depending on τ_b, a probability of one or zero that a given individual will be censored at a particular t. The implication of this is that the censoring mechanism is not MAR if the hazard rate also depends on τ_b.

This can be illustrated by means of an example. Suppose that, as a result of an increase in the labor supply of young people, the company being studied changed its promotion policy. More precisely, it made it more difficult to obtain a promotion during the first three years of employment. The result would be that the hazard rate of being promoted at the beginning of an individual's career would depend on τ_b, that is, on whether a given individual's employment started before or after the moment that the policy changed. Because the censoring times of cases like C ($\tau_1 - \tau_b$) depend on τ_b as well, this leads to a dependency between the censoring rate and the hazard rate. The solution to this problem is, however, very simple. The only thing that has to be done is to include τ_b as one of the regressors in the hazard model. By controlling for the calendar time of entry into the risk set, a form Type I censoring is obtained within the subgroups of persons who enter into the risk set at the same τ_b.

In general terms it can be stated that if censoring occurs at a particular calendar time, which is the most common type of censoring in social science research, the censoring mechanism and the process under study will have one potential common cause, i.e., the calendar time of entry into the risk set or the causes associated with that calendar time, such as the altered policy in the example. In demography, such an effect is called a cohort effect (see also section 4.6). Controlling for the calendar time of entry into the risk set or the causes associated with it makes the censoring mechanism (conditionally) independent of the duration distribution. In other words, it makes the missing data MAR.

The right censoring of observation D is the result of the same censoring mechanism applied to case C: The time at which the event of interest occurs is unknown because of the cessation of the observation period. Therefore, the same solution applies to this type of censored observations. However, it should be noted that if the time of entry into the risk set influences the hazard rate, the results of the study cannot be generalized to other observation periods. If, for example, an effect is found of the variable birth cohort on the hazard rate in a study on fertility behavior, the results cannot be generalized to future birth cohorts. Moreover, if an interaction effect is found between the time variable and cohort, the results cannot even be generalized to the same cohorts beyond the age at which they have been censored. In fact, this is a type of selection bias which is inherent in the study of social change.

Observation B is also right-censored but by a very different mechanism. It is removed from the risk set because an event other than the event of interest occurred during the observation period. In this case, the validity of the assumption of (conditionally) independent censoring depends on whether the event that led to censoring and the event under study have common causes which are not controlled, for instance, because they are not observed. If person B was removed from the risk set because he died as result of an accident, it can safely be assumed that censoring is independent of the event of getting promoted. If, however, person B stopped working at the company because of health problems, the independence of the censoring rate and the hazard rate of getting promoted is less clear. It is probable that less healthy individuals not only have a higher risk of losing their jobs, but also have a lower risk of getting promoted. If it is possible to control for health, again a (conditionally) independent censoring mechanism can be obtained, assuming that health is the only common cause of the two types of events. There are many other events that can lead to the type B censoring, such as a voluntary or involuntary move to another employer or retirement. The same arguments apply to these events. It is necessary to identify all of the causes that these 'censoring events' have in common with getting a promotion in order to be able to assume that the missing data are MAR.

The problems associated with the type B censoring are the same which occur when analyzing competing-risks data. Actually, the various kinds of events leading to censoring can be seen as risks which compete with the event under study. Section 4.7 discusses models for competing risks in more detail, including the problem of unobserved common risk factors leading to dependent risks.

Estimation Let T denote the time that an event or censoring occurred, and let δ denote a censoring indicator taking the value 1 if an event occurred and 0 if an observation was censored. If censoring can be assumed to be conditionally independent of the occurrence of an event, the joint probability density of the observed data, T and δ, is

$$P(T = t, \delta = 1|\mathbf{x}) = f(t|\mathbf{x})[1 - G(t|\mathbf{x})]$$

for non-censored cases, and

$$P(T = t, \delta = 0|\mathbf{x}) = g(t|\mathbf{x})[1 - F(t|\mathbf{x})]$$

for censored cases (Lagakos, 1979). Here, $f(t|\mathbf{x})$ and $F(t|\mathbf{x})$ are the density and the distribution function of the time that an event occurs (duration), given $\mathbf{x}$, and $g(t|\mathbf{x})$ and $G(t|\mathbf{x})$ are the density and the distribution function of the censoring time, given $\mathbf{x}$. The fact that censoring is independent, or equivalently, that the missing data are MAR, makes it possible to obtain the joint density of T and δ by multiplying the contributions of the censoring and duration distributions. For instance, the probability of experiencing an event at $T = t$ and observing this is obtained by multiplying the probability of an event taking place at $T = t$ and the probability of not being censored before $T = t$.

Using the joint density of T and δ given above yields the following likelihood function:

$$\mathscr{L} = \prod_{i=1}^{N} \{f(t_i|\mathbf{x}_i)[1 - G(t_i|\mathbf{x}_i)]\}^{\delta_i} \{g(t_i|\mathbf{x}_i)[1 - F(t_i|\mathbf{x}_i)]\}^{1-\delta_i}. \quad [4.30]$$

Here, $f(t_i|\mathbf{x}_i)[1 - G(t_i|\mathbf{x}_i)]$ is the contribution to the likelihood function of case i if the event was experienced. It denotes the product of the instantaneous probability of experiencing an event at t_i, given $\mathbf{x}$, and the probability of not being censored before t_i, given $\mathbf{x}$. The contribution of a censored observation to the likelihood function is $g(t_i|\mathbf{x}_i)[1 - F(t_i|\mathbf{x}_i)]$.

The likelihood function represented in Equation 4.30 can be broken down into a segment which depends on the determinants of the duration process of interest, and a segment which depends on the censoring mechanism, i.e.,

$$\mathcal{L} = \prod_{i=1}^{N} \left\{ f(t_i|\mathbf{x}_i)^{\delta_i} [1 - F(t_i|\mathbf{x}_i)]^{1-\delta_i} \right\} \left\{ g(t_i|\mathbf{x}_i)^{1-\delta_i} [1 - G(t_i|\mathbf{x}_i)]^{\delta_i} \right\} .$$

In order to be able to ignore the censoring mechanism when estimating the parameter of the hazard model an additional assumption has to be made, that is, that the parameters of the censoring model are distinct from the parameters of the hazard rate model. In other words, it must not be necessary to place restrictions between the time and covariate effects on the hazard rate and the time and covariate effects on the censoring rate. Note that the same assumption is made in the case of ignorable nonresponse, which was previously defined as the missing data being MAR and the parameters of the response mechanism and the parameters of the model of interest being distinct (see section 3.2).

If the parameters determining the duration distribution and the parameters determining the censoring distribution are distinct, maximum likelihood estimates for the parameters of the postulated hazard model can be obtained by maximizing the first part of the likelihood function

$$\mathcal{L} = \prod_{i=1}^{N} f(t_i|\mathbf{x}_i)^{\delta_i} [1 - F(t_i|\mathbf{x}_i)]^{1-\delta_i} ,$$

which can also be written completely in terms of the hazard rate $h(t_i|\mathbf{x}_i)$

$$\mathcal{L} = \prod_{i=1}^{N} h(t_i|\mathbf{x}_i)^{\delta_i} \exp\left(- \int_0^{t_i} h(u|\mathbf{x}_i)du \right) .$$

Using the missing data terminology introduced in Chapter 3, the missing data mechanism is ignored for likelihood-based inference about the parameters of interest. Instead of using the term independent censoring, it would be possible to use the term ignorable censoring mechanism. Analogous to the case of nonresponse, the censoring mechanism is non-ignorable if the censoring times and the survival times are correlated, in other words, if the probability of missing data depends on the value of the variable for which the scores are missing, or if the censoring mechanism and the process under study have common parameters (Rubin, 1976). If the censoring mechanism is nonignorable, the censoring and the event under study have to be analyzed simultaneously. This will be discussed in the next chapter.

4.5.2. Left censoring

Left censoring is a more complicated problem than right censoring. There are at least three possible strategies for dealing with left-censored observations: 1] deleting all left-censored observations; 2] treating τ_0 as τ_b, and 3] using estimation methods which make it possible to use left-censored observations.

The first strategy, deleting the left-censored observations (Allison, 1984), is the simplest of the three. Unlike the deletion of right-censored observations, this procedure does not result in biased parameter estimates (Yamaguchi 1991:7; Guo, 1993). The reason for this is that ignoring left-censored cases does not introduce selection with regards to T (Ridder, 1984). On the contrary, it prevents selection bias as will be demonstrated below. However, there is one important disadvantage to deleting the left-censored observations. It can lead to a huge loss of information, especially if the observation period is relatively short in comparison to the average survival time. In such cases, there will not only be a large number of left-censored observations, but they will also provide unique information on the hazard rates for durations which are longer than the observation period $\tau_1 - \tau_0$. Thus, the procedure is only recommendable if a small proportion of the sample is left-censored, even though deletion of left-censored cases does not introduce bias.

The second option is to assume that left-censored cases entered into the risk set at τ_0, that is, to assume that $\tau_b = \tau_0$. This amounts to assuming that the duration of nonoccurrence of an event, T, is equal to $\tau_e - \tau_0$. Clearly, this solution is only correct if the hazard rate is time independent. Unfortunately, the assumption of a constant hazard rate, or exponential survival, is often unrealistic while erroneously assuming an exponential survival distribution may lead to severe bias in parameter estimates (Heckman and Singer, 1985, 1986; Guo, 1993).

The third alternative is to use left-censored observations in the analysis as was done in the case of right-censored cases. There are, however, two problems associated with using left-censored observations for parameter estimation: It may introduce selection bias and it can prove difficult when the times of entry into the risk set are unknown.

Sample selection bias occurs whenever a sample is selected on the basis of the values of an endogenous variable (Heckman, 1979). Actually, left-censored cases are a selective sample of the individuals who entered into the risk set before τ_0. They form the group with lower hazard rates between τ_b and τ_0, the group with longer survival times T. For example, a sample of individuals who are unemployed at τ_0 will contain a relatively large proportion of persons who have a low probability of getting a job at short unemployment durations. This phenomenon is sometimes called length-bias sampling (Cox 1962, Flinn and Heckman, 1982). Using left-censored observations in the analysis may lead to a downwards bias of the duration effect for short durations. Therefore the deletion of all left-censored cases from the analysis prevents sample selection bias.

In left-censored cases, the exact time of entry into the risk set, τ_b, is often unknown. Sometimes, however, τ_b is known but there is no information on the values of the time-varying covariates between τ_b and τ_0. The latter situation is most likely to occur when the data are collected by means of a panel design in which an individual's time of entry into the state occupied at τ_0 is requested retrospectively. In the promotion-duration example, it would certainly be possible to obtain information on the date that employees started working at the company. On the other hand, collecting information on time-varying covariates may not be possible. Of course, if it were possible to collect all necessary information for both E and F, there would no longer be any left-censored cases.

It is clear that the solution to the left censoring problem depends on what is known about τ_b. In order to prevent biased estimates, moreover, the solution has to take into account that left-censored observations may have lower hazard rates or higher survival probabilities in the preobservation period than persons who entered into the risk set at the same point in time and who experienced the event before the start of the observation period.

Unknown τ_b Left-censored observations are more difficult to deal with when their time of entry into the risk set is unknown. Heckman and Singer discussed extensively what they call the 'problem of initial conditions' (Heckman and Singer, 1985, 1986). Ridder's work on the distribution of survival data also provided an important contribution to the treatment of left-censored observations (Ridder, 1984). More recently, Hamerle (1991) gave a comprehensive overview of methods for handling left-censored data.

Let R denote the length of the risk period before τ_0, $R = \tau_0 - \tau_b$, and let S denote the length of the risk period after τ_0, $S = \tau_e - \tau_0$. The total survival time T is $R + S$. According to Ridder (1984), the joint density of function of R and S is given by

$$f(r, s|\mathbf{x}, s > 0) = \frac{g(\tau_0 - r|\mathbf{x})f(r + s|\mathbf{x})}{\int_0^\infty g(\tau_0 - r|\mathbf{x})S(r|\mathbf{x})dr}.$$ [4.31]

Here, $g(\tau_0 - r|\mathbf{x})$ denotes the probability that someone with covariate values $\mathbf{x}$ will enter into the risk set at $\tau_0 - r$, that is, at τ_b. $S(r|\mathbf{x})$ denotes the probability of surviving until $T = r$ and $f(r + s|\mathbf{x})$ is equivalent to $f(t|\mathbf{x})$, that is, the density of T. In the denominator of Equation 4.31, the probability of entering into the risk set at $\tau_0 - r$ and surviving until τ_0 is integrated over all possible r. This results in the marginal probability of entering into the risk set before τ_0 and surviving to τ_0. The numerator expresses the probability of entering into the risk set at $\tau_0 - r$ and experiencing an event at $r + s$ which is t.

The density of S, given $\mathbf{x}$, the density of a left-censored survival time, is obtained by integrating $f(r, s|\mathbf{x}, s > 0)$ over r, the unobserved part of T,

$$f(s|\mathbf{x}, s > 0) = \frac{\int_0^\infty g(\tau_0 - r|\mathbf{x})f(r + s|\mathbf{x})dr}{\int_0^\infty g(\tau_0 - r|\mathbf{x})S(r|\mathbf{x})dr}.$$ [4.32]

Thus, the marginal density of S equals the probability of entering into the risk set before τ_0 and experiencing an event at $T = t = r + s$, divided by the probability of entering into the risk set before τ_0 and surviving until τ_0. This density no longer depends on the unknown values of R.

Unfortunately, the likelihood contribution on the basis of $f(s|\mathbf{x}, s > 0)$ not only involves the survival distribution of interest, but also depends on $g(\tau_0 - r|\mathbf{x})$, i.e., the distribution of the calendar time of entry into the risk set (τ_b). Therefore, the parameters of interest cannot be estimated without making additional assumptions with regard to entry rates $g(\tau_0 - r|\mathbf{x})$, except if there is some external information by which to estimate the entry rates empirically (Tuma and Hannan, 1984:132). In the analysis of the timing of divorces, for example, statistics on marriage rates may be used to estimate the rates of entry into the risk set for the event divorce.

One possible simplifying restriction is to assume that T is exponentially distributed. In that case, Equation 4.32 simplifies to $h(s|\mathbf{x})e^{-h(s|\mathbf{x})s}$, which is the same result obtained by the second solution for left censoring discussed above. This involves setting the time of entry into the risk set arbitrarily equal to τ_0 for all left-censored cases, and, moreover, assuming exponential survival. As was mentioned previously, erroneously assuming an exponential distribution, which is a quite common 'solution' to the left censoring problem, may lead to severe bias in the parameter estimates (Heckman and Singer, 1985, 1986).

Another possibility is to assume that the rate of entry is time invariant, i.e., that $g(\tau_0 - r|\mathbf{x}) = g(\mathbf{x})$. In that case, Equation 4.32 simplifies to

$$f(s|\mathbf{x}, s > 0) = \frac{\int_0^\infty f(r+s|\mathbf{x})dr}{\int_0^\infty S(r|\mathbf{x})dr} = \frac{\int_0^\infty f(r+s|\mathbf{x})dr}{E(T|\mathbf{x})} .$$

After making further parametric assumptions on the distribution of T (see section 4.3), this yields a likelihood function for estimating the parameters related to T which can be solved without too many problems. However, the validity of the results depends to a large degree on the validity of the assumption of a constant entry rate, given $\mathbf{x}$ (Guo, 1993).

Known τ_b If there is information on the time of entry into the risk set of left-censored observations, things are much less complicated. But, as mentioned above, treating left-censored observation in the same fashion as the other cases leads to an underestimation of the hazard rates for short durations. The only way to prevent this form of selection bias is to take the selection mechanism into account when estimating the model's parameters. In this case, we must take into account that a person can only belong to the sample if he/she did not experience the event of interest before τ_0. This can simply be accomplished by constructing the likelihood function with the conditional density of T given survival up to R rather than with the unconditional density of T (Tuma and Hannan, 1984:130-131). When R is known, this leads to the conditional maximization approach which was first proposed by Lancaster (Lancaster, 1979; Hamerle, 1991; Guo, 1993). The result is that only the information on a given individual which is not selective, that is, the survival information between r and t (or between τ_0 and τ_e), is used for estimating the parameters.

The conditional density of a left-censored case which, as in the case of F in Figure 4.1, experiences an event in the observation period is defined as (Lancaster, 1979; Tuma and Hannan, 1984; Guo, 1993)

$$f(t|T > r, \mathbf{x}) = \frac{h(t|\mathbf{x})S(t|\mathbf{x})}{S(r|\mathbf{x})} = \frac{h(t|\mathbf{x})\exp\left(-\int_0^t h(u|\mathbf{x})du\right)}{\exp\left(-\int_0^r h(u|\mathbf{x})du\right)}$$

$$= h(t|\mathbf{x})\exp\left(-\int_r^t h(u|\mathbf{x})du\right) . \qquad [4.33]$$

This conditional density is almost equal to the density for a noncensored observation. The only difference is that the ordinary survival probability is replaced by a conditional survival probability: The hazard rate is not integrated from 0 to t, but from r to t.

Apart from preventing selection bias, this procedure has the further advantage that no information is needed on the values of time-varying covariates between $T = 0$ and $T = r$. Since the conditional density function depends only on the covariate values in the observation period, the required data corresponds exactly to the data collected during the observation period. In that sense, the conditional density approach resembles the way in which period life tables are constructed (Guo, 1993).

Hamerle (1991) showed that the conditional density function used in the conditional likelihood method (Equation 4.33) can be also obtained by conditioning the joint density of R and S (Equation 4.31) on the marginal density of R without making additional assumptions with regard to $g(\tau_0 - r|\mathbf{x})$. Nevertheless, Ridder (1984) and Hamerle (1991) criticized the conditional likelihood approach. It would lead to considerable loss of efficiency because the information on R would only be used for eliminating selection bias and not for estimating the parameters of interest. More precisely, by conditioning on R and $\mathbf{X}$, the information in the joint distribution of $(R, \mathbf{X})$ is neglected. On the other hand, Guo (1993) states that there are two important disadvantages to using the joint density of R and S when R is known: The results may depend on the time-homogeneity assumption about $g(\tau_0 - r|\mathbf{x})$ and the procedure can only be used when all covariates are time-invariant. Thus, if it is taken into account that no assumptions need to be made on the distribution of τ_b, that the method can be used for estimating models with time-varying covariates, and that obtaining maximum likelihood estimates only requires a small modification of the standard procedures, it seems reasonable to state that when τ_b is known, the conditional likelihood method is preferable.

Computer programs The conditional maximization method for left-censored observations can be implemented using standard computer programs for estimating hazard models. It can be applied in continuous-time hazard models if the program concerned can deal with episode records. An episode record has a starting time that does not need to be equal to zero and an end time which does not need to be equal to t. Rohwer's TDA program is one such example (Rohwer, 1993). Since discrete-time methods always use episode records, that is, one record for every discrete time interval that a person is at risk, the conditional maximization procedure can easily be implemented in discrete-time hazard models. The only thing that has to be done is deleting all person-period records from $T = 0$ to $T = r$ for all left-censored observations.

In section 4.4, it was shown that the likelihood function for piecewise exponential survival models equals

$$\mathcal{L} = \prod_{i=1}^{N} \prod_{z=1}^{Z^*} h(z|\mathbf{x}_i)^{\delta_{iz}} \exp\left(-h(z|\mathbf{x}_i)e_{iz}\right)$$
$$= \prod_{abz} \theta_{abz}^{n_{abz}} \exp\left(\theta_{abz}E_{abz}\right),$$

where e_{iz} denotes the total time that person i belongs to the risk set in time interval z, and E_{abz} denotes the total exposure time in time interval z for persons with covariates values $A = a$ and $B = b$. When applying the conditional likelihood approach in combination with a piecewise exponential survival model, the exposure times e_{iz} are equal to zero until the time interval containing r, that is, until $t_{z-1} < r \leq t_z$. Of course, the changes in e_{iz} will also influence the cross-tabulated exposure times in E_{abz}. The only difference between the ordinary maximum likelihood method and the conditional maximum likelihood is that left-censored observations do not contribute to the total exposure times before $T = r$. In the ℓEM program (Vermunt, 1993), this procedure is implemented by allowing the user to specify the time of entry into the risk set.

4.6. Time-varying covariates, time, and time-covariate interactions

Until this point it was assumed, for the sake of simplicity, that the values of the explanatory variables used in hazard models do not change their values during the observation period. The only variable that was allowed to change its value was the time variable itself. However, dynamic analysis by means of event history analysis techniques not only implies that the hazard rates may change over time, but also that the values and the effects of covariates may change over time.

This section explains how to use time-varying covariates in hazard models. Special attention is paid to two special types of time-varying covariates: time and time-covariate interactions. Furthermore, some of the problems associated with the use of time-varying covariates are discussed.

4.6.1. Time-varying covariates

The chance to include explanatory variables which may change their values during the observation period is one of the great advantages of event history models. It is also one of the most difficult aspects of event history modeling since various mistakes can be made in the causal interpretation of the effects of time-varying covariates (Chamberlain, 1985; Lancaster, 1990:23-31; Yamaguchi, 1991:130-134).

Of course, as is true in all nonexperimental research, the initial distribution of the time-varying covariates may introduce selection bias when important covariates are not included in the model. However, *selection bias* may occur even if persons are randomized into the different categories of a time-varying covariate at $T = 0$, that is, if the covariate concerned is not correlated at $T = 0$ with possibly unobserved confounding factors. During the observation period, people may take on particular covariate values more often than other values as a result of unmeasured risk factors which are common for the covariate process and the dependent process.[10] More precisely, there may be unobserved factors that influence both the transitions in the time-varying covariates and the hazard rate of the event of interest. As a result, a part of the sample has both a higher probability of occupying a particular covariate state and a higher hazard rate. In such cases, the effect of a time-varying covariate on the hazard rate of the event under study is, at least partially, spurious.

Another possible pitfall with respect to the causal interpretation of the effects of time-varying covariates is the problem of *reverse causation*. One would expect that determining the causal order between covariates and the dependent process under study would be simpler in the case of dynamic analysis of event history data than in the case of static analysis. However, this is only true for the covariates that do not change their value during the observation period. Time-dependent covariates may be subject to reverse causation, that is, the process under study may influence the covariate process. The covariate process may be either influenced by the state occupied at the different points in time or by the size of the hazard rate. The former is called state dependence, the latter, rate dependence (Tuma and Hannan, 1984:268; Yamaguchi, 1991:137-139). Both forms of reverse causation may severely bias the results obtained from an event history analysis.

---

[10] Following Yamaguchi (1991:133), the term covariate process will be used to denote the changes which occur in the values of the time-varying covariates, and the term dependent process to denote the transitions in the dependent variable in the study concerned.

Exogenous versus endogenous covariates The problems of selection bias (or spuriousness) and reverse causation which are associated with the use of time-dependent covariates can be clarified using the distinction between exogenous and endogenous (time-varying) covariates proposed by Lancaster (1990:23-31). Endogenous covariates may be subject to spuriousness and reverse causation, while exogenous covariates do not have these problems. Lancaster derived the distinction between endogenous and exogenous covariates by writing down the joint probability distribution of the covariate process and the dependent process under study. Assume, for the sake of simplicity, that an event or censoring can only occur at discrete points in time and that there is only one time-varying covariate. Let t_l be the lth from L^* discrete time points, $x(t_l)$ a value on the time-varying covariate at the lth time interval, and $x(0, t_l)$ a complete covariate path from $T = 0$ through $T = t_l$. The joint probability of surviving through $T = t_l$ and having observed covariate values $x(0, t_l)$ can be written as

$$P(x(0, t_l), T > t_l) = \left\{ \prod_{k=1}^{l} P\left(x(t_k)|T > t_{k-1}, x(0, t_{k-1})\right) \right.$$

$$\left. \prod_{k=1}^{l} [1 - \lambda(t_k|x(0, t_k))] \right\}, \qquad [4.34]$$

and the joint probability of experiencing an event at $T = t_l$ and having covariate values $x(0, t_l)$

$$P(x(0, t_l), T = t_l) = \left\{ \prod_{k=1}^{l} P\left(x(t_k)|T > t_{k-1}, x(0, t_{k-1})\right) \right.$$

$$\left. \lambda(t_l|x(0, t_l)) \prod_{k=1}^{l-1} [1 - \lambda(t_k|x(0, t_k))] \right\}. \quad [4.35]$$

According to Lancaster (1990:28), the nature of a time-varying covariate is determined by the factor

$$P\left(x(t_l)|T > t_{l-1}, x(0, t_{l-1})\right), \qquad [4.36]$$

which describes the probability of having a particular covariate value at $T = t_l$, given survival through $T = t_{l-1}$ and the covariate path between $T = 0$ and $T = t_{l-1}$. Now, a covariate is exogenous if and only if

$$P\left(x(t_l)|T > t_{l-1}, x(0, t_{l-1})\right) = P\left(x(t_l)|x(0, t_{l-1})\right) \qquad [4.37]$$

for all t_l. Thus, a covariate is exogenous if the covariate process is independent of the process under study, that is, if the probability of having a particular value on a time-dependent covariate at time point t_l does not depend on the condition $T > t_{l-1}$, given the covariate history through $T = t_{l-1}$. In other words, an individual who did not experience an event at or before $T = t_{l-1}$ must have the same probability of having a particular value on a time-dependent covariate in $T = t_l$ as an individual who experienced an event at or before $T = t_{l-1}$, even after controlling for the covariate path through $T = t_{l-1}$. Note that the condition that $x(t_l)$ is independent of survival through $T = t_{l-1}$ is equivalent to stating that $x(t_l)$ is independent of the state occupied at $T = t_{l-1}$.

As can be expected, a covariate that is not exogenous is endogenous. This occurs whenever the covariate process is in some way related to the dependent process under study, that is, whenever experiencing of the event at or before t_{l-1} helps to predict an individual's covariate value at $T = t_l$, even after controlling for the complete covariate path up to t_{l-1}, $x(0, t_{l-1})$.

Chamberlain (1985) and Croughley and Pickles (1989) defined exogeneity in slightly different terms as

$$f(s(t_l)|x(0, t_{L^*})) = f(s(t_l)|x(0, t_l)),$$

where $s(t_l)$ denotes the state that a person occupies at the lth time point. Thus, exogeneity implies that the state occupied at a particular moment in time depends only on current and past covariate scores. On the other hand, if future covariate values possess additional predictive power, the exogeneity condition is not fulfilled. Note that this formulation of exogeneity is an inversion of Lancaster's formulation. While Equation 4.37 shows that survival up to t_l does not predict future covariate values, Equation 4.38 states that future covariate values do not predict survival up to t_l. Of course, these two seemingly different formulations are completely equivalent.

Covariates which take their values independently of whether a person survived or not are always exogenous. Kalbfleisch and Prentice (1980:121-122) called these covariates *external covariates*. They distinguished three types of external covariates, namely, time-constant covariates, defined covariates, and ancillary covariates. Time-constant covariates do not change their values during the observation period. Defined covariates are time-varying covariates for which the values are determined in advance for each subject at the different points in time.

Examples of defined covariates are time variables, such as age and duration, factors which are under control in an experimental setting, and interaction terms between time variables and time-constant covariates. Ancillary covariates are the output of a stochastic process that is external to the individuals under study, such as macro-level variables which influence the individual risk of becoming unemployed. Time-constant, defined, and ancillary covariates have in common that their values are not influenced by whether a person survives up to $T = t_{l-1}$. Moreover, external covariates have in common that they are defined, that is, that they have a value, irrespective of whether an event occurred or not.

Covariates which are defined only if the event under study does not occur, that is, the values can only be determined as long as a person survives, are by definition endogenous because the expression $P(x(t_l)|x(0, t_{l-1}))$ at the right-hand side of Equation 4.37 is a probability that cannot be evaluated at all values of T (Lancaster, 1990). Examples are an individual's wage in a study of the length of employment spells or an individual's general condition in a clinical trial. After all, upon becoming unemployed a person has no wage and after dying no general condition measure is available. Kalbfleisch and Prentice (1980:122-124) referred to such covariates as *internal covariates*. They defined an internal covariate as a time measurement taken on an individual that, as a result, requires survival of the individual for its existence. According to Kalbfleisch and Prentice (1980:124), internal covariates often act as intermediate variables. For instance, a medical treatment or another type of intervention may have an effect on the hazard rate of dying from a particular disease. However, after controlling for the time-varying covariate general condition, the effect may disappear. This may result from an indirect effect of the treatment on the risk of dying, that is, the treatment may improve the general condition and thus lower the risk of dying. The use of internal covariates can help to understand the process more precisely, but to understand the ongoing process completely the changes in the internal covariates themselves also have to be studied. For this reason, Manton, Woodbury, and Stallard (1988) strongly advocated models in which not only the process of interest – in their case mortality from different causes – is modelled, but in which also the evolution of risk factors is modelled. This makes it possible to improve the prediction of the effects of intervention in risk factors on the size of the hazard rate.

There are also covariates which are not defined externally to an individual subject, but which are not necessarily endogenous. For instance, in a study of unemployment, a person's marital status may be either an exogenous or endogenous covariate. The marital status is not internal according to the definition by Kalbfleisch en Prentice (1980) because it is still defined after an individual becomes unemployed. Whether marital status is endogenous or exogenous depends on whether the employment history up to $T = t_{l-1}$ helps us to predict an individual's marital status at t_l or not. Endogeneity can either be the result of reverse causation between employment and marital status, for instance because being employed makes the probability of a divorce smaller, or be the result of some common unobserved covariates which influence both the hazard of becoming unemployed and the hazard of divorce, such as, for instance, the stability of an individual's lifestyle.

Another example of a covariate that can be either exogenous or endogenous is the time-varying covariate of pregnancy in an analysis of the event marriage. The relationship between pregnancy and marriage may be the result of one of the following causal processes: pregnancy may be a reason to marry, women with a higher likelihood of marriage may have a higher risk of becoming pregnant, or the decision to marry and become pregnant may be taken simultaneously. In the first case, there is a direct effect of pregnancy on the hazard rate of marriage, which means that individuals with a high risk of premarital pregnancy at a young age will, as a result, have a higher risk of marrying young. In the second case, there may be reverse causation. More precisely, the rate of becoming pregnant may depend on the size of the rate of getting married. The latter case involves a spurious effect resulting from the fact that the rate of getting pregnant and the marriage rate are influenced by the same unobserved factors. It is not only difficult to determine which kind of process is at work, but an additional problem is that the three kinds of processes may each be valid for different subgroups.

4.6.2. Different dimensions of time

The previous sections discussed various methods for modeling the time dependency of the process under study. However, no attention was given to the operationalization of the variable time or to the interpretation of its effect. The operationalization of the time dependency of the hazard rate depends on the substantive research question which is to be answered. Hazard rates may be related to different kinds of time dimensions, such as age, calendar time, duration, and experience (Tuma and Hannan, 1984:189-197). However, normally, it is not correct to assume that the time variable has a direct causal effect on the hazard rate. Time dependence will generally be the result of unobserved factors which change in some systematic way together with the time dimension involved.

A time variable which is very often used, particularly in demographic research, is *age*. Age is, for instance, related to marriage, birth, and death rates. It seems plausible to explain the age dependence of marriage rates from social norms about the best age to marry. Birth rates are related to age both as a result of social norms and due to the physiological capacity to reproduce. In that case, there is a mixture of two types of age effects which can only be separated when at least one of them is operationalized in different fashion. And finally, death rates are related to age as a result of changing physiological conditions as individuals grow older.

Another time variable is *calendar time or period*. This variable generally indicates changing unmeasured macro conditions which influence the individual hazard rates. Divorce rates may be correlated to calendar time because of changed laws or changing social norms. In addition, the period dependence of the rate of becoming unemployed may be caused by fluctuations in the economy.

The time spent in the risk set, or *duration*, is also a useful time dimension. In the analysis of unemployment spells, a negative duration dependence is often found. This is explained by the fact that employers prefer to employ individuals who have only been unemployed for a short period of time. Duration is equivalent to the stigmatization of unemployment by society. The dependence of, for instance, divorce rates on the duration of marriage may be the result of a number of psychological aspects which influence the strength of a relationship.

Tuma and Hannan (1984:195) mentioned *experience* as another possible time variable. Experience is the total time spent in a particular state. Generally, it differs from duration only for the second and subsequent spells. In the analysis of employment spells, experience is the total time that an individual has been employed.

The last time dimension mentioned by Tuma and Hannan (1984:191) is *cohort*. Contrary to the above-mentioned time variables, cohort is not a time-varying variable. It is a variable that is constant during each particular spell. The variable cohort is often used in demographic research, but is useful in other fields as well. Cohort is generally defined as the period of entry into the risk set. Therefore, it is sometimes also called period-cohort. In the case of some specific life-course events, such as first marriage and first birth, it is simply someone's birth date or birth year. In the analysis of divorce, cohort may be the year of marriage, also referred to as a marriage-cohort. In the analysis of the length of the first job search after leaving school, cohort may be either the date of leaving school or the individual's year of birth. Generally, the variable cohort is used as an indicator for cumulated circumstances or experiences that particular subgroups of persons have in common.

Another constant time variable which is similar to cohort is the *age at the entry into the risk set*. It is also called the age cohort. The age at which an individual becomes unemployed may influence the hazard rate of becoming employed. The age that a women has her first child may influence the hazard rate of the second birth. Like the other time variables that were mentioned, this variable also serves as a correlate for particular unobserved factors.

Often, several time dependencies are at work simultaneously. For instance, divorce rates may depend on age, period, age at marriage, year of marriage, and duration of marriage. Unemployment rates may depend on age, experience, duration, and period. However, the number of time dependencies that can be included in a model is limited as a result of the well-known collinearity which also occurs in age-period-cohort models (Tuma and Hannan, 1984:196-197; Mason and Fienberg, 1985; Hagenaars, 1990:326-332).

A serious problem associated with the interpretation of the effects of time variables is that the observed time dependence may not only be the result of unobserved factors which change simultaneously with the time dimension being used in a particular model, but may also be influenced by unobserved factors which do not change with time. This is generally referred to as unobserved heterogeneity (Vaupel, Manton, and Stallard, 1979; Heckman and Singer, 1982, 1984; Trussell and Richards, 1985) and can easily be demonstrated. Suppose there are two subgroups with constant but different hazard rates. In that case, the relative size of the group with a lower hazard rate will increase with time. As a result, the mean hazard rate will decrease with time. This means that if this source of heterogeneity remains unobserved, there will be spurious negative time dependence (Elbers and Ridder, 1982).

The negative duration dependence of the hazard rate of becoming employed may result from the fact that those who are more capable find a job more easily, rather than from the fact that stigmatization by employers takes place. In addition, divorce rates may go down because individuals who know each other for a longer period before marrying have lower divorce rates, rather than because the quality of the relationship improves with the duration of marriage.

In general, unobserved heterogeneity leads to either an underestimation of positive time dependence or an overestimation of negative time dependence. An important difference with static regression models is, however, that in event history models unobserved factors influence the results even if they are uncorrelated with the observed variables at the time of entry into the risk set, that is, at $T = 0$. Although unobserved heterogeneity has the strongest impact on the duration effect, it may also influence the effects of observed covariates on the hazard rate.

4.6.3. Time-varying covariate effects

A strong point of event history models is that the effects of covariates may change with time, or equivalently, that the time effects may depend on covariate values. Such models, which are obtained by including interaction terms between time variables and covariates, are called non-proportional hazard models. Note that time-covariate interactions are also time-varying covariates.

These time-covariate interaction effects can be interpreted in different manners. The simplest interpretation is that the time dependence differs for subgroups. In other words, the unobserved factors which are associated with the time dimension concerned differ or function in a different manner for different observed subpopulations. For instance, women with different educational levels have their first child at different ages. This can occur because the social norm explanation for the effect of age only applies to less educated women. Highly educated woman may postpone the birth of their first child because they want to participate in the labor force and are subsequently confronted with both norms and physiological factors which determine the maximum age for starting a reproductive career.

On the other hand, time-covariate interaction effects can be interpreted as covariate effects that change with time. For instance, the interaction effect between age and educational level on the rate of first birth also means that the effect of the educational level on the rate of first birth changes with age. Suppose that at younger ages a higher educational level is a barrier to starting the reproductive career because the costs of having a child are too high. As time goes on, the relative costs for better educated women will go down in comparison to the costs for less educated women who have not yet had children. This phenomenon may lead to higher first-birth rates for less educated women than for highly educated women, but only at younger ages. At older ages, the birth rates may be equal for both groups, or may actually be higher for better educated women.

As is the case with time dependence itself, the interpretation of time-covariate interactions is not always straightforward: a significant interaction term between time and a time-constant covariate may also be the result of unobserved heterogeneity. Spurious time-covariate interaction effects occur when there is an unobserved variable which is correlated with the observed covariate concerned. This is the classic form of selection bias. In that case, the differences between the hazard rates for the categories of the observed covariate decline with time. The problem is even more complicated, since differences may still increase, but it is less so than if there is no selection bias.

For example, the interaction term between educational level and age discussed above will at least partially be the result of unobserved factors which are correlated with educational level. Suppose that the ethnic group that a woman belongs to influences her educational level: women from ethnic minorities, on average, have lower educational levels than women from the ethnic majority. This implies that at age 18, the proportion of childless women from an ethnic minority will be higher in the less educated group than in the more educated group. In addition, suppose that the variable 'ethnic group' is not observed and that women from ethnic minorities have higher first-birth rates than women from the ethnic majority. As a result, the proportion of women belonging to an ethnic minority in the risk set, thus without children, will decrease with age. However, since the less educated group contains more women belonging to an ethnic minority, the hazard rate for those with lower levels of education group will decrease faster than the hazard rate for the better educated group. This leads to a spurious age-education interaction.

Another example could be the interaction effect found between type of union (married/unmarried) and the duration of the union in the analysis of union dissolution. What is found is that at short durations unmarried couples have a much higher risk on separating than married couples, but at longer durations the difference between married and unmarried couples disappears (Manting, 1994). It is almost certain that this interaction effect is caused by unobserved factors which are strongly associated with the type of union such as, for instance, the stability of the relationship which could be operationalized as 'how long a couple has known each other at the start of the union'. If it were possible to control for such a factor, the difference in the duration of union between cohabiting couples and married couples might become much smaller.

4.6.4. Unobserved heterogeneity, selection bias, and spurious relationships

Above it was shown that the presence of unobserved heterogeneity may introduce bias in the parameters of hazard models in a number of different ways. In summary, unobserved heterogeneity usually has a downwards effect on the time dependence, even if the unobserved factors are uncorrelated with the values of covariates included in the model at $T = 0$. Moreover, covariate effects will be biased as well since the unobserved variables and the observed variable become correlated after $T = 0$. When the unobserved variable is related to other covariates at $T = 0$, that is, when there is some form of selection bias, spurious interaction effects between T and $\mathbf{X}$ will be found. Finally, the effect of (endogenous) time-varying covariates may be spurious as a result of the presence of unobserved risk factors which influence both the covariate process and the dependent process.

Of course, it is important to be aware of these phenomena. However, it would be even more useful to have instruments which could be used to minimize the distortion resulting from this type of problem. Various authors (Heckman and Singer, 1982, 1984; Vaupel, Manton, and Stallard, 1979) have proposed including a latent variable or a random effect in the hazard model to tackle the problem of unobserved heterogeneity. Normally, a latent variable with either a parametric or non-parametric distribution function is assumed to exist which is uncorrelated with the observed covariate values at $T = 0$. Under weak conditions, such a latent variable makes it possible to separate spurious from true time dependence (Elbers and Ridder, 1982; Heckman and Singer, 1984).

Spurious time dependence is, however, only one source of bias introduced by unobserved factors. The above-mentioned approach is limited because it does not allow the latent variable to be related to observed covariates. Therefore, it cannot be used to eliminate selection bias in general. Chapter 5 presents a more general approach which makes it possible to model the relationships between unobserved categorical or non-parametric covariates and observed covariates, including the initial states of the time-dependent covariates and the dependent process. This approach also makes possible the elimination of specific forms of selection bias.

Spurious effects of time-varying covariates, or selection bias in time-varying covariates, can be tackled by simultaneously analyzing the dependent process and the covariate process by means of the multivariate hazard models, which are discussed in section 2.7. By incorporating a latent variable which influences both the covariate process and the dependent process, it is possible to identify common unobserved risk factors and to recover the true effect of a time-varying covariate. This is only possible, of course, if the correlation between the dependent process and the covariate process does not result from reverse causation. In Chapter 5, these latent variable approaches are discussed more extensively.

4.6.5. Reverse causation

As mentioned previously, the causal interpretation of the effects of endogenous time-varying variables can be hampered by the existence of one of two forms of reverse causation, namely, state dependence or rate dependence (Tuma and Hannan, 1984:268).

State dependence occurs whenever the transition rates of the covariate process depend on the state occupied in the dependent process of interest. It leads to a correlation of the duration in the risk period with the state dependent covariate (Yamaguchi, 1991:137-139). In these circumstances, the time dependence and the effect of the covariate concerned can easily be confused. In other words, bias will be introduced in the covariate effect whenever the duration dependence is not modelled correctly. The only solution to this problem is a careful specification of the duration dependence of the process. The bias caused by state dependence is difficult to prevent because in many situations the time dependence is unknown.

Suppose employment status is used as a time-varying covariate in an analysis of the risk of divorce, and additionally it is known that married individuals have a lower risk of becoming unemployed than individuals who are not married. The result will be that the risk set will contain more employed people at longer durations than at shorter durations, not only because employed individuals have a lower risk of divorce, but also because married people have a higher probability of being employed. This leads to a correlation between duration and the time-varying covariate employment status.

Rate dependence, which means that the hazard rate of the covariate process depends on the value of the hazard rate of the dependent process, is an even more difficult form of reverse causation to tackle. Rate dependence can be illustrated by means of an example. In hazard models for the first birth, the employment status of a women is often used as a time-dependent covariate (Vermunt, 1991). What is generally found is that employed women have lower hazard rates of having children, while women who are not in the labor force have much higher rates. This effect may, however, be partially caused by the fact that some women stop working some time before the birth of their first child. They stop working because having children is seen as incompatible with a career. Thus, when a woman decides to have children, the hazard rate of first birth increases and, as a result of rate dependence, the risk of leaving the state of employment increases as well.

Yamaguchi (1991:138-139) mentioned a similar case. He found that people tended to stop using marijuana some time before they got married because of the perceived incompatibility of marijuana use and marriage. The consequence is that if using marijuana is used as a time-varying covariate for marriage, the effect will be, at least partially, the result of reverse causation: The hazard rate of abstinence from marijuana smoking increases as the hazard rate of getting married increases.

Actually, rate dependence results from a person's capacity to anticipate future or desired situations. When there is rate dependence, the causal order of events will no longer be in agreement with their time order (Marini and Singer, 1988). According to Yamaguchi (1991:139), a possible solution for rate dependence is to use a time-lag large enough for a possible rate dependent time-dependent covariate to make anticipation less probable. The main disadvantage of such an approach is that a true effect may disappear as a result of a too large time-lag. In fact, the only real solution is to perform additional research on the decision-making process governing the covariate value and the value of the dependent variable in order to understand the nature of the reverse causation. Do women stop working because they plan to have a baby? Do marijuana users stop using marijuana because they plan to marry? Such questions can only be answered by asking the actors concerned about their behavioral intentions (Marini and Singer, 1988:378; Willekens, 1991).

4.6.6. Estimation of hazard models with time-varying covariates

As demonstrated by Lancaster (1990:29-31), the estimation of hazard models with time-varying covariates is straightforward if the condition of exogeneity is fulfilled. In that case, Equation 4.36, which describes the dependence of the covariate process on the dependent process, does not contain information on the hazard parameters. More precisely, it is simply the marginal probability of the observed covariate path $\mathbf{x}(t_l)$. Therefore, the individual contribution to the likelihood function can be based on the second part of Equations 4.34 and 4.35, i.e.,

$$\prod_{k=1}^{l} [1 - \lambda(t_k|\mathbf{x}(t_k))] \,, \qquad [4.38]$$

$$\lambda(t_l|\mathbf{x}(t_l)) \prod_{k=1}^{l-1} [1 - \lambda(t_k|\mathbf{x}(t_k))] \,. \qquad [4.39]$$

These are probabilities given covariate values, which is the same interpretation as if all of the covariates are time-constant. However, if some time-dependent covariates are endogenous, this is not true. In that case, the expressions given in Equations 4.38 and 4.39 are factors in the joint probability of T and $\mathbf{x}(t_l)$, and are not probabilities conditional on the covariate path. According to Lancaster (1990:30), neglecting the last term of Equations 4.34 and 4.35 when the covariates are endogenous leads to a partial likelihood solution which can be seriously inefficient. In addition, if the endogeneity of time-varying covariates results from selection bias or reverse causation, the effects of these covariates will be biased.

Continuous time For continuous time, the likelihood function for a hazard model with time-varying covariates is given by

$$\mathcal{L} = \prod_{i=1}^{N} h(t_i|\mathbf{x}(t_i))^{\delta_i} \exp\left(-\int_{0}^{t_i} h(u|\mathbf{x}(u_i))du\right) . \qquad [4.40]$$

Equation 4.40 can also be written down in terms of episodes in which the covariates do not change their values. Let K_i be the number of episodes, K_i-1 the number of times that a change occurs in the covariate values of person i, and t_{k_i} the time point at with the kth change occurs. Moreover, t_{0_i} is the time point at which the first episode starts and t_{K_i} is the survival or censoring time. The censoring indicators δ_{k_i} are equal to 0 for all $k_i < K_i$ and have the usual meaning for $k_i = K_i$, that is, all episodes except the last one are always treated as censored. In terms of these K_i episodes for subjects i, the likelihood equals

$$\mathcal{L} = \prod_{i=1}^{N} \prod_{k=1}^{K_i} h(t_{k_i}|\mathbf{x}_{k_i})^{\delta_{k_i}} \exp\left(-\int_{t_{k_i-1}}^{t_{k_i}} h(u|\mathbf{x}_{k_i})du\right) . \qquad [4.41]$$

The advantage of splitting each record into K_i episodes is that these $N^* = \sum_{i=1}^{N} K_i$ episodes can be analyzed as if all of the covariates are time-constant. If each episode is treated as a left-censored case with a known starting time $R = r_j$ for episode j, Equation 4.41 can be simplified to

$$\mathcal{L} = \prod_{j=1}^{N^*} h(t_j|\mathbf{x}_j)^{\delta_j} \exp\left(-\int_{r_j}^{t_j} h(u|\mathbf{x}_j)du\right).$$

Maximizing this likelihood function is equivalent to the conditional maximization method for left-censored observations which was presented in section 4.5.

Log-rate model Like Equation 4.41, the likelihood for the piecewise exponential survival or log-rate model can be adjusted to allow for time-varying covariates (Trussell and Hammerslough, 1983). Suppose there is a model with two covariates A and B which may now be time-varying. This leads to

$$\mathcal{L} = \prod_{i=1}^{N} \prod_{k=1}^{K_i} \prod_{z=1}^{Z} h(z|\mathbf{x}_{k_i})^{\delta_{k_i z}} \exp\left(-h(z|\mathbf{x}_{k_i})e_{k_i z}\right)$$
$$= \prod_{abz} h_{abz}^{n_{abz}} \exp\left(-h_{abz}E_{abz}\right),$$

in which $e_{k_i z}$ denotes the total time that person i in episode k belongs to the risk set in time interval z. Although the likelihood in terms of the cross-tabulated number of events, n_{abz}, and the cross-tabulated exposure times, E_{abz}, seems to be equivalent to the situation in which there are no time-varying covariates (see Equation 4.21), it should be noted that in this case n_{abz} and E_{abz} are obtained in a different fashion:

$$n_{abz} = \sum_{i=1}^{N} \sum_{k=1}^{K_i} \delta_{k_i z} \gamma_{k_i ab}$$

$$E_{abz} = \sum_{i=1}^{N} \sum_{k=1}^{K_i} e_{k_i z} \gamma_{k_i ab}.$$

Here, $\gamma_{k_i ab}$ is an indicator variable taking the value 1 if person i has $A = a$ and $B = b$ in the kth episode and otherwise it takes the value 0.

Computer programs The estimation of the parameters of continuous-time hazard models with time-dependent covariates can easily performed by means of programs which permit the use of episode records as input. The TDA program which was developed by Rohwer (1993) can be used for that purpose.

The ℓEM program (Vermunt, 1993) can be used to estimate log-rate models with time-varying covariates. It allows the user to enter episode records as input. However, changing values of time-varying covariates can also be specified by defining the different covariate values as different states and utilizing the possibility of defining several transitions within one record. In that case, it is not necessary to perform episode splitting. This makes it relatively easy to analyze the covariate process simultaneously with the dependent process. The multivariate hazard models which can be used for this purpose are discussed more extensively in section 4.8.

Of course, the log-rate model with time-varying covariates can also be estimated by means of standard programs for log-linear analysis. In that case, the occurrence and the exposure matrix must be given as input.

4.7. Different types of events

Thus far, only hazard rate models for situations in which there is only one destination state were considered. In many applications it may, however, prove necessary to distinguish between different types of events or risks. In the analysis of the first-union formation, for instance, it may be relevant to make a distinction between marriage and cohabitation. In the analysis of death rates, one may want to distinguish different causes of death. And in the analysis of the length of employment spells, it may be of interest to make a distinction between the events voluntary job change, involuntary job change, redundancy, and leaving the labor force.

Before arguing the need for special models for analyzing event history data with more than one possible type event, a classification of multiple-risk situations is presented below. Then, the statistical concepts and the special types of models used in multiple-risk cases are presented. And finally, attention is given to the assumption of conditional independence of the survival times for the different types of events which can occur.

4.7.1. Classification of multiple-risk situations

In the sociological literature on competing risks, it is quite common to distinguish two ideal situations in which competing events can be analyzed with little methodological difficulty (Allison, 1984:42-44; Hachen, 1988; and Yamaguchi, 1991:169-171). Following Allison and Yamaguchi, they will be labeled as Type I and Type II situations. It is attractive to assume one of the two situations to be valid because in that case the same types of methods can be applied as are applied in the single-destination case. However, as will be argued below, it is almost always advisable to use a competing-risk model because none of the two situations is valid.

While the distinction between the above Type I and Type II situation is an important issue in the sociological literature on competing risks, in other fields, such as biometrics and demography, another problem associated with the analysis of different types of events is given a great deal of attention: the problem of dependence among competing risks (Tiatsis, 1975; Prentice and Kalbfleisch, 1979; Vaupel and Yashin, 1985; Yashin, Manton, and Stallard, 1986; Heckman and Honore, 1989). As is demonstrated below, the dependence or independence of competing risks strongly influences the range of interpretation of the results.

Type I and Type II situation In the *Type I* situation, the occurrence of one of the possible events is dominated by two separate independent steps. According to Allison (1984:42), such a situation occurs whenever the occurrence or nonoccurrence of an event, irrespective of its type, is determined by one causal process and, given that an event occurs, a second causal process determines which type of event occurs. The two steps are independent and governed by their own set of parameters.

The assumption of a Type I process can be valid, for instance, in consumer behavior research. One causal process determines whether an individual buys a particular product in $T = t$ and a second process determines the brand of the product. The aim of commercials may be either to influence the second step or to distort this two-step pattern. Likewise, the process leading to the first-union formation can be interpreted as being the outcome of such a two-step process. This is correct whenever one causal process determines the timing of the first-union formation and another determines the decision to marry or to cohabit, given that the first union will be formed.

If this Type I situation is valid, the two steps can be analyzed separately. The causal structure determining the occurrence or nonoccurrence of an event can be analyzed by means of a hazard model for one destination state. The second step can be analyzed using a discrete choice model, such as a logit or probit model, in which the kind of event is explained. If there are more than two risks, it is even possible to use a model for ordinal categorical data, such as a cumulative or sequential logit model (Tutz, 1995). The separate models for the hazard rate and the choice probabilities may contain common covariates.

A second ideal situation, which is called *Type II* by Allison (1984:43-44) and Yamaguchi (1991:171), occurs whenever the occurrence of each event type has a different causal structure. In that sense, it is the opposite of the Type I situation, in which it is assumed that the occurrence of an event, irrespective of its type, can be explained by a single causal process. Although the same covariates may be relevant, each event has an independent set of parameters, that is, the parameters for the different events are assumed to be distinct. Type II multiple-risk situations are often called competing risks (Kalbfleisch and Prentice, 1980: Chapter 7; Cox and Oakes, 1984: Chapter 9), since the occurrence of one type of event removes an individual not only from the risk set for the event concerned, but also from the risk set for the other events. This perception of situations in which there are different types of events is especially popular in biostatistics and demography.

The classical competing-risk example is death from competing causes. For instance, it is plausible to assume that different causal processes lead to death from heart disease and to death from cancer. In that case, a person dying of heart disease can be treated as being free of risk for dying of cancer. The same arguments could be applied in the analysis of employment spells if a distinction is made between voluntary and involuntary job changes. Different causal processes could be assumed to determine voluntary and involuntary job changes since different actors are involved in these two modes of leaving employment.

The process leading to a first-union formation could likewise be viewed as a competing-risk situation rather than a Type I situation. In the Type II situation, it would be assumed that there were no factors which influenced a first-union formation by marriage and a first-union formation by cohabitation in the same fashion. In other words, the two processes would be assumed to have no parameters in common.

If the process being studied takes place within a Type II situation, the different types of events can be analyzed separately, and the occurrence of one of the other possible events can be treated as a censored observation. There is, however, one exception: if a discrete-time logit model is used, the competing events must always be analyzed simultaneously (Allison, 1982). The reason for this is demonstrated below.

It appears attractive to assume one of the two ideal situations discussed above to be valid. In that case, it is not necessary to apply special instruments to the analysis of data on different types of events. The analysis can be performed in the same fashion as was discussed in the preceding sections of this chapter: in the Type I situation no distinction is made between the events and in the Type II situation the different kinds of events are analyzed separately. In social science research, however, neither of these two ideal situation is normally plausible. Most often, the occurrence of the events being studied is partially influenced in the same fashion by the same factors, and is partially influenced by unique factors or in a different fashion by the same factors. In other words, the process determining the occurrence of the events of interest is a mixture of Type I and Type II situations.

In the first-union example, it seems reasonable to assume that specific factors influence the timing of the first-union formation, regardless of the type of union, while other factors influence the risk of marriage and cohabitation is a different manner. Suppose that education is a factor of the former type and religion a factor of the latter type. This would imply that education determines the age at which a first union is formed and perhaps also influences the decision to marry or to cohabit, regardless of the age at which the union is formed. Thus, there is an effect of education on the overall hazard rate and possibly age-education and risk-education interaction effects as well. On the other hand, religion is assumed to have a different effect on the age-specific hazard rates of marriage and unmarried cohabitation. This implies that the model contains an age-risk-religion interaction.

A mixture of the two types is often the result of a Type I or Type II process being valid for different subpopulations. For instance, some individuals embark upon one type of union without the other type being a salient alternative, while others choose between marriage and cohabitation after deciding to form a first union.

Clearly, it is dangerous to choose the method of analyzing the data on the basis of a priori assumptions with regard to the mechanism which determines the occurrence of the events being studied. Therefore, it is recommended that a simultaneous analysis of the different events be performed using hazard models which are suited to that purpose. These techniques not only make it possible to specify models without the necessity of making assumptions on the type of multiple-risk situation, they can also be used to test these assumptions. Thus, even if it seems plausible to assume either Type I or Type II to be valid, it is not sensible to choose a particular way of analyzing the data without checking the validity of the assumption concerned.

When a simultaneous analysis is performed, the occurrence of a Type I or Type II situation can be detected on the basis of interaction effects which are included in the hazard model. If no interaction effect involving both duration and risk is significant, there is a Type I situation. If the interaction between duration and risk is significant and all covariate-risk interactions are significant as well, there is a Type II situation. In all other cases, there is a mixture of the two ideal situations.

Conditionally (in)dependent risks While the distinction between the Type I and Type II multiple-risk situations is especially relevant to the choice of the method for analyzing multiple-risk data, another distinction can be made on the basis of the range of interpretation of the results obtained from an analysis, namely, the distinction between independent and dependent competing risks.

In discussing the censoring problem in section 4.5, it was claimed that the estimation and interpretation of the parameters of hazard models was straightforward only if the censoring rate and the hazard rate could be assumed to be conditionally independent, given the covariates included in the model, of the event under study. This condition is fulfilled when there are no unobserved factors which influence both the hazard rate and the censoring rate. The independence of censoring and the occurrence of an event is so important because otherwise estimates of the hazard parameters would depend on which observations were censored.

The same argumentation can be applied to multiple-risk situations, particularly as it should be realized that censoring can be seen as a competing risk. When competing events are not independent, the size of the estimated hazard parameters for one type of event will be influenced by which cases experience which of the competing events, or in other words, the results will only be valid under current study conditions (Prentice and Kalbfleisch, 1979). However, it is often useful to be able to interpret the hazard rate of a particular event without having to take the sizes of the other risks into account. This makes it possible to predict the number of occurrences of each of the possible events under different assumptions about the values of the other hazard rates. For instance, it is possible to predict the substitution effect of the interest event when it becomes impossible for one of the other events to occur. A classic application of conditionally independent risks in the study of mortality is cause removal, or the estimation of overall mortality rates assuming that one cause of death could be eliminated (Manton and Stallard, 1987). But this is only allowable if the survival times are independent given the covariates included in the model, that is, when we have an independent competing-risk situation. Yashin, Manton, and Stallard (1986), for example, demonstrated that the effect of eliminating cancer and heart disease on survival is overestimated if the hazard model does not take dependencies between causes of death into account.

Hill, Axinn, and Thornton (1993) applied the principle of 'cause removal' to estimate the number of cohabiting couples if the probability of marriage would decrease as a result of changes in the law. Suppose that marriage rates and cohabitation rates are positively correlated, and that this correlation is completely captured by the covariates included in the model. This would imply that if marriage became less attractive, for example, because of changed legislation, cohabitation rates would rise since it could be expected that a segment of the individuals who would have married would now choose to cohabit. What happens is that marriage is partially substituted by cohabitation. On the other hand, if the dependence between the two events is not captured by the covariates included in the model, it is not possible to estimate this substitution effect correctly.

One major problem, however, is that although the conditional independence assumption is very attractive from a substantive point of view, it is difficult to test because only one of the possible durations, i.e., the shortest one, can be observed (Tiatsis, 1975; Heckman and Honore, 1989). Below, the (in)dependence among different types of events is discussed in more detail.

4.7.2. Statistical concepts in multiple-risk situations

As in the single destination situation, assume that for each individual there is a random survival time T. Suppose that, in addition, there is a random variable D indicating which of the possible events occurred. Of course, censored observations are also allowed. For the moment, covariate dependencies will not be taken into account. The multiple-risk equivalent of the hazard rate is given by

$$h_d(t) = \lim_{\Delta t \to 0} \frac{P(t \leq T < t + \Delta t, D = d | T \geq t)}{\Delta t}.$$

It denotes the instantaneous risks of experiencing an event of type d in the time interval $[t \leq T < t + \Delta t]$, given that no event occurs before $T = t$. Econometricians generally use the term transition intensity or transition rate for $h_d(t)$ (Lancaster, 1990:99-108), while biometricians use the terms crude hazard rate or cause-specific hazard rate (Cox and Oakes, 1984:143-145). The overall hazard rate can be obtained by summing the event-specific hazard rates, that is,

$$h(t) = \sum_d h_d(t).$$

The usual relationships between $h(t)$, $f(t)$, and $S(t)$ described in section 4.2) also apply in the multiple-risk situation.

The joint density of T and D, or the instantaneous probability that an event of type d will occur at $T = t$, is given by

$$f(T = t, D = d) = h_d(t)S(t) = h_d(t) \exp\left(-\int_0^t h(u)d(u)\right).$$

The marginal probability that the event is of type d is given by

$$P(D = d) = \int_0^\infty h_d(t) \exp\left(-\int_0^t h(u)d(u)\right) d(t).$$

Moreover, given that an event occurs at time t, the conditional probability that the event is of type d is

$$P(D = d|T = t) = f(D = d, T = t)/f(T = t) = h_d(t)/h(t).$$

An important special case occurs if

$$P(D = d|T = t) = P(D = d),$$

that is, if the type of event is independent of the time that an event occurs. In that case, the transition intensities for all d and t can be written as

$$h_d(t) = h(t)P(D = d).$$

In fact, this is the formal definition of the Type I situation presented above: there is no interaction between T and D, and T and D are independent of each other. Note that it is also a variant of the assumption of proportional hazard rates because the hazard rates of the various risks are in the same ratio for all t (Cox and Oakes, 1984:143). It is for this reason that Lancaster (1990:103-104) termed models of this type proportional intensity models.

Competing risks A slightly different treatment of situations including different types of events is what Cox and Oakes (1984:144) call the competing-risk approach. This approach assumes the existence of D^* random variables $T^{(1)}, \ldots, T^{(D^*)}$ denoting an individual's latent survival times, that is, one survival time for each of the D^* possible destination states assuming that the other types of events cannot occur. These survival times are called latent because the shortest one is the only one which is observed while the other ones remain unobserved. The relationship between the observable random variables T and D and the latent survival times is

$$T = \min(T^{(1)}, \ldots, T^{(D^*)}),$$

$$D = \arg\min(T^{(1)}, \ldots, T^{(D^*)}).$$

Thus, T is the minimum risk-specific survival time and D is the argument of the shortest $T^{(d)}$. In the competing-risk approach, the observable or crude hazard function is defined as

$$h_d(t) = \lim_{\Delta t \to 0} \frac{P\left(t \le T^{(d)} < t + \Delta t | T^{(w)} \ge t, w = 1, \ldots, D^*\right)}{\Delta t},$$

that is, as the instantaneous probability of occurrence of event d in the interval $[t \le T < t + \Delta t]$, given that all the latent survival times are greater than or equal to t.

Another important concept is the hazard function of the latent survival time $T^{(d)}$,

$$h^{(d)}(t) = \lim_{\Delta t \to 0} \frac{P\left(t \le T^{(d)} < t + \Delta t | T^{(d)} \ge t\right)}{\Delta t}.$$

This hazard rate is sometimes also called the net hazard function (Moon, 1991). Note that the net hazard rate is defined in exactly the same fashion as the hazard rate for a single destination state. According to Cox and Oakes (1984:145),

$$h_d(t) = h^{(d)}(t),$$

if the latent survival times $T^{(1)}, \ldots, T^{(D^*)}$ are mutually independent. This is, in fact, the formal definition of the independent competing-risk situation presented above. Thus, if the survival times for the various destination states are independent, the crude hazard rate $h_d(t)$ can be interpreted as a net hazard rate $h^{(d)}(t)$, that is, in the same fashion as a hazard rate for a single event. This means that removal from the risk set that is not caused by the event under study may be treated in the same fashion as independent censoring.

Note that both the Type I situation and the independent competing-risk situation, as defined here, are more restrictive than presented earlier. The reason for this is that the basic concepts are defined without using covariates. When covariates are introduced, the Type I situation occurs if

$$P(D = d|T = t, \mathbf{x}) = P(D = d|\mathbf{x}),$$

and

$$h_d(t|\mathbf{x}) = h(t|\mathbf{x})P(D = d|\mathbf{x}).$$

Furthermore, competing risks are conditionally independent if

$$h_d(t|\mathbf{x}) = h^{(d)}(t|\mathbf{x}),$$

that is, if crude and net hazard rates are equal, given covariate values.

4.7.3. Multiple-risk models and their estimation

Continuous-time models Continuous-time hazard rate models for different types of events have the same form as hazard rate models for a single type of event. Actually, a multiple-risk model consists of a hazard model for each destination state. For instance, a proportional log-linear hazard model for an event of type d is given by

$$h_d(t|\mathbf{x}) = h_d(t) \exp\left(\sum_j \beta_{dj} x_{dij}\right).$$

Nonproportional models can be obtained by allowing $h_d(t)$ to depend on particular covariates.

Maximum likelihood estimates for the parameters of a continuous-time hazard model for multiple destination states can be obtained by maximizing

$$\begin{aligned}
\mathcal{L} &= \prod_{i=1}^{N} \left(\prod_{d=1}^{D^*} h_d(t_i|\mathbf{x}_i)^{\delta_{di}} \right) \exp\left(-\int_0^{t_i} \sum_{d=1}^{D^*} h_d(u|\mathbf{x}_i)du \right) \\
&= \prod_{i=1}^{N} \prod_{d=1}^{D^*} h_d(t_i|\mathbf{x}_i)^{\delta_{di}} \exp\left(-\int_0^{t_i} h_d(u|\mathbf{x}_i)du \right),
\end{aligned}$$

in which δ_{di} is an indicator variable taking the value 1 if the event for person i is of type d, and otherwise taking the value 0. It can now easily be seen why the parameters of the risk-specific hazard models can be estimated separately in the Type II situation. Since $h_d(t)$ and β_{dj} are unequal for all d's in the Type II situation, the likelihood function can be factored into separate components for the different d's. Thus, if the parameters for the different types of event are distinct, each

$$\mathcal{L}_d = \prod_{i=1}^{N} h_d(t_i|\mathbf{x}_i)^{\delta_{di}} \exp\left(-\int_0^{t_i} h_d(u|\mathbf{x}_i)du \right),$$

can be maximized separately. Various standard computer programs exist which can be used to estimate parametric multiple-risk models with restrictions between the parameters across destination states. An example is the very flexible TDA program (Rohwer, 1993).

Discrete-time logit models Discrete-time models can also be adapted for analyzing data on different types of events (Allison, 1982). The probability that event d occurs in time interval t_l, given that no event occurred before t_l, can be related to a set of covariates by means of a multinomial logit model. A proportional hazard model would take the form

$$\lambda_d(t_l|\mathbf{x}) = \frac{\exp\left(\alpha_{dl} + \sum_j \beta_{dj} x_{dij} \right)}{1 + \sum_g \exp\left(\alpha_{gl} + \sum_j \beta_{gj} x_{gij} \right)}.$$

The likelihood function which is to be maximized equals

$$\mathcal{L} = \prod_{i=1}^{N} \left[\left\{ \prod_{d=1}^{D^*} \left(\frac{\lambda_d(t_{l_i}|\mathbf{x}_i)}{1 - \lambda(t_{l_i}|\mathbf{x}_i)} \right)^{\delta_{di}} \right\} \prod_{k=1}^{l_i} (1 - \lambda(t_k|\mathbf{x}_i)) \right],$$

in which the overall conditional probability of experiencing an event at t_k, $\lambda(t_k|\mathbf{x}_i)$, is defined as

$$\lambda(t_k|\mathbf{x}_i) = \sum_{d=1}^{D^*} \lambda_d(t_k|\mathbf{x}_i).$$

Contrary to the continuous-time likelihood function, this likelihood cannot be factored into separate components for each of the D^* events

(Allison, 1982). This is the result of the difference in definition of the survival probability,

$$S(t_l) = \prod_{k=1}^{l_i} (1 - \lambda(t_k|\mathbf{x}_i)) = \prod_{k=1}^{l_i} \left(1 - \sum_{d=1}^{D^*} \lambda_d(t_k|\mathbf{x}_i)\right).$$

The summation over d makes factorization impossible. Just as the single type of event model can be estimated by means of standard binomial logit programs, the multiple-risk model can be estimated by means of multinomial logit programs, which include programs for the log-linear analysis of frequency tables.

Log-rate models The log-rate model can also be adapted for analyzing data on different types of events (Larson, 1984). The extension to the multiple-risk case consists of including the type of event as an additional dimension to the tables with observed and expected number of events. Assuming that there is a model with two covariates denoted by A and B, and that Z and D denote the time variable and the type of event, respectively, the log-rate model for competing risks can be written as

$$\log m_{abzd} = \log E_{abz} + \sum_j \beta_{dj} x_{abdj}.$$

As in the single-event case, the data consists of a frequency table containing the number of events per level of A, B, Z and D, n_{abzd}, and a table with total exposure times, E_{abz}. It should be noted that, in most situations, the exposure matrix does not need to have an index for D, since the number of persons at risks is equal for each d: an individual who is at risk for one event will generally also be at risk for the other possible events.

As already mentioned above, a model is of the Type I form if it does not contain interaction terms involving both Z and D, that is, if the type of event that occurs does not depend on the time that an event occurs. An example of such a model is

$$\log m_{abzd} = \log E_{abz} + u + u_a^A + u_b^B + u_z^Z + u_d^D + u_{bz}^{BZ} + u_{ad}^{AD}. \quad [4.42]$$

Here, A, B, and Z influence the overall hazard rate, in which the effect of B is nonproportional. Moreover, A also influences the 'choice' between the different types of events. The log-rate model described in Equation 4.42 can also be written as

$$\frac{m_{abzd}}{E_{abz}} = \exp(u + u_a^A + u_b^B + u_z^Z + u_{bz}^{BZ})\exp(u_d^D + u_{ad}^{AD}). \quad [4.43]$$

The first part, at the right-hand side of Equation 4.43, defines the rate of occurrence of an event, irrespective of its type, at $Z = z$, given $A = a$ and $B = b$. The second part defines the probability of experiencing an event of type d. It can be seen that this probability is independent of the value of Z, which is simply the definition of the Type I situation.

A log-rate model is of the Type II form if it at least contains all of the two-variable interaction terms involving D. The reason for this is that the risk-specific models have no parameters in common and can, in principle, be estimated separately. An example of a model of the Type II form is

$$\log m_{abzd} = \log E_{abz} + u + u_a^A + u_b^B + u_z^Z + u_d^D + u_{ad}^{AD} + u_{bd}^{BD} + u_{zd}^{ZD}.$$

Clearly, the flexibility of the log-rate model with respect to the inclusion of interaction terms can be used to test whether the process under study is in agreement with one of the above-mentioned special types, or whether it is a mixture of the two types. This means that it is not necessary to make a priori assumptions about the nature of the process in order to simplify the analysis.

The log-rate model for multiple risks presented here can be estimated using standard programs for log-linear analysis. The ℓEM program (Vermunt, 1993) is, however, relatively easy to use because it does not require the occurrence and exposure matrices as input. These matrices are made by the program itself on the basis of information on covariate values, survival time, and type of event.

4.7.4. Conditionally (in)dependent risks

In presenting the different types of multiple-risk situations, some attention was given to the distinction between dependent and independent competing risks. Below, following the work of Vaupel and Yashin (1985), the implication of dependencies between risk-specific latent survival times, or equivalently, between risk-specific hazard rates is demonstrated.

Suppose that one of two types of events D can occur and that the latent survival times denoted by $T^{(1)}$ and $T^{(2)}$ have a common correlate X which has two categories. Let $h_1(t|1)$ and $h_2(t|1)$ denote the risk-specific hazard rates for $X = 1$, and $h_1(t|2)$ and $h_2(t|2)$ the risk-specific hazard rates for $X = 2$. Suppose, furthermore, that

$$0 > h_1(t|1) > h_1(t|2) \quad \text{for all } t,$$

and

$$0 > h_2(t|1) > h_2(t|2) \quad \text{for all } t.$$

Since the first group has higher hazard rates for both event 1 and event 2, the latent survival times $T^{(1)}$ and $T^{(2)}$, that is, the survival times that would be observed if the other event could not occur, will be positively correlated: individuals with $X = 1$ have shorter survival times for both events than individuals with $X = 2$.

The mean risk-specific hazard rates at $T = t$ are equal to

$$h_1(t) = \pi(t)h_1(t|1) + [1 - \pi(t)]\, h_1(t|2)\,,$$

and

$$h_2(t) = \pi(t)h_2(t|1) + [1 - \pi(t)]\, h_2(t|2)\,,$$

in which $\pi(t)$ denotes the proportion of the population at risk at $T = t$ with $X = 1$.

Furthermore, suppose that the hazard rate of the second event becomes very small (or perhaps even 0) and equal for both groups. This can be the result of, for example, a changed law in the analysis of union formation, a changed economic conjuncture in the analysis of employment, or the invention of a new medicine in the analysis of death. Not surprisingly, this will lead to a decrease in the mean hazard rate of the second event. However, it will also lead to an *increase* of the mean hazard of the first event. Since the decrease of $h_2(t|1)$ is greater than the decrease of $h_2(t|2)$, relatively more persons belonging to the first group will survive, in other words, $\pi(t)$ will increase. But, if $\pi(t)$ increases, $h_1(t)$ will also increase since $h_1(t|1) > h_1(t|2)$ (Vaupel and Yashin, 1985).

This is a general phenomenon. If the latent survival times of competing risks are correlated as a result of common risks factors, a change in one risk-specific hazard rate will influence the other risk-specific hazard rates as well (Hill, Axinn, and Thornton, 1993). If, as in the example, two risk-specific hazard rates are positively correlated, a decrease in one hazard rate will lead to an increase in the other hazard rate. On the other hand, if two events are not correlated, that is, if they do not have common risk factors, a change in the hazard rate of one event will not influence the mean hazard rate of the other event.

The implications of this phenomenon for the interpretation range of the results obtained from a particular analysis are considerable. If it is not possible to observe one or more of the common factors causing the correlation between the risk-specific hazard rates, the results obtained for one type of event will be only valid given the observed occurrence of the other events, or, as Prentice and Kalbfleisch (1979) state it, the risk-specific regression coefficients describe covariate effects on the risk-specific hazard rates under current study conditions (see also Hachen, 1988). Often, however, researchers want to answer questions about the implication of changes in the occurrence of one type of event for the occurrence of another type of event. For instance, to what extent would other causes of death increase if one cause could be eliminated? Will the rate of voluntary job changes increase if the rate of involuntary job changes decreases? To what extent will unmarried cohabitation substitute an expected decrease in the hazard rate of married cohabitation? Of course, if the dependencies between the hazard rates are captured by including the right covariates in the model, if the hazard rates are conditionally independent, these kinds of questions can be answered quite adequately (see, for example, Manton, Woodbury, and Stallard, 1988).

The above-mentioned example also illustrates the importance of the independent censoring assumption. Censoring can be considered one of the possible events. If the censoring mechanism is not conditionally independent of the causal process underlying the event(s) under study, the results from a particular study are only valid given the observed censoring rates. In other words, different results will be obtained with other observed censoring rates. This would, of course, enormously devaluate the results of an analysis.

Common unobserved risk factors In section 4.6, the implication of unobserved heterogeneity for the parameter estimates of hazard rate models was discussed for one kind of event. But, as demonstrated above, the implications of unobserved heterogeneity may be even larger in models for competing risks since there may be unobserved factors which are shared by the different risks.

Two strategies have been proposed to identify possible common unobserved risk factors: the inclusion of one or more unobserved variables which influence the risk-specific hazard rates (Vaupel and Yashin, 1985; Heckman and Honore, 1989) in the hazard model and the use of nested logit models (Hill, Axinn, and Thornton, 1993). The former strategy can be used with both continuous-time and discrete-time data, the latter only with discrete-time data.

Actually, including unobserved covariates, or random terms, in a multiple-risk hazard model is the same type of solution for unobserved heterogeneity as the one presented in section 4.6 for the situation in which there is only one type of event. A difference is, however, that now it is necessary to specify a model for the joint distribution of the risk-specific unobserved latent variables since these variables may be correlated. The simplest specification is to assume the same unobserved factor to be relevant for all events, in other words, to assume that the risks-specific unobserved factors are perfectly correlated. Vaupel and Yashin (1985) proposed using a general unobserved factor together with risk-specific unobserved factors. They assumed these latent variables to be gamma-distributed and mutually independent. Moon (1991) showed how to include non-parametric unobserved heterogeneity in a competing-risk model, including a mover-stayer specification. However, he did not consider dependencies among the latent variables. Butler, Anderson and Burkhauser (1988) presented a competing-risk model with semi-parametric unobserved heterogeneity: A discrete bivariate distribution was used as a numerical approximation of an underlying continuous joint distribution of two unobserved factors. The general non-parametric latent variables approach presented in Chapter 5 makes it possible to specify the relationships between the latent variables influencing the risk-specific hazard rates in many different ways, including the specifications proposed by Vaupel and Yashin (1985) and by Butler, Anderson, and Burkhauser (1988).

The second method for handling shared unobserved risk factors among competing risks has recently been proposed by Hill, Axinn and Thornton (1993). Their solution consists of a modification of the discrete-time logit model which is based on using a nested logit model developed in the field of discrete choice modeling (McFadden, 1981) rather than an ordinary (multinomial) logit model. In nested logit models, it is assumed that the choice alternatives can be grouped into stochastically independent sets, the individual members of which may be correlated with each other. In other words, nested logit models allow relaxation of the IIA (Independence of Irrelevant Alternatives) assumption which underlies ordinary (multinomial) logit models. The difference with the ordinary discrete-time logit model is the inclusion of an additional parameter called the index of dissimilarity for each subset of alternatives. This parameter, which is denoted by ρ and which takes values between 0 and 1, captures the unmeasured dependence among the different kinds of events. More precisely, the unmeasured correlation among alternatives within the subset concerned equals $(1 - \rho^2)$.

Suppose there is a nested discrete-time logit model in which the dependent competing risks belong to the same subset. In that case, the regression model for the overall conditional probability of experiencing an event at t_l is specified as

$$\lambda(t_l|\mathbf{x}) = \frac{\left[\sum_d \exp\left(\sum_j \beta_{dj}/\rho\, x_{dij}\right)\right]^\rho}{1 + \left[\sum_d \exp\left(\sum_j \beta_{dj}/\rho\, x_{dij}\right)\right]^\rho},$$

in which, for simplicity of notation, the time parameters are incorporated in the β's. The probability that the event that occurred at t_l is of type d equals

$$P(D = d|T = t, \mathbf{x}) = \frac{\exp\left(\sum_j \beta_{dj}/\rho\, x_{dij}\right)}{\sum_g \exp\left(\sum_j \beta_{gj}/\rho\, x_{gij}\right)}.$$

The conditional probability of experiencing an event of type d at t_l can be simply obtained by combining the two above equations, i.e.,

$$\lambda_d(t_l|\mathbf{x}) = \lambda(t_l|\mathbf{x})\, P(D = d|T = t, \mathbf{x}).$$

In an application on union formation, with marriage and unmarried cohabitation as competing events, Hill, Axinn, and Thornton (1993) found a value of 0.44 for ρ. They demonstrated that when the event marriage is less likely to occur, a model including the dependence parameter leads to considerably more substitution of marriage by cohabitation than a model that does not take the dependence between the alternatives into account.

4.8. Multivariate hazard models

Up to now, it was assumed that each individual experiences no more than one event. The information that was used to estimate a hazard model consisted, besides the covariate information, of one survival time and an indicator variable indicating whether censoring or an event occurred. In the case of multiple risks, information on the type of event that occurred was also needed. This section presents models for simultaneously analyzing several events per unit of analysis, that is, for analyzing event histories.

First, the different kinds of multivariate event history data are presented. Then an explanation is given on how to analyze repeatable events of one type. After that, the multiple-state model is presented, including the Markov and the semi-Markov chain model which are special cases of it. It is shown that the multiple-state generalization of the discrete-time logit model (Allison, 1982) leads to a model that is equivalent to the discrete-time Markov model introduced in section 2.9. Subsequently, hazard models for some other kinds of multivariate survival data are presented. And finally, attention is given to methods that can be used to take dependencies among survival times into account.

4.8.1. Multivariate event history data

Most events studied in social sciences are repeatable, and most event history data contains information on *repeated events* for each individual. This is in contrast to biomedical research, where the event of greatest interest is death. Examples of repeatable events are job changes, having children, arrests, accidents, promotions, and residential moves. It is not surprising that most of the work on methods for simultaneous analysis of repeatable events is done by sociologists, economists, and demographers (Tuma and Hannan, 1984; Hamerle, 1989; Lancaster, 1990; Heckmann and Singer, 1982, 1985; Hoem and Jensen, 1982).

Often events are not only repeatable but also of different types, that is, we have a *multiple-state* situation. When people can move through a sequence of states, events cannot only be characterized by their destination state, as in competing risks models, but they may also differ with respect to their origin state. An example is an individual's employment history: an individual can move through the states of employment, unemployment, and out of the labor force. In that case, six different kinds of transitions can be distinguished which differ with regard to their origin and destination states. Of course, all types of transitions can occur more than once. Other examples are people's union histories with the states living with parents, living alone, unmarried cohabitation, and married cohabitation (Manting, 1994), or people's residential histories with different regions as states (Mulder, 1993). Special multiple-state models are the well-known Markov and semi-Markov chain models (Coleman, 1981; Tuma and Hannan, 1984:91-115, Hoem and Jensen, 1982).

Hazard models for analyzing data on repeatable events and multiple-state data are special cases of the general family of multivariate hazard rate models. Another application of these multivariate hazard models is the simultaneous analysis of different life-course events, or as Willekens (1989) calls it, parallel careers. For instance, it can be of interest to investigate the relationships between women's reproductive, relational, and employment careers, not only by means of the inclusion of time-varying covariates in the hazard model, but also by explicitly modeling their mutual interdependence. Manton, Woodbury, and Stallard (1988) stressed the importance of simultaneously modeling the process of interest and the evolution of risk factors to be able to predict the effect of intervention in risk factors on survival. Multivariate hazard models which make it possible to simultaneously model changes in the value of the dependent variable and changes in the values of the time-varying covariates can also be used to detect spurious effects of time-varying covariates and particular forms of reverse causation.

Another application of multivariate hazard models is the analysis of *dependent or clustered observations*. Observations are clustered, or dependent, when there are observations from individuals belonging to the same group or when there are several similar observations per individual. Examples are the occupational careers of spouses, educational careers of brothers (Mare, 1994), child mortality of children in the same family (Guo and Rodriguez, 1991), or in medical experiments, measures of the sense of sight of both eyes or measures of the presence of cancer cells in different parts of the body. In fact, data on repeatable events can also be classified under this type of multivariate event history data, since in that case there is more than one observation of the same type for each observational unit as well.

The different types of multivariate event history data have in common that there are dependencies among the observed survival times. These dependencies may take several forms. The occurrence of one event may influence the occurrence of another event. Events may be dependent as a result of common antecedents. And, survival times may be correlated because they are the result of the same causal process, with the same antecedents and the same parameters determining the occurrence or nonoccurrence of an event.

Multivariate event history data can also be viewed as a form of multilevel data (Goldstein, 1987; Bryk and Raudenbuch, 1992; Yang and Goldstein, 1996). It is always possible to distinguish at least two levels. This can either be an individual and the different observations on an individual, or a group and the different observations on individuals belonging to a group.

4.8.2. Analyzing repeated events

There are three approaches for analyzing data on repeated events, multiple spells, or multiple cycles as Lancaster (1990:108) called it, namely: 1] performing separate analyses of subsequent events, 2] performing a pooled analysis in which every spell is treated as a separate observation, and 3] analyzing the events simultaneously taking dependencies among the separate events into account.

The first strategy, *analyzing each subsequent event separately*, is a rather simple one. For employment spells, it would imply that a separate analysis is performed for the first employment spell, for the second employment spell, and so on. Such an approach requires no special assumptions, and is especially useful when the events are actually of a different type, in other words, when each spell-specific hazard model has its own set of parameters. However, when the causal process is essentially the same across subsequent spells, doing a separate analysis is both tedious and statistically inefficient (Allison, 1984:51). In the analysis of employment spells, this procedure will generally not be followed. But when analyzing the timing of births, it is quite common to perform separate analyses for different parities. The main disadvantage of this procedure is that no restrictions can be imposed on the parameters across the parity-specific hazard rate models. Moreover, it makes it impossible to identify unobserved risk factors which are the same for all spells.

The second strategy, *performing a pooled analysis* in which each event is treated as a separate case, is also very simple. From a substantive point of view, this approach is just the opposite of the first strategy in that the factors determining the occurrence or nonoccurrence of an event are assumed to be equal for each of the subsequent events. In other words, all parameters are restricted to be equal across spells (Hamerle, 1989). For employment spells this may be a realistic assumption, but in many other cases the causal process may depend at least partially on the ranking of the event.

When performing a pooled analysis, the different events for one individual are treated as statistically independent observations. In most cases, there is good reason to think that the independence assumption is false, at least to some degree (Allison, 1984:54). In general, it can be expected that people having short employment spells, will continue to have short employment spells because for some reason they have high probabilities of becoming unemployed. This does, however, not violate the (conditional) independence assumption as long as the dependence is captured by the explanatory variables included in the model. But, in most situations it is unrealistic to assume that all heterogeneity is taken into account by the observed covariates. If the assumption of statistical independence is not fulfilled, parameter estimates are biased and their standard errors are underestimated.

Another problem associated with the pooled analysis approach is that the only time dimension that can be used is the time since the last event or since the entry into the risk set for the event concerned (Hamerle, 1989). When discussing the different kinds of time variables, this time dimension was called duration. But, sometimes it is necessary to use other kinds of time variables, such as age or calendar time. And if duration is used as the principal time dimension, for the first event this will generally not be possible, and even if it is possible, the duration dependence of the first event will probably be different from the duration dependence of the subsequent events. For example, the time dimension for a second or subsequent birth can be duration since the previous birth, but for the first birth it is more logical to use age or duration since marriage or unmarried cohabitation as the time dimension. It will be clear that pooled analysis seriously limits the treatment of the time dependence of the process.

Another disadvantage of the approach concerned is that it does not use information on the correlations among the durations of subsequent spells. These correlations are not only statistically problematic, they also make it possible to identify sources of unobserved heterogeneity. By treating spells as separate observations this valuable information in the data is neglected.

The third approach for analyzing repeatable events is *to perform a simultaneous analysis* of the several events recorded per individual taking similarities, differences and dependencies among events into account. This makes it possible to restrict particular parameters to be equal across subsequent events, to use different kinds of time dimensions, to use information about the previous history as independent variables, and to identify unobserved heterogeneity by means of the local independence assumption.

As mentioned above, the choice of the appropriate time dimension is always problematic when analyzing repeated events. Often, it is advisable to use several time dimensions at the same time. In section 4.6, which introduced the different types of time variables, it was demonstrated that for repeatable events, additional time dimensions can be defined containing information on the previous history, such as the mean duration of the previous spells, total time spent in the risk set for the event concerned (experience), age at occurrence of the previous event (age-cohort), calendar time at occurrence of the previous event (cohort), and time since the previous event (duration). Of course, linear dependencies among the potential time dimensions restrict the number of time dimensions that can actually be used at the same time.

Since hazard models for a single type of repeated event are special cases of the multiple-state models to be discussed in the next subsection, they are not discussed separately.

4.8.3. Multiple-state models

The advantages of the simultaneous analysis of data on repeated events was demonstrated above. Of course, the same arguments apply to situations in which there is not only information on the occurrence of more than one event per observational unit, but in which different types of events can occur. Below models for analyzing such multiple-state data are presented. These multiple-state models are very similar to the multiple-risk models discussed in section 4.7. There are, however, three important differences, namely: 1] there may be more than one origin state, 2] there may be more than one spell per person, and 3] not only time or duration and covariate values may influence the transition rates, but also the previous history.

Statistical concepts The notation must be extended to make the above-mentioned three extensions possible. Let M be an indicator variable denoting the episode or spell number and M_i^* the total number of observed episodes for person i. Let O^m be an indicator variable denoting the origin state in the mth spell, O^* the number of origin states, and o^m a value of O^m, with $1 \le o^m \le O^*$. For the destination states the same notation is used as in the previous chapter. The only difference is that analogous to O^m and o^m, D and d are replaced by a spell-specific destination state indicator D^m and a spell-specific destination state value d^m. Note that generally $O^m = D^{m-1}$. Moreover, the number of origin states will generally be equal to the number of destination states, that is, $O^* = D^*$. Let T^m be the time that the mth event occurred or the censoring time if $m = M_i^*$. If an individual is in episode m, his previous history of the process is collected in ω^{m-1}, i.e., $\omega^{m-1} = \{t^0, o^1, t^1, d^1, \ldots, t^{m-1}, d^{m-1}\}$. It contains information on the previous states and the time points that transitions occurred. It is often referred to as a sample path (Tuma and Hannan, 1984:48).

The hazard rate or transition intensity for a change from $O^m = o^m$ to $D^m = d^m$, given previous history, can be defined as

$$h_{od}^m(t|\omega^{m-1}) =$$
$$\lim_{\Delta t \to 0} \frac{P\left(t \le T^m < t + \Delta t, D^m = d^m | T^m \ge t, O^m = o^m, \omega^{m-1}\right)}{\Delta t}.$$

This quantity can be interpreted as an origin and destination-specific hazard rate. Note that here, the transition intensity is postulated as dependent on T^m, a time dimension that is not reset to zero after each particular transition.

Let U^m be a random variable denoting the duration or the waiting time at which the mth event occurred, i.e., $U^m = T^m - T^{m-1}$. Equivalently, the transition intensities can be specified as dependent on the waiting time U^m rather than T^m, i.e.,

$$h_{od}^m(u|\omega^{m-1}) =$$
$$\lim_{\Delta u \to 0} \frac{P\left(u \le U^m < u + \Delta u, D^m = d^m | U^m \ge u, O^m = o^m, \omega^{m-1}\right)}{\Delta t}.$$

It should be noted that the definition of the hazard rate is very similar to the definition that was used for multiple risks (see section 4.7). The only difference is the appearance of $O^m = o^m$ and ω^{m-1} as additional conditions in the definition of the hazard rate. The overall hazard rate of leaving origin state o^m in the mth spell is

$$h_o^m(t|\omega^{m-1}) = \sum_{d=1}^{D^*} h_{od}^m(t|\omega^{m-1}),$$

$$h_o^m(u|\omega^{m-1}) = \sum_{d=1}^{D^*} h_{od}^m(u|\omega^{m-1}),$$

and the spell and origin-specific survival probability is

$$S_o^m(t|\omega^{m-1}) = \exp\left(-\int_{t^{m-1}}^t \sum_{d=1}^{D^*} h_{od}^m(v|\omega^{m-1})d(v)\right),$$

$$S_o^m(u|\omega^{m-1}) = \exp\left(-\int_0^u \sum_{d=1}^{D^*} h_{od}^m(v|\omega^{m-1})d(v)\right).$$

The other relevant functions, such as the joint probability of either T^m or U^m and D^m, the marginal probability that $D^m = d^m$, the conditional probability that $D^m = d^m$, given t^m or u^m, and the net hazard rate, are defined analogous to the case of multiple risks as well. The only modification of the definition as presented in section 4.7 is the conditioning on o^m and ω^{m-1}.

Markov and semi-Markov chain models As mentioned above, transition rates may depend either on time or on duration since the previous event, on the spell number, and on information of the previous history. For the moment, we will not consider the influence of covariates on the spell, origin, and destination-specific hazard rates.

Markov chain models are special cases of the multiple-state models. The key assumption of the Markov chain model is that the transition intensities do not depend on either the previous history or the spell number (Tuma and Hannan, 1984:92-94). The hazard rates or transition intensities are only allowed to depend on the origin state, the destination state, and T^m:

$$h_{od}^m(t|\omega^{m-1}) = h_{od}(t).$$

Note that in Markov models, by definition, the use of waiting times (U^m) instead of process times (T^m) is not allowed. Markov models also forbid self-transitions, in other words, $h_{oo}(t) = 0$. The Markov model given above is a non-stationary or time-inhomogeneous Markov model since the rates depend on T^m. However, often an additional assumption is made, namely, that the transition intensities do not vary with time:

$$h_{od}(t) = h_{od}.$$

This gives a stationary or time-homogeneous Markov chain model.

Semi-Markov models or Markov renewal models are similar to Markov models. In the semi-Markov model, the transition intensities are restricted either as

$$h_{od}^m(t|\omega^{m-1}) = h_{od}(t|t^{m-1}),$$

or as

$$h_{od}^m(u|\omega^{m-1}) = h_{od}(u|t^{m-1}).$$

This implies that, unlike the Markov model, the transition intensities may also depend on waiting time, and, moreover, on the calendar time at which the previous event occurred. Another difference with the Markov model is that self-transitions are allowed. This makes the model suited for analyzing repeatable events of the same type as discussed above. In that case, the model is also called a renewal model (Lancaster, 1990:88-97). A special case of the renewal process occurs when the hazard rate is time-homogeneous. In that case, a Poisson model is obtained (Lancaster, 1990:85-88). Another special case of the semi-Markov occurs when there are two different states and self transitions are not permitted. This gives an alternating renewal model (Lancaster, 1990:97-98; Tuma and Hannan, 1984:106).

When the transition rates are allowed to depend on covariates, the same definitions apply. However, in that case, Markov and semi-Markov models are generally called modulated or heterogeneous Markov and semi-Markov models.

Continuous-time models Event history models for multiple-state situations are very similar to the multiple-risk models discussed in section 4.7. In principle, a separate model is specified for each combination of o, d, and m. A proportional log-linear hazard model for a transition from o to d in the mth spell is given by

$$h_{od}^m(t|\mathbf{x}^m) = h_{od}^m(t) \exp\left(\sum_j \beta_{odj}^m x_{odij}^m\right),$$

$$h_{od}^m(u|\mathbf{x}^m) = h_{od}^m(u) \exp\left(\sum_j \beta_{odj}^m x_{odij}^m\right),$$

where $\mathbf{x}^m$ is the spell-specific covariate vector which may also contain information on the previous history. Nonproportional models can be obtained by allowing $h_{od}^m(t)$ or $h_{od}^m(u)$ to depend on $\mathbf{x}^m$. Maximum likelihood estimates of the β_{odj}^m parameters can be obtained by maximizing

$$\mathcal{L} = \prod_{i=1}^N \prod_{m=1}^{M_i^*} \prod_{o=1}^{O^*} \left[\left\{\prod_{d=1}^{D^*} h_{od}^m(t_i^m|\mathbf{x}_i^m)^{\delta_{di}^m}\right\} \exp\left(-\int_{t_i^{m-1}}^{t_i^m} h_o^m(v|\mathbf{x}_i^m)dv\right)\right]^{\epsilon_{oi}^m},$$

$$\mathcal{L} = \prod_{i=1}^N \prod_{m=1}^{M_i^*} \prod_{o=1}^{O^*} \left[\left\{\prod_{d=1}^{D^*} h_{od}^m(u_i^m|\mathbf{x}_i^m)^{\delta_{di}^m}\right\} \exp\left(-\int_0^{u_i^m} h_o^m(v|\mathbf{x}_i^m)dv\right)\right]^{\epsilon_{oi}^m},$$

where δ_{di}^m is an indicator variable taking the value 1 if a transition to d occurred for person i in the mth spell, and ϵ_{oi}^m is an indicator variable taking the value 1 if the origin state is o for person i in the mth spell. Otherwise, δ_{di}^m and ϵ_{oi}^m are equal to zero.

Since the likelihood function can be factored into separate components for each combination of o, d, and m, the spell and type of transition-specific models can be estimated separately if the parameters are postulated to be distinct, that is, if no restrictions are imposed across spells. However, generally it is of interest to impose restrictions across spells and across different types of events, which implies that the above likelihood function has be to maximized without factorizing it.

There are various standard computer programs which can be used to estimate parametric multiple-state models with restrictions on the parameters across origin and destination states and across spells. The best known is the RATE program (Tuma, 1979). Another example is the very flexible TDA program (Rohwer, 1993).

Log-rate models Log-rate models can also be used to specify multiple-state models. The only difference with the log-rate models for a single nonrepeatable event is that the table to be analyzed contains three additional dimensions. Let O denote the origin state, D the destination state, M the spell number, Z the time dimension which can be either process or waiting time, and A and B two categorical covariates. In its most general form, the multiple-state variant of the log-rate model can be written as

$$\log m_{abzodm} = \log E_{abzom} + \sum_j \beta_{odmj} x_{abodmj} .$$

The data which is needed to estimate this model consists of a frequency table containing the number of events per value of A, B, Z, O, D, and M, n_{abzodm}, and a table with total exposure times, E_{abzom}. Note that, as in the case of competing risks, the exposure matrix has no index d, since in most situations the number of persons at risk is equal for each d. If this is not true, the index d has to be added to the table with exposure times.

It will be clear that the log-rate model is very flexible for analyzing multiple-state data. Equality restrictions can easily be imposed on the time and covariate effects across types of transitions and spells. This can simply be accomplished by leaving out particular interaction terms of the model.

The multiple-state log-rate model can be estimated relatively easily by means of the *ℓEM* program (Vermunt, 1993). The program allows specification of different origin and destination states, and, moreover, more than one spell per record. Of course, it is also possible to use a standard program for log-linear analysis.

4.8.4. Discrete-time Markov chain models

The discrete-time logit model can also be adapted for analyzing multiple-state data (Allison, 1982). It can be shown that if the transition rates are in agreement with a Markov chain model, the discrete-time logit model is equivalent to the discrete-time Markov model which was presented in section 2.9. In order to distinguish between these two models, the latter will be called the classical Markov model. This subsection discusses the differences and similarities between these two models.

According to the definition of a Markov chain model presented above, a discrete-time logit model which fulfills the Markov assumption can be defined as

$$\lambda_{od}(t_l|\mathbf{x}) = \frac{\exp\left(\alpha_{odl} + \sum_j \beta_{odj} x_{odij}\right)}{1 + \sum_g \exp\left(\alpha_{ogl} + \sum_j \beta_{ogj} x_{ogij}\right)} . \qquad [4.44]$$

Note that the time dimension is process time (T) and not waiting time (U). Since the transition probabilities are not allowed to depend on the spell number, $\lambda_{od}(t_l|\mathbf{x})$ does not contain the superscript m. For the sake of simplicity, the model for $\lambda_{od}(t_l|\mathbf{x})$ does not contain time-covariate interactions and time-varying covariates.

Let δ_d^m and ϵ_o^m be spell-specific indicator variables taking value 1 if a transition to destination state d occurs and if the origin state equals o, respectively, and otherwise taking value 0. Using these indicator variables, the probability density function of the discrete-time survival data is given by

$$f(t_1, d_1, \ldots, t_M, d_M | o_1, \mathbf{x}) = \prod_{m=1}^{M^*} \prod_{o=1}^{O^*} \left[\left\{ \prod_{d=1}^{D^*} \left(\frac{\lambda_{od}(t_m|\mathbf{x})}{1 - \lambda_o(t_m|\mathbf{x})} \right)^{\delta_d^m} \right\} \right.$$
$$\left. \prod_{t_k=t_{m-1}}^{t_m} (1 - \lambda_o(t_k|\mathbf{x})) \right]^{\epsilon_o^m} , \qquad [4.45]$$

where $\lambda_o(t_k|\mathbf{x})$ is the probability of leaving state O, irrespective of the destination state.

Using the same notation as in section 2.9, for the classical Markov model, the joint probability of the observed covariate values and the states a person occupies at the different points in time is given by

$$\pi_{\mathbf{x}s_0 s_1 \ldots s_{L^*}} = \pi_{\mathbf{x}} \pi_{s_0|\mathbf{x}} \prod_{l=1}^{L^*} \pi_{s_l|\mathbf{x}s_{l-1}} . \qquad [4.46]$$

Here, s_l denotes a value of S_l, the state occupied at the lth point in time, S_0 is the starting position or the initial states, and L^* is the total number of time points. The total number of states is denoted by S^*.

As a result of a different type of notation, the density functions described in Equations 4.45 and 4.46 seem to be quiet different. However, if the length of the observation period is the same for all persons, the density function for discrete-time survival data (Equation 4.45) can also be written as a product of time-point-specific transition probabilities rather than spell-specific densities. As above, let L^* be the length of the observation period, and S_l be the state occupied at t_l. In that case, the density function of the discrete-time survival data given in Equation 4.45 can also be written as follows:

$$f(s_1, \ldots, s_{L^*}|s_0, \mathbf{x}) = \prod_{l=1}^{L^*} \lambda_{s_{l-1}s_l}(t_l|\mathbf{x})^{\delta_l} \left\{1 - \lambda_{s_{l-1}}(t_l|\mathbf{x})\right\}^{(1-\delta_l)}, \quad [4.47]$$

in which δ_l is an indicator variable indicating whether a transition occurred in t_l or not, and in which

$$\lambda_{s_{l-1}}(t_l|\mathbf{x}) = \sum_{g=1}^{S^*} \lambda_{s_{l-1}g}(t_l|\mathbf{x}) \qquad \text{if } s_l = s_{l-1} \;,$$

$$\lambda_{s_{l-1}s_l}(t_l|\mathbf{x}) = 0 \qquad \text{if } s_l = s_{l-1} \;.$$

Now it can be seen that the density function given in Equation 4.47 is equivalent to the last part of Equation 4.46, since

$$\pi_{s_l|\mathbf{x}s_{l-1}} = \lambda_{s_{l-1}s_l}(t_l|\mathbf{x}) \qquad \text{if } s_l <> s_{l-1} \;,$$

$$\pi_{s_l|\mathbf{x}s_{l-1}} = 1 - \lambda_{s_{l-1}}(t_l|\mathbf{x}) \qquad \text{if } s_l = s_{l-1} \;.$$

This reflects that, if the length of the observation period is the same for all individuals, the models are very similar.

The parameters of the classical discrete-time Markov model are the conditional probabilities which appear in Equation 4.46. More restricted models are specified by means of equality and fixed-value restrictions on these probabilities (Van de Pol and Langeheine, 1990). The different parameterizations make the classical Markov model and the discrete-time logit model look rather different. However, by using the logit parameterization of (conditional) probabilities discussed in section 2.9, in other words, by treating the classical Markov model as a modified path model (Goodman, 1973; Hagenaars, 1990), a version is obtained that is equivalent to the discrete-time logit model. Yamaguchi (1990) already recognized the similarity between Goodman's causal log-linear model for categorical variables and the discrete-time logit method. The logit parameterization of the transition probabilities appearing in Equation 4.46 can, as in Equation 4.44, be parameterized as

$$\pi_{s_l|s_{l-1},\mathbf{x}} = \frac{\exp\left(\alpha_{s_{l-1}s_l} + \sum_j \beta_{s_{l-1}s_lj} x_{s_{l-1}s_lij}\right)}{\sum_g \exp\left(\alpha_{s_{l-1}g} + \sum_j \beta_{s_{l-1}gj} x_{s_{l-1}gij}\right)} . \qquad [4.48]$$

As always, identifying restrictions have to be imposed on the log-linear parameters. In discrete-time logit models, these restrictions have very specific form. As can be seen from the logit model described in Equation 4.44, within every level of O, the category no event is the reference category. This is the reason that the denominator contains the term 1 for the reference category and that the summation is over all possible events, given the value of O. As a result, the α and β parameters in the discrete-time logit model represented in Equation 4.44 can be interpreted as effects on transition probabilities. To obtain the same parameterization when using a modified path model with steps of the form given in Equation 4.48, the one-variable parameters of S_l have to be left out of the model and the α's and β's in which $S_l = S_{l-1}$ have to be fixed to zero. The result is that, as in Equation 4.44, the stayers are treated as the reference category within each origin state s_{l-1}. These identifying restrictions guarantee that the modified path model gives parameters identical to the discrete-time logit model, namely, time and covariate effects on the transition probabilities rather than on the probability that $S_l = s_l$. In other words, the model consists of transition-specific main and covariate effects for each point in time.

A difference between the discrete-time logit model and the classical discrete-time Markov model is that in the latter the observation period is assumed to be the same for all persons. Generally, there are no facilities to handle observations which are censored during the observation period. However, by using the missing data methods discussed in Chapter 3, censoring, partial nonresponse, and panel attrition can be handled without any problem. Chapter 5 will demonstrate how to deal with different kinds of partially observed event history information when using the modified path analysis approach for analyzing discrete-time event history data.

Another difference between the two methods is that in the classical model described in Equation 4.46, the marginal distribution of the covariates, π_x, and the marginal distribution of the initial state, $\pi_{s_0|x}$, appear in the model. This means that restrictions can be imposed on them as well. As will be demonstrated in the next chapter, the ability to specify a model for the covariates and the initial state can be an important feature. For instance, in the hazard modeling tradition, unobserved heterogeneity is generally assumed to be independent of the covariate values and of the initial position. However, when it is possible to model the covariate structure and the initial position, it is no longer necessary to make such assumptions. Then, it is just one of the possible model specifications.

Although both models are based on the Markov assumption, in the hazard modeling tradition the Markov assumption is never explicitly tested. When using the classical Markov model, the Markov assumption can be explicitly tested by means of, for instance, the likelihood-ratio chi-squared statistic. This is the result of the fact that when all covariates are categorical, the data can be represented in a frequency table.

The last difference to be mentioned between the two models is that in the classical discrete-time Markov model the basic time dimension is always process time. As demonstrated earlier, in hazard models the time dimension can also be duration or waiting time, although in that case it is no longer a Markov model, but a semi-Markov model. It is possible to accommodate the classical model to allow the transition rates to depend on waiting time as well.

To summarize, a strong point of the discrete-time hazard model is the logit parameterization of the transition probabilities which makes it possible to specify parsimonious models for covariate dependence of the process to be studied. Another strong point, of course, is the way it handles censored observations. Some weak points are, however, that the covariate values and the initial position are always treated as fixed quantities and that the Markov assumption is never tested explicitly.

It can be concluded that the classical discrete-time Markov model is, in fact, an event history model as well. It is identical to the discrete-time logit model when it is parameterized as a modified path model and when partially observed data can be included in the analysis. This implies, for instance, that the latent variables techniques presented in Chapter 3 can easily be transferred to discrete-time logit models. This is an interesting feature which will be used in Chapter 5.

The logit parameterization of the transition probabilities of classical discrete-time Markov model, including the potential for using partially observed data and the latent variable techniques mentioned above, is implemented in the *ℓEM* program (Vermunt, 1993).

4.8.5. Other kinds of multivariate hazard models

In section 4.6, some problems associated with the use of time-varying covariates in hazard models were discussed. More precisely, it was shown that the effect of a time-dependent covariate may be (partially) spurious as a result of unobserved factors influencing both the covariate process and the dependent process. Another problem associated with the use of time-varying covariates is reverse causation.

Multivariate hazard models make it possible to detect dependencies among *different life-cycle transitions* which are caused by common antecedents. Moreover, they make it possible to analyze the simultaneous relationships among two or more processes. This implies that multivariate hazard models can help to tackle some of the problems associated with the use of time-varying covariates. An example of an application of such a multivariate hazard model is Yamaguchi's analysis of the interdependence between marijuana use and marriage (Yamaguchi, 1990).

The use of multivariate event history techniques for studying the relationships among different life-cycle transitions rather than investigating their relationships by means of the use of time-varying covariates is also richer from a substantive point of view. Willekens (1989) promoted these kinds of models for the analysis of interdependencies among parallel careers, where the term parallel careers refers to different aspects of life, such as place of residence, union type, birth of children, education and occupation. Manton, Woodbury, and Stallard (1988) stressed the importance of simultaneously modeling the process of interest – in their case death from different causes – and the evolution of risk factors to be able to predict the effect of intervention in risk factors on survival.[11]

There is, however, also a statistical reason to model several life-cycle transitions simultaneously. According to Lancaster (1990:30), using information on the covariate process of endogenous covariates, improves the efficiency of the parameter estimates.

The analysis of *dependent or clustered observations* is another field of application of multivariate hazard models. Examples of dependent ob-

---

[11] They proposed modeling changes in discrete and continuous variables by means of a continuous-time multivariate Gaussian stochastic model (see also Manton and Woodbury, 1985). The main difference between their approach and the approach presented in this subsection is that the latter assumes that all the variables are discrete.

servations are employment histories of husbands and wives, infant mortality of children from the same family (Guo and Rodriguez, 1991), and school transitions of brothers (Mare, 1994). For clustered or dependent observations, the same arguments in favor of simultaneous analysis apply as the ones that were mentioned when discussing the analysis of repeatable events. Actually, data on repeatable events is a particular type of clustered data.

Models Let us use the term cluster in the most general sense. More precisely, a cluster can consist of: 1] a number of observations of the same type on different individuals belonging to the same group, 2] a number of observations of the same type on one individual, or 3] a number of observations of different types on one individual. Examples of these three types of clustered observations are data on school transitions of brothers, measurements of different parts of the body in a clinical trial, and data on a woman's occupational, reproductive and relational career, respectively.

Let M indicate a particular observation within a cluster. Assume, for simplicity of exposition, that there is data on one single kind of event for each within-cluster observation. This assumption can easily be relaxed by defining a multiple-state model for within-cluster observations. In principle, a separate hazard model can be specified for each within-cluster observation, i.e.,

$$h^m(t|\mathbf{x}^m) = h^m(t) \exp\left(\sum_j \beta_j^m x_{ij}^m\right).$$

For clustered observations of the types 1 and 2, restrictions are generally imposed on the parameters across m's. The hazard model could, for instance, be of the form

$$h^m(t|\mathbf{x}^m) = h(t) \exp\left(\sum_j \beta_j x_{ij} + \sum_k \beta_k^m x_{ik}^m\right).$$

Here, both the time dependence and the effects of the covariates which have the same value for all observations belonging to the same cluster are assumed to be equal.

Models for clustered observations of the third type will generally include information on one type of observation as a time-varying covariate in the hazard model for another type of observation. Suppose we perform a simultaneous analysis of women's reproductional, occupational and relational histories. In that case, a woman's employment and relational status can be used as time-varying covariates in the hazard rate model for the first birth, probably with some time-lag to prevent the effects which are found being the result of reversed causation (see section 4.6). In addition, the number of children and marital status can be used as time-varying covariates in the hazard rate model for employment transitions.

The estimation of the model parameters is performed in the same way as in the case of repeatable events, which as already mentioned, are clustered observations as well.[12]

A strong point of the simultaneous analysis of clustered observations in the way proposed here, is that dependencies among observations which are not described by the observed covariates included in the model can be captured by means of the latent variables techniques to be discussed in the next chapter. Below the problem of conditionally dependent observations is introduced.

4.8.6. Conditional dependence among observations

The maximum likelihood methods for estimating multivariate event history models discussed so far are based on the assumption of conditional independence. More precisely, the observations within every unit of observation are assumed to be independent given the covariate information which is used in the multivariate hazard model. However, in most situations, this assumption is not very realistic. As a result of common unobserved risk factors, the spells, the different kinds of transitions for a particular person, or the observations within a particular cluster may remain correlated, even after controlling for observed risk factors.

Since dependencies among observations lead to biased parameter estimates and underestimated standard deviations (Allison, 1984:54), detecting dependencies among observations belonging to the same cluster is important from a statistical point of view. However, detecting common unobserved risk factors is also important from a substantive point of view

---

[12] Recently, Petersen (1995) compared three alternative approaches for dealing with interdependent event history data of the third type, data on different types of life-cycle transitions. He demonstrated that as long as events cannot occur at the same point in time, the three approaches are equivalent to one another and to using one type of history as a time-varying covariate in the hazard model for another type of history. On the other hand, if it is possible to experience more than one type of transition at the same time, the three approaches yield different results due to the fact that each of them specifies the risk of the simultaneous occurrence of events is a slightly different way.

(Mare, 1994). It helps us to answer the following kinds of questions: Are there common unobserved variables influencing different types of life-cycle transitions? How are survival times of the different observations within one unit related?

There are three types of methods which can be used to detect and to control for dependencies among observations belonging to the same cluster: random-effects methods, fixed-effects methods, and methods which are based on using association parameters.

Random-effects approach The random-effects approach is based on the introduction of a latent variable having the same value for all observations belonging to the same cluster (Heckman and Singer, 1982; Guo and Rodriguez, 1992; Clayton and Cuzick, 1985).[13] This latent variable, whose distribution may have either a parametric or non-parametric functional form, is included in the hazard model as one of the covariates. The random-effects approach (Yamaguchi, 1986) is, in fact, very similar to the way unobserved heterogeneity is handled in univariate hazard models (see section 4.6). An important difference is, however, that the local independence assumption, that is, the assumption that the observations belonging to one cluster are independent given the latent variable included in the model, makes it easier to identify the model. Note that the local independence assumption is identical to the basic assumption of latent structure models (see section 3.1).

Chamberlain (1985) and Yamaguchi (1986) stated that random-effects methods have two important disadvantages. First, the functional form of the distribution of the unobserved variable may strongly influence the results. Therefore, Heckman and Singer (1982, 1984, 1985) recommended using a non-parametric approach which is similar to a latent class model. A second problem is that the latent variable is generally assumed to be independent of the observed covariates and of the initial position. But, in most cases it is unrealistic to assume that the unobserved factors influencing the hazard rate are not correlated with the observed factors and with the state occupied at $T = 0$. In the next chapter, a random-effects approach is presented which overcomes the two weak points mentioned by Chamberlain and Yamaguchi: it is non-parametric and makes it possible to relate the latent variable capturing the unobserved heterogeneity to the observed covariates and to the state occupied at $T = 0$.

---

[13] Recently, Petersen, Andersen, and Gill (1996) proposed decomposing the random-effect into two independent components: a common factor within a cluster and a unique factor of the observations within a cluster.

Fixed-effects approach   A second method for dealing with dependencies among observations consists of including cluster-specific effects, or incidental parameters, in the model (Chamberlain, 1985; Yamaguchi, 1986)). In fact, a categorical variable is included in the hazard model which indicates to which cluster a particular observation belongs. Thus, observations belonging to the same cluster have the same value for this variable while observations belonging to different clusters have different values. This approach, which is called the fixed-effects method for treating unobserved heterogeneity, can only be applied with multivariate survival data, that is, when there is more than one observation for the largest part of the observational units.

The advantage of using fixed-effects methods to correct for unobserved heterogeneity is that they circumvent the two objections against random-effects methods which were presented above: No functional form needs to be specified for the unobserved heterogeneity and the unobserved heterogeneity is automatically related to both the initial state and the time-constant covariates.

The major limitation of the fixed-effects approach is that since each cluster has its own incidental parameter, no parameter estimates can be obtained for the effects of covariates which have the same value for the different observations belonging to the same cluster. Only the effect of observation-specific, or in the case of repeatable events, of time-varying covariates can be estimated. Another problem is that the incidental parameters cannot be estimated consistently, since by definition they are based on a limited number of observations regardless of the sample size. This inconsistency may be carried over to the other parameters if the parameters are estimated by means of maximum likelihood methods (Yamaguchi, 1986).

The maximum likelihood estimation of the fixed-effects model can be performed by means of standard programs for event history analysis. The only thing that has to be done is to include in the hazard model a categorical covariate having a different value for each cluster or observational unit. Because the number of incidental parameters is generally very large, it may be difficult to estimate the model parameters by means of Newton-Raphson-like methods. Yamaguchi (1986) proposed estimating the fixed-effects model by means of the Newton-Raphson algorithm after removing the incidental parameters from the likelihood function. This is possible only if the time-varying covariates, including the time variable itself, are step functions of T or U. Another option is to use the iterative proportional fitting algorithm or the uni-dimensional Newton algorithm which were presented in Chapter 2 and which are implemented in, for instance, the *ℓEM* program (Vermunt, 1993).

Alternative procedures for estimating the parameters of hazard models with these kinds of incidental parameters are marginal likelihood (Chamberlain, 1985), conditional likelihood (Cox and Lewis, 1966) and partial likelihood (Chamberlain, 1985) methods. These approaches allow us to obtain a likelihood function which is independent of the incidental parameters by imposing additional restrictions on the duration dependence of the process and the types of covariates which may be used in the regression model (Yamaguchi, 1986). Although these alternative procedures do not have the inconsistency problem of the maximum likelihood method, the additional restrictions strongly limit their applicability.

When there are two completed survival times for each unit of observation, the partial likelihood approach for estimating fixed-effects models can simply be implemented using a logistic regression model (Kalbfleisch and Prentice, 1980:190-192). A variable has to be defined which takes the value 1 for the shorter of the two spells and the value 0 for the longer of the two spells. Applying a fixed-effect approach involves using this variable as the dependent variable in a logistic regression model in which the time-varying covariates are used as regressors.

Using association parameters A third approach for modeling dependencies among survival times consists of including additional parameters in the hazard model describing the associations among the observed survival times. Clayton and Cuzick (1985) proposed that the association between two survival times be described by means of one parameter denoted by θ. This parameter has a direct interpretation in terms of hazard rates, i.e.,

$$h(t_1|T_2 = t_2) = \theta\, h(t_1|T_2 > t_2),$$
$$h(t_2|T_1 = t_1) = \theta\, h(t_2|T_1 > t_1).$$

Here, T_1 and T_2 denote the first and second survival time, respectively. It can be seen that the hazard rate for observation 1 at a particular point in time is θ times higher if T_2 equals t_2 than if T_2 is greater than t_2. In fact, θ is a continuous generalization of the well-known continuation ratio in the contingency table literature (Clayton and Cuzick, 1985).

Winship (1986) and Mare (1994) modelled the association between discrete survival times by means of a (conditional) quasi-symmetry model. This model is well known in the contingency table literature as well. But it is also possible to use other kinds of models for investigating the associations among discrete survival times, such as, for instance, the log-multiplicative association models discussed in section 2.7.

The main limitation of modeling the conditional dependence among survival times by means of association parameters is that no causal interpretation can be given to the parameters (Whitehead, 1985). This is in contrast to the random-effects approach, in which the additional parameters can be interpreted as the effects of unobserved common risk factors.

5 Event History Analysis With Latent Variables and Missing Data

The previous chapter introduced models for the analysis of event history data and discussed various problems associated with the analysis of event history data, most of which are caused by missing information. In section 4.6, it was demonstrated that unobserved heterogeneity hampers the interpretation of the effects of time-varying covariates, time variables, and time-covariate interactions. More precisely, unobserved heterogeneity biases the duration dependence downward, even if it is not correlated with the observed covariates. If the unobserved risk factors are correlated with the time-constant covariates included in the model, in other words, if there is selection bias, not only are the model parameters biased, but there will also be spurious time-covariate interactions. If there are unobserved risk factors which also have an effect on changes in the values of particular endogenous time-dependent covariates, the effects of these covariates will be at least partially spurious. In section 4.7, it was demonstrated that unobserved common risk factors may lead to dependent competing risks. And finally, as discussed in 4.8, unobserved heterogeneity may invalidate the assumption of conditional independence in models for repeatable events or other types of clustered observations, and may lead to spurious effects of time-varying covariates.

In the field of event history analysis, techniques have been developed to tackle some of these problems. In particular, the problem of spurious time dependence has received a lot of attention (Heckman and Singer, 1982, 1984; Flinn and Heckman, 1982; Vaupel, Manton and Stallard, 1979; Manton, Vaupel and Stallard, 1986; Trussell and Richards, 1985). Also, some work has been done on the problem of dependent observations (Mare, 1994; Guo and Rodriguez, 1994; Yamaguchi, 1986; Clayton and Cuzick, 1985) and on the problem of dependent competing risks (Vaupel and Yashin, 1985; Heckman and Honore, 1989). However, some other problems, such as the selection bias problem, remain unresolved since the latent covariates introduced in the hazard models are always assumed to be independent of the observed covariates and of an individual's initial state (Yamaguchi, 1986, 1991:132). The general latent variable approach that is presented in this chapter does not have this limitation. Therefore, it can also help to resolve some of the remaining problems, especially the problems of selection bias and of spuriousness of effects of time-varying covariates.

In Chapter 3, two other kinds of missing data problems were discussed: measurement error, and partially missing data. It was shown that the problem of measurement error in categorical covariates can be handled by means of latent class models (Goodman, 1974; Haberman, 1979: Chapter 10). Measurement error is a problem which may also occur when collecting event history data. The covariates may be measured with error, which, as is known for ordinary regression models, leads to biased covariate effects. But duration, or more generally, the states that individuals occupy at different points in time, may be measured with error as well.

Lancaster (1990:59-61) showed that in particular situations measurement error in recorded regressors and durations can, in addition to the above-mentioned omitted variables problems, be an argument to use a mixture model. If the hazard is of a Weibull or exponential form and the random measurement error in the recorded duration is multiplicative, the error generates a mixture model. If the hazard is proportional and log-linear and the error in the covariates is additive, a mixture model is also obtained. In the latter case, the mixture distribution depends on the value of the covariate concerned.

Here, another more general approach to measurement error in recorded states and in recorded durations is used which is based on the latent class techniques discussed in section 3.1. A latent class model can be used to relate the latent or true score to one or more observed variables by a set of conditional response probabilities, which may be restricted by means of a logit model. When covariates are measured with error, or when covariates can only be measured indirectly, one or more categorical latent variables can be used as covariates in the event history model instead of the unreliable observed covariates concerned. A related approach was proposed by Gong, Whittemore, and Grosser (1990) who presented a method for handling misclassification in covariates with a restricted latent class model. Their approach is actually a special case of the approach that is presented here, that is, a situation in which the mechanism leading to measurement error is known.

In the field of event history analysis, correcting for measurement error in recorded states is very rare. However, as already mentioned in section 3.1, in the field of discrete-time Markov modeling, the idea of correcting measurement error in the observed states is very old (Wiggins 1955, 1973; Lazarsfeld and Henry, 1968), and has been worked out more recently by Poulsen (1982) (see also Van de Pol and De Leeuw, 1989; Van de Pol and Langeheine, 1990; and Vermunt, Langeheine, and Böckenholt, 1995). In latent Markov models, the latent unobserved states at the different points in time are related to the observed states using a latent class model with as many latent variables as observed ones. A Markov model is specified for the relationships among these latent variables. This way, it is possible to distinguish true changes from changes which are caused by measurement error in the recorded states. As demonstrated in section 4.8, discrete-time Markov models are equivalent to discrete-time logit models, especially if a logit parameterization of the transition probabilities is used. As a result, discrete-time event history models with error in recorded states can be formulated by means of the latent class methods discussed in Chapter 3. The same methods can be used to correct for measurement error in time-varying covariates.

Another type of missing data problem is partially missing information. Of course, researchers may be confronted with this problem in event history analysis as well. Both covariate values and information on the dependent process may be missing for some individuals. Schluchter and Jackson (1989) proposed using the information of subjects with partially missing time-constant covariates in a hazard analysis using a method which is similar to the one proposed by Fuchs (1982) for log-linear models. Their approach can easily be extended when using the models for nonresponse proposed by Fay (1986, 1989) which were introduced in section 3.2. This makes it possible to specify nonignorable response models for the partial nonresponse on particular covariates. Recently, Baker (1994) applied these models for nonresponse in a discrete-time logit model with a partially missing covariate.

Besides time-constant covariates, information on the dependent process can be partially missing as well. Censoring is, of course, the best known form of missing information on the process to be studied. As demonstrated in section 4.5, censoring can easily be dealt with as long as the censoring mechanism is independent of the process to be studied, in other words, as long as the response mechanism is ignorable. However, when the censoring mechanism is nonignorable, other methods for handling censored observation must be used. For that purpose, it is possible to use Fay's causal models for nonresponse (Fay, 1986, 1989). The models for nonresponse can be used not only to deal with censoring, but also to deal with event history data with nonnested missing data patterns. The same methods can be used to handle partially missing information on time-dependent covariates.

This chapter presents a unifying framework for dealing with unobserved heterogeneity, measurement error, and partially missing data in the context of event history analysis. The general model that is used for this purpose consists of two parts, a log-linear model in which the relationships among the observed, partially missing, and unobserved covariates are specified, and a event history model for those events whose occurrence has to be explained. The event history model can be either a piecewise exponential survival model, which is also known as log-rate model, or a discrete-time logit model. This means that only models which can be handled within the framework of log-linear analysis are used in this chapter. The advantage of this restriction is that the models are mathematically simple and that it is not necessary to assume parametric functional forms for the covariate and survival distributions. When necessary, parametric models can be approximated by imposing restrictions on the log-linear parameters. In spite of the restriction to models which can be handled within the framework of log-linear modeling, the main principles of the general approach can be transferred to parametric models for the covariates and the duration process.

Although above the general approach to be discussed in this chapter was presented as a tool for handling different kinds of missing data problems in event history analysis, it can also be seen as an extension of the log-linear path model. By combining the log-linear path models presented in Chapters 2 and 3 with event history models, it becomes possible to use information on the timing of events in a modified path model. One possible application concerns the construction of typologies by means of

TABLE 5.1 Special cases of the general missing data approach presented in this chapter

1. Unobserved heterogeneity	5.2
- a. a single nonrepeatable event	5.2.4
- b. dependent competing risks	5.2.5
- c. repeatable events and multiple-state processes	5.2.6
- d. clustered or dependent observations	5.2.7
- e. spurious effects of time-varying covariates	5.2.8
2. Measurement error	5.3
- a. in covariates	5.3.1
- b. in recorded states	5.3.2
3. Partially missing data	5.4
- a. information on covariates	5.4.1
- b. event history data	5.4.2

latent class models which contain information on the timing of events as indicators.

After the general model is presented in section 5.1, attention is given to the three above-mentioned types of missing data problems: unobserved heterogeneity, measurement error, and partially missing data. Table 5.1 gives an overview of the special cases of the general model that are presented in this chapter. As can be seen, the three main types of missing data problems, unobserved heterogeneity, measurement error, and partially missing data, are dealt with in sections 5.2, 5.3, and 5.4, respectively. Within these missing data categories, different special cases are distinguished which are discussed in separate subsections. As already mentioned, unobserved heterogeneity may introduce spurious time dependence when analyzing a single nonrepeatable event, (5.2.4), may lead to dependence among competing risks (5.2.5), may complicate the analysis of repeatable events, multiple-state processes (5.2.6), and other types of dependent observations (5.2.7), and may lead to spurious effects of time-varying covariates (5.2.8). Measurement error may occur in the covariates which are used in the hazard model (5.3.1) and in the states occupied at the different points in time (5.3.2). The same applies to partially missing data (5.4.1 and 5.4.2).

Unlike the previous chapters, which described the techniques on which the general missing data approach is based, in this chapter many applications are presented using real-world data sets from different substantive fields to illustrate the potentials of the general missing data approach.

5.1. General model

The general model which is used for dealing with missing data in event history analysis consists of two parts. The first part is a model for the time-constant covariates used in the event history model. These covariates may be observed, unobserved, or partially unobserved. A variable indicating the initial state may also be included in this part of the model. For the covariates, we will use a causal log-linear model of the type discussed in Chapters 2 and 3. This implies that, as in modified path models, all endogenous variables have to be categorical. The second part of the general model is a multiple-state event history model, which can be used not only to model the dependent process to be studied, but also the transitions occurring in the time-varying covariates. Here, we will use either a log-rate model or a discrete-time logit model in the second part of the model.

If only information on time-constant covariates is missing, the model can be written in its most compact form as

$$\sum_{\mathbf{x}_{mis}} P(\mathbf{x}, \mathbf{t}, \delta) = \sum_{\mathbf{x}_{mis}} P(\mathbf{x})P(\mathbf{t}, \delta|\mathbf{x}).$$ [5.1]

The joint probability function of the time-constant covariates ($\mathbf{x}$) and the times that transitions occur ($\mathbf{t}, \delta$) is decomposed into a part containing the covariate information and a part containing the event history information, given the covariate values. Of course, to obtain the density for the incompletely observed data, one has to sum over the missing data, denoted by $\mathbf{x}_{mis}$.

As in other types of regression models, the relationships between the covariates are normally not investigated in event history analysis. This means that only the second part at the right-hand side of Equation 5.1, $P(\mathbf{t}, \delta|\mathbf{x})$, is considered. However, by specifying a log-linear path model for the covariates, it not only becomes possible to investigate the relationships among the covariates, but also to handle all kinds of missing data problems concerning the covariates using the techniques discussed in Chapter 3.

If, apart from ignorable censoring, no missing information appears in the second part of the model, it is possible to use any of the event history models discussed in the previous chapter. However, if there is measurement error in the recorded states or if there is a more general form of partially missing information on the dependent process, it is most tractable to use a discrete-time model. The same applies if some information on time-varying covariates is missing. The reason for this is that for continuous-time models, such as the log-rate model, measurement error in the recorded states and general forms of partially missing information on the dependent process cannot easily be dealt with yet. Here, we will only use discrete-time logit models in such situations. Because the discrete-time logit model is also a modified path model (see subsection 4.8.4), it is possible to use the missing data techniques developed in the field of log-linear analysis for dealing with missing information on the dependent process.

Thus, the models that are used in this chapter may consist of three different types of models for the event history part. If only information on some time-constant covariates is missing, the event history model may be either a log-rate model or a discrete-time logit model. If event history information is missing, the event history model is a discrete-time logit model which is extended with the missing data methods developed for the modified path model discussed in Chapter 3, that is, in which the states at the different points in time may be latent or partially observed. In the latter case, the general model can be written as

$$\sum_{\mathbf{x}_{mis},\mathbf{s}_{mis}} P(\mathbf{x},\mathbf{s}) = \sum_{\mathbf{x}_{mis},\mathbf{s}_{mis}} P(\mathbf{x})P(\mathbf{s}|\mathbf{x}). \qquad [5.2]$$

Here, $\mathbf{s}$ denotes the observed and unobserved states of an individual at the different points in time, and $\mathbf{s}_{mis}$ the missing information in these states. As demonstrated in section 4.8, the density function of discrete-time event history model can also be written in terms of states occupied at different point in time, instead of survival times and censoring indicators.

Estimation   Maximum likelihood estimation of event history models with missing data can be performed by various means, including the EM algorithm which was introduced in Chapter 3 in the context of log-linear modeling with missing data (Dempster, Laird and Rubin, 1979). The E step of the algorithm involves completing the data on the basis of the observed data and the parameter values from the previous iteration.[1] In the M step, the same estimation methods can be used to compute

---

[1] It should be noted that the general definition of the E step is the computation of the expectation of the complete data likelihood. However, if the density function of the complete data belongs to the exponential family, the E step simplifies to the estimation of the complete-data sufficient statistics (see, for instance, Tanner, 1993: Chapter 4). Since all the models which are discussed in this chapter belong to the exponential family, we can use this simpler definition of the E step.

improved estimates of the model parameters as when there is no missing data. The event history model and the model for the covariates can be estimated separately by means of the algorithms discussed in Chapter 2, i.e., iterative proportional fitting, Newton-Raphson, and uni-dimensional Newton.

To complete the data in the E step, the probability of the missing data given the observed data and the parameters estimates from the last iteration has to be computed. These conditional probabilities, which are sometimes also called posterior probabilities, are obtained by

$$P(\mathbf{x}_{mis}|\mathbf{x}_{obs}, \mathbf{t}, \delta) = \frac{P(\mathbf{x}, \mathbf{t}, \delta)}{\sum_{\mathbf{x}_{mis}} P(\mathbf{x}, \mathbf{t}, \delta)}, \qquad [5.3]$$

$$P(\mathbf{x}_{mis}, \mathbf{s}_{mis}|\mathbf{x}_{obs}, \mathbf{s}_{obs}) = \frac{P(\mathbf{x}, \mathbf{s})}{\sum_{\mathbf{x}_{mis}, \mathbf{s}_{mis}} P(\mathbf{x}, \mathbf{s})}. \qquad [5.4]$$

Equation 5.3 refers to situations in which only data on time-constant covariates is missing; Equation 5.4 refers to situations in which also event history information is missing.

This EM algorithm has been implemented in the computer program ℓEM (Vermunt, 1993). The program allows the user to specify a log-linear path model for the covariates and a hazard model for the dynamic process under study. In the M step of the EM algorithm, both the iterative proportional fitting and the one-dimensional Newton algorithm can be used. In this way, not only hierarchical log-linear models can be specified, but also models with all kinds of restrictions on the parameters as discussed in Chapter 2. Contrary to Newton-Raphson and Fisher's scoring, the EM algorithm does not automatically supply standard errors for the parameter estimates. The ℓEM program computes standard errors via numerical approximation of the observed information matrix (see Appendix G).

An advantage of the EM algorithm is that it is very stable: Under quite weak conditions it converges to at least a local maximum of the log-likelihood function. A disadvantage is, however, that it may converge slowly in the neighborhood of the maximum. It is well known that Newton-type methods perform very well near to the maximum. Therefore, in models with not too many parameters, it may be more efficient to switch to a Newton-type algorithm after some EM iterations. When using ℓEM, it is possible to switch to the Newton-Raphson, Broyden-Fletcher-Goldfarb-Shanno (BFGS), or Levenberg-Maquardt method (Press et. al., 1986).

5.2. Unobserved heterogeneity

The implications of unobserved heterogeneity or omitted variables in the context of event history analysis was discussed in sections 4.6, 4.7, and 4.8 of the previous chapter. To summarize, it was demonstrated that unobserved heterogeneity biases the duration dependence downward, even if it is not correlated with the observed covariates. If the unobserved risk factors are correlated with the time-constant covariates included in the model, in other words, if there is selection bias, not only are the model parameters biased, but there will also be spurious time-covariate interactions. If there are unobserved risk factors which also have an effect on changes in the values of particular endogenous time-dependent covariates, the effects of these covariates will be, at least partially, spurious. In addition, unobserved common risk factors may lead to dependent competing risks. And finally, unobserved heterogeneity may invalidate the assumption of conditional independence in models for repeatable events or other types of clustered observations and may lead to spurious effects of time-varying covariates.

Because of the serious implications of unobserved heterogeneity in hazard models, it is not surprising that in the last two decades a great deal of work has been done on this subject (Vaupel, Manton, and Stallard, 1979; Manton, Vaupel and Stallard, 1981, 1986; Vaupel and Yashin, 1985; Heckman and Singer, 1982, 1984; Flinn and Heckman, 1982; Trussell and Richards, 1985; Mare, 1994; Guo and Rodriguez, 1994; Yamaguchi, 1986; Clayton and Cuzick, 1985; Heckman and Honore, 1989). In the above-mentioned sections of Chapter 4, the most important methods for dealing with unobserved heterogeneity were mentioned. One approach, also known as the random effects methods, involves the introduction of one or more latent covariates in the event history model. In this section, these random effects methods are discussed in more detail. First, the parametric and non-parametric latent variable approaches which have become standard tools for dealing with unobserved heterogeneity in event history analysis are discussed. Then, a more general non-parametric latent variable approach is presented, which is a special case of the general model presented in section 5.1. Subsection 5.2.3 discusses the identifiability of the parameters in hazard models with latent covariates. And finally, in subsections 5.2.4-5.2.8, it is shown how to use the general latent variable approach to detect spurious time dependence when analyzing a single nonrepeatable event, how to identify dependencies among competing risks, how to analyze repeatable events and other types of dependent observations, and how to detect spurious effects of time-varying covariates. These last five subsections contain several examples in which real-world data sets from different substantive fields are used.

5.2.1. Latent variable approaches to unobserved heterogeneity

Parametric mixture distributions Vaupel, Manton, and Stallard (1979) proposed correcting for unobserved heterogeneity, or as they called it 'frailty', in the life-table analysis of mortality rates (see also Manton, Vaupel and Stallard, 1981). They were especially concerned about the effect of unobserved heterogeneity on the size of the observed mortality rates at higher ages. Individuals who are alive at a specific age form a selective group of the birth cohorts to which they belong, namely, the individuals who are less frail. As a result, observed age-specific mortality rates, which equal the mean of the mortality rates of the persons who are still alive, will be lower than the age-specific mortality rates for someone with average frailty. Vaupel and Yashin (1985) described this phenomenon nicely as: "Individuals age faster than heterogeneous cohorts". In section 4.6, this phenomenon was described as the downwards bias of the duration dependence resulting from unobserved heterogeneity.

To be able to estimate the age-specific mortality rates of someone with average frailty, Vaupel, Manton and Stallard (1979) proposed including a continuous latent variable in a hazard model. The value of this latent variable was assumed to be constant during an individual's life, and, moreover, the latent variable was assumed to have a multiplicative and proportional effect on the hazard rate, i.e.,

$$h(t|\theta) = h(t)\theta. \qquad [5.5]$$

Here, θ denotes a value of the latent variable, which is assumed to have a particular distributional form. Since the hazard rate is not allowed to take negative values, θ must be greater than or equal to zero. This must be taken into account when choosing a particular distributional form for θ. The amount of unobserved heterogeneity is determined by the size of the standard deviation of the distribution of the latent variable: The larger the standard deviation of θ, the more unobserved heterogeneity there is.

The model represented in Equation 5.5 is, in fact, a mixture model as discussed in the context of latent class analysis (see section 3.1). The only difference is that the mixture variable is assumed to have a particular continuous distribution function, while in latent class analysis, there is a discrete mixture variable with an unspecified distributional form. Below, a non-parametric approach to unobserved heterogeneity is presented which, like latent class analysis, is based on the use of a finite mixture model.

Since θ cannot be observed, the hazard rate $h(t)$ which appears in Equation 5.5 is also unobservable. The observable hazard rate is the marginal hazard rate at $T = t$, i.e.,

$$\bar{h}(t) = \int_0^\infty h(t)f_t(\theta)d\theta = h(t)\bar{\theta}(t). \qquad [5.6]$$

Here, $f_t(\theta)$ denotes the density function of θ at $T = t$ and $\bar{\theta}(t)$ the mean value of the latent variable at $T = t$. The mean value of θ at $T = 0$, $\bar{\theta}(0)$, can be arbitrarily set to 1. Note that $\bar{h}(t)$ is the hazard rate that is modeled when the unobserved heterogeneity is not taken into account. It can easily be seen from Equation 5.6, that, except at $T = 0$, the individual hazard rates $h(t)$ are higher than the marginal hazard rates. The reason is that the mean value of θ declines with time since the individuals with a higher θ have higher hazard rates at all t.

Vaupel, Manton, and Stallard (1979) proposed using a gamma distribution for θ, with a mean of 1 and a variance of $1/\gamma$, where γ is the unknown parameter to be estimated. Several other authors have proposed incorporating a gamma distributed multiplicative random term in event history models (Tuma and Hannan, 1984:177-179; Tuma, 1985; Lancaster, 1979, 1990:65-70). According to Vaupel, Manton and Stallard (1979), the gamma distribution was chosen because it is analytically tractable and readily computational. Moreover, it is a flexible distribution that takes on a variety of shapes as the dispersion parameter γ varies: When $\gamma = 1$, it is identical to the well-known exponential distribution; when γ is large, it assumes a bell-shaped form reminiscent of a normal distribution. Multiplicative frailty cannot be negative, and the gamma distribution is, along with the log-normal and Weibull distribution, one of the most commonly used distributions to model variables that are necessarily positive.

The estimation of the parameters of hazard models with a gamma disturbance term is relatively easy for particular conditional survival distributions such as the exponential model, the Weibull model and the Gompertz model. This results from the fact that after integrating out the mixture distribution, simple expressions remain for the hazard and survival functions appearing in the likelihood function to be maximized. For instance, when an exponential survival model is postulated, the marginal hazard and survival functions for person i with covariate values $\mathbf{x}_i$ are

$$\bar{h}(t|\mathbf{x}_i) = \frac{\exp(\sum_j \beta_j x_{ij})\gamma}{\exp(\sum_j \beta_j x_{ij})t + \gamma},$$

$$\bar{S}(t|\mathbf{x}_i) = \left(\frac{\gamma}{\exp(\sum_j \beta_j x_{ij})t + \gamma}\right)^{\gamma}.$$

Note that the hazard rate depends on the time variable T even though in the exponential model the individual hazard rates are time independent (Tuma and Hannan, 1984:177-179). Several computer programs contain an option to specify parametric hazard models with gamma distributed unobserved heterogeneity, two of which are Tuma's RATE program (Tuma, 1979) and Rohwer's TDA program (Rohwer, 1993).

Although the assumption of a gamma distribution has been dominant, other distributions have also been advocated. Heckman and Singer (1982) used both a log-normal and a normal mixture distribution. Hougard (1984, 1986a, 1986b) proposed the inverse Gaussian distribution and other kinds of positive stable distributions. Wrigley (1990) proposed a beta or multivariate-beta (Dirichlet) form for the mixing distribution in combination with a discrete-time logit model. The beta-logistic model is a heterogeneity model which is often used in the context of discrete choice modeling (Heckman and Willis, 1977).

Non-parametric mixture distributions Heckman and Singer (1982, 1984) demonstrated by an analysis of one particular data set that the results obtained from continuous-time hazard models can be very sensitive to the choice of the functional form of the mixture distribution. Therefore, they proposed using a non-parametric characterization of the mixing distribution by means of a finite set of so-called mass points, or points of support, whose number, locations, and weights are empirically determined. In this approach, the continuous mixing distribution of the parametric approach is replaced by a discrete density function defined by a set of empirically identifiable mass points which are considered adequate to characterize fully the form of the heterogeneity. Laird's work provides the theoretical underpinnings of this non-parametric mass points method (Laird, 1978). In fitting models of this type, one typically starts with two points of support and proceeds to add more as long as the estimated relative risks are distinct and the weights are positive (Laird, 1978). Often, two or three points of support suffice (Guo and Rodriguez, 1992).

It should be noted that the arguments of Heckman and Singer (1982) against the use of parametric mixing distributions have been criticized by other authors who claimed that the sensitivity of the results to the choice of the mixture distribution was caused by the fact that Heckman and Singer misspecified the duration dependence in the hazard model they formulated for the data set they used to demonstrate the potentials of their non-parametric approach. (Blossfeld, Hamerle, and Mayer, 1989:97). Trussell and Richards (1985) demonstrated that the results obtained with Heckman and Singer's non-parametric mixing distribution can severely be affected by a misspecification of the functional form of the distribution of T. Newman and McCulloch (1984) found no strong influence of the choice of the mixing distribution on the results in an analysis of the timing of births. Ridder and Verbakel (1983) showed, by means of a simulation study, that the results are much more sensitive to the choice of the conditional survival distribution than to the choice of mixture distribution. These results indicate that the specification problem is not solved simply by using a non-parametric rather than a parametric mixture distribution. Irrespective of the type of mixture distribution, a lot of attention has to be given to the specification of the duration dependence of the process under study.

Actually, the non-parametric unobserved heterogeneity model proposed by Heckman and Singer (1982, 1984) is, in fact, strongly related to latent class analysis (Goodman, 1974a, 1974b). As in latent class analysis, the population is assumed to be composed of a finite number of exhaustive and mutually exclusive groups formed by the categories of a latent variable. Suppose Z is a categorical latent variable with Z^* categories, and z is a particular value of Z. If there are no observed covariates, the non-parametric hazard model with unobserved heterogeneity can be formulated as follows:

$$h(t|\theta_z) = h(t)\theta_z .$$

Here, θ_z denotes the (multiplicative) effect on the hazard rate for latent class z. The marginal hazard rate at $T = t$ is now defined as

$$\bar{h}(t) = \sum_{z=1}^{Z^*} h(t)\pi_z(t)\theta_z = h(t)\bar{\theta}_z(t) ,$$

where $\pi_z(t)$ is the proportion of the population belonging to latent class z at $T = t$ and $\bar{\theta}_z(t)$ the mean value of θ_z at $T = t$. In the terminology used by Heckman and Singer (1982), the number of latent classes (Z^*), the latent proportions ($\pi_z(t)$), and the effects of Z (θ_z) are called the number of mass points, the weights, and the mass points locations, respectively.

Recently, Lindsay, Clogg, and Grego (1991) demonstrated the equivalence between restricted latent class models and non-parametric mixture models in the context of the Rasch model. The latent class model and the non-parametric heterogeneity model are both applications of finite mixture distributions (Everitt and Hand, 1981; Titterington, Smith, and Makov, 1985; Wedel and DeSarbo, 1994, 1995). The only difference between them is, in fact, the purpose for which they were developed: Models with non-parametric unobserved heterogeneity were developed to approximate a continuous mixing distribution with an unknown form, while latent class models were originally developed to construct measurement models with discrete latent variables.[2]

Davies (1987) and Wrigley (1990) showed that it is also possible to incorporate non-parametric unobserved heterogeneity in discrete-time logit models. Wrigley proposed the standard incorporation of a θ_z of zero for each origin state. Such a specification leads to a mover-stayer structure with one class of stayers for each origin state (Goodman, 1961). Although Heckman and Singer (1982) also mentioned the possibility of specifying mover-stayer models, they never gave examples of this interesting special case of their non-parametric approach. Farewell (1982) proposed using the mover-stayer model in combination with either a discrete-time logit model or a Weibull model for separating the probability of the occurrence on the event of interest from its timing among the persons who experience the event.[3] For the discrete-time Markov model, the use of a finite mixture distribution, including the mover-stayer model, has been advocated by Poulsen (1982) and Van de Pol and Langeheine (1990).

A strongly related application of the latent class model was proposed by Wedel et al. (1993) and Böckenholt (1993). They apply the latent class model in a Poisson regression model. As demonstrated in section 4.8, the Poisson model is equivalent to a continuous-time event history model for repeatable events assuming a constant hazard rate, that is, assuming exponential survival. Wedel et al. (1995) included non-parametric unobserved heterogeneity in a piecewise exponential survival model or

---

[2] Recently, Heinen (1993, 1996) demonstrated that linearly restricted latent class models can be used to estimate latent trait models by approximating the assumed continuous distribution of the latent trait variable with a discrete distribution.

[3] Kuk and Chen (1992) used the same type of mover-stayer specification in combination with a Cox proportional hazard model, while Yamaguchi (1992) and Yamaguchi and Ferguson (1995) combined it with an accelerated failure-time model.

log-rate of the form presented in section 4.4. Recently, Böckenholt and Langeheine (1996) proposed including a categorical time-varying latent variable to correct for unobserved heterogeneity in a Poisson regression model in which the Poisson rate was assumed to be constant within periods of time.

The estimation of non-parametric heterogeneity models is a bit more complicated than, for instance, the gamma model because it is not possible to obtain simple expressions for the hazard and survival functions by integrating out the mixture distribution. Heckman and Singer (1982, 1984) proposed estimating non-parametric models by means of the EM algorithm (Dempster, Laird and Rubin, 1977). Poulsen (1982) and Langeheine and Van de Pol (1990, 1994) also used the EM algorithm to estimate their mixed Markov models.

Limitations The use of parametric mixture distributions is relatively simple in models for a single nonrepeatable event. However, when there is more than one (latent) survival time per observational unit, that is, when there is a model for competing risks, a model for repeatable events, or another type of multivariate hazard model, this is generally not true anymore. It is not so easy to include several possibly correlated parametric latent variables in a hazard model because that makes it necessary to specify the functional form of the multivariate mixture distribution. Therefore, in such cases, most applications use either several mutually independent cause, spell, or transition-specific latent variables, or one latent variable that may have a different effect on the several cause, spell or transition-specific hazard rates. The former approach was adopted, for instance, by Tuma and Hannan (1984:177-183), and the latter, for instance, by Flinn and Heckmann (1982) in a study in which they used a normal mixture distribution.

The two above-mentioned specifications of the unobserved factors have also been used in models with non-parametric unobserved heterogeneity (Heckman and Singer, 1985; Moon, 1991). However, the latent class approach which is presented in the next subsection is much more general. It can also be used to specify models with several latent variables which are mutually related without the necessity of specifying the distributional form of their joint distribution since the joint distribution of the latent variables is non-parametric as well. If necessary, the joint distribution can be restricted by means of a log-linear parameterization of the latent proportions.

Another important drawback of the usual way of modeling unobserved heterogeneity is caused by the fact that the mixture distribution is assumed to be independent of the observed covariates.[4] This is, in fact, in contradiction to the omitted variables argument which is often used to motivate the use of mixture models. If one assumes that particular important variables are not included in the model, it is usually implausible to assume that they are completely unrelated to the observed factors. In other words, by assuming independence among unobserved and observed factors, the omitted variable bias, or selection bias, will generally remain (Chamberlain, 1985; Yamaguchi, 1986, 1991:132). This is, in fact, Chamberlain's main argument for using fixed effects methods to correct for unobserved heterogeneity. However, as was shown in section 4.8, fixed effects methods have serious limitations as well. They can only be used when there is more than one observed survival time for the largest part of the sample, and they do not allow for getting estimates for the effects of time-constant covariates.

To solve the selection bias problem, Blossfeld, Hamerle, and Mayer (1989:98) proposed regressing an individual's score on the latent variable θ on the covariates included in the model. In his TDA program, Rohwer (1993) implemented an option to regress the coefficient of variation of the gamma distribution on covariate values, which is a first attempt to relate a parametric mixture distribution to observed covariates. However, by regressing the coefficient of variation on covariates, the mean value of θ is still equal for all individuals, irrespective of their covariate values. Therefore, Rohwer's approach does not solve the above-mentioned problem.

5.2.2. A more general non-parametric latent variable approach to unobserved heterogeneity

To overcome the limitations of the latent variable approaches which were discussed above, a more general non-parametric latent variable approach to unobserved heterogeneity was developed which is based on the general hazard model with missing data presented in section 5.1. The main difference between this latent variable approach and Heckman and Singer's model is that different types of specifications can be used for the joint distribution of the observed covariates, the unobserved

---

[4] An exception is the mover-stayer model proposed by Farewell (1982), in which the probability of belonging to the class of stayers is regressed on a set of covariates by means of a logit model (see also Yamaguchi, 1992). Recently, Brüderl and Diekman (1995) and Land, McCall, and Nagin (1996) developed log-logistic and Poisson models, respectively, which contain a probit model for the probability of being a mover.

covariates, and the initial state. This means that it becomes possible to specify hazard models in which the unobserved factors are related to the observed covariates and to the initial state. A special case is, for instance, the mover-stayer model proposed by Farewell (1982), in which the probability of belonging to the class of stayers is regressed on a set of covariates by means of a logit model. Moreover, when hazard models are specified with several latent covariates, different types of specifications can be used for the relationships among the latent variables, one of which leads to a time-varying latent variable as proposed by Böckenholt and Langeheine (1996). By means of a multivariate hazard model, the latent covariates can also be related to observed time-varying covariates.

Like the general model presented in section 5.1, the model that is used for dealing with unobserved heterogeneity consists of two parts: a log-linear path model in which the relationships among the time-constant observed covariates, the initial state, and unobserved covariates are specified, and an event history model in which the determinants of the dynamic process under study are specified.

Suppose there is a model with three time-constant observed covariates denoted by A, B, and C, and two unobserved covariates denoted by W and Y. In the *first part* of the model, the relationships between these five variables are specified by means of a log-linear path model as presented in sections 2.9 and 3.1. Let π_{abcwy} denote the probability that an individual belongs to cell (a, b, c, w, y) of the contingency table formed by the variables A, B, C, W, and Y. As was demonstrated in section 2.9, specifying a modified path model for π_{abcwy} involves two things, namely, decomposing π_{abcwy} into a set of conditional probabilities on the basis of the assumed causal order among A, B, C, W, and Y, and specifying log-linear or logit models for these conditional probabilities. At least three meaningful specifications for the causal order among A, B, C, W, and Y are possible, namely, all the variables are of the same order, the latent variables are posterior to the observed variables, and the observed variables are posterior to the latent variables. In the first specification, π_{abcwy} is not decomposed in terms of conditional probabilities. The second specification is obtained by

$$\pi_{abcwy} = \pi_{abc}\,\pi_{wy|abc}\,,$$

and the third one by

$$\pi_{abcwy} = \pi_{wy}\,\pi_{abc|wy}\,.$$

Suppose that the second specification is chosen. In that case, π_{abc} and $\pi_{wy|abc}$ can be restricted by means of a non-saturated (multinomial) logit model. A possible specification of the dependence of the unobserved covariates on the observed covariates is, for instance,

$$\pi_{wy|abc} = \frac{\exp\left(u_w^W + u_y^Y + u_{aw}^{AW} + u_{bw}^{BW} + u_{cw}^{CW}\right)}{\sum_{wy} \exp\left(u_w^W + u_y^Y + u_{aw}^{AW} + u_{bw}^{BW} + u_{cw}^{CW}\right)}.$$

Here, W depends on A, B, and C, while Y is assumed to be independent of W and the observed covariates. Other specifications are, for instance,

$$\pi_{wy|abc} = \frac{\exp\left(u_w^W + u_y^Y + u_{wy}^{WY}\right)}{\sum_{wy} \exp\left(u_w^W + u_y^Y + u_{wy}^{WY}\right)} = \pi_{wy},$$

where the joint latent variable is assumed to be independent of the observed variables, and

$$\pi_{wy|abc} = \frac{\exp\left(u_w^W + u_y^Y\right)}{\sum_{wy} \exp\left(u_w^W + u_y^Y\right)} = \pi_w \pi_y,$$

in which the two latent variables are mutually independent and independent of the observed variables. It should noted that for these latter specifications it does not matter which assumption is made about causal order between A, B, C, W, and Y since the same models can be obtained by imposing restrictions on π_{abcwy} or $\pi_{abc|wy}$ rather than $\pi_{wy|abc}$.

The *second part* of the model with non-parametric unobserved heterogeneity consists of an event history model for the dependent process to be studied. The event history models which are used here are log-rate models (section 4.4) and discrete-time logit models (section 4.3).

As demonstrated in section 4.8, in its most general form, the hazard rate for the log-rate model in which the variables A, B, C, W, and Y are used as regressors is denoted by $h_{od}^m(z|a, b, c, w, y)$, where o denotes the origin state, d the destination state, and m the spell or episode number. In discrete-time models, the transition probability from $O = o$ to $D = d$ is denoted by $\lambda_{od}^m(t_l|a, b, c, w, y)$. When the discrete-time logit model is a Markov model, the transition probability may also be denoted by $\pi_{s_l|abcwys_{l-1}}$, where s_l is the state that an individual occupies at the lth point in time.

Estimation To obtain maximum likelihood estimates of the parameters of a hazard model with the observed covariates A, B, and C and latent covariates W and Y, the following likelihood function has to be maximized:

$$\mathcal{L} = \prod_{i}^{N} \sum_{wy} \pi_{abcwy} \mathcal{L}_i^*(h), \qquad [5.7]$$

in which $\mathcal{L}_i^*(h)$ denotes the contribution of person i to the complete data likelihood function for the hazard model, and a, b, c are the observed values of A, B, and C for person i. More information about the exact form of $\mathcal{L}_i^*(h)$ can be found in section 4.8. Since the likelihood function described in Equation 5.7 is based on the general density function represented in Equation 5.1, as already mentioned in section 5.1, the parameters can be estimated with the EM algorithm.

The posterior probabilities which are needed in the E step to compute the complete-data sufficient statistics can be obtained by means of Equation 5.3. Here, we need the probability that person i belongs to latent class (w, y) is

$$P(w, y|i) = \frac{\pi_{abcwy} \mathcal{L}_i^*(h)}{\sum_{wy} \pi_{abcwy} \mathcal{L}_i^*(h)}.$$

When using a log-rate model, these posterior probabilities are used to obtain estimates of the number of events and the total exposure times, i.e.,

$$\hat{n}_{abcwyzodm} = \sum_{i=1}^{N} \delta_{izod}^m P(w, y|i)\, \gamma_{iabc},$$

$$\hat{E}_{abcwyzom} = \sum_{i=1}^{N} e_{izo}^m P(w, y|i)\, \gamma_{iabc}.$$

Here, γ_{iabc} and δ_{izod}^m, are indicator variables taking the value one if a particular condition is fulfilled, and which are otherwise equal to zero. More precisely, γ_{iabc} indicates whether person i has covariate values (a, b, c), and δ_{iodz}^m whether person i experienced a transition from $O = o$ to $D = d$ in time interval z in the mth spell. And finally, e_{izo}^m is the total time that person i spent in the origin state o in time interval z in the mth spell.

In the M step of the EM algorithm, the completed tables $\hat{n}_{abcwyzodm}$ and $\hat{E}_{abcwyzom}$ are used to obtain improved estimates for the hazard parameters as if it were completely observed data. The completed data which is needed to update the estimates for the parameters of the log-linear part of the model is obtained in the E step by

$$\hat{n}_{abcwy} = \sum_{i=1}^{N} P(w, y|i) \, \gamma_{iabc} \, .$$

As demonstrated in section 4.8, the discrete-time logit model is equivalent to a modified path model. This means the estimation of discrete-time logit models with latent covariates can be performed with the same version of the EM algorithm presented in section 3.1.

5.2.3. Identifiability

Elbers and Ridder (1982) proved that the parameters of hazard models with unobserved heterogeneity for a single nonrepeatable event are identifiable if three conditions are fulfilled, namely, if the model is a proportional hazard model with at least one regressor, if the mixture distribution has a finite mean, and if the duration dependence is parameterized. Heckman and Singer (1984) showed, however, that regressors are not necessary for identification provided that the hazard function is assumed to be a member of particular parametric families. They proved identifiability for a class of Box-Cox hazard rate models from which the Weibull, the Gompertz, and the exponential models are special cases, and for the log-logistic model. Heckman and Singer also showed that non-parametric mixture models are identifiable if the time dependence is parameterized.

If the time-dependence is not parameterized, that is, if the hazard model is a semi-parametric model, it is possible to identify the mixture distribution in models for repeatable events, clustered observations, or other kinds of multivariate survival times which can be assumed to have equal random terms (Clayton and Cuzick, 1985; Klein, 1992; Nielsen et al., 1992; Petersen, Andersen, and Gill, 1996). Van de Pol and Langeheine (1990) showed that the parameters of discrete-time mixed Markov models, which are also models for repeatable events, can be identified without imposing restrictions on the time dependence or on the mixture distribution. Recently, Kortram et al. (1995) demonstrated that for identification it suffices that the model is a proportional hazard model.

This means that in proportional hazard models, it is not necessary to parameterize the time dependence or the mixing distribution, or to have multivariate survival times.

In summary, the parameters of event history models with unobserved heterogeneity can be identified by ensuring that at least one of the following conditions is fulfilled: 1] the model is a proportional hazard model; 2] the duration dependence is parameterized; 3] the mixing distribution is parameterized; or 4] the model is a multivariate hazard model.

One factor determining identifiability has not yet been mentioned. Contrary to the usual practice, in the approach that is used here, it is not necessary to assume the latent variable capturing the unobserved heterogeneity to be independent of the observed covariates. Limited experience with this approach has shown that the inclusion of additional parameters in the model describing the relationships between latent and observed covariates does not lead to identification problems as long as one of the above-mentioned sufficient conditions is fulfilled.

When using non-parametric unobserved heterogeneity, it is not known beforehand how many latent classes can be identified on the basis of the data. Laird (1978) proposed starting with two latent classes and adding more classes as long as the estimated relative risks are distinct and the weights are greater than zero. Often, two or three latent classes suffice (Guo and Rodriguez, 1992). In some situations, it is even impossible to identify two latent classes. This occurs, for instance, if exponential survival is assumed in a model for a single nonrepeatable event, while the data shows a positive time dependence. The reason for this is that if survival is exponential, unobserved heterogeneity must lead to spurious negative duration dependence. Thus, in fact, the observed positive duration dependence is in contradiction with the postulated model. The same occurs when there is a positive duration dependence within time intervals in a piecewise constant hazard model.

A well-known method to ensure local identifiability in latent class models is to run the same model using different sets starting values (Goodman, 1974b; Hagenaars, 1990:111-112; Formann, 1992). This is the simplest way to check identifiability when using the EM algorithm to estimate the parameters. If two different sets of starting values yield different parameter estimates but the same values for the log-likelihood function, the model parameters which are different are not identifiable. Note that when both parameter estimates and likelihood values are different, the solution with the lower likelihood value is either a local maximum or a boundary solution. Another more formal method for checking identifiability is by means of the information matrix. Local identifiability is ensured if this matrix is positive definite (see Appendix G).

5.2.4. A single nonrepeatable event

Above, a general approach to the unobserved heterogeneity problem in the analysis of event history data was introduced. In this subsection, two applications are presented to demonstrate how to deal with unobserved heterogeneity when analyzing a single nonrepeatable event. The first application uses a log-rate model for the analysis of first-birth rates. The second application uses a discrete-time logit model for the analysis of school transition.

Example 1: Timing of the first birth

The use of hazard models for the analysis of demographic transitions is increasingly becoming standard practice. However, as was demonstrated above, the results can be influenced by the presence of unobserved risk factors. An example is presented in which a latent covariate is included in a log-rate model for the timing of the first birth. It should be mentioned that the example serves mainly as an illustration of the use of the latent variable methods introduced above. The intention is not to present an accurately real-world model for the timing of first births.

Data The data for the example was obtained from a Dutch family and fertility survey called ORIN[5] (NIDI, 1989) which was conducted in 1983. The data set contains information on the fertility histories of 846 18-54 year-old women. The time variable which was used is age measured in years. The time axis was divided into 23 intervals indicating all different ages between 18 and 40 years. Because two age groups are empty, there are 21 different ages at which the event under study occurred. A very small number of women in the sample already had a first child at age 18.

Two observed covariates were used in the log-rate model. The first is a woman's educational level, with 4 categories: 1] primary school, 2] secondary school, 3] vocational education and 4] university or polytechnic. In demographic research, educational level is often used as an indicator of either the occupational aspirations of a woman (Vossen, 1989;

---

[5] The name ORIN stands for Onderzoek Relatievorming in Nederland (Survey on Union Formation in the Netherlands). This study was conducted by the NIDI institute in The Hague.

Willekens, 1991; Vermunt, 1991a) or the opportunity costs of children (Becker, 1981). Women with a higher educational level can be expected to have a lower probability of having a first child because they have work aspirations which conflict with having children and because their relative costs of having children are higher, assuming that they have to stop working after the birth of their first child. The second covariate is an attitude item on the importance of family and children in one's life. This indicator was used to operationalize the concept of familism which is thought to influence fertility behavior (Lesthaege and Meekers, 1986; Vermunt, 1991b). The familism item is classified into three categories: 1] familistic 2] neither familistic nor non-familistic, and 3] non-familistic.

Model As explained when presenting the hazard model with unobserved heterogeneity, the models to be specified consist of two parts: a log-linear path model for the covariates and a hazard model for the dependent process to be studied. Let A denote a woman's educational level, B familism, and W a latent variable which is assumed to capture the unobserved heterogeneity. The general form of the model which is used in this example to describe the relationships between the covariates is

$$\pi_{abw} = \pi_{ab}\, \pi_{w|ab}\,.$$

This means that the latent variable W is seen as an intervening variable between the observed covariates and the hazard rate of having a first child. So, W stands for intervening variables influencing the rate of first birth which are not included in the model, such as having a partner, wanting to have children, and being employed.

Although it is possible, the joint distribution of the observed covariates A and B, π_{ab}, is not restricted in this example. Note that here we just want to show which types of specifications can be used for the unobserved heterogeneity rather than how to model the relationships between observed covariates. Measurement models in which the joint distribution of the observed covariates is restricted as well will be discussed in section 5.3. To be able to specify more restricted models for $\pi_{w|ab}$, it is parameterized by means of a logit model,

$$\pi_{w|ab} = \frac{\exp\left(u_w^W + u_{aw}^{AW} + u_{bw}^{BW}\right)}{\sum_w \exp\left(u_w^W + u_{aw}^{AW} + u_{bw}^{BW}\right)}\,. \qquad [5.8]$$

This is the least restrictive model that will be used for $\pi_{w|ab}$. Note that it is not a saturated model because it does not contain the three-variable interaction term u_{abw}^{ABW}.

On the basis of the model described in Equation 5.8, it is possible to specify more restrictive models with regard to the effects of A and B on W by imposing particular restrictions on the u_{aw}^{AW} and u_{bw}^{BW} parameters. One constraint that is used below is to fix both u_{aw}^{AW} and u_{bw}^{BW} to zero, which yields a model in which the unobserved heterogeneity is independent of the observed heterogeneity, that is, $\pi_{w|ab} = \pi_w$. This specification, which is how unobserved heterogeneity is usually modeled in event history analysis, will be denoted as an 'independent' unobserved heterogeneity model.

Another set of restrictions which may be used to reduce the number of parameters of the model for the covariates is

$$u_{aw}^{AW} = (a - \bar{a})(w - \bar{w})\, \beta^{AW}\,,$$
$$u_{bw}^{BW} = (b - \bar{b})(w - \bar{w})\, \beta^{BW}\,.$$

These restrictions lead to a linear-by-linear association between A and W and B and W (see section 2.5). Below, the reason for using such a specification is explained in more detail.

Several different types of specifications may be used for the event history part of the model. In its most general form, the log-rate model that will be used is

$$h(z|a, b, w) = \frac{m_{abwz}}{E_{abwz}} = \exp\left(v + v_a^A + v_b^B + v_w^W + v_z^Z + v_{wz}^{WZ}\right)\,, \quad [5.9]$$

where the variable Z with index z denotes the time intervals. It should be noted that here, unlike in the presentation of the log-rate model in section 4.4, the hazard parameters are denoted by v instead of u to distinguish them from the parameters of the covariate part model. As can be seen, the hazard model described in Equation 5.9 does not contain higher-order interaction terms involving A or B; only the simplest specification for the dependence of the first-birth rate on A and B is used. As discussed in the previous section, the assumption that the covariate effects are proportional is sufficient for identifying a model, irrespective of the choice of specification for the unobserved heterogeneity.

Different types of hazard models are specified by restricting v_z^Z and v_{wz}^{WZ}. An exponential model is obtained by fixing both v_z^Z and v_{wz}^{WZ} to zero. Fixing only v_{wz}^{WZ} to zero yields a proportional hazard model, in which different kinds of specifications for v_z^Z can be used. When no further restrictions are imposed on v_z^Z, a model is obtained which is equivalent to Cox's proportional hazard model (see section 4.4). Another specification which is used for v_z^Z is quadratic time dependence, which is a rather common way to describe the age pattern in the timing of the first birth, i.e.,

$$v_z^Z = z \, \beta_1^Z + z^2 \, \beta_2^Z \,,$$

where β_1^Z is the linear effect of Z and β_2^Z quadratic effect of Z on the hazard rate. And finally, in some models both v_z^Z and v_{wz}^{WZ} are restricted to a quadratic functional form. This results in a nonproportional model with different quadratic time dependencies for the different values of W.

Testing The test results for the estimated models are presented in Table 5.2. In the first set of models (Models 1a to 3b), the latent variable W is assumed to be independent of the observed covariates; in other words, u_{aw}^{AW} and u_{bw}^{BW} are fixed to zero. Moreover, the effect of the latent variable on the hazard rate is assumed to be proportional, which means that v_{wz}^{WZ} is fixed to zero. This is the standard way of correcting for unobserved heterogeneity in hazard models.

A comparison of the log-likelihood values of the models with one latent class, that is, the models without heterogeneity, shows that there is duration dependence. The conditional likelihood test between Model 1a and Models 1b and 1c show that the exponential model, which assumes no duration dependence, fits a lot worse than the Cox and quadratic models ($L_{1a|1b}^2 = 56.37, df = 20, p = .000$ and $L_{1a|1c}^2 = 42.41, df = 2, p = .000$).[6] The quadratic model captures the time dependence rather well using only two time parameters since it does not fit significantly worse than the Cox model ($L_{1c|1b}^2 = 28.08, df = 18, p > .06$).

Including a second latent class does not improve the log-likelihood value of the exponential model (Model 2a) as there is a positive duration dependence, while, as already mentioned in subsection 5.2.3, the exponential model can only capture unobserved heterogeneity if there is a (spurious) negative duration dependence. As can be seen from the comparison of the two-class Cox model (Model 2b) and the two-class quadratic model (Model 2c) with their no-unobserved heterogeneity variants, the log-likelihood decreases a bit more for the Cox model. Includ-

---

[6] The likelihood-ratio chi-square statistic $L_{r|u}^2$ to compare nested models can be computed by taking 2 times the difference between the log-likelihood value of the *u*nrestricted model and of the *r*estricted model (section 2.4). The number of degrees of freedom can be obtained by taking the difference in the number of parameters of the models concerned. However, as already mentioned in section 3.1, models with different numbers of latent class cannot be compared this way because of difficulties associated with parameter space boundaries (Titterington, Smith and Makov, 1985).

TABLE 5.2 Test results for the estimated models for the timing of the first birth

Model		log-likelihood	# parameters
Independent/proportional			
1a.	1 class exponential	-3497.95	18
1b.	1 class Cox	-3441.58	38
1c.	1 class quadratic	-3455.54	20
2a.	2 class exponential	-3497.95	20
2b.	2 class Cox	-3437.95	40
2c.	2 class quadratic	-3453.12	22
3a.	3 class Cox	-3437.48	42
3b.	3 clas quadratic	-3452.83	24
Independent/nonproportional			
4a.	2 class Cox	-3429.14	60
4b.	2 class quadratic	-3449.08	24
5a.	3 class Cox	-3426.84	82
5b.	3 class quadratic	-3445.55	28
Dependent (AW, BW)/proportional			
6a.	2 class Cox	-3430.39	45
6b.	2 class quadratic	-3444.87	27
7a.	3 class Cox	-3422.25	52
7b.	3 class quadratic	-3438.15	34
Dependent (AW, BW linear)/proportional			
8a.	2 class Cox	-3435.32	42
8b.	3 class Cox	-3432.53	44
8c.	mover-stayer Cox	-3437.13	41
8d.	2 movers Cox	-3433.47	43

ing a third class does not have much influence on either the Cox model (Model 3a) or the quadratic model (Model 3b).

The first extension of the usual way of modeling unobserved heterogeneity is the specification of models in which the latent variable W is allowed to have a nonproportional effect on the hazard rate, in other words, the interaction term v_{wz}^{WZ} is included in the model (Models 4a-5b). Including the interaction effects between duration and the unobserved covariate in the Cox model leads to so many extra parameters that the improvement of the fit is no longer significant. This applies to both the two- and three-class models (Models 4a and 5a): $L_{2b|4a}^2 = 17.62$, $df = 20$, $p > .99$ and $L_{3a|5a}^2 = 21.28$, $df = 40$, $p > .61$. But, the quadratic two- and three-class models both improve significantly by assuming nonproportionality (Models 4b and 5b): $L_{2c|4b}^2 = 8.08$, $df = 2$, $p < .02$ and $L_{3b|5b}^2 = 14.56$, $df = 4$, $p < .01$.

In Models 6a-7b, the assumption that the unobserved factor W is independent of the observed covariates is relaxed. This is another important extension of the usual way of modeling unobserved heterogeneity. For simplicity of exposition, the effect of W on the hazard rate is again assumed to be proportional ($v_{wz}^{WZ} = 0$). Table 5.2 shows that the inclusion of the u_{aw}^{AW} and u_{bw}^{BW} interaction terms in the covariate model leads to a significant increase in log-likelihood value for Models 6a, 6b, 7a and 7b compared to their 'independent' unobserved heterogeneity variants: $L_{2b|6a}^{2} = 15.12$, $df = 5$, $p < .01$, $L_{2c|6b}^{2} = 16.50$, $df = 5$, $p < .005$, $L_{3a|7a}^{2} = 30.46$, $df = 10$, $p < .001$, and $L_{3b|7b}^{2} = 29.36$, $df = 10$, $p < .002$. It must be stated that although the models fit very well, many local maxima were encountered when fitting these models. This indicates that one has to be cautious with these kinds of models. One cannot even be sure that the final solutions presented in the table are the global maximum likelihood solutions. Nevertheless, the fact that several sets of starting values lead to the same log-likelihood value and the same parameter estimates demonstrates that the models are identified. This is confirmed by the fact that the information matrix is positive definite for Models 6a-7b.

Models 6a-7b are not only problematic because of the occurrence of local maxima, but, as will be demonstrated below, the parameter estimates of these of models are also rather strange. It seems that to get more stable results, a more restricted specification for the relationships between the observed covariates and the latent variable has to be used. To be able to specify more restrictive models, substantive hypotheses are needed about the nature of the unobserved heterogeneity. One option is to assume that particular covariates influence the unobserved covariate but not the hazard rate (Heckman, 1979). Such a solution is, in fact, very similar to using the observed covariates as indicators for the latent variables, as in the measurement models that will be discussed in section 5.3. Another option is to restrict the relationship between the covariates and the latent variables to have a more systematic pattern. To demonstrate this option, the relationships between A and W and between B and W are restricted to linear-by-linear (see Equation 5.8). The main reason for choosing this specification here is that the parameter estimates of the nonrestricted covariate parts of Models 6a-7b are very difficult to interpret. It is not possible to detect any systematic pattern in the u_{aw}^{AW} and u_{bw}^{BW} parameters, which is strange if one realizes that both A and B are ordinal variables. By the rather restrictive linear-by-linear specification it was hoped to get more interpretable results. Other less restrictive specifications that could be used are, for instance, row or column association models or log-multiplicative association models (see sections 2.5 and 2.7).

For simplicity of exposition, the linear-by-linear β^{AW} and β^{BW} terms (see Equation 5.9) are only included in the Cox proportional models with two and three latent classes (Models 8a and 8b). Now, only the three-class model fits significantly better than the 'independent' unobserved heterogeneity model concerned (Models 2b and 3a): $L^2_{2b|8a} = 5.26, df = 2, p > .07$ and $L^2_{3a|8b} = 9.90, df = 2, p < .008$. Furthermore, both Models 8a and 8b are restricted by fixing the log-linear hazard parameter for one class to be equal to $-\infty$.[7] In other words, the models become mover-stayer models with one class (Model 8c) or two classes (Model 8d) of movers, respectively. This mover-stayer structure is interesting from a substantive point of view, because the proportion of stayers can be interpreted as the proportion of women that remain childless. Note that testing the mover-stayer restriction using the likelihood-ratio statistic is not allowed since the v_w^W parameter concerned is fixed on a boundary value. Nevertheless, the small decrease in the likelihood of Models 8c and 8d compared to Models 8a and 8b indicates that the mover-stayer structure performs quite well.

Parameters Table 5.3 presents the estimates for the covariate effects on the hazard rate and for the parameters describing the relationships among the covariates for some of the model in Table 5.3. When there is no unobserved heterogeneity, the effects of A and B on the hazard rate are very similar for the different specifications of the duration dependence (Models 1a, 1b, and 1c). Inclusion of a two-class independent unobserved heterogeneity component in the model, leads to stronger effects of A and B (Models 2b and 2c). In other words, 'independent' heterogeneity attenuates the hazard parameters. Again, the hazard parameters for the Cox model (Model 2b) and the quadratic model (Model 2c) are very similar. Also, the class proportions and the effects of the latent variable are almost the same for the two models. Both models identified two latent groups, one with a low hazard rate and one with a much higher hazard. In Models 2b and 2c, the ratio of the hazard rates of the two groups is .12 $(= \exp(-1.059 - 1.059))$ and .17 $(= \exp(-.892 - .892))$, respectively.

---

[7] Fixing a log-linear parameter to $-\infty$ is the same as fixing the multiplicative parameter concerned to zero. When using the IPF or the uni-dimensional Newton algorithm discussed in Chapter 2, a multiplicative parameter can simply be fixed to zero by using zero as starting value for the parameter concerned. This will lead to structural zero cells in the table concerned.

In the three-class 'dependent' unobserved heterogeneity models (Models 7a and 8d), the parameter estimates are very different from Models 2b and 2c and also from one another. In the three-class model with unrestricted interaction terms u_{aw}^{AW} and u_{bw}^{BW} (Model 7a), the hazard parameters for the covariates become very extreme. For instance, someone with $A = 2$ has a 100 ($=\exp(1.653 - -2.951)$) times higher hazard rate than someone with $A = 4$. Similar extreme effects are found for covariate B. However, at the same time, the parameters describing the effects of A and B on W indicate that the extremely low-risk groups, $A = 4$ and $B = 3$, have a very high probability of belonging to latent class number three, the class with an extremely high risk of a first birth. The opposite is true for $A = 2$ and $B = 1$, the groups with the highest risks.[8] They have a very low probability of belonging to the high-risk class. Thus, what actually happens is that class membership and covariate effects compensate one another, which makes the results obtained from Model 7a very difficult to interpret.

In the restricted 'dependent' model (Model 8d), the hazard parameters for A are very similar to the 'independent' models (Models 2b and 2c). The effect of B, however, becomes much larger: Familistic women have a much higher risk of a first birth than the other two groups, which are now quite close to one another. The linear effects of A and B on W indicate that both educational level and familism are negatively related to the latent variable. Women with a low educational level and with a familistic attitude have a much lower probability of belonging to class one, the group that remains childless, than highly educated non-familistic women. This is consistent with what one expects to find. Actually, the only result in Model 8d that is difficult to interpret is the fact that the hazard parameters for levels two and three of W are not in the 'correct' order. Thus, although we specified linear-by-linear effects of the observed covariates on W, W is not an ordered variable. The more extreme effect of B on the rate of first birth can be explained by the fact that persons with $B = 1$ are too often classified in the low-risk class $W = 3$. The large standard errors of the parameter estimates concerning B indicate that there is a strong dependence between them.

---

[8] It should be noted that - as indicated by the extremely high negative value of the u_{42}^{AW} parameter - the probability of being in latent class two given that one has educational level four is near to zero. When a parameter estimate is so near to the boundary of the parameter space, it is not possible to compute one of the standard errors of the set of parameters concerned. That is the reason that no standard errors is given for u_{32}^{AW}.

TABLE 5.3 Some parameter estimates for models for the timing of the first birth

	Model 1a		Model 1b		Model 1c		Model 2b		Model 2c		Model 7a		Model 8d	
log-rate parameters														
v	-2.777	(0.057)	-2.981	(0.114)	-3.879	(0.157)	-2.519	(0.199)	-4.295	(0.318)	-2.551	(0.163)	-2.669	(0.270)
v_1^A	0.536	(0.102)	0.555	(0.102)	0.554	(0.102)	0.860	(0.166)	0.798	(0.165)	1.275	(0.205)	0.731	(0.146)
v_2^A	0.286	(0.084)	0.302	(0.084)	0.302	(0.084)	0.450	(0.129)	0.397	(0.122)	1.653	(0.216)	0.446	(0.125)
v_3^A	-0.022	(0.077)	-0.025	(0.077)	-0.025	(0.077)	-0.042	(0.107)	-0.060	(0.100)	0.023	(0.209)	-0.089	(0.098)
v_4^A	-0.801		-0.833		-0.831		-1.268		-1.135		-2.951		-1.087	
v_1^B	0.291	(0.078)	0.305	(0.079)	0.303	(0.079)	0.402	(0.114)	0.379	(0.115)	1.430	(0.219)	1.108	(0.707)
v_2^B	-0.084	(0.064)	-0.083	(0.065)	-0.082	(0.065)	-0.142	(0.092)	-0.127	(0.089)	-0.222	(0.183)	-0.590	(0.477)
v_3^B	-0.208		-0.222		-0.221		-0.260		-0.252		-1.208		-0.519	
v_1^W							-1.059	(0.187)	-0.892	(0.193)	-2.394	(0.285)	$-\infty$	
v_2^W							1.059		0.892		-0.053	(0.123)	1.000	(0.362)
v_3^W											2.447		-1.000	
latent proportions														
π_1^W							0.597		0.587		0.311		0.115	
π_2^W							0.403		0.413		0.392		0.558	
π_3^W											0.296		0.327	

effects of A and B on W

u_{11}^{AW}	-1.067	(0.552)
u_{12}^{AW}	2.366	(0.301)
u_{13}^{AW}	-1.299	
u_{21}^{AW}	0.106	(0.612)
u_{22}^{AW}	2.126	(0.374)
u_{23}^{AW}	-2.233	
u_{31}^{AW}	-1.363	(0.478)
u_{32}^{AW}	2.811	(———)
u_{33}^{AW}	-1.449	
u_{41}^{AW}	-2.324	
u_{42}^{AW}	-7.304	
u_{43}^{AW}	4.900	
u_{11}^{BW}	1.721	(0.723)
u_{12}^{BW}	0.203	(0.686)
u_{13}^{BW}	-1.924	
u_{21}^{BW}	-0.255	(0.477)
u_{22}^{BW}	-0.113	(0.361)
u_{23}^{BW}	0.368	
u_{31}^{BW}	-1.466	
u_{32}^{BW}	-0.091	
u_{33}^{BW}	1.557	
β^{XA}	-0.362	(0.195)
β^{XB}	-3.567	(3.633)

To summarize, this example showed how to deal with unobserved heterogeneity using the general approach presented in subsection 5.2.2. Two extensions of the usual way of modeling unobserved heterogeneity, which can be routinely handled within the general hazard model, were applied, namely, the effect of the unobserved variable was allowed to be nonproportional and the unobserved heterogeneity was allowed to be related to the observed covariates. The latter extension seems to be problematic in that the results are sensitive to the specification that is used for the relationships among A, B, and W. This means that it is necessary to have some a priori information to be able to decide which of the specifications is the correct one. This cannot simply be decided on the basis of the model fit. The specification problem also shows that the independent unobserved heterogeneity model which is just one of the possible models may be misspecified as well.

Example 2: School transitions

Data and model The application of the latent variable approach when time is a discrete variable is illustrated using data published in a recent paper by Mare (1994). The data is a cross-tabulation of the educational attainments of 18,563 men, their fathers, and their oldest brothers obtained from the 1973 Occupational Changes in a Generation II Survey (Featherman and Hauser, 1975). Further on, in subsection 5.2.7 on models for dependent or clustered observations, both the respondents' and the oldest brothers' information on school transitions will be used. Here, only the respondents' information is used.

Mare (1994) proposed analyzing data on school transitions by means of discrete-time hazard models. As in the analyses of Mare, the time axis is not formed by time or age, but by the qualitative stages of the schooling process. The actual amount of calendar time that it takes an individual to get through a particular school level is assumed to be irrelevant. The time axis or the respondent's schooling is classified into three levels: did not finish high school, finished high school, and completed some post-secondary schooling. The event whose occurrence is explained is dropping out of school, that is, not finishing the next school level, given that one has finished the previous level. Dropping out may either occur after finishing primary school or after finishing high school. Mare used one observed covariate, the educational level of the father of the respondent which is measured in five categories (0-8, 0-11,12,13-15 and $\geq$ 16 years). In the application presented by Mare, a latent covariate was used in a simultaneous analysis of respondents' and brothers' school transitions. Here, we demonstrate how to incorporate a latent covariate into a discrete-time logit model for a single event.

Let A denote the observed covariate father's schooling and W the unobserved covariate. As in Example 1, two types of specifications are used for the relationship between the observed and unobserved covariate. The unobserved covariate, denoted by W, may be either independent of or dependent on A. If it is dependent, the relationship is restricted to linear-by-linear because otherwise the model is not identifiable.

In its most general form, the discrete-time logit model which is used equals

$$\lambda(t_l|a, w) = \frac{\exp\left(v + v_a^A + v_w^W + v_l^L + v_{al}^{AL} + v_{wl}^{WL}\right)}{1 + \exp\left(v + v_a^A + v_w^W + v_l^L + v_{al}^{AL} + v_{wl}^{WL}\right)} .$$

Here, $\lambda(t_l|a, w)$ denotes the probability of dropping out of school at the *l*th school level, given an individual's scores on A and W.

Because of identification problems it is not always possible to include all the hazard parameters (v's) in the model at once. To identify the model parameters when W is included in the model, both v_{al}^{AL} and v_{wl}^{WL} must be assumed to be equal to zero for all a, w, and l. In other words, the covariate effects on the probability of dropping out must be assumed to be proportional. As will be demonstrated later on, these restrictions are not necessary when the respondent's and brother's schooling histories are analyzed simultaneously.

The discrete-time event history data for this example can be organized into a contingency table format because the length of the observation period is the same for all individuals and because all covariates are categorical. This makes it possible to test the fit of the models by means of the Pearson's and the likelihood-ratio chi-square statistics. Therefore, L^2 values and number of degrees of freedom are presented instead of log-likelihood values and number of parameters.

Results Table 5.4 presents the test results for the models which are estimated with the respondents' schooling data. Models 1, 2, and 3 do not include unobserved heterogeneity. In Model 1, it is assumed that A has no effect on the probability of dropping out, in other words, it contains only the main effect v. This model fits very badly ($L^2 = 4195.36, df = 8, p = .000$). In Model 2, the effect of fathers' education (A) on the rate of dropping out of school (v_a^A) is included and in Model 3, this effect is allowed to be nonproportional, which involves including v_{al}^{AL}. The conditional L^2 tests between the three models without unobserved heterogeneity show that both the main effect of fathers' educational level on

TABLE 5.4 Test results for the estimated models for respondents dropping out of school

Model		L^2	df	p
1.	no covariates	4195.36	8	.0000
2.	A proportional	175.42	4	.0000
3.	A nonproportional	0.00	0	-
4.	Model 2 + 2 class	16.59	2	.0002
5.	Model 2 + mover-stayer	17.30	3	.0006
6.	Model 5 + linear AW	15.65	2	.0004

the probability of dropping out ($L^2_{1|2} = 4019.94, df = 4, p = .000$) and the interaction of fathers' education with duration ($L^2_{2|3} = 175.42, df = 4, p = .000$) are highly significant. Thus, only the saturated model fits the data well. However, as demonstrated in section 4.6, this nonproportionality can also be caused by unobserved heterogeneity.

Model 4 is a proportional hazard model with a two-class latent covariate which is independent of A. Although its absolute fit is not perfect ($L^2 = 16.59, df = 2, p < .0003$), it fits much better than Model 2, using only two additional parameters. Model 4 can be simplified by imposing a mover-stayer structure on the effect of the latent variable, that is, by restricting the hazard parameter for one class to be equal to $-\infty$. The fit of the mover-stayer model (Model 5) is not worse than the unrestricted two-class model ($L^2 = 17.30, df = 3, p < .0006$). It should be noted that although Model 5 does not describe the data perfectly, it performs quite well if the huge sample size (18563 cases) is taken into account. Finally, a linear-by-linear effect of A on W was included in the mover-stayer model (Model 6). The conditional test between Models 5 and 6 shows that this effect of A on W is not significant ($L^2_{5|6} = 1.65, df = 1, p > .19$).

Table 5.5 reports the parameter estimates for three different proportional hazard models. As in Example 1, the effect of the observed covariate becomes somewhat stronger after correcting for unobserved heterogeneity. Not surprisingly, correcting for unobserved heterogeneity also increases the positive duration dependence. The hazard parameters of the mover-stayer model (Model 5) and the unrestricted two-class model (Model 4) are very similar. In the mover-stayer model, one group containing 12.5 percent of the respondents is identified having a dropout probability of zero. The other 87.5 percent have a 'mean' probability of dropping out of .20 ($= \exp(-.521 - .869)/(1 + \exp(-.521 - .869))$) and .59 ($= \exp(-.521 + .869)/(1 + \exp(-.521 + .869))$) at the first and second school level, respectively.

TABLE 5.5 Parameter estimates for some models for respondents dropping out of school

	Model 2		Model 4		Model 5	
discrete-time logit parameters						
v	-0.826	(0.022)	-2.269	(0.592)	-0.521	(0.030)
v_1^A	1.168	(0.026)	1.606	(0.062)	1.570	(0.042)
v_2^A	0.826	(0.032)	1.109	(0.059)	1.082	(0.049)
v_3^A	-0.030	(0.033)	-0.154	(0.041)	-0.150	(0.039)
v_4^A	-0.664	(0.056)	-0.921	(0.072)	-0.898	(0.065)
v_5^A	-1.300		-1.641		-1.604	
v_1^L	-0.506	(0.013)	-0.897	(0.048)	-0.869	(0.033)
v_2^L	0.506		0.897		0.869	
v_1^W			1.825	(0.496)	0.000	
v_2^W			-1.825		$-\infty$	
latent proportions						
π_1^W			0.833		0.875	
π_2^W			0.167		0.125	

The example on school transitions demonstrated that a more parsimonious description of the data can be obtained when correcting for unobserved heterogeneity. Instead of assuming a nonproportional effect of father's education on the probability of dropping out at a particular school level, the data could be described almost as well by means of a mover-stayer model which contained only one parameter more than a proportional model without heterogeneity.

5.2.5. Dependent competing risks

As mentioned in section 4.7, the latent variable techniques can also be used to model conditional dependence among different types of events. Dependence among competing risks can be modelled either by allowing the different types of events to depend on the same unobserved factor or by specifying event- or risk-specific unobserved factors which are allowed to be related to one another. Below an example is presented in which the events becoming employed and leaving the labor force are treated as competing risks for individuals who are unemployed (Example 3). A discrete-time logit model with a latent covariate is used to capture the dependence between these two transitions. In a second example (Example 4), the first birth example discussed in subsection 5.2.4 is extended by treating censoring as a dependent competing risk, in other words, by relaxing the independent censoring assumption.

Example 3: Transition from unemployed to employed or out of the labor force

Data and models This example investigates the determinants of the process of leaving the state of 'unemployed', with destination states 'employed' and 'out of the labor force' being treated as competing risks. It seems unrealistic to assume that, even given covariate values, becoming employed and leaving the labor market are independent events. Certainly, there will be unobserved individual factors influencing both the probability of finding employment and of leaving the labor force. This example is used to show how to take possible dependencies among competing risks into account by means of the general latent variable approach introduced in subsection 5.2.2.

The data are taken from the well-known 'Survey of Income and Program Participation' (SIPP). This survey is a panel study in which every three months information is gathered on the respondents' employment histories during the preceding three months. The information which is used for this example is obtained from a group of individuals who were followed during the years 1986 and 1987. Not all available employment information is used, only a person's employment status in the middle of the month before the interview. For the group of individuals concerned, complete information is available for 6 points in time for 4,597 people. Section 5.4 shows how the partially observed employment histories can also be used for parameter estimation.

To analyze the transition from unemployed to either employed or out of the labor force, the first unemployment spell is selected for each person in the sample. Of course, it would also be possible to use all unemployment spells. In that case, the dependencies among the spells have to be taken into account, which is the subject of the next subsection. For this example, in which the problem of dependencies among competing risks is the central issue, it is sufficient to use only the first unemployment spell for each individual. In total, 535 persons were either unemployed at the beginning of the observation period or became unemployed during the observation period. These 535 persons form the risk set for the competing events of interest.

The discrete-time logit model which is used contains three observed covariates: sex (male, female), ethnic group (non-black, black), and age at the beginning of the observation period or cohort (47-66, 27-46, < 27).

The age group above 66 years is not used in the analysis, because only very few of them belonged to the risk set of unemployed persons. The observed covariates are denoted by A, B and C, respectively. Also an unobserved covariate is included in the model to take unobserved risk factors into account. As in the examples presented above, this latent covariate, denoted by W, can be either independent of or dependent on the observed covariates.

For simplicity of exposition, the event- or risk-specific transition probabilities are assumed to be constant over time. Note that if these probabilities depend on some time dimension which is unknown as a result of left censoring, such as the length of the current unemployment spell, it is only possible to perform the analysis correctly if there is some external information on the distribution of the time of entry into the risk set (see section 4.5). Of course, it would have been possible to postulate the risk-specific transition probabilities as dependent on some known time dimension, such as age or calendar time.

The most general model which is used for destination state d is given by

$$\lambda_d(t_l|a,b,c,w) = \frac{\exp\left(v_d^D + v_{ad}^{AD} + v_{bd}^{BD} + v_{cd}^{CD} + v_{wd}^{WD}\right)}{1 + \sum_d \exp\left(v_d^D + v_{ad}^{AD} + v_{bd}^{BD} + v_{cd}^{CD} + v_{wd}^{WD}\right)}. \quad [5.10]$$

If $D = 1$, the event is finding a job, and if $D = 2$, the event is leaving the labor force. The fact that this model does contain the one-variable effects for A, B, C, and W does not mean that it is a non-hierarchical model. As explained in section 4.8, the two-variable effects v_{ad}^{AD}, v_{bd}^{BD}, v_{cd}^{CD}, and v_{wd}^{WD} are parameterized in such a way that they can be directly interpreted as the risk-specific covariate effects.[9] Note that the model represented in Equation 5.10 is already a restricted model since many interactions are excluded from it. Of course, it is possible to specify models which contain, for instance, three-variable interaction terms, such as v_{acd}^{ACD}.

Results The test result for the estimated models are given in Table 5.6. Model 1 contains only the main effect v_d^D, and Model 2a also contains the two-variable interactions v_{ad}^{AD}, v_{bd}^{BD}, and v_{cd}^{CD}. By comparing these two models without unobserved heterogeneity, it can be seen that the observed covariates have a significant effect on the probability of leaving

---

[9] The parameters v_{ad}^{AD}, for instance, can be interpreted as the effect of A on the probability of the occurrence of event d at t_l if $\sum_a v_{ad}^{AD} = 0$. In other words, the identifying restriction which is used is that the two-variable terms sum to zero within each level of D.

TABLE 5.6 Test results for the estimated competing risks models for leaving the state of unemployment

Model		log-likelihood	# parameters
1.	no covariates	-1930.59	14
2a.	1 class	-1903.19	22
2b.	2 class	-1891.94	25
2c.	3 class	-1891.29	28
3a.	1 stayer + 1 mover	-1899.77	23
3b.	1 stayer + 2 movers	-1891.99	26
4a.	2 class + *AW, BW, CW*	-1882.91	29
4b.	2 class + linear *AW, BW, CW*	-1884.89	28
4c.	3 class + *AW, BW, CW*	-1879.29	36
4d.	3 class + linear *AW, BW, CW*	-1882.71	31

unemployment ($L^2_{1|2a} = 54.8$, $df = 8$, $p < .0001$). Although not demonstrated here, separate tests for sex, ethnic group, and age show that all three variables have a significant effect on both transition probabilities.

Models 2b-3b contain a latent variable which is postulated to be independent of the observed covariates. By comparing the log-likelihood values of Models 2a, 2b, and 2c, it can be seen that the two-class solution (Model 2b) captures almost all unobserved heterogeneity. The decrease of the log-likelihood by including a third latent class (Model 2c) is negligible. The likelihood values of the mover-stayer models[10] indicate that both the model with one class of movers (Model 3a) and the model with two classes of movers (Model 3b) detect unobserved heterogeneity. However, the fit of Model 3b is almost identical to the fit of Model 2b. This is caused by the fact that in Model 3b, the estimated probability of belonging to the class of stayers is almost zero, which makes it almost identical to the two-class model.

In Models 4a-4d, the assumption that the unobserved heterogeneity models is independent of the observed covariates is relaxed by including direct effects of *A*, *B*, and *C* on *W* in the model. As in Example 1, several local maxima were encountered for these 'dependent' heterogeneity models. Conditional tests show that both the two-class model (Model 4a) and the three-class model (Model 4c) improve significantly by including these additional effects: $L^2_{2b|4a} = 18.06$, $df = 4$, $p < 0.002$ and $L^2_{2c|4c} = 24.00$, $df = 8$, $p < 0.003$. The same applies to the models with linear-by-linear effects on *W* rather than unrestricted two-variable

---

[10] The mover-stayer models (Models 3a and 3b) are obtained by fixing one v^{WD}_{wd} parameter to $-\infty$ within each level of *D*.

TABLE 5.7 Parameter estimates for some competing risks models for leaving the state of unemployment

	Model 2a		Model 2b		Model 4a	
transition to employed $(D = 1)$						
v	-0.107	(0.135)	-0.138	(0.640)	-0.866	(0.266)
$v_1^A, -v_2^A$	-0.247	(0.091)	-0.275	(0.128)	-1.522	(0.538)
$v_1^B, -v_2^B$	0.445	(0.128)	0.594	(0.190)	0.769	(0.188)
v_1^C	-0.473	(0.157)	-0.594	(0.221)	-0.529	(0.288)
v_2^C	0.158	(0.127)	0.209	(0.176)	0.666	(0.245)
v_3^C	0.315		0.385		-0.137	
$v_1^W, -v_2^W$			-1.275	(0.207)	-2.162	(0.447)
transition out of the labor force $(D = 2)$						
v	-0.158	(0.125)	0.013	(0.323)	-0.214	(0.154)
$v_1^A, -v_2^A$	-0.450	(0.102)	-0.465	(0.109)	-1.081	(0.424)
$v_1^B, -v_2^B$	-0.117	(0.120)	-0.060	(0.136)	-0.012	(0.136)
v_1^C	-0.072	(0.163)	-0.115	(0.178)	-0.071	(0.183)
v_2^C	-0.136	(0.144)	-0.131	(0.154)	0.004	(0.173)
v_3^C	0.208		0.246		0.067	
$v_1^W, -v_2^W$			-0.525	(0.294)	-0.850	(0.453)
latent proportions						
π_1^W			0.410		0.268	
π_2^W			0.590		0.732	
effects of A, B and C on W						
$u_{11}^{AW}, -u_{21}^{AW}, -u_{12}^{AW}, u_{22}^{AW}$					-0.819	(0.209)
$u_{11}^{BW}, -u_{21}^{BW}, -u_{12}^{BW}, u_{22}^{BW}$					0.159	(0.165)
$u_{11}^{CW}, -u_{12}^{CW}$					0.122	(0.224)
$u_{21}^{CW}, -u_{22}^{CW}$					0.368	(0.206)
$u_{31}^{CW}, -u_{32}^{CW}$					-0.490	

effects (Models 4b and 4d): $L_{2b|4b}^2 = 14.10, df = 3, p < 0.003$ and $L_{2c|4d}^2 = 17.16, df = 3, p < 0.001$.

Table 5.7 reports the parameter estimates for Models 2a, 2b, and 4a. The comparison between the no unobserved heterogeneity model (Model 2a) and the two-class 'independent' unobserved heterogeneity model (Model 2b) with respect to the effects of the observed covariates on the event-specific transition probabilities shows that, as in the previous examples, most effects become slightly stronger by correcting for the unmeasured risk factor. The only exception is the effect of C on the probability of leaving the labor force at t_l. Furthermore, the parameters of Model 2b show that the unobserved risk factors for the two kinds of events are strongly positively related. Both the risk of becoming employed and the risks of leaving the labor force is much higher for the second class than for the first class.

The parameter estimates of the competing-risk model differ a great deal between the 'dependent' two-class model (Model 4a) and Model 2b. The covariate effects on W indicate that persons with $A = 1$ (men) and $C = 3$ (< 27) more often belong to the high-risk class $W = 2$ while persons with $C = 2$ (27-46) more often belong to the low-risk class $W = 1$. As can be expected, this reduces (makes more negative) the effects of $A = 1$ and $C = 3$ on the transition probabilities and increases (makes more positive) the effect of $C = 2$.

As in Example 1, this shows that the results are strongly influenced by the specification that is used for the nature of the unobserved heterogeneity. It should be noted that besides assuming the unobserved heterogeneity to be independent of all the observed covariates or to be dependent on all the observed covariates, there are many other possible specifications. For instance, W could be assumed to depend on age (C) but not on sex (A) and ethnic group (B). Theoretical considerations must determine which of the possible specifications should be preferred.

Example 4: Timing of the first birth with dependent censoring

When discussing the example on first births (Example 1), the censoring mechanism was assumed to be conditionally independent of the process under study. In other words, it was assumed that there are no unobserved risk factors influencing both censoring and the occurrence of an event. Of course, assuming independent censoring is the usual way of performing such an analysis. However, by treating censoring as a competing risk, it is possible to test the independent censoring assumption. That is, we can investigate whether there are common unobserved risk factors for censoring and the occurrence of a first birth.

For this example, the same ORIN data as in the example on first births discussed above is used. For simplicity of exposition, the latent variable is assumed to be independent of the observed covariates. In Example 1, the possibility of relaxing this assumption was discussed. The hazard model is similar to Cox's proportional hazard model in that the covariate effects are assumed to be proportional and the time dependencies of the processes concerned is not restricted. This gives the following log-rate

TABLE 5.8 Test results for the estimated models for the timing of the first birth in which censoring is treated as a competing risk

Model		log-likelihood	# parameters
1.	1 class	-4753.33	65
2.	2 class	-4749.50	68
3.	3 class	-4748.99	71
4.	4 class	-4748.99	74

model:

$$h_d(z|a, b, w) = \frac{m_{abwzd}}{E_{abwz}} = \exp\left(v_d^D + v_{ad}^{AD} + v_{bd}^{BD} + v_{wd}^{WD} + v_{zd}^{ZD}\right).$$

The event is a first birth if $D = 1$ and censoring if $D = 2$. The same identifying restrictions are imposed on the two-variable parameters as in the preceding example.

The test result given in Table 5.8 show that a two-class solution (Model 2) suffices in describing the unobserved heterogeneity in the competing risks, first birth and censoring. Table 5.9 presents the parameter estimates for the model without an unobserved heterogeneity component (Model 1) and the two-class model (Model 2). The opposite sign of the hazard parameters of the latent variable W for first birth and for censoring indicates that there is a (weak) negative dependence between the competing risks, first birth and censoring. Women belonging to the class with a lower risk of having a first child run a bit higher risk of being censored. The parameter estimates for the two-class model are very similar to the ones for Model 2b in Example 1 (see Table 5.2.4), where there was no correction for dependencies between censoring and first birth. Apparently, the weak negative dependence between the occurrence of an event and censoring does not influence the parameter estimates very much. The only difference of some importance is the small increase from 59.7 to 63.0 percent of the size of the class with a lower risk of experiencing a first birth. If the 'event' censoring could be removed, that is, if there were no censored observations, the hazard rate of having a first child would be slightly lower than the one that is currently observed.

5.2.6. Repeatable events and multiple-state processes

The two preceding subsections illustrated the use of the latent variable approach to unobserved heterogeneity in situations in which each

TABLE 5.9 Parameter estimates for two models for the timing of the first birth in which censoring is treated as a competing risk

	Model 1				Model 2			
	first birth $(D=1)$		censoring $(D=2)$		first birth $(D=1)$		censoring $(D=2)$	
log-rate parameters								
v	-2.981	(0.114)	-2.891	(0.581)	-2.492	(0.199)	-3.016	(0.627)
v_1^A	0.555	(0.102)	-0.702	(0.199)	0.872	(0.167)	-0.725	(0.202)
v_2^A	0.302	(0.084)	0.047	(0.114)	0.467	(0.133)	0.031	(0.117)
v_3^A	-0.025	(0.077)	0.288	(0.093)	-0.042	(0.109)	0.285	(0.093)
v_4^A	-0.833		0.368		-1.297		0.410	
v_1^B	0.305	(0.079)	-0.083	(0.109)	0.408	(0.114)	-0.095	(0.111)
v_2^B	-0.083	(0.065)	-0.014	(0.074)	-0.147	(0.093)	-0.005	(0.076)
v_3^B	-0.222		0.097		-0.261		0.010	
v_1^W					-1.065	(0.181)	0.157	(0.251)
v_2^W					1.065		-0.157	
latent proportions								
π_1^W					0.6301			
π_2^W					0.3699			

individual can experience only one event. However, when events are repeatable, the problem of unobserved heterogeneity is even more serious. As demonstrated in section 4.8, in such a case unobserved heterogeneity may not only introduce spurious time dependence and selection bias, but may also lead to a violation of one of the principal assumptions on which the maximum likelihood estimation of the model parameters is based, that is, the assumption that the different events for one individual are independent given the covariates which are included in the hazard model.

Fortunately, it is relatively easy to detect dependencies among different spells for the same observational unit. When events are not repeatable, the detection of omitted variables can be rather sensitive to model assumptions, such as proportionality of covariate effects, parameterization of the time dependence, and specification of the relationships between observed and unobserved covariates. Since in repeatable events situations it is generally plausible to assume that the unobserved risk factors are the same for all events, there is much more information to identify unobserved heterogeneity. More precisely, dependencies among observed survival times can be used to detect common unobserved risk factors. Actually, this is the same principle used in standard latent class models in which the relationships between the indicators are used to identify the latent variables. As with latent class models where the indicators are assumed to be independent of one another given the latent variable(s), here the spell-specific duration distributions are assumed to be independent of one another after controlling for their common unobserved risk factor(s).

Below, the modeling of dependencies among events is illustrated by means of an application to the timing of the first, second, and third birth, and by means of an application to labor market transitions. The former application uses a log-rate model, the latter one a discrete-time logit model.

Example 5: Timing of the first, second, and third birth

Data and model This example extends Example 1 on the timing of the first birth by simultaneously analyzing the occurrence or nonoccurrence of the first, second, and third birth. For this purpose the same ORIN data is used. Although the parity-specific births can be seen as repeatable events, it is implausible to assume that the parameters determining the three different processes are the same. This means that the hazard parameters will almost certainly depend on the number of previous events, which is sometimes also called occurrence dependence (Heckman and Singer, 1985). Rather than seeing birth as a repeatable event, it can be seen as a multiple-state process in which only particular transitions are possible. More precisely, the only transitions which are possible are forward transitions in which no parities are skipped. Such a process in which individuals pass through different stages is sometimes referred to as a staging process (Chiang, 1984: Chapter 12; Willekens, 1990).

A special problem in analyzing repeatable events is the choice of the time axis. In this example, the number of years after turning 18 is used as the time variable for the first birth, while the duration since the previous birth is used as the time variable for the second and third births. Using such different types of time variables is not problematic as long as one does not want to make the time dependency equal across spells. Instead of, or in addition to duration, it would also have been possible to use, for instance, age and calendar time as additional time variables in the transition-specific hazard models. Of course, in a more extended application it would be preferable to perform the analysis using different kinds of time variables. For this illustrative example, however, it is sufficient to include one single type of time variable in the hazard model.

The specification that is used for the covariate part of the model is the same as in Example 1 (see Equation 5.8). Apart from the latent variable W, the models contain two observed covariates: educational level (A) and familism (B). As in Example 1, three different specifications are used for the covariate part of the model, namely: models with an 'independent' latent variable, models in which W depends on A and B, and models in which W is linearly related to A and B.

For the hazard model only the simplest specification is used, that is, a proportional hazard model in which there is a separate duration parameter for each duration category. The log-rate model for the application concerned is given by

$$h^m(z|a, b, w) = \exp\left(v_m^M + v_{am}^{AM} + v_{bm}^{BM} + v_{wm}^{WM} + v_{zm}^{ZM}\right) .$$

As in section 4.8, superscript m of $h^m(z|a, b, w)$ is used to denote a particular spell. The variable indicating the spell number is denoted by M. In this case, $1 \leq m \leq 3$, that is, the first, the second, or the third birth. As can be seen from the specification of the log-linear parameters included in the hazard model, the effects of A (education), B (familism), and W on the hazard rates are assumed to be unequal for the different events.

Results Table 5.10 presents the test results for the models that are estimated. When the latent variable is assumed to be independent of the observed covariates, each additional latent class leads to an increase in the likelihood function (Models 1a-1d). It can be seen that the increase becomes smaller for each next latent class. Again, the fit of the models can be greatly improved by including the unrestricted direct effects of the observed covariates on the latent variable W (Models 2a-2c). But, as in Example 1, these models are very unstable. Many different sets of starting values were needed to obtain the solutions presented here, and many local maxima were encountered. Also in the linearly restricted 'dependent' models, we found several local solutions, but less than in the unrestricted models. In the two-class model (Model 3a), the linear effects of A and B on W are, however, not significant ($L_{1b|3a}^2 = 5.92, df = 2, p > .05$). On the other hand, the fit of the three- and four-class models (Models 3b and 3c) improves by including the linear effects of the observed covariates on the latent variable: $L_{1c|3b}^2 = 13.28, df = 2, p < .002$; and $L_{1d|3c}^2 = 15.98, df = 2, p < .001$.

The parameter estimates for Models 1a, 1b, and 3b are reported in Table 5.11. The parameter estimates for the model without an unobserved

TABLE 5.10 Test results for the estimated models for the timing of the first, second, and third births

Model		log-likelihood	# parameters
independent *W*			
1a.	1 class	-4734.89	73
1b.	2 class	-4726.61	77
1c.	3 class	-4723.75	81
1d.	4 class	-4721.14	85
W related to *A* and *B*			
2a.	2 class	-4719.57	82
2b.	3 class	-4704.88	91
2c.	4 class	-4697.82	100
W linearly related to *A* and *B*			
3a.	2 class	-4723.62	79
3b.	3 class	-4717.11	83
3c.	4 class	-4713.15	87

heterogeneity component (Model 1a) indicate that the effect of educational level is strongest for the first birth and weakest for the second birth. The effect of the familism indicator is strongest for the third birth and weakest for the second birth. Including a two-class 'independent' unobserved heterogeneity component in the model (Model 1b) slightly increases the hazard parameters of the observed covariates for the second and third births. The hazard parameters of the latent variable *W* indicate that the two-class latent variable captures the positive dependence between the second and the third event: Class one has both a lower risk of a second birth and a lower risk of a third birth than class two. The two latent classes do not differ with respect to the hazard rate for the first birth. Seemingly, Model 2b does not capture the unobserved heterogeneity that was encountered in the example on the occurrence or nonoccurrence of the first birth. In Example 1, two latent classes were identified which differed strongly with respect to the risk of the first birth. Although not demonstrated here, the 'independent' three-class solution (Model 2c) detects the unobserved heterogeneity in the first birth. In addition, the hazard parameters for the first birth are similar to the ones of the 'independent' two-class model in Example 1.

The parameter estimates for the 'linearly dependent' three-class model (Model 3b) are rather different from the other two models. The first class consists of women with the lowest risk of a first birth and the highest risk of a second and third birth. Class two has an intermediate risk of a first

TABLE 5.11 Parameter estimates for some models for the timing of the first, second, and third births

	Model 1a		Model 1b		Model 3b	
first birth ($M = 1$)						
v	-2.981	(0.114)	-2.983	(0.115)	-2.205	(0.181)
v_1^A	0.555	(0.102)	0.553	(0.103)	0.111	(0.229)
v_2^A	0.302	(0.084)	0.303	(0.084)	0.179	(0.124)
v_3^A	-0.025	(0.077)	-0.024	(0.077)	0.127	(0.107)
v_4^A	-0.832		-0.832		-0.417	
v_1^B	0.305	(0.079)	0.306	(0.079)	0.511	(0.122)
v_2^B	-0.083	(0.065)	-0.084	(0.065)	-0.087	(0.074)
v_3^B	-0.222		-0.222		-0.425	
v_1^W			0.030	(0.220)	-1.454	(0.381)
v_2^W			-0.030		-0.632	(0.206)
v_3^W					2.086	
second birth ($M = 2$)						
v	-2.075	(0.154)	-1.660	(0.256)	-1.642	(0.199)
v_1^A	-0.091	(0.114)	-0.123	(0.139)	0.112	(0.149)
v_2^A	0.113	(0.092)	0.085	(0.112)	0.275	(0.120)
v_3^A	-0.161	(0.089)	-0.175	(0.107)	-0.195	(0.109)
v_4^A	0.139		0.214		-0.193	
v_1^B	0.166	(0.088)	0.181	(0.115)	0.097	(0.106)
v_2^B	-0.123	(0.073)	-0.115	(0.091)	-0.144	(0.080)
v_3^B	-0.043		-0.066		0.047	
v_1^W			-0.642	(0.165)	0.917	(0.211)
v_2^W			0.642		-0.558	(0.142)
v_3^W					-0.359	
third birth ($M = 3$)						
v	-2.852	(0.174)	-2.905	(0.441)	-2.479	(0.245)
v_1^A	0.173	(0.149)	0.233	(0.213)	0.605	(0.278)
v_2^A	-0.200	(0.135)	-0.216	(0.177)	0.209	(0.259)
v_3^A	-0.287	(0.134)	-0.434	(0.179)	-0.453	(0.207)
v_4^A	0.314		0.417		-0.361	
v_1^B	0.342	(0.124)	0.439	(0.166)	0.244	(0.176)
v_2^B	-0.011	(0.111)	-0.005	(0.142)	-0.026	(0.131)
v_3^B	-0.332		-0.434		-0.218	
v_1^W			-1.001	(0.341)	1.028	(0.394)
v_2^W			1.001		-0.953	(0.252)
v_3^W					-0.075	
latent proportions						
π_1^W			0.547		0.292	
π_2^W			0.453		0.657	
π_3^W					0.051	
linear effects of A and B on W						
β^{AW}					-1.478	(0.441)
β^{BW}					0.733	(0.343)

birth and the lowest risk of a second and third birth. Class three has the highest risk of a first child and an intermediate risk of a second and third child. Thus, women belonging to class one either remain childless or have a large family, women belonging to class two have the highest probability of having only one child, while almost all women belonging to class three have at least one child. The direct effects of A and B on W indicate that there is a strong negative relationship between educational level and W and a strong positive relationship between familism and W, where one has to be aware of the fact that familism is coded from familistic to non-familistic. Familistic highly educated women have the highest probability of belonging to class one, while non-familistic women with a low education have the highest probability of belonging to class three. Comparison of the hazard parameters of Model 3b with the ones of Model 1b shows that the effect of A on rate of first birth becomes weaker, while its effect on the second and third birth becomes both stronger and more consistent in the sense that the educational levels are almost in the 'correct' order. The effect of B on the rate of first birth increases and its effects on the rate of third birth decreases. With respect to the covariate effects on the rate of first birth, it should be noted that the increase of the direct effect of A and the decrease of the direct effect of B partially compensate the strong indirect effects via W.

The example on the timing of the first, second, and third birth showed that a substantial amount of unobserved heterogeneity may be detected using the dependencies among spells. Although the models in which the latent variable was assumed to be related to the observed covariates fitted significantly better than the model with an 'independent' latent variable, there are several problems associated with the former type of model. If the relationships between the observed covariates and the latent variable are not restricted, the models may become unstable. Another problem is that indirect effects of the observed covariates via the latent variable and direct effects of the observed covariates on the hazard rates may compensate one another.

Example 6: Labor market transitions

This example demonstrates how unobserved heterogeneity can be dealt with when analyzing multiple-state data as in the case of labor market transitions. In a particular period of time, individuals may move several times through the states of employed, unemployed, and out of the labor force. As in the preceding examples, the goal is not to build a model that explains as well as possible the processes that are going on in reality, but to demonstrate the flexibility of the latent variable approach to unobserved heterogeneity which was introduced in subsection 5.2.2.

Data and model Example 6 uses the SIPP data which were introduced in Example 3. As in that example, information on a respondent's employment status at six points in time with a mutual distance of three months is selected from the available 1986-1987 SIPP data. For the sake of simplicity, only two different states are distinguished: employed and not employed, where not employed can be either unemployed or out of the labor force. The analysis presented below concerns the transitions between these two states. The observed covariates race, sex, and age that are used in the model for the transition probabilities are the same as in Example 3. The only difference is that now the information on the oldest age group is also used. As a result, there are four age/cohort categories instead of three ($> 66, 47 - 66, 27 - 46, < 27$).

The time dimension that is used in the discrete-time logit model is calendar time. This means that the transition probabilities are assumed not to depend on the duration in a particular state. So, in fact, a discrete-time Markov model is used. When working with this kind of panel data, it is very difficult to allow the transition probabilities to depend on duration. The reason for this is that the observations are left-censored, which means that no information is available on the time of entry into the state occupied at the time of the first interview (see section 4.5). Although the Markov assumption also implies that the transition probabilities depend only on the origin state at the time point concerned, this assumption can easily be relaxed.

Actually, the combined covariate model and discrete-time Markov model used to analyze the SIPP data is a modified path model with a latent mixture variable, sometimes also referred to as a mixed Markov model (Poulsen, 1982; Van de Pol and Langeheine, 1990). The joint distribution of the observed covariates (A, B, and C), the unobserved covariate (W), the initial state (S_0), and the states occupied from $T = 1$ up to $T = 5$ (S_1, S_2, S_3, S_4, and S_5) can be written as

$$\pi_{abcws_0s_1s_2s_3s_4s_5} = \pi_{abc}\,\pi_{w|abc}\,\pi_{s_0|abcw}\prod_{l=1}^{5}\pi_{s_l|abcws_{l-1}}, \qquad [5.11]$$

If $S_l = 1$, an individual is employed at $T = t_l$, and if $S_l = 2$, an individual is not employed at $T = t_l$. Thus, if $S_{l-1} \neq S_l$, $\pi_{s_l|abcws_{l-1}}$ is the probability of experiencing one of the possible transitions at the lth point in time.

It can be seen that in the model represented in Equation 5.11, the latent variable W capturing the unobserved heterogeneity is assumed to intervene between the observed covariates A, B, and C, and the dependent process of interest. In this particular situation, such a specification seems to be the most logical one since it is more plausible that an individual's sex, race, and age influence unobserved factors which are relevant for employment transitions than the other way around. Possible intervening variables which are not included in the model and which, as a result, may introduce unobserved heterogeneity are educational level, human capital, work-related attitudes, and position in the household in which one lives. The most general model that is used for $\pi_{w|abc}$ is

$$\pi_{w|abc} = \frac{\exp\left(u_w^W + u_{aw}^{AW} + u_{bw}^{BW} + u_{cw}^{CW}\right)}{\sum_w \exp\left(u_w^W + u_{aw}^{AW} + u_{bw}^{BW} + u_{cw}^{CW}\right)}. \qquad [5.12]$$

This means that in the 'dependent' unobserved heterogeneity models, only the two-variable interaction terms between W and the observed covariates are included. An 'independent' unobserved heterogeneity model is obtained by fixing the two-variable interactions u_{aw}^{AW}, u_{bw}^{BW}, and u_{cw}^{CW} to zero.

From Equation 5.11, it can be seen that the state that an individual occupies at $T = 0$ is included as one of the variables in the model. This makes it possible to specify a model for the relationship between the unobserved covariate and the initial state. Two specifications are used for the relationship between S_0 and W: models containing the two-variable interaction term $u_{ws_0}^{WS_0}$ and models in which $u_{ws_0}^{WS_0}$ is fixed to zero. The relationships between A, B, C, and S_0 are not restricted.

The model that is used for the transition probabilities is

$$\pi_{s_l|abcws_{l-1}} = \qquad [5.13]$$

$$\frac{\exp\left(v_{s_ls_{l-1}}^{S_lS_{l-1}} + v_{as_ls_{l-1}}^{AS_lS_{l-1}} + v_{bs_ls_{l-1}}^{BS_lS_{l-1}} + v_{cs_ls_{l-1}}^{CS_lS_{l-1}} + v_{ws_ls_{l-1}}^{WS_lS_{l-1}}\right)}{\sum_{s_l} \exp\left(v_{s_ls_{l-1}}^{S_lS_{l-1}} + v_{as_ls_{l-1}}^{AS_lS_{l-1}} + v_{bs_ls_{l-1}}^{BS_lS_{l-1}} + v_{cs_ls_{l-1}}^{CS_lS_{l-1}} + v_{ws_ls_{l-1}}^{WS_lS_{l-1}}\right)},$$

where

$$v_{s_ls_{l-1}}^{S_lS_{l-1}} = v_{as_ls_{l-1}}^{AS_lS_{l-1}} = v_{bs_ls_{l-1}}^{BS_lS_{l-1}} = v_{cs_ls_{l-1}}^{CS_lS_{l-1}} = v_{ws_ls_{l-1}}^{WS_lS_{l-1}} = 0 \text{ if } S_l = S_{l-1}.$$

So, actually, the discrete-time logit model which is used to model the transitions from state S_{l-1} to state S_l is a modified path model with modified path steps of the form given in Equation 5.14. However, as demonstrated in subsection 4.8.4, to obtain the same parameter estimates as in the standard discrete-time logit model, the v parameters cannot be identified by the usual ANOVA-like restrictions, but the v parameters in which $S_l = S_{l-1}$ must be fixed to zero. Within each level of S_{l-1} the stayers are treated as reference category. These identifying restrictions give parameters that can be interpreted as covariate effects on the transition probabilities rather than covariate effects on the probability that $S_l = s_l$. In other words, the model consists of transition-specific main effects and covariate effects for each l.

The discrete-time logit model represented in Equation 5.14 is already a restricted model since it does not contain higher-order interaction terms involving more than one covariate. This does not mean, however, that it is not possible to include these higher-order interaction terms in the model. In addition, more restricted models can be specified on the basis of this one. For instance, a stationary Markov model is obtained by assuming both the main effects and the covariate effects to be equal across time points. Moreover, a proportional model is obtained by assuming the covariate effects to be equal across time points.[11]

Because in the SIPP panel the observation period is the same for all persons, and all the covariates included in the model are categorical, the data can be organized into a contingency table. This makes it possible to test the fit of the estimated models by means of the likelihood-ratio chi-square statistic L^2.

Testing Table 5.12 presents the test results for the models that are estimated using the SIPP data. Models 1a and 1b are without covariate effects. Models 2a-2e contain the effects of the observed covariates and of the unobserved covariate, which is assumed to be independent of both the initial position and the observed covariates. In Models 3a-3g, the unobserved heterogeneity is assumed to be related to the initial position, and in Models 4a-4d, it is assumed to be related to both the initial position and the observed covariates.

The stationarity assumption can be tested by comparing the stationary and nonstationary models without covariates (Models 1a and 1b). The conditional test of Model 1a against Model 1b indicates that, although the nonstationary model fits significantly better than the stationary model

---

[11] Assuming parameters to be equal across time points involves restricting parameters to be equal across modified path steps. Appendix E.3 explains how to estimate models with such restrictions.

TABLE 5.12 Test results for the estimated models for the transitions between employed and not employed

Model		L^2	df	p
no covariates				
1a.	stationary	3390.59	990	0.000
1b.	nonstationary	3349.01	982	0.000
independent W				
2a.	1 class	1919.82	980	0.000
2b.	2 class	1198.27	977	0.000
2c.	3 class	1116.78	974	0.001
2d.	4 class	1101.91	971	0.002
2e.	5 class	1077.53	968	0.008
W related to S_0				
3a.	2 stayer + 1 mover	1573.99	978	0.000
3b.	2 stayer + 2 mover	1098.98	974	0.003
3c.	2 stayer + 3 mover	963.86	970	0.550
3d.	2 stayer + 4 mover	945.33	966	0.677
3e.	2 class	1183.44	976	0.000
3f.	3 class	964.59	972	0.561
3g.	4 class	945.54	968	0.691
W related to S_0, A, B and C				
4a.	2 class	1064.04	971	0.019
4b.	3 class	851.85	962	0.996
4c.	4 class	795.82	953	1.000
4d.	2*2 class	876.56	963	0.978

($L^2_{1a|1b} = 41.58$, $df = 8$, $p < .001$), the fit does not improve very much by assuming nonstationarity, especially if one compares it with the improvement of the fit that occurs by including the effects of the observed covariates on the two transition probabilities in the stationary model (Model 2a). The conditional test between Models 1a and 2a shows that the L^2 value falls from 3390.58 to 1919.82 using only 10 degrees of freedom. Therefore, for the sake of simplicity, in all the other models the Markov process is assumed to be stationary.

The test results for the 'independent' unobserved heterogeneity models (Models 2b-2e) show that there is a large improvement of L^2 when a latent covariate is included. Compared to 2a, the two-class model has an L^2 value more than 700 points lower using only three additional parameters. Also, the third class captures a substantial amount of unobserved heterogeneity. Even after including a fifth class (Model 2e) the L^2 value goes down. Apparently, there is a substantial amount of unobserved heterogeneity in the data.

It seems implausible to assume that the unobserved risk factors influence the transition probabilities, or equivalently, the states occupied from $T = t_1$ to $T = t_5$, but not the state occupied at $T = t_0$. Therefore, a direct effect of W on S_0 is included in the model (Models 3a-3g). Including such an effect makes it possible to specify a mover-stayer structure as proposed by Wrigley (1990), that is, a model with one class of stayers for every origin state. Models 3a-3d are models with two classes of stayers, one for the state employed and one for the state not employed, while Models 3e-3g are unrestricted. As in the example on the transition out of the state of unemployment (Example 3), the mover-stayer models become almost equal to the non-restricted models if the number of classes increases. This is caused by the fact that the latent proportions in the classes of stayers become rather small very quickly. In this example, the unrestricted three-class model (Model 3e) fits as well as the model with two classes of stayers and three classes of movers (Model 3c), and the four-class model (Model 3f) fits as well as the model with two classes of stayers and four classes of movers (Model 3d). It has to be concluded that in this particular situation the mover-stayer structure does not function very well.

Comparison of Model 3e with Model 2b shows that the fit of the two-class model does not improve as much as one would expect by including a direct effect of W on S_0 ($L^2_{2b|3e} = 14.83$, $df = 1$, $p < .001$). On the other hand, the three- and four-class models improve a great deal. This can be seen by comparing Model 3f with Model 2c ($L^2_{2c|3f} = 152.19$, $df = 2$, $p = .000$) and Model 3g with Model 2d ($L^2_{2d|3g} = 156.38$, $df = 3$, $p = .000$).

As in the previous examples, it is possible to relax the assumption that the unobserved heterogeneity is independent of the observed heterogeneity. This can be accomplished by including direct effects of the observed covariates on the latent variable in models as described in Equation 5.12.[12] The test results of Models 4a-4c compared with those of Models 3e-3g indicate that inclusion of the two-variable interactions u^{AW}_{aw}, u^{BW}_{bw}, and u^{CW}_{cw} greatly improves the fit, irrespective of the number of latent classes: $L^2_{3e|4a} = 119.40$, $df = 5$, $p = .000$; $L^2_{3f|4b} =$

---

[12] It should note that, like in the previous examples of 'dependent' unobserved heterogeneity models, several local solutions were found when estimating Models 4a-4d. This means that when using these types of models one must try out several sets of random starting values.

112.74, $df = 10$, $p = .000$; and $L^2_{3g|4c} = 149.72$, $df = 15$, $p = .000$. Here, the linear-by-linear model is not used because two covariates are dichotomous and the third covariate, age, cannot be expected to have a linear effect on W.

The models presented so far contained one latent variable influencing both the transition from employed to not employed and the transition from not employed to employed. So, in fact, it was assumed that the unobserved risk factors are the same for both transitions. Whether the unobserved factors which influence the two transition probabilities are the same or not can be tested by using a specification with two latent variables, each of which is assumed to influence one of the two transitions. Model 4d contains two related dichotomous latent variables, one influencing the transition from employed to not employed and one influencing the transition from not employed to employed. Although the fit of Model 4d is better than the two-class model with only one latent variable (Model 4a), it is worse than that of Model 4b, which has almost the same number of parameters as Model 4d. So, assuming origin state-specific latent variables does not lead to a simpler and better fitting model.

Parameters Table 5.13 reports the parameter estimates for Model 2a and for three variants of the well-performing three-class model (Models 2c, 3f, and 4b). In the model without unobserved heterogeneity (Model 2a), females, blacks, and persons belonging to the oldest and the youngest age groups have the highest risk of experiencing a transition from employed to not employed. On the other hand, males, non-blacks, and persons belonging to the two youngest age groups have the highest risk of moving from not employed to employed.

In Model 2c, most parameter estimates are somewhat more extreme than those in Model 2a. This is the same result as in the other examples with an 'independent' latent variable. The effects of the latent variable on the transition probabilities indicate that the largest class, containing 61 percent of the population, consists of persons with a low risk of becoming not employed and a low risk of finding a job after becoming not employed. Actually, it is a class of stayers in either the position employed or the position not employed. The first class, with a latent proportion of 29 percent, consists of persons with a high risk of becoming not employed and a moderate risk of becoming employed. And finally, the smallest class is a class of frequent movers, that is, persons that have both a high risk of becoming not employed and a high risk of finding a job.

TABLE 5.13 Parameter estimates for some models for the transitions between employed and not employed

	Model 2a		Model 2c		Model 3f		Model 4b	
employed to not employed ($S_{l-1} = 1$ and $S_l = 2$)								
v	-2.232	(0.064)	-3.458	(0.166)	-1.830	(0.132)	-1.335	(0.201)
$v_1^A, -v_2^A$	-0.139	(0.033)	-0.185	(0.047)	-0.243	(0.051)	-0.104	(0.096)
$v_1^B, -v_2^B$	-0.202	(0.054)	-0.198	(0.079)	-0.298	(0.082)	-0.365	(0.148)
v_1^C	0.435	(0.131)	0.221	(0.171)	0.663	(0.171)	0.687	(0.332)
v_2^C	-0.330	(0.071)	-0.281	(0.097)	-0.144	(0.102)	-0.644	(0.221)
v_3^C	-0.653	(0.064)	-0.656	(0.087)	-0.943	(0.096)	-0.588	(0.173)
v_4^C	0.548		0.716		0.424		0.545	
v_1^W			2.520	(0.227)	2.027	(0.102)	1.157	(0.139)
v_2^W			1.885	(——)	-0.052	(0.134)	0.819	(0.220)
v_3^W			-4.405		-1.975		-1.976	
not employed to employed ($S_{l-1} = 2$ and $S_l = 1$)								
v	-2.546	(0.073)	-2.076	(0.158)	-2.394	(0.135)	-1.728	(0.209)
$v_1^A, -v_2^A$	0.266	(0.036)	0.219	(0.054)	0.304	(0.057)	-0.037	(0.083)
$v_1^B, -v_2^B$	0.274	(0.056)	0.324	(0.083)	0.333	(0.091)	0.616	(0.111)
v_1^C	-2.339	(0.151)	-3.394	(0.282)	-3.645	(0.250)	-1.510	(0.432)
v_2^C	-0.217	(0.082)	-0.190	(0.150)	-0.365	(0.141)	0.111	(0.243)
v_3^C	1.120	(0.072)	1.626	(0.132)	1.798	(0.139)	1.625	(0.201)
v_4^C	1.436		1.958		2.212		-0.226	
v_1^W			-0.500	(0.134)	-0.479	(0.121)	0.680	(0.155)
v_2^W			3.043	(0.274)	2.798	(0.216)	-2.989	(0.158)
v_3^W			-2.543		-2.319		2.309	
latent proportions								
π_1^W			0.292		0.188		0.140	
π_2^W			0.100		0.217		0.334	
π_3^W			0.608		0.596		0.525	

(to be continued)

In Model 3f, the latent variable was allowed not only to influence the transition probabilities but also the initial position; in other words, W was allowed to have an indirect effect on the states occupied after $T = t_0$ via the value of S_0. As can be seen, this slightly increases the effects of the observed covariates on the transition probabilities. The effect of W on the initial position indicates that persons belonging to the first class have a relatively high probability of starting in the position

TABLE 5.13 (*Continued*)

	Model 2a	Model 2c	Model 3f	Model 4b	
effects of observed covariates on W					
$u_{11}^{AW}, -u_{21}^{AW}$				0.243	(0.059)
$u_{12}^{AW}, -u_{22}^{AW}$				-0.463	(0.048)
$u_{13}^{AW}, -u_{23}^{AW}$				0.220	
$u_{11}^{BW}, -u_{21}^{BW}$				-0.198	(0.095)
$u_{12}^{BW}, -u_{22}^{BW}$				0.126	(0.075)
$u_{13}^{BW}, -u_{23}^{BW}$				0.073	
u_{11}^{CW}				$-\infty$	(0.479)
u_{12}^{CW}				1.298	(0.242)
u_{13}^{CW}				-1.298	
u_{21}^{CW}				-0.477	(0.241)
u_{22}^{CW}				0.305	(0.130)
u_{23}^{CW}				0.172	
u_{31}^{CW}				-0.503	(0.115)
u_{32}^{CW}				-0.253	(——)
u_{33}^{CW}				0.756	
u_{41}^{CW}				0.879	
u_{42}^{CW}				-1.300	
u_{43}^{CW}				0.420	
effect of W on initial position (S_0)					
$u_{11}^{WS_0}, -u_{12}^{WS_0}$		-0.737	(0.063)	-0.308	(0.074)
$u_{21}^{WS_0}, -u_{22}^{WS_0}$		0.607	(0.069)	-1.027	(0.093)
$u_{31}^{WS_0}, -u_{32}^{WS_0}$		0.130		1.334	

not employed, while persons belonging to the second class have a relatively high probability of starting in the position employed. Apparently, these unequal initial positions of persons belonging to the different latent classes have two consequences. First, the latent distribution changes considerably, and second, the effect of the latent variable becomes less strong. The first class now has a much higher risk of becoming not employed than the other two groups, and although the risk of becoming not employed for the third class is not so low any more as in Model 2a, it is still much lower than for the other two classes. The effect of W on the transition from employed to not employed does not change very much.

The parameter estimates for Model 4b indicate that including direct effects of the observed covariates on the latent variable W has the strongest impact on the covariate effects on the transition from not employed to employed. If we look at the log-linear parameters indicating the covariate effects on W, we can see that women ($A = 2$) belong more often to class two than men ($A = 1$). This class has a low probability of finding a job and a high probability of becoming not employed. The inclusion of this indirect effect of sex on the transition probabilities leads to a decrease of the negative effect of sex on the transition from employed to not employed and a disappearance of the positive effect of sex on the transition from employed to not employed. The effect of B on W indicates that blacks ($B = 2$) belong more often to class one that non-blacks ($B = 1$). This class has the highest risk of becoming not employed and an intermediate risk of becoming employed. The increased positive effect of B on the probability of becoming employed indicates that the indirect effect of B via W overestimates the probability of finding a job for blacks. The effect of age (C) on W shows that the oldest age group ($C = 1$) never belongs to class one. Most of them belong to $W = 2$. Also the largest proportion of individuals in the second age group belong to class two. The third age group is overrepresented in class three, while most people of the youngest age belong to either class one or three. If we look at the effect of C on the probability of getting employed, we can see that especially the parameter estimate for $C = 4$ changes dramatically. The fact that the strong positive effect of $C = 4$ disappears is caused by the fact that the youngest age group belongs to either classes one or three, which have the highest probability of getting employed. Moreover, the negative effect for $C = 1$ decreases because the oldest age group has the highest probability of belonging to the low-risk class two. With respect to the effect of C on the probability of becoming not employed, it can be seen that the parameter estimates for the low-risk groups $C = 2$ and $C = 3$ become almost equal to one another.

This example demonstrates the importance of correcting for unobserved heterogeneity when analyzing multiple-state data. The 'independent' unobserved heterogeneity models detected a substantial amount of interdependence between the different spells of one individual. In addition, it was shown that the latent variable approach which is proposed here is very flexible: Several specifications can be used for the latent variable capturing unobserved heterogeneity. Besides the standard 'independent' unobserved heterogeneity specification, the latent variable capturing the unobserved heterogeneity may be related to both the observed covariates and the initial position. Moreover, models with several mutually related latent variables can be specified. It was also shown that the results may be strongly influenced by the specification which is chosen. This illustrates that substantive arguments must guide the choice of model specification.

5.2.7. Dependent or clustered observations

As demonstrated in section 4.8, not only models for repeatable events and multiple-state processes, but also models for dependent or clustered observations belong to the family of multivariate hazard models. Clustered survival data occurs in many situations. Instances of clustered data are observations of members of the same household, observations of spouses or brothers, observations of different parts of the body of one individual or animal in medical trials, observations of different parts of a machine, etc. Repeatable events can also be seen as a specific form of clustered observations since, in that case, there are several observations of the same individual too. Like repeatable events, clustered survival times can generally not be treated as independent observations, even after controlling for the observed covariates which are included in the hazard model. The reason for this is that there will be unobserved heterogeneity which the observations belonging to the same cluster have in common.

This subsection demonstrates how to use the general latent variables approach to unobserved heterogeneity when analyzing bivariate survival data. For this purpose, Example 2 (on dropping out of school) is extended: the respondents' school careers as well as the school careers of their brothers are analyzed. Although the example concerns a situation in which each cluster consists of exactly two observations, the approach used here can also be applied when clusters contain more than two observations, possibly with clusters of unequal sizes.

Example 7: School transitions of brothers

Data and model The example of respondents' school careers (Example 2) is extended by analyzing simultaneously the school histories of respondents and their brothers. As mentioned above, Mare (1994) used the data on the schooling of brothers to demonstrate how to use a latent class approach to detect dependencies between survival times when observations are dependent or clustered. The model proposed by Mare is a special case of the hazard model with unobserved heterogeneity which was presented in subsection 5.2.2. Mare specified a bivariate discrete-time logit model with a dichotomous 'independent' latent variable which was assumed to have a proportional and equal effect on respondents' and their oldest brothers' probabilities of dropping out of school.[13]

Here, part of Mare's analysis is repeated, but also several types of extensions are presented which lead to models fitting much better than the latent class models presented by Mare. In addition, it is demonstrated that the discrete-time event history model proposed by Mare can be specified in a much easier and efficient way when it is treated as a modified path model with latent variables.

Apart from the observed covariate father's education denoted by A, the bivariate discrete-time logit model contains two latent variables W and Y denoting the unobserved respondent's (W) and brother's (Y) factors influencing the risk of dropping out of school, where W and Y are assumed to be associated with each other. As in the previous examples, the unobserved variables are assumed to be intervening variables. This implies that, in the covariate part of the model, a model has to be specified for $\pi_{wy|a}$. The most general model that is used for $\pi_{wy|a}$ is

$$\pi_{wy|a} = \frac{\exp\left(u_w^W + u_y^Y + u_{aw}^{AW} + u_{ay}^{AY} + u_{wy}^{WY}\right)}{\sum_{wy} \exp\left(u_w^W + u_y^Y + u_{aw}^{AW} + u_{ay}^{AY} + u_{wy}^{WY}\right)}. \qquad [5.14]$$

It can be seen that the three-variable interaction term u_{awy}^{AWY} is assumed to be zero.

Several kinds of specifications can be obtained by restricting the two-variable interactions appearing in the model described in Equation 5.14. The latent variables can either be assumed to be independent of or dependent on A. When they are independent of A, all u_{aw}^{AW} and u_{ay}^{AY} parameters must be fixed to zero. Dependence of W and Y on A is modeled by means of linear-by-linear interaction terms. This specification is used because it forces the effects of the ordinal variable father's education on the intervening unobserved factors to have systematic patterns.

In the discussion below, the relationship between W and Y is modeled in several ways. The simplest one is to assume all nondiagonal elements of the conditional distribution of WY given A to be empty,

$$\pi_{wy|a} = 0 \quad \text{if } w \neq y, \qquad [5.15]$$

---

[13] Information is available on the school careers of respondents and their oldest brothers. It should be noted that a respondent's oldest brother is not necessarily older than the respondent.

that is, to assume all u_{wy}^{WY} terms in which $w \neq y$ to be equal to $-\infty$. This boils down to assuming that the unobserved factors influencing the risk of dropping out of school are the same for respondents and brothers. In other words, W and Y are actually identical, and it is more efficient then to use only one latent variable instead of two.

Other possible specifications of the conditional distribution of W and Y given A are symmetry and quasi-symmetry. A symmetry model is obtained by restricting

$$u_{wy}^{WY} = u_{yw}^{WY} \text{ and } u_w^W = u_y^Y, \qquad [5.16]$$

and quasi-symmetry by

$$u_{wy}^{WY} = u_{yw}^{WY}. \qquad [5.17]$$

The likelihood-ratio test of the symmetry model against the quasi-symmetry model can be used to test the assumption of marginal homogeneity of W and Y (Bishop, Fienberg and Holland, 1975: Chapter 8; Hagenaars, 1986, 1990:156-162). Thus, it is not only possible to test the strong assumption that W and Y are identical, it is also possible to test the weaker assumption that W and Y have the same marginal distribution.

The event history part of the model consists of separate discrete-time logit models for oldest brothers and respondents,

$$\lambda^1(t_l|a, w) = \frac{\exp\left(v_1^M + v_{l1}^{LM} + v_{a1}^{AM} + v_{y1}^{YM} + v_{al1}^{ALM} + v_{yl1}^{YLM}\right)}{1 + \exp\left(v_1^M + v_{l1}^{LM} + v_{a1}^{AM} + v_{y1}^{YM} + v_{al1}^{ALM} + v_{yl1}^{YLM}\right)}, \qquad [5.18]$$

$$\lambda^2(t_l|a, y) = \frac{\exp\left(v_2^M + v_{l2}^{LM} + v_{a2}^{AM} + v_{w2}^{WM} + v_{al2}^{ALM} + v_{wl2}^{WLM}\right)}{1 + \exp\left(v_2^M + v_{l2}^{LM} + v_{a2}^{AM} + v_{w2}^{WM} + v_{al2}^{ALM} + v_{wl2}^{WLM}\right)}. \qquad [5.19]$$

Here, $\lambda^1(t_l|a, w)$ is the brother's probability of dropping out of school at the lth point in time, while $\lambda^2(t_l|a, w)$ is the same probability for the respondent. To distinguish the parameters of the two discrete-time logit models a variable M is introduced, taking value 1 for the oldest brother and value 2 for the respondent. Variable A denotes the father's education, W and Y are the latent covariates, and L is the discrete time interval.

Equality restrictions can be imposed on the parameters across the two models represented in Equations 5.18 and 5.19. For simplicity of exposition, the models that are presented here differ only from each other with respect to the specification of the effects of W and Y. The specification of the duration effects and the effects of father's schooling is based on Mare's best fitting model. This means that the duration effects are not restricted and that the effects of father's schooling are assumed to be nonproportional, but equal for respondents and brothers. In other words, the restrictions that

$$v_{a1}^{AM} = v_{a2}^{AM} \quad \text{and} \quad v_{al1}^{ALM} = v_{al2}^{ALM} \qquad [5.20]$$

are imposed.

Mare (1994) estimated the bivariate discrete-time logit model with Haberman's NEWTON program (Haberman, 1988), which is a program for estimating latent class models and other kinds of log-linear models with latent variables. It can be demonstrated that the model formulated in Equations 5.14, 5.18, and 5.19 is similar to a latent class model or, more precisely, to a latent class model with direct effects between indicators. When a specification is used in which W is identical to Y (see Equation 5.15), using the modified path notation introduced in sections 2.9 and 3.1, the probability density function of the above bivariate survival model can also be written as

$$\pi_{aws_{11}s_{12}s_{21}s_{22}} = \pi_a \pi_{w|a} \pi_{s_{11}|aw} \pi_{s_{12}|aws_{11}} \pi_{s_{21}|aw} \pi_{s_{22}|aws_{21}}. \qquad [5.21]$$

Here, S_{11}, S_{12}, S_{21}, and S_{22} denote the states occupied by the brother (S_{11}, S_{12}) and the respondent (S_{21}, S_{22}) at the two points in time. It will be clear that the model represented in Equation 5.21 is a modified path model with a latent variable. As a result, it must be estimated in the same way as the modified path models described in section 3.1.

It can be seen that, in fact, the variables S_{11}, S_{12}, S_{21}, and S_{22} serve as indicators for the latent variable W. The model differs from an ordinary latent class model in that the states occupied at the second point in time depend on the states occupied at the first point in time. In this sense the model is similar to a latent class model with direct effects between indicators as proposed by Hagenaars (1988). Here, these direct effects are, however, fixed a priori by means of structural zero probabilities, or equivalently, by log-linear parameters fixed to be equal to $-\infty$, because the state dropped out is an absorbing state: If someone drops out at the first point in time, the probability of being a dropout at the second point in time is one. Another difference between the model described in Equation 5.21 and a standard latent class model is the presence of an external variable (A) that is assumed to be related to the indicators.

Because Mare (1994) used the NEWTON program to estimate the bivariate logit model, he specified it in a different way. Although Winship and Mare (1989) showed that it is possible to specify modified path models by means of NEWTON, normally the model parameters are estimated in the complete table, that is, in the table containing all variables. For a standard latent class model, this is not a problem. Because of the assumed local independence among indicators, it does not matter whether the parameters are estimated in the separate marginal tables containing an indicator and the corresponding latent variable or in the complete table. This results from the collapsibility theorem (Bishop, Fienberg, and Holland, 1975:47-48). However, in this example it does matter whether W is specified to be independent of A in the marginal table AW or in the complete table. This results from the fact that both A and W are supposed to have a direct effect on S_{11}, S_{12}, S_{21}, and S_{22}. By specifying W to be independent of A in the table including S_{11}, S_{12}, S_{21}, and S_{22}, Mare (1994) made the latent covariate conditionally independent of A, that is, given the values of S_{11}, S_{12}, S_{21}, and S_{22}. Such a specification is not in agreement with the usual way of specifying unobserved heterogeneity and, moreover, it is a bit strange since normally it makes no sense to set conditions on something that is posterior. As will be demonstrated below, Mare's specification may yield estimates which differ a great deal from the ones obtained with the specification described in Equation 5.21.

Testing Table 5.14 gives the test results for the models that are estimated with the brothers' schooling data. Model 1, which is used as a reference model, does not contain unobserved heterogeneity. The model for the risk of dropping out is of the form given in Equations 5.18 and 5.19, with the restriction described in Equation 5.20. In other words, the effect of fathers' schooling on the dropout probability for respondents and their oldest brothers is assumed to be nonproportional and equal for respondents and their brothers. Model 1 fits very badly ($L^2 = 4381.64$, $df = 28$, $p = .000$). Apparently, the assumption of conditional independence between brothers' and respondents' schooling must be rejected. Note that here it is possible to test explicitly the conditional independence assumption by means of the likelihood-ratio chi-square. However, when using continuous-time models, such a test does not exist. This is perhaps the reason why most researchers use event history models without being concerned about possible dependencies among observations.

TABLE 5.14 Test results for the estimated models for respondents' and oldest brothers' dropping out of school

Model		L^2	df	p
1.	1 class	4381.64	28	0.000
2.	2 class	689.26	26	0.000
3a.	3 class	256.07	24	0.000
3b.	3 class with linear effect of W	257.61	25	0.000
4a.	4 class	186.76	22	0.000
4b.	4 class with linear effect of W	199.22	23	0.000
5a.	Model 3b + linear AW	132.20	24	0.000
5b.	Model 3b + unequal effects of W	214.47	24	0.000
5c.	Model 3b + nonproportional effects of W	244.13	24	0.000
6a.	2*3 class unrestricted WY	163.45	19	0.000
6b.	2*3 class symmetric WY	234.55	22	0.000
6c.	2*3 class quasi-symmetric WY	164.94	20	0.000
7a.	Model 6c + linear AW and AY	26.73	18	0.083
7b.	Model 6c + linear $AW = AY$	28.84	19	0.069
7c.	Model 6c + unequal effects of W and Y	155.18	19	0.000
7d.	Model 6c + nonproportional effects of W and Y	159.75	19	0.000
8.	Model 7d - effect of A + unrestricted $AW = AY$	50.26	19	0.000

The next set of models contains one latent variable to be denoted by W. As mentioned above, this is equivalent to assuming that the association between W and Y is perfect (see restriction 5.15). For the moment, the effects of the latent variable in the discrete-time logit model are assumed to be equal for respondents and brothers and proportional, that is, $v_{w1}^{WM} = v_{w2}^{WM}$ and $v_{wl1}^{WLM} = v_{wl2}^{WLM} = 0$, and W is assumed to be independent of A.

As can be seen from Table 5.14, including a two-class latent covariate in the bivariate logit model (Model 2) improves the fit a great deal compared to Model 1 ($L^2 = 689.26$) with only two additional parameters: a latent class proportion and the effect of W on the transition probabilities. A two-class model of this form is the most extended model with unobserved heterogeneity presented by Mare (1994). But, as mentioned above, an important difference with the approach presented here is that Mare estimated the model parameters in the complete table, which gives an L^2 value of 877.65 instead of 689.26.

By including a third latent class (Model 3a), the fit improves again a great deal ($L^2 = 256.07$). Even including a fourth class in the model (Model 4a) improves the fit considerably ($L^2 = 186.76$), especially if one realizes that only two additional parameters are used for each additional latent class. To test whether the latent variable has a linear effect on the transition probability, in Models 3b and 4b, the effects of W are restricted to be linear. The fit of the three-class model does not deteriorate by this additional restriction ($L^2_{3b|3a} = 1.52, df = 1, p > .21$). Although in the four-class model the linear restriction leads to a significantly worse model, the increase in L^2 is moderate ($L^2_{4b|4a} = 12.54, df = 2, p < .002$), especially if the huge sample size of 18,563 cases is taken into account.

Because the gain of incorporating a fourth class is relatively small compared to the gain of incorporating a second and third class, an effort can be made to improve the well-performing three-class model (Model 3b) by relaxing one by one the underlying assumptions of this model with regard to the nature of the unobserved heterogeneity. These assumptions are: an equal effect of W on the probability of dropping out for the respondent and his brother, proportionality of the effect of W, W independent of A, and identical unobserved risk factors for the respondent and his oldest brother. The first three assumptions can be relaxed using models with only one latent variable W (Models 5a-5c). To relax the other assumption, it is necessary to specify models with two latent variables W and Y (Models 6a-6c).

Inclusion of a linear direct effect of A on W in the model (Model 5a) greatly improves the fit of the model compared to Model 3b ($L^2_{3b|5a} = 125.41, df = 1, p = .000$). Also, relaxing only the assumption that the effect of W is equal for respondents and brothers (Model 5b) leads to a considerably better fit ($L^2_{3b|5b} = 43.14, df = 1, p = .000$). Although the improvement is relatively less important, allowing the effect of W to be nonproportional (Model 5c) leads to a significantly better fitting model as well ($L^2_{3b|5c} = 13.48, df = 1, p = .000$). So, all three assumptions concerned seem to be violated.

To check whether the unobserved risk factors are the same for respondents and their brothers, a model is specified with two latent variables denoted by W and Y (Model 6a). As mentioned above, W is assumed to capture the respondent's unobserved factors and Y the brother's unobserved factors. Actually, compared to Model 3b, only the restrictions described in Equation 5.15 are relaxed. Because these restrictions involve fixing parameters to their boundary values, it is not possible to test Model 3b against Model 6a by means of a likelihood-ratio test. Nevertheless, the large difference in L^2 between Model 6a and Model 3b – 94.14 using six additional parameters – indicates that the assumption that the unobserved risk factors for the respondent and the brother are exactly the same, is too strong.

Besides the unrestricted specification of the relationship between W and Y which is used in Model 6a, more restricted specifications can be used. In Model 6b, the relationship between W and Y is assumed to be symmetric, and in Model 6c, it is specified to be quasi-symmetric. The restrictions to obtain these two models are described in Equations 5.16 and 5.17, respectively. The conditional test of the quasi-symmetry model (Model 6c) against Model 6a demonstrates that the relationship between W and Y can be described very well by a quasi-symmetry model ($L^2_{6c|6a} = 1.49, df = 1, p > .22$). On the other hand, the symmetry model (Model 6b) performs very badly compared to Model 6a ($L^2_{6b|6a} = 71.10, df = 3, p = .000$). The test of the symmetry model against the quasi-symmetry model provides us with the well-known conditional test for marginal homogeneity (Bishop, Fienberg and Holland, 1975: Chapter 8; Hagenaars, 1990:156-162). This test leads to a significant result as well ($L^2_{6b|6c} = 69.61, df = 2, p = .000$). Thus, the conclusion can be that respondents and their oldest brothers do not have exactly the same unobserved factors and that, moreover, W and Y have different marginal distributions.

By means of Models 5a-6c it was tested whether the fit of Model 3b could be improved by relaxing one by one the underlying assumptions of this model with regard to the nature of the unobserved heterogeneity. The next set of models (Models 7a-7d) investigate the effect of relaxing these assumptions simultaneously. The starting-point is Model 6c: the model with a quasi-symmetric relation between W and Y, with equal, linear, and proportional effects of W and Y on the transition probabilities, and without direct effects of A on W and Y.

Including a direct linear effect of A on W and Y (Model 7a), greatly improves the fit of Model 6c ($L^2_{6c|7a} = 138.21, df = 2, p = .000$). If the relationships AW and AY are assumed to be equal (Model 7b), the fit does not deteriorate at all ($L^2_{7b|7a} = 2.11, df = 1, p > .14$). Allowing for unequal effects of W and Y (Model 7c) and nonproportional effects of W and Y on the transition probabilities (Model 7d) leads to better fitting models as well ($L^2_{6c|7c} = 9.76, df = 1, p < .002$; and $L^2_{6c|7d} = 5.19, df = 1, p < .03$). The improvement of the fit is, however, not so spectacular as with Models 7a and 7b.

Thus, as the final model could serve the very well-fitting Model 7b ($L^2 = 28.84, df = 19, p > .06$). This model contains a quasi-symmetric relationship between W and Y and equal and linear effects of A on W and Y. Model 7b is a parsimonious model that can be interpreted easily: The schooling histories of respondents and their brothers are conditionally independent of one another given their fathers' educational level and the person-specific unobserved risk factors. These unobserved factors have equal, linear, and proportional effects on the logit of probability of dropping out for respondents and their oldest brothers. Moreover, the unobserved factors W and Y are associated, and are equally and linearly influenced by the fathers' schooling.

But, as will be demonstrated below, Model 7b yields are rather strange effects of fathers' education on the probability of dropping out. To illustrate that the specification of the nature of the unobserved heterogeneity used in Model 7b is just one of the possible specifications leading to a well-fitting model, another quite different specification is used in Model 8. Because the strange parameters obtained from Model 7b are probably the result of the assumed linearity of the relationship between A and Y, and between A and W, this assumption is relaxed in Model 8. However, because of the bad experience with models with both unrestricted indirect effects and unrestricted direct effects of observed covariates of the transition probabilities (see Example 1), the direct effect of A on the transition probabilities is excluded from Model 8. To compensate for the nonproportionality of the effect of A that was found in the other models, the effects of Y and W are allowed to be nonproportional. So, Model 8 is a model without a direct effect of A on the respondent's and brother's probability of dropping out, with unrestricted but equal AW and AY interaction terms, and with equal and linear but nonproportional effects of W and Y. Although its fit is not as good as for Model 7b, Model 8 performs rather well ($L^2 = 50.26$, $df = 19$, $p = .000$), especially if the huge sample size (18,563) is taken into account. As will be shown below, the parameter estimates for Model 8 can be easily interpreted.

Parameters Table 5.15 reports the parameter estimates for Model 1 and for four different three-class models. It must be noted that, to be able to compare directly the mean of the logit of the transition probability for brothers and respondents at the two points in time, the main effect v_m^M is absorbed in v_{lm}^{LM}. As can be seen from the v_{lm}^{LM} parameters of Model 1, at both school levels the risk of dropping out is somewhat lower for respondents ($M = 2$) than for their oldest brothers ($M = 1$). Furthermore, as could be expected, the effect of fathers' schooling shows a monotonic pattern at both points in time. The nonproportionality of the effect of A results from the fact that the differences between the transition probabilities of adjacent categories of A change strongly between $T = t_1$ and $T = t_2$: The distances between the first three categories of A are much smaller at the second school level, while the distance between the third and fourth categories of A are much larger at the second school level.

TABLE 5.15 Parameter estimates for some models for respondents' and oldest brothers' dropping out of school

	Model 1		Model 3b		Model 6c		Model 7b		Model 8	
discrete-time logit parameters										
v_{11}^{LM}	-1.338	(0.030)	-2.841	(0.054)	-2.906	(0.076)	-9.291	(2.895)	-8.977	(0.248))
v_{21}^{LM}	-0.142	(0.025)	-0.596	(0.054)	-0.086	(0.132)	11.814	(0.263)	1.809	(0.270))
v_{12}^{LM}	-1.543	(0.030)	-3.171	(0.057)	-3.035	(0.076)	-2.284	(0.763)	-1.620	(0.228)
v_{22}^{LM}	-0.256	(0.024)	-0.805	(0.053)	0.101	(0.125)	11.600	(0.238)	2.633	(1.196)
v_{11}^{AL}	1.486	(0.029)	2.224	(0.048)	2.547	(0.076)	1.148	(0.724)		
v_{21}^{AL}	0.942	(0.035)	1.359	(0.059)	1.395	(0.093)	1.555	(0.709)		
v_{31}^{AL}	-0.424	(0.042)	-0.771	(0.057)	-0.868	(0.069)	-3.611	(2.828)		
v_{41}^{AL}	-0.662	(0.068)	-1.021	(0.091)	-1.127	(0.097)	0.185	(0.777)		
v_{51}^{AL}	-1.342		-1.791		-1.947		0.723			
v_{12}^{AL}	0.945	(0.025)	1.872	(0.047)	2.706	(0.090)	0.715	(0.071)		
v_{22}^{AL}	0.797	(0.034)	1.523	(0.056)	1.975	(0.111)	1.036	(0.125)		
v_{32}^{AL}	0.215	(0.030)	0.199	(0.055)	0.089	(0.070)	0.153	(0.086)		
v_{42}^{AL}	-0.615	(0.049)	-1.148	(0.110)	-1.572	(0.149)	-0.464	(0.103)		
v_{52}^{AL}	-1.342		-2.446		-3.198		-1.440			
β^{W}, β^{Y}			3.079	(0.059)	3.253	(0.096)	13.073	(——)		
$\beta_{1}^{WL}, \beta_{1}^{YL}$									11.464	(——)
$\beta_{2}^{WL}, \beta_{2}^{YL}$									5.544	(0.832)
latent proportions										
π_{11}^{WY}			0.079		0.178		0.279		0.151	
π_{12}^{WY}					0.053		0.027		0.073	
π_{13}^{WY}					0.041		0.061		0.036	
π_{21}^{WY}					0.000		0.042		0.042	
π_{22}^{WY}			0.555		0.376		0.162		0.245	
π_{23}^{WY}					0.000		0.126		0.149	
π_{31}^{WY}					0.020		0.023		0.004	
π_{32}^{WY}					0.000		0.030		0.030	
π_{33}^{WY}			0.366		0.332		0.251		0.270	

(to be continued)

From the parameters of Model 3b, it can be seen that including an 'independent' three-class latent covariate in the discrete-time logit model leads to more extreme parameters. The differences between respondents and brothers, between the two time points, and between the categories of A are larger than in Model 1. It is important to note that these results are exactly the opposite of the results obtained by Mare (1994).

TABLE 5.15 (*Continued*)

	Model 1	Model 3b	Model 6c	Model 7b		Model 8	
effect of A on W and Y							
β^{AW}, β^{AY}				- 0.285	(0.011)		
u_{11}^{AW}, u_{11}^{AY}						-0.700	(0.018)
u_{21}^{AW}, u_{21}^{AY}						-0.526	(0.022)
u_{31}^{AW}, u_{31}^{AY}						0.068	(0.020)
u_{41}^{AW}, u_{41}^{AY}						0.383	(0.028)
u_{51}^{AW}, u_{51}^{AY}						0.773	
u_{12}^{AW}, u_{12}^{AY}						-0.014	(0.020)
u_{22}^{AW}, u_{22}^{AY}						0.096	(0.024)
u_{32}^{AW}, u_{32}^{AY}						0.270	(0.024)
u_{42}^{AW}, u_{42}^{AY}						-0.097	(0.037)
u_{52}^{AW}, u_{52}^{AY}						-0.253	
u_{13}^{AW}, u_{13}^{AY}						0.714	
u_{23}^{AW}, u_{23}^{AY}						0.430	
u_{33}^{AW}, u_{33}^{AY}						-0.339	
u_{43}^{AW}, u_{43}^{AY}						-0.286	
u_{53}^{AW}, u_{53}^{AY}						-0.520	

It was checked whether the differences are caused by the additional latent class, but this is not the case. Also in the two-class model (Model 2) the parameters are more extreme than in Model 1. So, the fact that Mare estimated the bivariate logit model in the complete table instead of using a modified path model not only leads to a worse model fit, but also to completely different substantive results.

The latent proportions and effects of W on the transition probabilities show that there is a group containing 37 percent of the population with an extremely high risk of dropping out of school.[14] Persons belonging to class two, the modal class, have a low risk of dropping out of school, and a small group containing 8 percent of the population has an extremely low risk of dropping out of school.

In the quasi-symmetry model (Model 6c), the distribution of the unobserved factors for respondents (W) and brothers (Y) was allowed to be different. This leads to even more extreme differences between the time categories and among the levels of father's education. However, the dif-

---

[14] Note that the scores that were used for W and Y in the linear effects β^W and β^Y are -1, 0, and 1. Therefore, the parameters for categories 1, 2, and 3 of W and Y are 3.079, 0.0000, and 3.079, respectively.

ferences between the mean of the logit of the transition probabilities for respondents and their brothers disappear. At the second point in time, brothers have an even lower risk of dropping out than respondents. This is not surprising, because brothers, who, as we saw, have a higher risk of dropping out of school, less often belong to the low-risk class (class one) than respondents (0.19 versus 0.27). Note that these probabilities can be calculated from the cell probabilities of the joint latent distribution of W and Y.

As demonstrated above, by allowing W and Y to depend linearly and equally on A, the fit of the model improved a great deal. But, as can be seen from Table 5.14, the parameters of the discrete-time logit model for Model 7b are rather different from the parameters for Models 1, 3b, and 6c. Particularly the effect of fathers' education is very difficult to interpret since the monotonic pattern disappeared completely. From the covariate part of Model 7b, it can be seen that the effect of A on W and Y is rather strong. For instance, the ratio of the odds of belonging to class one rather than to class three between persons with less and highly educated fathers is $\exp(8 * -0.285) = .102$.[15] In other words, individuals with highly educated fathers will belong to class one more often, while persons with less educated fathers will belong to class three in more cases.

The latent probabilities show that now brothers belong more often to the high-risk class (class three) than respondents (.44 versus .30). On the basis of the size of the direct effects of W and Y on the transition probabilities (13.073), it can be concluded that persons belonging to class one are stayers, while persons belonging to class three certainly drop out, where the probability of dropping out at the first point in time is higher for respondents than for brothers. Note that the linear effect of 13.073 means that the effects are $-1 * 13.073$ for class one, $0 * 13.073$ for class two, and $1 * 13.073$. for class three.[16] However, the larger number of brothers in class three is partially compensated by a lower mean transition probability at the first point in time.

Most of the effects of fathers' education on the risk of dropping out are weaker than in Model 6c. This is to be expected when an observed covariate is allowed to have an indirect effect on the transition probabilities via a latent variable. The effects of A are no longer monotonic,

---

[15] For the levels of W and Y the scores -1, 0, and 1 were used, and for the levels of A the scores -2, -1, 0, 1, and 2.

[16] No standard error is reported for this effect because, as will be explained below, we have a boundary solution in which several probabilities become (almost) equal to one or zero.

TABLE 5.16 Estimated probabilities of dropping out of school for respondents' and oldest brothers' according to Models 7b and 8

W/Y	A	$\lambda^1(t_1\|a, y)$	$\lambda^1(t_2\|a, y)$	$\lambda^2(t_1\|a, w)$	$\lambda^2(t_2\|a, w)$
Model 7b					
1	1	0.000	0.367	0.000	0.319
1	2	0.000	0.444	0.000	0.393
1	3	0.000	0.249	0.000	0.211
1	4	0.000	0.152	0.000	0.126
1	5	0.000	0.063	0.000	0.052
2	1	0.000	1.000	0.243	1.000
2	2	0.000	1.000	0.325	1.000
2	3	0.000	1.000	0.003	1.000
2	4	0.000	1.000	0.109	1.000
2	5	0.000	1.000	0.174	1.000
3	1	0.993	1.000	1.000	1.000
3	2	0.995	1.000	1.000	1.000
3	3	0.543	1.000	0.999	1.000
3	4	0.981	1.000	1.000	1.000
3	5	0.989	1.000	1.000	1.000
Model 8					
1		0.000	0.023	0.000	0.052
2		0.000	0.860	0.165	0.933
3		0.923	1.000	1.000	1.000

however, with the parameter v_{31}^{AL} (-3.611) being a real outlier. This problem, which makes the effect of A difficult to interpret, can be expected to be caused by the fact that the effect of A on Y and W was restricted to linear-by-linear. This probably resulted in a too high number of people with $A = 3$ in the high-risk classes, which is compensated by an extremely low direct effect on the transition probability.

The estimated transition probabilities for Model 7b, which are reported in Table 5.16, demonstrate the implication of the extreme values of the hazard parameters. Although the first class is clearly a low-risk class, contrary to what would be expected on the basis of the effects of W and Y on the transition probabilities, it is not a class of stayers. In the second time interval, both brothers and respondents have a considerable risk of dropping out, where the size of the transition probabilities also depends on the value of A. The second class surely drops out at $T = t_2$. However, the risk of dropping out at $T = t_1$ differs for brothers and respondents. Respondents belonging to class two have a much higher probability of dropping out in the first time interval than their oldest brothers. The probability of dropping out also depends on A, where persons with $A = 3$ clearly have the lowest risks. Finally, class three has a very high risk of dropping out at the first time interval. There is, however, one exception: For brothers with a father belonging to the middle educational category, the probability of dropping out is much lower. The persons of class three that do not drop out at the first point in time surely drop out at the second point in time. Thus, it can be concluded that the much lower mean transition probability at $T = t_1$ for brothers leads to significantly lower transition probabilities only for brothers belonging to class two. Moreover, the extremely low value of v_{31}^{AL} leads to much lower transition probabilities for brothers belonging to class three and respondents belonging to class two. In fact, the linear-by-linear effects AY and AW result in too many brothers with $A = 3$ in class three instead of class two and too many respondents with $A = 3$ in class two instead of class one.

From the reported transition probabilities for Model 7b, it can also be seen that we have a boundary solution for the effect of the latent variables on the transition probabilities. In each column of Table 5.16, there is only one set of probabilities that is not equal to one or zero. Thus, we could specify the same model with a priori ones and zeros rather than with a direct effect of W and Z on the transition probabilities. This is reason that no standard errors can be calculated for β^W (and β^Y).

Because of the problems associated with Model 7b, a specification in which the relationships between A and the unobserved risk factors are not linearly restricted was tested. In Model 8, the association between W and Y is similar to that in Model 7b, although fewer persons belong to class one, and more to class two. The direct effects of A on W and Y show a quite regular pattern. Persons with less educated fathers more often belong to class one and persons with highly educated fathers are more often found in class three. The middle category of A has the highest probability of belonging to class two. From the hazard parameters, it can be seen that, as in Model 7b, the larger number of brothers in the high-risk class is partially compensated by a much lower mean of the logit of the transition probabilities at $T = t_1$. The effect of the latent variables W and Y on the risk of dropping out is again very strong.[17] Therefore, class three could be labeled as certain movers and class one as stayers. From the estimated probabilities in Table 5.16 it can be seen that class one is indeed almost a class of stayers. Only

---

[17] For β_1^{WL} (and β_1^{YL}), we again have a solution which is too near to the boundary of the parameter space to be able to obtain its standard error.

at the second point in time, do persons belonging to class one have a small risk of dropping out. Class two has a much higher dropout probability, where the risk is higher for respondents than for their brothers. And finally, all members of class three drop out, where brothers have a somewhat higher probability of dropping out at $T = t_2$ instead of $T = t_1$.

It will be clear that, although Model 7b fits better, Model 8 is much easier to interpret. Moreover, the assumption that a background variable such as fathers' education has only an indirect effect on the school behavior of sons can be very well defended. It should, however, be noted that Model 8 differs substantially from the usual way of correcting for unobserved heterogeneity. But, to correct for selection bias, strong a priori assumptions about the selection mechanism are needed. As already mentioned, such an assumption could be that a particular covariate influences the unobserved factor but has no direct effect on the risk of dropping out.

This example demonstrated the potentials of the general latent variable approach to correct for unobserved heterogeneity when analyzing survival data from dependent observations. The inclusion of a latent covariate in the model for dropping out of school showed that there is a strong dependence between the dropout risks of respondents and their oldest brothers. In addition, it was demonstrated how to relax some of the assumptions which are generally made when correcting for unobserved heterogeneity: The unobserved heterogeneity was allowed to depend on the observed covariate, to be partially different for respondents and brothers, and to have nonproportional effects on the risk of dropping out of school. It will also be clear from the example that it is not a problem to obtain a model that describes the data well. However, only on the basis of substantive arguments can it be decided whether a particular specification for the unobserved heterogeneity makes sense.

5.2.8. Simultaneous modeling of the dependent process and the covariate process

As explained in 4.6 in the discussion of the problems associated with the use of time-varying covariates, the effect of a time-varying covariate on the hazard rate of the event of interest may be partially spurious. If there are unobserved factors that influence both the covariate process and the dependent process,[18] systematic selection into categories of the time-varying covariate concerned will occur, and, as a result, the effect of the covariate concerned will be (partially) spurious.

Here, we will demonstrate how to disentangle true and spurious effects of time-varying covariates by simultaneously modeling the covariate process and the dependent process. Using a multivariate hazard model, the existence of a latent variable can be postulated which influences both the transition rates of a time-dependent covariate and the transition rates of the event(s) under study. Furthermore, by including a direct effect of the time-varying covariate on the hazard rate, it is possible to check whether a significant direct effect remains after controlling for the common unobserved risk factor(s). Note that such a latent variable approach not only allows us to disentangle true and spurious effects of time-varying covariates, it also makes it possible to detect unobserved factors influencing the occurrence of the event to be studied.

Example 8: School transitions of brothers with direct effects between processes

Data and model To demonstrate how to perform a simultaneous analysis of the covariate and dependent processes, the previous example (Example 7) is modified. In this example, the respondent's schooling is not only explained by his father's schooling, but also by his oldest brother's schooling. Actually, the schooling of the oldest brother is included in the model for the respondent as a time-varying covariate having two possible values: dropped out or not at the school level concerned. It is expected that if the older brother dropped out at or before a particular school level, the respondent will have a higher risk of dropping out at that school level.

The time-varying covariate indicating whether a respondent's oldest brother dropped out of school is not an exogenous covariate (see section 4.6). As a result of the existence of common unobserved family factors influencing both school careers, a respondent's survival in t_l will help to predict the covariate value in t_{l+1}. Therefore, the relationship between brothers' and respondents' schooling will at least partially be spurious. As in the previous example, the latent class approach is used to control for common unobserved risk factors. In fact, the only difference with

---

[18] The terms dependent process and covariate process are used to denote changes that occur in the value of the dependent variable of interest and changes that occur in the values of the time-varying covariates, respectively.

the analyses presented in the previous subsection is that the schooling of the oldest brother is allowed to have a direct effect on the respondent's dropout rate.

It must be noted that, although in the data set that is used most oldest brothers are older than the respondents, in some cases the oldest brother is younger that the respondent (Mare, 1994). To perform the analysis correctly, in such cases one should reverse the status of oldest brother and respondent because, logically, only the schooling of the older one can influence the schooling of the younger one and not the other way around. But, there is no information available to determine whether the brother or the respondent is older. So, in principle, the correctness of the causal inference is not only threatened by unobserved risk factors but also by this partial reverse causation. However, for simplicity of exposition, the analysis is performed as if the oldest brother is always older than the respondent. Although this may somewhat distort the substantive conclusions, it does not influence the illustrative relevance of this example.

Because the main purpose of this example is to show how to disentangle the true and the spurious effects of a time-varying covariate, only the simplest specification for the nature of the unobserved risk factors is used. The unobserved risk factors are assumed to be the same for the respondents and their brothers, which, as was demonstrated in Example 7, is equivalent to using one single latent variable. Moreover, the latent variable is assumed to be independent of the father's education.

The discrete-time logit model for the brother's dropping out is the same as the one which is used in Example 7. The model for the respondent's dropping out differs in that a time-varying covariate is included in the model, i.e., his brother's dropout status at the time point or school level concerned. The discrete-time logit models are given by

$$\lambda^1(t_l|a, w) = \frac{\exp\left(v_1^M + v_{l1}^{LM} + v_{a1}^{AM} + v_{w1}^{WM}\right)}{1 + \exp\left(v_1^M + v_{l1}^{LM} + v_{a1}^{AM} + v_{w1}^{WM}\right)}, \quad [5.22]$$

$$\lambda^2(t_l|a, w, s_{1l}) = \frac{\exp\left(v_2^M + v_{l2}^{LM} + v_{a2}^{AM} + v_{w2}^{WM} + v_{s_{1l}}^{S_{1l}}\right)}{1 + \exp\left(v_2^M + v_{l2}^{LM} + v_{a2}^{AM} + v_{w2}^{WM} + v_{s_{1l}}^{S_{1l}}\right)}, \quad [5.23]$$

in which $v_{s_{1l}}^{S_{1l}}$ denotes the effect of the dropout status of the oldest brother at time point t_l on the respondent's probability of dropping out at time point t_l. In other words, the effect $v_{s_{1l}}^{S_{1l}}$ describes whether the oldest brother's dropping out before finishing secondary school influences the respondent's dropout probability at this school level, and the effect $v_{s_{12}}^{S_{12}}$ describes whether the oldest brother's dropping out before completing some post-secondary education influences the probability that respondents drop out at this level. Particularly interesting is whether the direct effect of the time-varying covariate brother's dropout status on the respondent's risk of dropping out declines when one controls for unobserved risk factors influencing both the covariate process and the dependent process.

From the model represented in Equations 5.22 and 5.23, it can be seen that the effect of the latent variable W and of the father's education (A) is assumed to be proportional. An additional restriction that is imposed on the parameters is that the effects of W and A are equal for brothers and respondents, i.e., $v_{a1}^{AM} = v_{a2}^{AM}$ and $v_{w1}^{WM} = v_{w2}^{WM}$.

Note that, as in the previous example, the combined covariate and hazard model can be written as a modified path model, that is,

$$\pi_{aws_{11}s_{12}s_{21}s_{22}} = \pi_a \, \pi_{w|a} \, \pi_{s_{11}|aw} \, \pi_{s_{12}|aws_{11}} \, \pi_{s_{21}|aws_{11}} \, \pi_{s_{22}|aws_{21}s_{12}} \, .$$

The only difference with the modified path model described in Equation 5.21 is that here it is assumed that there are also direct effects of S_{11} on S_{21} and of S_{12} on S_{22}.

Results The models for which the test results are presented in Table 5.17 differ with respect to the number of latent classes and the specification of $v_{s_{1l}}^{S_{1l}}$. Models 1a, 2a, 3a, and 4a have one, two, three, and four latent classes, but without a direct effect of the brother's dropout status on the respondent's risk of dropping out. In Models 1b, 2b, 3b, and 4b, a direct effect of the brother's dropout status on the respondent's probability of dropping out is included, but this effect is assumed to be equal at both school levels, i.e., $v_{s_{11}}^{S_{11}} = v_{s_{12}}^{S_{12}}$. And finally, in Models 1c, 2c, 3c, and 4c, this effect is allowed to be nonproportional.

The test results show that the model fit can be greatly improved by including a direct effect of brother's schooling on respondent's schooling in the model. The proportional effect of brother's schooling remains significant after controlling for common unobserved risk factors, irrespective of the number of latent classes. Moreover, the effect seems to be nonproportional. Including a nonproportional direct effect of brother's schooling on respondent's schooling in the model without unobserved heterogeneity decreases the L^2 value dramatically from 4381.6 (Model 1a) to 596.9 (Model 1c). Although not so extreme, the decrease in the L^2 value is significant in the two-, three-, and four-class models as well.

TABLE 5.17 Test results and parameter estimates for the estimated models for respondent's schooling in which oldest brother's schooling is used as a time-varying covariate

Model	L^2	df	$v_{s_{11}}^{s_{11}}$		$v_{s_{12}}^{s_{12}}$	
1a. 1 class no $v_{s_{1l}}^{s_{1l}}$	4381.64	28	0.000		0.000	
1b. 1 class proportional	647.33	27	0.816	(0.014)	0.816	(0.014)
1c. 1 class nonproportional	596.90	26	0.894	(0.018)	0.692	(0.022)
2a. 2 class no $v_{s_{1l}}^{s_{1l}}$	689.26	26	0.000		0.000	
2b. 2 class proportional	219.56	25	0.493	(0.023)	0.493	(0.023)
2c. 2 class nonproportional	218.01	24	0.525	(0.034)	0.472	(0.028)
3a. 3 class no $v_{s_{1l}}^{s_{1l}}$	256.07	24	0.000		0.000	
3b. 3 class proportional	174.86	23	0.344	(0.039)	0.344	(0.039)
3c. 3 class nonproportional	154.45	22	0.410	(0.038)	0.201	(0.048)
4a. 4 class no $v_{s_{1l}}^{s_{1l}}$	186.76	22	0.000		0.000	
4b. 4 class proportional	156.44	21	0.257	(0.044)	0.257	(0.044)
4c. 4 class nonproportional	144.99	20	0.344	(0.048)	0.175	(0.049)

Note that only in the two-class model does the proportionality assumption not need to be rejected ($L_{2b|2c}^2 = 1.55, df = 1, p > .21$).[19]

Table 5.17 also provides the estimates for the direct effects of the brother's dropout status on the respondent's risk of dropping out. When one controls for common unobserved heterogeneity, the size of the effect decreases considerably. In Model 1c, the time-specific effects are .89 and .69, which implies that the odds of dropping out rather than not dropping out are 5.93 (= exp[2 ∗ .89]) and 3.97 (= exp[2 ∗ .69]) times higher if a respondent's brother dropped out at or before the school type or the time point concerned than if the brother did not drop out. In Model 4c, these effects decline to .34 and .18, or in terms of the odds ratios, to 1.97 (= exp[2 ∗ .34]) and 1.43 (=exp[2 ∗ .18]). Thus, although an important direct effect of the oldest brother's schooling on the respondent's schooling remains, the effect is much weaker than if no correction for common unobserved risk factors is carried out. In other words, the effect found in Model 1c seems to be partially spurious.

Usually, event histories on different types of life-cycle transitions are routinely related to each other by using one type of history as a time-varying covariate in a hazard model in which transitions in another type of history are explained. For example, a woman's employment and re-

---

[19] Because this could be the result of a local maximum, Model 2c was estimated using different sets of starting values. However, all sets of starting values gave the L^2 reported in the table, which indicates that it is not a local solution.

lational histories are used to explain the timing of the birth of her first child (Vermunt, 1991a). Like in the brothers' schooling example, such a practice may lead to parameter estimates which are at least partially spurious. This example demonstrated that by modeling simultaneously the dependent process and the covariate process, it is possible to identify and to control for common unobserved risk factors influencing both the covariate process and the dependent process. This makes it possible to distinguish the true and the spurious effects of a time-varying covariate.

5.3. Measurement error

The previous section demonstrated how to use the event history model with missing data introduced in section 5.1 to correct for unobserved heterogeneity. On the one hand, standard approaches, such as the 'independent' unobserved heterogeneity models proposed by Heckman and Singer (1982, 1984), Wrigley (1990), and Mare (1994), were presented as special cases of the combined log-linear and hazard modeling approach. On the other hand, it was shown how to extend these 'independent' unobserved heterogeneity models, for instance, by allowing the unobserved factor(s) to be related to observed covariates and to the initial position. Other extensions of the usual way of treating unobserved heterogeneity that were discussed are models with several possibly related latent covariates and models for the simultaneous analysis of the covariate process and the dependent process. All these models have in common that they concentrate on the traditional use of models with latent variables in the field of event history analysis, namely, correcting for unobserved heterogeneity.

Another interesting application of models with latent variables, which, moreover, has more in common with the latent variable models discussed in Chapter 3, is correcting for measurement error. In Chapter 3, the latent class model, which was originally proposed by Lazarsfeld (1950a, 1950b), was presented as a tool for correcting for measurement error in observed variables. In addition, some extensions of the standard latent class model were discussed, with the modified path model with latent variables as the most general 'latent class model' (Hagenaars, 1985, 1990:135-142, 1993; Vermunt, 1994). As was indicated in Figure 5.1, this section explains how to apply latent class models and modified path models with latent variables to correct for measurement error in the observed categorical covariates which are used in event history models and in the observed states at the different points in time in discrete-time event history models.

As in the models discussed in the previous section, correcting for measurement error in the observed covariates involves including one or more latent variables as covariates in a hazard model. There are, however, two important differences with the use of latent variables to correct for unobserved heterogeneity. First, when latent variable models are used to correct for measurement error in observed covariates, the latent variable must always be related to one or more observed covariates which, moreover, are generally assumed to be mutually independent given a particular value of the latent variable. Second, the observed variables serving as indirect measures for the latent covariate will generally not be used as regressors in the hazard model. In other words, the 'indicators' and the survival distribution(s) are assumed to be conditionally independent, that is, independent given the latent variable(s) concerned. Thus, a latent class model is specified in which a number of unreliable measures are used to identify one or more latent covariates, which are used as regressors in a hazard model.

Gong, Whittemore, and Grosser (1990) proposed specifying a latent class-like model for the covariates in a log-rate model to deal with the problem of misclassification in covariates. In a model for survival of breast cancer, they used the stage of the disease at diagnosis as a covariate, but it was known that for a part of the sample the stage of the disease was underestimated by one level. Although Gong, Whittemore, and Grosser did not call it by that name, they proposed to correct for the misclassification in the covariate by means of a restricted latent class model in which only the conditional response probabilities in which the observed stage equals the true stage or is one stage lower than the true state were not fixed to zero. This application of a latent class model in the covariate part of an event history model is a special case of the more general approach that is presented below.

Latent class models or, more precisely, modified path models with latent variables can also be used to correct for measurement error in the observed states occupied at the different points in time when time is assumed to be a discrete variable. For that purpose, an extension of the discrete-time latent Markov model proposed by Wiggins (1955, 1973) is used. In section 4.8, it was shown that the parameterization of the discrete-time Markov model as a modified path model yields a specification which is equivalent to a discrete-time logit model. By parameterizing the latent Markov model in a similar way, that is, as a modified path model with latent variables, a discrete-time logit model is obtained which can be used to analyze transitions between latent states. In other words, an event history model is obtained that can be used to correct for measurement error in the observed states at the different points in time.

Although the methods for correcting for measurement error in the observed states that are discussed here can only be used if time is a discrete variable, there are also models which can be used in continuous-time settings. Coleman (1964) showed how to estimate continuous-time Markov models with panel data subject to measurement error. The unreliable measurements, or uncertain responses, as Coleman called them, were assumed to be measured at particular time points, while the underlying duration process was assumed to be continuous. Also Lancaster (1990:59-60) proposed a method to correct for measurement error in observed duration. He demonstrated that in specific situations measurement error in recorded continuous durations can be dealt with using mixture models as discussed in the previous section.

Below we will demonstrate how to use the modified path model with latent variables to correct for measurement error in observed categorical covariates in both discrete-time and continuous-time models, and to correct for measurement error in observed states in discrete-time event history models. As in the previous section, a number of applications based on real-world data sets are used to illustrate these two variants of the general approach to missing data problems in event history analysis.

5.3.1. Measurement error in covariates

As demonstrated in section 5.1, the general model for dealing with missing data problems in event history analysis consists of two parts: a part in which the relationships among the covariates are specified and a part in which the event history model of interest is specified. Correcting for measurement error in observed covariates involves specifying a latent class model in the covariate part of the model, and using the latent indirectly measured variable as a regressor in the hazard model.

Suppose there is a hazard model with two time-constant covariates denoted by A and W, where A is observed and W is latent or measured indirectly. Four observed variables B, C, D, and E serve as indicators for the latent variable W. Suppose, furthermore, that the latent covariate (W) is posterior to observed covariate (A). In this case, the covariate part of the model, specifying the relationships among A, B, C, D, E, and W, equals[20]

$$\pi_{abcdew} = \pi_a \, \pi_{w|a} \, \pi_{bcde|w} \,, \qquad [5.24]$$

where, as a result of the local independence assumption,

$$\pi_{bcde|w} = \pi_{b|w} \, \pi_{c|w} \, \pi_{d|w} \, \pi_{e|w} \,. \qquad [5.25]$$

As shown in section 3.1, all kinds of restricted latent class models can be specified by parameterizing the conditional response probabilities appearing in Equation 5.25 as logit models.

Although here only one observed and one latent covariate is used in the hazard model, it is not a problem to specify models with several observed and several indirectly measured covariates. The only difference is that in such a case, the modified path model in which the relationships between observed covariates, indirectly observed covariates, and indicators are specified becomes a bit more complicated.

The event history part of the model is exactly the same as in models with unobserved heterogeneity. Again, the hazard model may be either a discrete-time logit model or a continuous-time log-rate model of the most general form, that is, a multiple-state model.

Obtaining maximum likelihood estimates of the parameters of a hazard model with A and W as covariates, and with B, C, D, and E as indicators for W involves maximizing the following likelihood function:

$$\mathcal{L} = \prod_i^N \sum_w \pi_{abcdew} \mathcal{L}_i^*(h) \,, \qquad [5.26]$$

in which $\mathcal{L}_i^*(h)$ denotes the contribution of person i to the complete data likelihood function for the hazard model, and a, b, c, d, and e are the values of A, B, C, D and E for person i. More information about the exact form of $\mathcal{L}_i^*(h)$ can be found in section 4.8. Since the likelihood function described in Equation 5.26 is based on the general density function represented in Equation 5.1, as already mentioned in section 5.1, the parameters can be estimated with the EM algorithm. In subsection 5.2.2, more details were given about the E step and the M step when the hazard model is a log-rate model.

---

[20] If no a priori assumption is made about the causal ordering between A and W, the term $\pi_a \, \pi_{w|a}$ appearing in Equation 5.24 has to be replaced by π_{aw}, and if W is assumed to precede A, by $\pi_w \, \pi_{a|w}$.

Example 9: An indirectly measured covariate in the analysis of the timing of the first, second, and third births

Data and model This example illustrates the use of indirectly observed covariates by means of a hazard model for the timing of the first, the second, and the third birth. It differs from Example 5 in that, instead of introducing a latent variable to correct for unobserved heterogeneity, here an indirectly measured variable is introduced which influences the hazard rate. This indirectly measured covariate is assumed to measure a woman's family and work attitude. It is well known that work-orientedness and familism are important determinants of fertility behavior (Bernhardt, 1986; Lesthaege en Meekers, 1986; Vermunt, 1991a, 1991b). In fact, the single familism item which was used as a covariate in the hazard model is replaced by a latent variable indicating familism and work-orientedness.[21]

The observed covariate educational level will again be denoted by A, the indicators by B, C, D, and E, and the latent covariate by W. The items B and C serve as indicators for familism, and the items D and E serve as indicators for work-orientedness. The wording of the four attitude items is as follows: B] Marriage is the most unique relationship in a person's lifetime (1=fully agree and 3=totally disagree); C] In our modern world the only place where you can feel completely happy and at ease is at home, with your own family and children (1=fully agree and 3=totally disagree); D] How positively or negatively do you feel about financial independence for a conjugal or intimate two-person relationship? (1=negative and 3=positive); E] For a married woman with school children working outside the home is ... (1=objectionable, 2=not objectionable, and 3=recommendable). Item C is the one that was used as the covariate indicating 'familism' in Examples 1, 4, and 5.

The covariate part of the model is exactly the same as in the model described in Equations 5.24 and 5.25. So, apart from a measurement model for W, educational level is assumed to influence a woman's familism and work-orientedness. The models to be estimated only differ from one another with respect to the number of latent classes.

For the hazard model, only one specification is used as well, that is, a proportional hazard model with unrestricted time dependence. The effects of W, A, and the time variable Z are assumed to be different for

---

[21] Two labels (work-orientedness and familism) are used for the same latent variable because originally two types of indicators were used with the intention of identifying two different dimensions. However, the analysis presented below shows that the indicators measured the same dimensions.

TABLE 5.18 Test results for the estimated models for the timing of the first, second, and third births with an indirectly measured covariate

Model		log-likelihood	# parameters	BIC	AIC
1.	1 class	-7241.69	67	14935.0	14617.4
2.	2 class	-7003.12	82	14559.0	14170.2
3.	3 class	-6943.13	97	14540.1	14080.3
4.	4 class	-6911.18	112	14577.3	14046.4
5.	5 class	-6898.90	127	14653.8	14051.8

the first, the second, and the third birth. This gives the following rather simple transition or event-specific log-rate model:

$$h^m(z|a, w) = \left(v_m^M + v_{am}^{AM} + v_{wm}^{WM} + v_{zm}^{ZM} \right).$$

The variable M with index m is used denote the spell number, in this case the parity of the birth.

Results Table 5.18 shows the test results for the models with one to five latent classes (Models 1-5). It can be seen that inclusion of each additional latent class decreases the likelihood function using fifteen additional parameters. However, the decrease becomes smaller with each next latent class. Because on the basis of the log-likelihood function it is difficult to decide which model performs best, Table 5.18 also reports the BIC and AIC values for the models concerned.[22] It can be seen that on the basis of the BIC criterion Model 3 should be preferred, while on the basis of the AIC criterion it should be decided that Model 4 performs best.

Table 5.19 reports the parameter estimates for the covariate part of Model 4. The estimates for the conditional response probabilities $\pi_{b|w}$, $\pi_{c|w}$, $\pi_{d|w}$ and $\pi_{e|w}$ can be used to label the latent classes with respect to their familism (items B and C) and work-orientedness (items D and E). The fact that class one has the highest probability of giving positive answers to the familism items and negative answers to the work-orientedness items indicates that this class consists of the most familistic and the least work-oriented women. Class number four is the least familistic and the most work-oriented group. The other two classes take

---

[22] The definitions of BIC and AIC which are used here are given in Equations 2.10 and 2.9, respectively. Using these definitions, the smaller the value of BIC and AIC, the better the model performs.

TABLE 5.19 Parameter estimates for the covariate part of Model 4 for the timing of the first, second, and third births with an indirectly measured covariate

$\pi_{w|a}$	$A = 1$	$A = 2$	$A = 3$	$A = 4$	total
$W = 1$	0.541	0.358	0.147	0.070	0.225
$W = 2$	0.199	0.340	0.241	0.006	0.212
$W = 3$	0.223	0.233	0.326	0.416	0.311
$W = 4$	0.037	0.069	0.286	0.508	0.252
$\pi_{b|w}$	$W = 1$	$W = 2$	$W = 3$	$W = 4$	
$B = 1$	0.651	0.258	0.104	0.027	
$B = 2$	0.294	0.651	0.858	0.429	
$B = 3$	0.055	0.091	0.038	0.545	
$\pi_{c|w}$	$W = 1$	$W = 2$	$W = 3$	$W = 4$	
$C = 1$	0.666	0.105	0.028	0.000	
$C = 2$	0.233	0.730	0.760	0.257	
$C = 3$	0.101	0.165	0.212	0.743	
$\pi_{d|w}$	$W = 1$	$W = 2$	$W = 3$	$W = 4$	
$D = 1$	0.387	0.203	*0.022	*0.048	
$D = 2$	0.255	0.477	0.648	0.194	
$D = 3$	*0.358	*0.320	0.330	0.757	
$\pi_{e|w}$	$W = 1$	$W = 2$	$W = 3$	$W = 4$	
$E = 1$	0.568	0.511	0.150	0.046	
$E = 2$	0.383	0.487	0.765	0.668	
$E = 3$	*0.049	*0.003	0.084	0.286	

an intermediate position, where class two is more familistic and less work-oriented than class three.

Actually, the classes can be ordered on one single dimension since the conditional response probabilities are almost consistent with the ordinal latent class model proposed by Croon (1990). In an ordinal latent class model, the cumulative conditional response probabilities for adjacent classes are not allowed to cross each other. Only three pairs of response probabilities, which are marked with *, show small discrepancies from the perfect ordinal latent class model.

From the estimated conditional probabilities that $W = w$ given that $A = a$ it can be seen that the latent variable is strongly related to educational level. Women with a high educational level have the highest probability of belonging to the non-familistic work-oriented class (class four), while women with a low educational level have the highest probability of belonging to the familistic non-work-oriented class (class one).

TABLE 5.20 Hazard parameters for the model for the timing of the first, second, and third births with an indirectly observed covariate (Model 4)

	$M = 1$		$M = 2$		$M = 3$	
v	-3.000	(0.171)	-1.792	(0.184)	-2.859	(0.209)
v_1^A	0.589	(0.149)	-0.251	(0.136)	-0.013	(0.165)
v_2^A	0.521	(0.152)	-0.006	(0.112)	-0.354	(0.152)
v_3^A	-0.001	(0.131)	-0.132	(0.112)	-0.258	(0.153)
v_4^A	-1.109		0.389		0.625	
v_1^W	0.622	(0.144)	0.127	(0.141)	0.480	(0.197)
v_2^W	-1.136	(0.364)	0.940	(0.278)	0.776	(0.355)
v_3^W	0.692	(0.185)	-0.589	(0.148)	-0.424	(0.277)
v_4^W	-0.178		-0.478		-0.832	

The estimated hazard parameters for Model 4, which are given in Table 5.20, indicate that the categories of W are not ordered with respect to the risk of experiencing subsequent births. Classes one and three have the highest risk of a first birth, while class two has the lowest risk of a first birth. So, class two contains the highest proportion of women that remain childless. Given that a first birth occurred, class three has the highest risk of a second and a third birth. Classes two and four have the lowest risk of a second and third birth.

From a substantive point of view, the results of this example are somewhat disappointing. It would have been nice if the latent classes had shown some regular pattern with respect to the hazard rates of the first, second, and third births. That this is not so may be due to the fact that the hazard regression model itself is very simplistic. For instance, important time dimensions, such as cohort and age at the previous birth, were not included in the model and, moreover, the covariate effects were not allowed to be nonproportional. Nevertheless, it will be clear that the latent class approach exemplified here provides us with a powerful tool for correcting for measurement error in observed covariate values.

5.3.2. Measurement error in observed states

When the observed states at the different points in time are subject to measurement error, the observed transitions are a mixture of true and spurious transitions resulting from measurement error. Generally, such unreliable measurements inflate observed changes (Van de Pol and De

Leeuw, 1986). Thus, if a correction for unreliability in the recorded states takes place, fewer individuals will be found to experience transitions than if no correction for this type of error takes place (Coleman, 1964; Hagenaars, 1992). It should, however, be noted that this rule is only valid if the errors made at the successive points in time are assumed to be uncorrelated.

Here, a method for correcting for measurement error is presented that is based on an extension of the discrete-time latent Markov model originally proposed by Wiggins (1955, 1973). In section 4.8 it was shown that by parameterizing the manifest discrete-time Markov model as a modified path model, a model is obtained that is equivalent to a discrete-time logit model. By parameterizing the latent Markov model in a similar way, that is, as a modified path model with latent variables, a discrete-time logit model is obtained which can be used to model transitions between latent states. In this model, the observed states at the different points in time are related to the latent states by means of a set of conditional response probabilities capturing the measurement error in the recorded states.

The discrete-time logit model for latent transitions is similar to the multiple-group latent Markov model which was proposed by Van de Pol and Langeheine (1990) to make it possible to take observed heterogeneity into account. The multiple-group latent Markov model has, however, two important limitations (Vermunt, Langeheine, and Böckenholt, 1995). First, since each level of the joint independent variables has its own set of parameters, the number of parameters to be estimated may become very large as the number of explanatory variables increases. A second limitation is that it cannot be used with time-varying covariates. The approach to be presented below overcomes these two limitations by allowing the specification of a logit regression model with time-constant and time-varying covariates for the latent transition probabilities.

In the previous discussions on discrete-time models, the state that an individual occupies at $T = t_l$ was denoted by S_l, where l denotes a particular point in time. This notation should be extended to be able to distinguish true or latent states from observed or manifest states. The observed states will be denoted by S_l, with values s_l, and the latent states by Φ_l, with values ϕ_l. Although in this case each latent variable, Φ_l, has only one indicator, S_l, it is also possible to specify models with several indicators per occasion (Vermunt and Georg, 1995). Assuming that the model contains three observed covariates denoted by A, B, and C, the joint distribution of the observed covariates, the observed states from $T = t_0$ up to $T = t_{L^*}$ and the true states from $T = t_0$ up to $T = t_{L^*}$ is given by

$$\pi_{abcs_0s_1\ldots s_{L^*}\phi_0\phi_1\ldots\phi_{L^*}} = \pi_{abc}\pi_{\phi_0|abc}\prod_{l=1}^{L^*}\pi_{\phi_l|abc\phi_{l-1}}\prod_{l=0}^{L^*}\pi_{s_l|abc\phi_l}. \qquad [5.27]$$

Here, π_{abc} forms the covariate part of the model. Although, for the sake of simplicity, all the covariates are assumed to be time constant and observed, the latent discrete-time model may also contain unobserved, indirectly observed, and time-varying covariates.

The event history part of the model represented in Equation 5.27 contains three types of parameters: $\pi_{\phi_0|abc}$ is the conditional probability of a particular true initial state given the categories of A, B, and C, $\pi_{\phi_l|abc\phi_{l-1}}$ is the conditional probability of being in the true state ϕ at the lth point in time given the values of the observed covariates and the true state occupied at the $l - 1$th point in time, and $\pi_{s_l|abc\phi_l}$ is a conditional response probability describing the amount of measurement error in Φ_l.

Although generally in latent Markov models $\pi_{\phi_0|abc}$ is not restricted, it is possible to restrict the initial latent distribution given the observed covariates. For instance, by assuming $\pi_{\phi_0|abc}$ to be equal to π_{ϕ_0} for all a, b, and c, a model is obtained in which the latent distribution at $T = t_0$ is assumed to be equal for all the levels of the joint variable ABC.

If $\Phi_l \neq \Phi_{l-1}$, $\pi_{\phi_l|abc\phi_{l-1}}$ is a transition probability, though now between latent states instead of observed states. As in the manifest case, $\pi_{\phi_l|abc\phi_{l-1}}$ can be parameterized by means of a logit model. For example, a possible logit model for the latent transition probabilities is

$$\pi_{\phi_l|abcw\phi_{l-1}} = \qquad [5.28]$$

$$\frac{\exp\left(v_{\phi_l\phi_{l-1}}^{\Phi_l\Phi_{l-1}} + v_{a\phi_l\phi_{l-1}}^{A\Phi_l\Phi_{l-1}} + v_{b\phi_l\phi_{l-1}}^{B\Phi_l\Phi_{l-1}} + v_{c\phi_l\phi_{l-1}}^{C\Phi_l\Phi_{l-1}} + v_{w\phi_l\phi_{l-1}}^{W\Phi_l\Phi_{l-1}}\right)}{\sum_{\phi_l}\exp\left(v_{\phi_l\phi_{l-1}}^{\Phi_l\Phi_{l-1}} + v_{a\phi_l\phi_{l-1}}^{A\Phi_l\Phi_{l-1}} + v_{b\phi_l\phi_{l-1}}^{B\Phi_l\Phi_{l-1}} + v_{c\phi_l\phi_{l-1}}^{C\Phi_l\Phi_{l-1}} + v_{w\phi_l\phi_{l-1}}^{W\Phi_l\Phi_{l-1}}\right)},$$

where the following identifying restrictions are imposed on the v parameters:

$$v_{\phi_l\phi_{l-1}}^{\Phi_l\Phi_{l-1}} = v_{a\phi_l\phi_{l-1}}^{A\Phi_l\Phi_{l-1}} = v_{b\phi_l\phi_{l-1}}^{B\Phi_l\Phi_{l-1}} = v_{c\phi_l\phi_{l-1}}^{C\Phi_l\Phi_{l-1}} = v_{w\phi_l\phi_{l-1}}^{W\Phi_l\Phi_{l-1}} = 0 \text{ if } \Phi_l = \Phi_{l-1}.$$

In fact, the logit model that is specified for the latent transitions is of the same form as the discrete-time logit models that were used for manifest transitions.[23]

---

[23] It should be noted that in many situations particular transitions are impossible to occur. In the analysis of births, for example, a woman with two children can only experience

From the conditional response probabilities, $\pi_{s_t|abc\phi_t}$, appearing in Equation 5.27, it can be seen that the observed states are assumed to be conditionally independent of each other given the joint latent variable $\Phi_0 \Phi_1 \ldots \Phi_{L^*}$. So, in fact, the latent Markov model is a latent class model in which the latent distribution is restricted to have a Markovian change structure (Hagenaars, 1992). Another slightly different and perhaps easier way to view the latent Markov model is as a model with L^* mutually related latent variables, each with only one indicator.

As in latent class models, it is possible to relax the local independence assumption by including direct effects between observed states (Hagenaars, 1988; Bassi et al., 1995). The measurement errors at successive points in time may, for instance, be assumed to be correlated because people tend to be consistent with regard to their reported states, irrespective of their true states. In such a case, the response probabilities $\pi_{s_t|abc\phi_t}$ appearing in Equation 5.27 have to be replaced by $\pi_{s_t|abcs_{t-1}\phi_t}$ for all $T \geq t_1$.

Also the conditional response probabilities describing the measurement part of the model can be parameterized by means of a logit model. The simplest specification for $\pi_{s_t|abc\phi_t}$ is to assume the measurement error to be independent of the observed covariates and the point in time, that is,

$$\pi_{s_t|abc\phi_t} = \pi_{s|\phi} = \frac{\exp\left(q_{s\phi}^{S\Phi}\right)}{\sum_s \exp\left(q_{s\phi}^{S\Phi}\right)},$$

where q denotes a log-linear parameter of the measurement model.[24] This gives time-homogeneous and equal reliability for all the values of A, B, and C. Another possible specification is

$$\pi_{s_t|abc\phi_t} = \pi_{s|abc\phi} = \frac{\exp\left(q_{s\phi}^{S\Phi} + q_{as\phi}^{AS\Phi} + q_{bs\phi}^{BS\Phi} + q_{cs\phi}^{CS\Phi}\right)}{\sum_s \exp\left(q_{s\phi}^{S\Phi} + q_{as\phi}^{AS\Phi} + q_{bs\phi}^{BS\Phi} + q_{cs\phi}^{CS\Phi}\right)}.$$

Here, the error rates also depend on A, B, and C, but not on higher-order interactions among the three covariates. For the q parameters,

---

one type of event, namely, getting a third child. This yields specifications with structural zero transitions which are similar to the latent class stage-sequential models proposed by Collins and Wugalter (1992).

[24] The log-linear parameters of the measurement part of the discrete-time model are denoted by q to be able to distinguish them from the u parameters of the covariate part of the model and the v parameters of the discrete-time logit model.

the same kinds of identifying restrictions are used as for the v parameters, that is, all the effects in which $\Phi_l = S_l$ are fixed to zero. With such identifying restrictions, each q parameter indicates the main or covariate effect on the 'transition' from a particular true state to another observed state, in other words, on the size of the measurement error. It will be clear that the log-linear parameterization of the measurement model for the latent states is very flexible. When there are several indicators per occasion, the logit models may, for instance, be used to specify measurement models which are discrete approximations of latent trait models (Heinen, 1992; Vermunt and Georg, 1995).

To be able to identify the model parameters of the model represented in Equation 5.27, it is necessary to impose certain restrictions on either the latent transition probabilities or the conditional response probabilities. This is not surprising, especially if one realizes how many latent variables the model contains. According to Van de Pol and Langeheine (1990), in a latent Markov model the response probabilities for the first occasion $T = t_0$ and last occasion $T = t_{L^*}$ are not identified. However, it is sufficient for identification to assume them to be equal to the response probabilities for the nearest occasions, i.e., $\pi_{s_0|\phi_0} = \pi_{s_1|\phi_1}$ and $\pi_{s_{L^*}|\phi_{L^*}} = \pi_{s_{L^*-1}|\phi_{L^*-1}}$. Note that this means that the latent Markov model can only be identified if there are observations for at least three points in time. Another procedure to achieve identification, which can be used if there are at least four occasions, is to impose restrictions on the first and the last set of transition probabilities, for instance, by assuming time-homogeneity of the latent Markov chain. But, if one does not want to impose these kinds of identifying restrictions, the parameters of latent Markov models can only be identified by using more than one indicator for the time-specific latent states (Bassi et al., 1995).

Estimation of the latent discrete-time logit model can be performed by means of the EM algorithm which is implemented in the ℓEM program (Vermunt, 1993). The contribution to the likelihood function for an individual with covariate values a, b, and c, and observed states $s_0, s_1, \ldots s_{L^*}$ can be based on the probability density function given in Equation 5.27. Since this density function is of the form given in Equation 5.2, the posterior probabilities needed in the E step of the EM algorithm are given in Equation 5.4. In this particular case, they are obtained by

$$P(\phi_0, \phi_1, \ldots, \phi_{L^*}|a, b, c, s_0, s_1, \ldots, s_{L^*}) =$$
$$\frac{\pi_{abcs_0s_1\ldots s_{L^*}\phi_0\phi_1\ldots\phi_{L^*}}}{\sum_{\phi_0\phi_1\ldots\phi_{L^*}} \pi_{abcs_0s_1\ldots s_{L^*}\phi_0\phi_1\ldots\phi_{L^*}}}.$$

Because the model for latent transitions is a modified path model with latent variables, the same version of the EM algorithm may be used to estimate its parameters as was presented in section 3.1.

There is one important limitation with respect to the practical applicability of the discrete-time logit model for latent transitions. In the E step of the EM algorithm, for each non-zero observed cell entry, the corresponding cell entries of the table including the joint latent dimension $\Phi_0\Phi_1 \ldots \Phi_{L^*}$ have to be computed. Since the number of cell entries of the joint latent dimension increases exponentially with the number of time points, computational limitations make it impossible to estimate latent Markov models with a large number of time points.[25]

Another restrictive feature of the event history model for latent transitions is that it can only be applied if the length of the observation period is the same for all the individuals involved in the study. This is, in fact, the same condition as for applying the classical latent Markov model as implemented in, for instance, the PANMARK program (Van de Pol, Langeheine, and De Jong, 1988). It must, however, be noted that this condition can easily be relaxed by using the missing data methods to be discussed in the next section.

Example 10: A model for latent labor market transitions

Data and models To illustrate the use of models for transitions between latent states, the example on labor market transitions (Example 6) is extended. As in Example 6, the transitions between the states employed and not employed are analyzed, but the difference is that now the measurements of the states occupied at the six different points in time are no longer assumed to be completely reliable. The covariates which are used in the model are sex (A), ethnic group (B), and cohort/age (C).

Because the stationary Markov model performed rather well in the manifest case, here the transition probabilities are assumed to be time homogeneous as well. This makes the event history part of the model simple so that the example can focus on the specification of the measurement model for the latent states. Another advantage of assuming stationarity of the transition probabilities is that under this condition identification of all the parameters is guaranteed, irrespective of the model that is specified for the conditional response probabilities. The model that is

---

[25] If the latent variables are dichotomous, it is possible to deal with eight to ten time points, but if the latent variables have five categories, three or four is the maximum number of occasions that can be dealt with (Vermunt, Langeheine, and Böckenholt, 1995).

TABLE 5.21 Test results for the estimated models for latent labor market transitions

Model		L^2	df	p
1.	no error	1919.82	980	0.000
2a.	saturated heterogeneous	784.68	788	0.527
2b.	simple heterogeneous	1393.49	968	0.000
2c.	2th order heterogeneous	1074.40	938	0.001
2d.	3th order heterogeneous	893.53	908	0.628
3a.	saturated homogeneous	1021.15	948	0.049
3b.	simple homogeneous	1433.30	978	0.000
3c.	2th order homogeneous	1180.13	973	0.000
3d.	3th order homogeneous	1042.76	968	0.047
4a.	2th order homogeneous correlated	1140.80	972	0.000
4b.	3th order homogeneous correlated	981.46	966	0.358

used for the latent transitions is of the form given in Equation 5.29, with the only difference that the parameters are assumed not to depend on the point in time. So, in fact, the model not only assumes the transition probabilities to be time homogeneous, but that the covariate effects are proportional as well.

Testing Table 5.21 reports the test results for four types of models: a model without measurement error (Model 1), heterogeneous models or models in which the measurement error differs per occasion (Models 2a-2d), homogeneous models or models in which the measurement error is assumed to be equal for the different points in time (Models 3a-3d), and homogeneous models with correlated errors or direct effects between observed states (Models 4a and 4b).

Model 1 and Model 2a give the upper and lower bound L^2 values for the stationary latent Markov model with uncorrelated measurement errors. Model 1 is the stationary model without measurement error, while Model 2a is the model with completely unrestricted $\pi_{s_l|abc\phi_l}$'s. By correcting for (uncorrelated) measurement errors, at maximum the L^2 value can go down 1135.14 points using 192 degrees of freedom. The excellent fit of Model 2a indicates that if, from a substantive point of view, it is sensible to assume that the true states are not measured completely reliable, the lack of fit of the stationary Markov model can, to a large extent, be attributed to measurement errors in the recorded states.

In Model 2b, labeled as the simple heterogeneous model, the response probabilities do not depend on the observed covariates A, B, and C, in other words, $\pi_{s_l|abc\phi_l} = \pi_{s_l|\phi_l}$. Model 2b captures almost half of the difference in L^2 values between Model 1 and Model 2a using only 12 degrees of freedom ($L^2_{2b|2a} = 526.33$). Model 2c contains, besides the direct effect of Φ_l on S_l, the two-variable interactions between the covariates and the observed states S_l, that is, q_{as_l}, q_{bs_l}, and q_{cs_l}. This means that the covariates are allowed to influence directly the value of the observed states, irrespective of the true state. These two-variable effects have a very specific meaning in terms of the state-specific measurement errors. Suppose, for instance, that q_{as_l} is negative. In this case, $\Phi_l = 1$ will be measured less reliably for $A = 1$ than for $A = 2$, while $\Phi_l = 2$ will be measured more reliably for $A = 1$ than for $A = 2$. In other words, the covariate concerned is assumed to have exactly the reverse effect on the measurement error for the states employed and not employed, which is a rather strong assumption. The fact that Model 2c fits significantly better than Model 2b ($L^2_{2b|2c} = 310.09, df = 30, p = .000$) indicates that the reliability of the measurements depends on the covariate values. When the three-variable interactions $q_{as_l\phi_l}$, $q_{bs_l\phi_l}$, and $q_{cs_l\phi_l}$ are included in the measurement model, in other words, when the covariates are allowed to influence the state-specific reliabilities in a non-reversed way (Model 2d), the model greatly improves again ($L^2_{2c|2d} = 180.87, df = 30, p = .000$). Moreover, since Model 2d does not fit significantly worse than Model 2a ($L^2_{2d|2a} = 97.54, df = 120, p < .93$), it seems that it is not necessary to include higher-order interaction terms in the measurement model.

The heterogeneous models presented above have one important disadvantage: They use many parameters to describe the unreliability in the recorded states. However, often it is realistic to assume the measurement error to be equal across points in time. Models 3a-3d are time-homogeneous variants of Models 2a-2d. All the conditional L^2 tests of the homogeneous models against the matching heterogeneous models are significant, which implies that the measurement error is not stable across time points. However, the much more parsimonious homogeneous models do not perform that badly if their L^2 values are compared with heterogeneous models with the same number of degrees of freedom. Model 3d, for instance, has the same df as Model 2b, but a much lower L^2 value. Comparison of the L^2 values of Models 3c and 3d ($L^2_{3c|3d} = 137.87, df = 5, p = .000$) indicates again that the covariate effects on the state-specific measurement errors are not exactly reversed.

Because often it is unrealistic to assume that the measurement errors at the different points in time are uncorrelated, two models are specified with a direct effect of S_{l-1} on S_l. Model 4a is the same as Model 3c, except that it contains the two-variable interaction terms $q_{s_l s_{l-1}}$. Model 4b is obtained by including the three-variable interaction terms $q_{s_l s_{l-1} \phi_l}$

into Model 3d. Models 4a and 4b fit significantly better than Models 3c and 3d, respectively: $L^2_{3c|4a} = 39.33$, $df = 1$, $p = .000$; and $L^2_{3d|4b} = 81.30$, $df = 2$, $p = .000$. This indicates that, if from a substantive point of view it is sensible to assume correlated measurement errors between successive occasions, it can be an important source of lack of fit of the manifest Markov model (Model 1) as well.

Parameters The parameter estimates reported in Table 5.22 show that the parameters of the event history model depend rather strongly on the specification of the error structure for the true states. Consider first the parameters of the measurement part of Model 3b. The q parameters for Model 3b indicate that the measurement error is rather small. The mean error probabilities for the state employed and not employed are .027 ($= \exp(-3.571)/[1 + \exp(-3.571)]$) and .013 ($= \exp(-4.369)/[1 + \exp(-4.369)]$), respectively. But even with this rather small amount of measurement error, correcting for measurement error decreases the transition probabilities considerably. The mean probability of a transition from employed to not employed declines from .097 in Model 1 to .055 in Model 3b, while the mean of the other transition probability declines from .073 to .032.[26] Furthermore, all the covariate effects on the transition probabilities become somewhat stronger, except for the effect of sex (A) on the transition from not employed to employed. This is in agreement with what is found most often, that is, that measurement error attenuates the strength of the relationships between variables.

In Model 3d, the covariates were allowed to influence the error rates. Since the same identifying restrictions are used for the q parameters as for the parameters of the discrete-time logit model, they indicate the influence on the 'transition' from a true state to another observed state, in other words, the influence on the sizes of $\pi_{2|abc1}$ and $\pi_{1|abc2}$, respectively. As can be seen from the q parameters for Model 3d, males ($A = 1$), whites ($B = 1$), and persons belonging to the middle two age groups ($C = 2$ and $C = 3$) have the lowest error rates for the state employed, while females, non-whites, and the two oldest age groups have the lowest error rates for the state not employed. Moreover, the effect of age on both error rates is much stronger than the effects of sex and ethnic group.

---

[26] The mean transition probability within the levels of the covariates can be obtained from the main effect v. For example, $.097 = \exp(-2.232)/[1 + \exp(-2.232)]$.

TABLE 5.22 Parameter estimates for some models for latent labor market transitions

	Model 1		Model 3b		Model 3d		Model 4b	
employed to not employed ($\Phi_{l-1} = 1$ and $\Phi_l = 2$)								
v	-2.232	(0.064)	-2.845	(0.090)	-3.170	(0.111)	-5.773	(0.293)
$v_1^A, -v_2^A$	-0.139	(0.033)	-0.139	(0.051)	-0.267	(0.077)	-0.312	(0.100)
$v_1^B, -v_2^B$	-0.202	(0.054)	-0.266	(0.078)	-0.249	(0.011)	-0.022	(0.169)
v_1^C	0.435	(0.131)	0.508	(0.175)	0.993	(0.169)	3.468	(0.335)
v_2^C	-0.330	(0.071)	-0.345	(0.104)	0.001	(0.113)	2.224	(0.287)
v_3^C	-0.653	(0.064)	-0.976	(0.104)	-0.883	(0.129)	0.987	(——)
v_4^C	0.548		0.813		-0.111		-6.679	
not employed to employed ($\Phi_{l-1} = 2$ and $\Phi_l = 1$)								
v	-2.546	(0.073)	-3.424	(0.137)	-3.700	(0.156)	-4.611	(0.579)
$v_1^A, -v_2^A$	0.266	(0.036)	0.118	(0.054)	0.025	(0.079)	0.004	(0.168)
$v_1^B, -v_2^B$	0.274	(0.056)	0.333	(0.085)	0.319	(0.130)	0.761	(0.572)
v_1^C	-2.339	(0.151)	-2.530	(0.291)	-2.130	(0.269)	-1.700	(0.299)
v_2^C	-0.217	(0.082)	-0.420	(0.154)	-0.090	(0.153)	-0.174	(0.247)
v_3^C	1.120	(0.072)	0.956	(0.131)	0.990	(0.137)	0.921	(0.225)
v_4^C	1.436		1.994		1.230		0.953	
measurement error for employed ($\Phi_l = 1$ and $S_l = 2$)								
q			-3.571	(0.072)	-3.338	(0.134)	-2.314	(0.151)
$q_1^A, -q_2^A$					-0.160	(0.073)	-0.194	(0.070)
$q_1^B, -q_2^B$					-0.109	(0.124)	-0.226	(0.107)
q_1^C					0.404	(0.224)	0.127	(0.232)
q_2^C					-0.243	(0.136)	-0.115	(0.129)
q_3^C					-0.442	(0.122)	-0.434	(0.121)
q_4^C					0.281		0.422	
$q_1^{S_{l-1}}, -q_2^{S_{l-1}}$							-0.888	(0.096)
measurement error for not employed ($\Phi_l = 2$ and $S_l = 1$)								
q			-4.370	(0.171)	-4.420	(0.432)	-3.808	(0.544)
$q_1^A, -q_2^A$					0.358	(0.077)	0.256	(0.072)
$q_1^B, -q_2^B$					0.256	(0.107)	0.174	(0.089)
q_1^C					-3.919	(1.248)	-4.082	(1.581)
q_2^C					-0.485	(0.481)	-0.561	(0.585)
q_3^C					1.828	(0.438)	1.943	(0.543)
q_4^C					2.576		2.700	
$q_1^{S_{l-1}}, -q_2^{S_{l-1}}$							0.560	(0.078)

The event history parameters for Model 3d indicate that when the structure of the measurement error is specified more precisely, there is even less change. In Model 3d, the mean probability of becoming not employed is .040, and the mean probability of finding a job is .024. Furthermore, because of the strong effect of age on the error rates, it is not surprising that the effects of age are affected most by allowing reliability to depend on the covariate values. The most striking change occurs in the effect for the youngest age group ($C = 4$) on the transition from employed to not employed. While in Models 1 and 3b the youngest age group had the highest risk of becoming not employed, in Model 3d the probability for this age group is around the mean level. Other differences between the parameters for Models 3b and 3d are the weaker effects of A and C on the transition from not employed to employed, and the stronger effect of A on the transition from employed to not employed.

In Model 4b, the measurement errors were allowed to be correlated between successive time points. By including direct effects of the preceding observed states on the error rates, the covariate effects on the measurement error change most for the true state employed. The error rates for whites ($B = 1$) and persons belonging to the oldest age group ($C = 1$) become lower, while the error rates for persons belonging to the youngest age group become higher. Moreover, the effects of sex and ethnic group on the measurement errors for the state not employed become somewhat smaller. The signs of the direct effects of the observed state on the previous occasion on the state-specific reliabilities indicate that persons with $S_{l-1} = 1$ have a lower error rate for the true state employed and a higher error rate for the true state not employed, while persons with $S_{l-1} = 2$ have a higher error rate for the state employed and a lower error rate for the state not employed. So, people tend to be consistent in their reported employment status, irrespective of their true state. This leads to a more reliable measurement if the true state corresponds with the observed state, and a less reliable measurement if the true state does not correspond with the observed state.

The most important change in the event history parameters compared with the model with uncorrelated errors (Model 3d) is the change in the probability of becoming not employed for persons with $C = 4$. This group has a probability of nearly zero ($\exp(-5.773 - 6.679)/[1 + \exp(-5.77 - 6.679)]$) of becoming not employed, which indicates that the solution is on or very close to the boundary of the parameter space. From a substantive point of view, this implies that all the observed transitions from employed to not employed of persons belonging to the youngest age group can be attributed to measurement error. Also the effect of ethnic group on the two transition probabilities changes quite a lot: The difference between whites and non-whites in the probability of becoming not employed disappears, while the difference in the probability of becoming employed increases.

Although on the basis of the model fit it can be concluded that Model 4b performs very well, the extremely low probability of becoming not employed for the youngest age group indicates that it probably overestimates the amount of measurement error. It is very implausible that the youngest age group really has a probability of zero of becoming unemployed or going out of the labor force. Thus, as always, substantive arguments must determine the choice from among the many different possible specifications for the structure of the measurement error. This example demonstrated the flexibility of approach for dealing with measurement error in the observed states, which was presented in this section. It can be used to test different types of assumptions about measurement error, such as whether the measurement error is stable over time, whether the measurement error depends on an individual's covariate values, and whether the measurement error is correlated between successive points in time.

5.4. Partially missing data

The two previous sections presented event history models with latent variables, in other words, models in which the information on some variables is completely missing. This section deals with another type of missing data problem. Event history models are presented which can be used when covariate values are partially missing or when event history information is partially missing. The lack of some information can, for instance, be the result of nonresponse or panel attrition, but it can also be caused by the data collection design itself. In clinical trials, sometimes it is very expensive or even impossible to collect additional covariate information for the individuals who are already involved in the study. Social surveys are also often subject to partial nonresponse.

The approach for dealing with partially observed data discussed here is based on the missing data techniques developed in the field of log-linear modeling. Schluchter and Jackson (1989) applied the approach of Fuchs (1982) to use cases with partially observed covariate values in a log-rate model with categorical covariates. However, as demonstrated in section 3.2, Fuchs's approach has the disadvantage that the nonresponse mechanism must be assumed to be ignorable. Moreover, Schluchter and Jackson (1989) only specified a saturated model for the covariate part of the model. Here, Schluchter and Jackson's method is extended by using Fay's approach to nonresponse (Fay, 1986) instead of Fuchs's approach. This makes it possible to relax the assumption that the response mechanism is ignorable. Recently, Baker (1994) applied models for nonresponse in combination with a discrete-time logit model. Furthermore, since the covariate part of the event history model used is a modified path model, different kinds of log-linear models can be specified for the covariates, such as the models with latent variables discussed in the previous two sections. It should be noted that Schluchter and Jackson already mentioned the possibility of extending their hazard model with partially observed covariates with a more general model for the covariates and with a model for response mechanism.

Not only the covariate values, but also the event history data may be partially missing. The best known forms of missing data on the occurrence or nonoccurrence of the event(s) under study are, of course, left and right censoring. As demonstrated in section 4.5, one of the strong points of hazard rate models is that right-censored observations can be used for the estimation of the parameters, and that, in specific situations, the same applies to left-censored observations. However, the standard treatment of censored observations is only valid if the censoring mechanism is independent (Kalbfleisch and Prentice, 1980) or noninformative (Lagakos, 1979), that is, if the missing data mechanism is ignorable for likelihood-based inference. By means of the above-mentioned methods for handling missing data, it is possible to relax this assumption for discrete-time event history models; more precisely, it is possible to specify models in which the dependent process and the censoring process are related to each other. The approach presented here has two other advantages compared to the standard way of dealing with missing event history information. First, it can be used with more general patterns of nonresponse than left censoring and right censoring: Missing data may occur at every point in time, that is, not only at the beginning or the end of the observation period. Second, it can also be used for dealing with missing information on time-varying covariates.

It should be noted that the models for nonresponse can only be used for dealing with missing event history information if time is treated as a discrete variable. The reason for this is that the models for nonresponse are based on defining an event history model as a modified path model with missing data, which is only possible for a discrete-time logit model. If time is continuous, other types of methods have to be used to deal with nonignorable censoring. One method, which was illustrated in Example 4, is treating censoring as a dependent competing risk.

One of the strongest points of the approach to be presented here is that it is embedded in the general missing data framework introduced in section 5.1. This makes it possible to use the missing data techniques to be discussed below in conjunction with unobserved heterogeneity, indirectly observed covariates, and latent transitions. The next two subsections demonstrate the way in which to use Fay's causal models for nonresponse to deal with partially observed covariates and with partially observed discrete-time event history data.

5.4.1. Partially observed covariates

In section 3.2, the method proposed by Fay (1986) for handling partially observed data in log-linear models was discussed. Fay's method can also be used for dealing with partially observed covariates in event history models by simultaneously specifying a causal log-linear model with response indicators and a hazard model for the time variable of interest. Thus, a model consists again of two parts: a part in which the relationships between the covariates and the response mechanism is specified, and a part in which the dependent process of interest is specified. In fact, the solution for this type of missing data problem is very similar to the solution that was applied for completely unobserved covariates in sections 5.2 and 5.3.

Suppose there is a hazard model for one single type of event with four observed covariates A, B, C, and D. Furthermore, suppose that the scores on D are missing for some persons, and that the indicator variable R indicates whether D is observed ($R = 1$) or not ($R = 2$). Using the terminology introduced in section 3.2, there are two subgroups of persons on whom the same kind of information is available. For subgroup $ABCD$, all covariates are observed, while for subgroup ABC, only A, B, and C are observed. In addition, for all persons there is information on the survival time and on whether one experienced an event or not.

The covariate part of the model is a causal model for nonresponse as proposed by Fay (1986), i.e.,

$$\pi_{abcdr} = \pi_{abcd}\, \pi_{r|abcd} \, . \tag{5.29}$$

Although, for the sake of simplicity, π_{abcd} will not be restricted, it is possible to postulate a model for the covariates as well.

The mechanism causing the missing data can be specified by means of a logit model for conditional probability $\pi_{r|abcd}$. It should be noted that it is even necessary to impose some restrictions on $\pi_{r|abcd}$ because otherwise the model is not identified. It is not possible to include the effects of all completely and partially observed covariates, including all their higher-order interaction terms, in the model for the response mechanism. The simplest response model is obtained by the following logit model:

$$\pi_{r|abcd} = \pi_r = \frac{\exp\left(u_r^R\right)}{\sum_r \exp\left(u_r^R\right)}. \qquad [5.30]$$

From the fact that the model for $\pi_{r|abcd}$ does not contain interaction terms of R and the covariates, it can be seen that the probability of nonresponse is assumed to be independent of all the covariates included in the model. Using the missing data terminology introduced in section 3.2, the missing data is assumed to be missing completely at random (MCAR). Another possible specification is

$$\pi_{r|abcd} = \pi_{r|abc} = \frac{\exp\left(u_r^R + u_{ra}^{RA} + u_{rb}^{RB} + u_{rc}^{RC}\right)}{\sum_r \exp\left(u_r^R + u_{ra}^{RA} + u_{rb}^{RB} + u_{rc}^{RC}\right)}. \qquad [5.31]$$

Here, R is assumed to depend on A, B, and C, but not the higher-order interactions between these variables. Since R depends only on variables which are observed for all individuals, the response model represented in Equation 5.31 assumes the missing data to be missing at random (MAR). Note that it is a 'non-saturated' MAR model because the higher-order interaction terms are not included in the model.

The response models described in Equations 5.30 and 5.31 both assume the response mechanism to be ignorable because the value of the response indicator R does not depend on the variable which is missing for some persons. A simple nonignorable nonresponse model would be

$$\pi_{r|abcd} = \pi_{r|d} = \frac{\exp\left(u_r^R + u_{rd}^{RD}\right)}{\sum_r \exp\left(u_r^R + u_{rd}^{RD}\right)}. \qquad [5.32]$$

This is a nonignorable response model because the probability of nonresponse depends on a variable which is not observed for all individuals.

The second part of the model can be either a log-rate model or a discrete-time logit model. The log-rate model may be of the form

$$h(z|a, b, c, d) = \exp\left(v + v_a^A + v_b^B + v_c^C + v_d^D + v_z^Z\right), \qquad [5.33]$$

which is a proportional hazard model. It should be noted that the response indicator can be included as a regressor in the hazard model as well. Although in most applications it is not very sensible, in some situations it may be of interest to test whether the nonresponse is related to the dependent process.

Estimation of the parameters of the log-linear model for the covariates, the response model, and the hazard model can again be performed by means of the EM algorithm. Since the model described in Equations 5.29 and 5.33 is a special case of the general model defined in Equation 5.1, the posterior probabilities which are needed in the E step of the EM algorithm for obtaining the complete data are of the form given in Equation 5.3. In this particular example, the E step involves computing the probability that $D = d$ given the observed covariate and survival information and the current parameter estimates for individuals with a missing value on D. This posterior probability can be obtained by

$$P(d|i) = \frac{\pi_{abcd2} \mathcal{L}_i^*(h)}{\sum_d \pi_{abcd2} \mathcal{L}_i^*(h)},$$

where a, b, and c are the observed covariate values of person i, and $\mathcal{L}_i^*(h)$ is the contribution of person i to the complete data likelihood function for the event history part of model.

Example 11: A hazard model for the incidence of high blood pressure with partially observed covariates

Data and model Schluchter and Jackson (1989) illustrated their approach to partially observed covariates in log-rate models by means of an example on the incidence of high blood pressure. Example 11, which is based on the same data set, demonstrates some of the possible extensions of their method when using the general missing data approach presented above. After repeating a part of Schluchter and Jackson's analysis, we will show how to specify nonignorable response models and models in which the relationships between the covariates are restricted by means of a latent class model.

The data concern 6,942 men who enrolled in the Institute for Aerobic Fitness in Dallas, Texas, between 1970 and 1982 (Blair et al., 1984). At the initial visit, the men were examined, and baseline data were collected. In 1982, data was collected on the incidence of high blood pressure during the period between the initial visit and the moment of the interview. Schluchter and Jackson defined the time variable for their hazard model as the time between the year of the initial visit to the center and the year a person was diagnosed to have high blood pressure. As covariates they used age ($\leq 40, > 40$), systolic blood pressure (≤ 120 mm Hg, > 120 mm Hg), treadmill stress test time (≤ 11 minutes, > 11 minutes), and percentage body fat as determined by hydrostatic weighing ($\leq 16, > 16$), which will here be denoted by A, B, C, and D, respectively. The variable percentage of body fat (D) was the only variable with partially missing information. It was not observed in 53 percent of the men enrolled in the study.

The model for the covariates and the response model are of the form given in Equation 5.29. For the time of being, a saturated model is assumed for the relationships between the covariates. To test different assumptions about the response mechanism different specifications are used for response probability $\pi_{r|abcd}$, such as the ones described in Equations 5.30-5.32.

For the hazard part of the model only one specification is used, that is, a piecewise constant proportional hazard model with three time intervals: 0-3 years, 4-6 years, and 7-12 years. The log-rate model concerned is equivalent to the model described in Equation 5.33. From the analyses performed by Schluchter and Jackson, it is known that this simple model fits very well. So, the only part that is varied is the model for the response mechanism.

Results Table 5.23 shows the test results for the models that are presented below. Model 1, which is Schluchter and Jackson's final model, is of the form given in Equation 5.30; in other words, it assumes the missing data to be MCAR. Models 2 and 3 are two other ignorable response models. Model 2 is the 'saturated' MAR model; in other words, the model in which R depends on all completely observed covariates, including all their higher-order interaction terms.[27] From the conditional likelihood-ratio test of Model 1 against Model 2, it can be seen that the missing data is clearly not MCAR: $L_{1|2}^2 = 145.44, df = 7, p = .000$. Model 3 is the 'non-saturated' ignorable response model described in Equation 5.31: It contains only the two-variable terms of R and A, B, and C, respectively. Since Model 3 does not fit worse than Model 2 ($L_{3|2}^2 = 4.84, df = 4, p > .31$), the higher-order interaction terms are not significant. Although not presented in Table 5.23, separate tests show that all two-variable effects are significant.

---

[27] In this particular case, a log-linear model for nonresponse can be specified which is equivalent to the 'saturated' ignorable response mechanism because of the nested pattern of nonresponse (see also section 3.2).

TABLE 5.23 Test results for the estimated models for the incidence of high blood pressure with missing data on one of the covariates

Model	log-lik.	# par.
simple hazard model		
1. MCAR $\{ABCD, R\}$	-16839.38	24
2. saturated MAR $\{ABCD, ABCR\}$	-16766.16	31
3. second order MAR $\{ABCD, AR, BR, CR\}$	-16768.58	27
4. nonignorable $\{ABCD, DR\}$	-16779.57	25
latent class hazard model		
5. 2 class nonignorable $\{AW, BW, CW, DW, RW\}$	-16869.51	16
6. 3 class nonignorable $\{AW, BW, CW, DW, RW\}$	-16775.94	23

In Model 4, the response mechanism is of the form described in Equation 5.32, which is a nonignorable model since it contains a direct effect of D on R. As can be seen from the difference in values of the log-likelihood functions, Model 4 fits much better than Model 1, using only one additional parameter ($L^2_{1|4} = 119.62$, $df = 1$, $p = .000$). Moreover, it fits almost as well as Model 3.[28] Of course, substantive arguments have to determine the choice between an ignorable and a nonignorable response model. It will be clear, however, that, using Fay's approach, it is relatively easy to specify nonignorable models for nonresponse. And, in terms of fit, this model performs rather well in this example. Often one does not know whether the missing data mechanism is ignorable or not. In such cases, it is advisable to investigate whether the structural parameters of interest are sensitive to the specification which is used for the mechanism causing the missing data.

Table 5.24 reports the parameter estimates for some of the models for nonresponse. The first column gives the estimates of the hazard parameters which are obtained when only complete cases are used. The second column presents the parameter estimates for Model 3, the 'nonsaturated' MAR model. But, since any ignorable response model gives the same hazard parameters, the reported hazard parameters for Model 3 are at the same time the hazard parameters for Models 1 and 2. It can be seen that the parameter estimates change when using incomplete data in the analysis. The effect of age (A) on the risk of high blood pressure becomes weaker, whereas the effects of systolic blood pressure (B)

---

[28] Models 3 and 4 cannot be tested against each other by means of a likelihood-ratio test because they are not nested.

TABLE 5.24 Parameter estimates for the models for the incidence of high blood pressure under different assumptions about the response mechanism

	Complete data		Model 3		Model 4		Model 6	
log-rate parameters								
v	-5.250	(0.150)	-5.281	(0.115)	-5.229	(0.112)	-5.1470	(0.122)
$v_1^A,-v_2^A$	-0.204	(0.078)	-0.124	(0.058)	-0.122	(0.059)		
$v_2^B,-v_2^B$	-0.768	(0.101)	-0.831	(0.081)	-0.828	(0.081)		
$v_3^C,-v_2^C$	0.206	(0.116)	0.295	(0.092)	0.309	(0.092)		
$v_4^D,-v_2^D$	-0.195	(0.091)	-0.196	(0.091)	-0.156	(0.082)		
v_1^W							-0.793	(0.232)
v_2^W							-0.520	(0.192)
v_3^W							1.313	
v_1^Z	0.187	(0.104)	0.080	(0.075)	0.082	(0.075)	0.077	(0.075)
v_2^Z	0.168	(0.109)	0.132	(0.081)	0.123	(0.082)	0.120	(0.081)
v_3^Z	-0.355		-0.212		-0.205		-0.197	
response parameters								
u_1^R			-0.128	(0.015)	-0.075	(0.017)	-0.070	(0.015)
u_{11}^{RA}			-0.065	(0.013)				
u_{11}^{RB}			-0.074	(0.012)				
u_{11}^{RC}			0.104	(0.015)				
u_{11}^{RD}					-0.362	(0.041)		
u_{11}^{RW}							-0.246	(0.028)
u_{12}^{RW}							0.031	(0.024)
u_{13}^{RW}							0.215	

and treadmill stress test time (C) become stronger. The effect of percentage of body fat (D), the variable with missing data, remains almost equal. And finally, the negative time dependence becomes weaker.

From the parameter estimates for the response model of Model 3, it can be seen that the high-risk groups ($A = 2$, $B = 2$, and $C = 1$) have the highest probability of nonresponse. Although the effects are weak, the nonresponse is clearly selective in the sense that it is related to the dependent process under study.

The parameters for the response model of Model 4 indicate that there is a rather strong relationship between D and the probability of observing or not observing D. Nevertheless, the hazard parameters for this nonignorable model are very similar to the ones for the ignorable models.

Only the effect of D becomes somewhat weaker when a nonignorable response mechanism is postulated instead of an ignorable one. Thus, in this particular case, it is more important to use the partially observed data than to specify correctly the mechanism causing the missing data.

To show that the approach for dealing with incompletely observed co-variates can easily be applied together with the latent variable models discussed in the previous two sections, two additional models are formulated which, from a substantive point of view, seem to be interesting as well. Suppose that the variables A, B, C, and D are indicators for the latent variable 'physical condition', denoted by W. In this case, the model for the joint distribution of A, B, C, D, W, and R may be:

$$\pi_{abcdwr} = \pi_a \, \pi_{w|a} \, \pi_{b|w} \, \pi_{c|w} \, \pi_{d|w} \, \pi_{r|w} \, .$$

This is, in fact, a latent class model in which B, C, and D serve as indicators for W, and in which A (age) is used as an exogenous variable. Moreover, W is assumed to determine the probability of observing D. Note that such a response model gives a nonignorable response mechanism because the response indicator depends on a variable which is not observed for all persons. The hazard rate is assumed to depend only on W, where the effect is assumed to be proportional.

As can be seen from the test results reported in Table 5.23, the model with a two-class latent variable (Model 5) performs very badly. However, the three-class model performs very well (Model 6). The value of the log-likelihood function is very near to the ones for Models 2 and 4. Model 6 has, however, less parameters than these two models and, moreover, the parameter estimates can be interpreted very easily.

The hazard parameters for Model 4, which are reported in Table 5.24, show that the latent class model identified three groups with clearly different risks of being diagnosed as having high blood pressure. The hazard rate for persons belonging to the third class is more than eight times higher than for the persons belonging to the first class. Moreover, the parameter estimates for the response model show that the group with the highest hazard rate also has the highest probability of missing data on D. This is, of course, consistent with the findings from Models 3 and 4.

Table 5.25 gives the parameter estimates for the covariate part of Model 6. The estimated marginal distribution of W shows that almost 40 percent of the persons belong to the high-risk class. Furthermore, it can be seen that there is a rather strong relationship between age and W. Almost 50 percent of the individuals who are older than 40 years of age

TABLE 5.25 Parameter estimates for the covariate part of the latent class model for the incidence of high blood pressure with a nonignorable response mechanism (Model 6)

$\pi_{w\mid a}$	$A = 1$	$A = 2$	*total*
$W = 1$	0.508	0.199	0.328
$W = 2$	0.231	0.321	0.283
$W = 3$	0.262	0.480	0.388
$\pi_{b\mid w}$	$W = 1$	$W = 2$	$W = 3$
$B = 1$	0.541	1.000	0.001
$B = 2$	0.459	0.000	0.999
$\pi_{c\mid w}$	$W = 1$	$W = 2$	$W = 3$
$C = 1$	0.383	0.964	0.933
$C = 2$	0.617	0.036	0.067
$\pi_{d\mid w}$	$W = 1$	$W = 2$	$W = 3$
$D = 1$	0.808	0.148	0.137
$D = 2$	0.192	0.852	0.863

belong to high-risk class three, while only 26 percent of the youngest age group belongs to the high-risk class. The conditional 'response' probabilities $\pi_{b\mid w}$, $\pi_{c\mid w}$, and $\pi_{d\mid w}$ show that W is most strongly related to B. Almost all persons belonging to class three have a high systolic blood pressure ($B = 2$), which is quite different from the two low-risk classes. The relationships between W and the other two observed variables, C and D, are less clear. Although most persons belonging to class three have a low treadmill stress time ($C = 1$), most persons belonging to class two have a low treadmill stress time as well. The same applies to the risk factor high percentage of body fat ($D = 2$). Actually, high systolic blood pressure, short treadmill stress time, and high percentage of body fat seem to be risk factors only if, as in class three, they occur in combination with each other.

5.4.2. Partially observed event history data

The missing data methods developed in the field of log-linear modeling can be used not only for dealing with partially observed covariates, but also for dealing with partially missing discrete-time event history data. This is not surprising, since the discrete-time logit model is, in fact, a modified path model.

Event history models are very well suited for using one particular type of missing data in the analysis, i.e., censored observations (see section

4.5). However, the models with response indicators proposed by Fay (1986) have a number of advantages over the usual way of dealing with censored observations. The most important one is that they make it possible to relax the assumption that the censoring mechanism is independent of the process under study. Nonignorable missing data mechanisms, or dependent censoring mechanisms, can be specified by allowing the response indicators to depend on the variables with missing data, that is, on the states occupied at the different points in time. A second advantage of Fay's approach is that partially observed data can be used for parameter estimation, irrespective of the pattern of the missing data. In other words, non-nested patterns of missing data can be handled without any problem. A third important feature is that the procedure can be used not only with missing data on the dependent process, but also with missing data on time-varying covariates.

Although Fay's procedure has not yet been applied in order to deal with partially observed event history data,[29] causal models for nonresponse have been applied many times in the context of longitudinal analysis of categorical data, that is, in combination with modified path models. Hagenaars (1990:181-200) demonstrated the usefulness of these methods for the analysis of panel data; Vermunt (1988, 1994, 1996) applied causal models for nonresponse to a long-term panel study on social mobility, while Conaway (1992, 1993) used these models for analyzing partially missing longitudinal labor market data and longitudinal data on victimization.

Suppose there is a discrete-time logit model with three observed covariates A, B, and C. Let, as in the other applications on discrete-time models, S_l be the state that a person occupies at $T = t_l$, where l indicates a particular point in time. Furthermore, let R_l be a response indicator denoting whether S_l is observed ($R_l = 1$) or missing ($R_l = 2$). No a priori assumptions are made about the pattern of the missing data: For each individual, any S_l may be either observed or missing. The simultaneous model for the covariates, the dependent process, and the response mechanism is given by

$$\pi_{abcs_0s_1,\ldots,s_{L^*}r_0r_1,\ldots,r_{L^*}} = \quad\quad\quad [5.34]$$

$$\pi_{abc}\, \pi_{s_0|abc}\, \pi_{r_0|abcs_0} \prod_{l=1}^{L^*} \left(\pi_{s_l|abcs_{l-1}}\, \pi_{r_l|abcs_0,\ldots,s_lr_0,\ldots,r_{l-1}} \right).$$

---

[29] Baker, Wax, and Patterson (1993) used a similar procedure for dealing with informative censoring. The difference is, however, that they used additional information on censored observations obtained by double sampling.

For simplicity of exposition, the covariate part of the model, π_{abc}, is not restricted, and, moreover, it is assumed that all covariates are time constant. The only difference between Equation 5.35 and a standard discrete-time logit model is the inclusion of a set of conditional probabilities in which the response indicators appear as dependent variables: $\pi_{r_0|abc}$ denotes the conditional probability of observing or not observing the initial state S_0, while $\pi_{r_l|abcs_0,...,s_lr_0,...,r_{l-1}}$ denotes the conditional probability of observing or not observing S_l. It can be seen that the value of R_l may depend on the covariates, the previous states, the current state, and the previous values of the response indicators. As recommended by Fay (1986), it will be assumed that the values of response indicators do not influence the values of other variables included in the model.[30] Although, from a substantive point of view, this seems rather logical, technically it is not a problem to change the structure of Equation 5.35 in such a way that each response indicator influences, for instance, the state occupied at the next point in time.

Like the other probabilities appearing in Equation 5.35, the nonresponse probabilities, $\pi_{r_l|abcs_0,...,s_lr_0,...,r_{l-1}}$, can be restricted by means of a logit parameterization. It is even necessary to impose some restrictions on these probabilities because not all effects can be identified at the same time. More precisely, if the model includes a direct effect of S_l on R_l, some of the other effects must be left out of the model.

Because of the non-nested pattern of the missing data, it is not possible to specify a causal log-linear model for nonresponse which is equivalent to the 'saturated' MAR model. The 'saturated' MAR model is the ignorable response model which uses all degrees of freedom which are gained by incorporating the incomplete tables in the analysis. However, as already demonstrated in section 3.2, the L^2 value under a 'saturated' MAR model can be obtained in an indirect way (Fuchs, 1982). By specifying a saturated log-linear model for the covariates and the states occupied between $T = t_0$ and $T = t_{L^*}$ in combination with an MCAR response model, the L^2 and df are obtained for the MCAR response model. Note that an MCAR response model is obtained by restricting the nonresponse probabilities to depend only on the preceding response indicators. Subtracting the L^2 and df of this MCAR model from the L^2

---

[30] According to Fay (1986), a response indicator appearing in a model for nonresponse may only be used either as a dependent variable or as an independent variable in a logit model for another response indicator. In other words, response indicators may not be used as explanatory variables in a logit model for a variable which is not a response indicator.

and df that are obtained from an event history model which is also estimated under the MCAR assumption gives a conditional test for the estimated model under a 'saturated' MAR nonresponse model. The parameter estimates for the discrete-time logit model are the same for any ignorable response mechanism, which is exactly the definition of ignorability.

When a log-linear model is specified for the response mechanism, it will very quickly become a nonignorable response model. A nonignorable response model – in other words, a response model that influences the estimates of the structural parameters of interest – is obtained by allowing the response indicators to depend on variables which are missing for some persons. In this case, a nonignorable response model is obtained if the model contains direct effects of the S_l's on the R_l's, for instance, if S_{l-1} is assumed to influence R_l. Thus, contrary to what perhaps would be expected on the basis of the term 'nonignorable nonresponse', a log-linear response model may yield a nonignorable response mechanism even if the response indicators are not directly influenced by the variables which lack of information they indicate. An exception to this rule occurs when the nonresponse has a nested pattern. In that case, the response mechanism will be ignorable as long as the response model does not contain direct effects on the response indicators of the variables which lack of information they indicate (see also section 3.2).

Because the model given in Equation 5.35 is a modified path model, the same version of the EM algorithm can be used for obtaining maximum likelihood estimates of its parameters as the version described in the section 3.2. Model testing can be performed by means of the L^2 statistic.

Example 12: A discrete-time logit model for partially observed labor market transitions

Data and models This example illustrates the use of the log-linear models for nonresponse when data is missing on the states that persons occupy at the different points in time. For this purpose, the SIPP data on labor market transitions which was introduced in Example 3 is used. Both complete and incomplete data is used in the analysis, and the mechanism causing the missing data is investigated.

The SIPP rotation group from which the data was also used in some of the previous examples consists of 6,754 persons. For 4,597 persons there is complete information on the states occupied from $T = t_0$ to

$T = t_5$. Thus, by using only complete cases, the available information for 32 percent of the cases is not used. Since there are observations for six points in time, theoretically there are 64 (2^6) distinct patterns of nonresponse. In the data set, 52 of these 64 pattern occur. This means that there is clearly no nested pattern in the missing data. From the 2,157 persons with missing data, 964 persons have missing data on all the S_l after the first occurrence of nonresponse. These 964 persons do not include the 17 persons who have missing data on all S_l. Another group of 582 respondents starts participating in the study after $T = t_0$, and continues to participate until the end of the study. The remaining 504 persons have less regular missing data patterns.

The model that is used is of the form given in Equation 5.35. For the sake of simplicity, only one specification is used for the discrete-time logit model. As in Example 11, the transition probabilities are assumed to be constant over time and the effects of the covariates sex (A), race (B), and age (C) are assumed to be proportional; in other words, the model is a stationary Markov model. The example focuses on the specification of the model for nonresponse rather than the event history model itself.

Results Table 5.26 reports the test results for the models that are estimated using the complete and incomplete SIPP data. Models 1 and 2 are two reference models in which the missing data is assumed to be MCAR. In Model 1, a saturated model is specified for the event history part of the model, while Model 2 is the stationary Markov of interest. As mentioned above, the L^2 value for the stationary Markov model assuming 'saturated' MAR missing data (Model 3) can be obtained by subtracting the L^2 value of Model 1 from the L^2 value of Model 2. Thus, 2081.66 is the lower bound value for L^2 that can be obtained by specifying a model for the response mechanism, while 4770.68 is the upper bound value, that is, the value for the most restrictive missing data mechanism, MCAR. The difference between the two, 2689.02, can be bridged using 10,577 degrees of freedom.

Model 4 is the most extended ignorable model that can be specified with the log-linear models for nonresponse. The values of the response indicators R_l are assumed to depend on the values of all previous response indicators and the values of the three covariates A, B, and C, including all their higher-order interaction terms. Model 4 has an L^2 value which is 1080.27 lower than for Model 2 using 945 additional parameters ($p < .002$). Model 5 includes only the two-variable terms between R_l and A, B, and C, respectively. Comparison of this rather parsimonious

TABLE 5.26 Test results for the estimated models for labor market transitions with missing data on the dependent process

Model		L^2	df
saturated model			
1.	MCAR	2689.02	10577
hazard model with ignorable response mechanisms			
2.	MCAR or $\{R_0..R_l\}$	4770.68	11557
3.	'saturated' MAR	2081.66	980
4.	$\{R_0..R_l ABC\}$	3690.41	10612
5.	$\{R_0..R_l, R_l A, R_l B, R_l C\}$	4255.29	11527
6.	$\{R_0..R_l, R_l R_{l-1} A, R_l R_{l-1} B, R_l R_{l-1} C\}$	4221.70	11502
7.	$\{R_0..R_l, R_l ABC\}$	4195.53	11467
8.	$\{R_0..R_l, R_0 C\}$	4310.07	11554
9.	$\{R_0..R_l, RA, RB, RC\}$	4592.20	11552
hazard model with nonignorable response mechanisms			
10.	$\{R_0..R_l, R_l A, R_l B, R_l C, R_l S_{l-1}\}$	4250.18	11522
11.	$\{R_0..R_l, R_l A, R_l B, R_l C, R_l S_l\}$	4237.45	11521
12.	$\{R_0..R_l, R_l A, R_l B, R_l C, R_l S_{l-1} S_l\}$	4212.53	11511

ignorable model with the 'saturated' MAR model (Model 2) shows that Model 5 captures an important part of the process causing nonresponse: $L^2_{5|2} = 515.39$, $df = 30$, $p = .000$. In Models 6 and 7, an attempt is made to improve the fit of Model 5 in two different ways. Model 6 contains the three-variable interactions among R_l, R_{l-1}, and the covariates, which means that the effect of responding or not on the previous occasion is assumed to depend on covariate values. Model 7 contains all the higher-order interaction terms among R_l and the covariates. Conditional tests show that neither Model 6 nor Model 7 fits better than Model 5: $L^2_{5|6} = 33.59$, $df = 25$, $p > .11$; and $L^2_{5|7} = 59.76$, $df = 60$, $p > .48$.

Since the parameter estimates for Model 5 indicate that, except for the effect of age (C) on R_0, all the covariate effects on the nonresponse probabilities are very weak, a response model is specified that, apart from the interactions among the response indicators, only contains a direct effect of C on R_0 (Model 8). The strong decrease in L^2 compared to Model 2 ($L^2_{2|8} = 460.61$) indicates that indeed $u_{r_0 c}^{R_0 C}$ is the most important covariate effect in the model for the nonresponse. However, the other effects included in Model 5 are still significant: $L^2_{8|5} = 54.78$, $df = 27$, $p < .002$. And lastly, another ignorable model more parsimonious than Model 5 is tested, namely, a response model in which the effects of the covariates on the response indicators are assumed to be equal for all points in time (Model 9). Model 9 fits much worse than Model 5 ($L^2_{9|5} = 363.91, df = 25, p = .000$), which means that the probability of nonresponse is not time-homogeneous.

Taking Model 5 as a starting-point, some nonignorable response models are tested. Model 10 contains the direct effects of the state occupied at $T = t_{l-1}$ on the probability of responding or not at $T = t_l$. The conditional test against Model 5 indicates that these effects are not significant: $L^2_{5|10} = 5.11, df = 5, p > .40$. In Model 11, the response probabilities are allowed to depend on the state occupied at the same moment in time. These effects are significant: $L^2_{5|11} = 17.84, df = 6, p < .001$. And finally, Model 12 contains the three-variable interactions among R_l, S_l, and S_{l-1}, which implies that the nonresponse probabilities are assumed to depend on whether a transition took place or not, and also on the type of transition.[31] Model 12 fits significantly better than Model 11: $L^2_{11|12} = 24.92, df = 10, p < .006$.

Because most of the parameters of the log-linear models for nonresponse are very small, only the parameters of the event history part of the model are considered. These parameters are obtained using only complete cases, assuming ignorable nonresponse (Model 2-9), and assuming nonignorable nonresponse (Model 12) are given in Table 5.27. It can be seen that in this particular case the parameter estimates are rather invariant under the different assumptions about the response mechanism. The only parameters that change somewhat by including the partially observed data in the analysis are the effects of age (C) on both transition probabilities. The main effect for the transition from employed to not employed also increases slightly. Apparently, persons with missing data have a higher risk of becoming not employed than persons without missing data. As can be expected, the standard errors of the parameter estimates are smaller when using all available information. Comparison of the parameters of the ignorable models with those of the nonignorable model demonstrates that in this particular case it does not matter which model is specified for the response mechanism. This is, of course, important to know.

---

[31] Since nonignorable response models may not be identified, different sets of starting values have been used for Models 10-12 to check the identifiability of all their parameters. All these different sets of starting values gave the same solution, which indicates that the models are identified.

TABLE 5.27 Parameter estimates for the models for labor market transitions under different assumptions about the nonresponse mechanism

	Complete cases		Models 2-9		Model 12	
employed to not employed ($S_{l-1} = 1$ and $S_l = 2$)						
v	-2.232	(0.064)	-2.137	(0.057)	-2.157	(0.059)
$v_1^A, -v_2^A$	-0.139	(0.033)	-0.113	(0.029)	-0.115	(0.029)
$v_1^B, -v_2^B$	-0.202	(0.054)	-0.191	(0.047)	-0.184	(0.047)
v_1^C	0.435	(0.131)	0.503	(0.119)	0.511	(0.120)
v_2^C	-0.330	(0.071)	-0.426	(0.066)	-0.417	(0.066)
v_3^C	-0.653	(0.064)	-0.652	(0.058)	-0.652	(0.058)
v_4^C	0.548		0.575		0.558	
not employed to employed ($S_{l-1} = 2$ and $S_l = 1$)						
v	-2.546	(0.073)	-2.536	(0.065)	-2.512	(0.069)
$v_1^A, -v_2^A$	0.266	(0.036)	0.256	(0.032)	0.252	(0.031)
$v_1^B, -v_2^B$	0.274	(0.056)	0.247	(0.048)	0.242	(0.047)
v_1^C	-2.339	(0.151)	-2.330	(0.140)	-2.332	(0.139)
v_2^C	-0.217	(0.082)	-0.144	(0.076)	-0.140	(0.076)
v_3^C	1.120	(0.072)	1.165	(0.065)	1.170	(0.065)
v_4^C	1.436		1.309		1.302	

5.5. Conclusions

This chapter presented a general approach to missing data problems in event history analysis which can be used to correct for unobserved heterogeneity, to correct for measurement error in observed covariate values and in the observed states, and to deal with partially missing information on covariate values and on the states occupied at the different points in time. This very flexible approach was based on the use of log-linear models or, more precisely stated, on the simultaneous specification of a modified path model with latent or partially missing variables for the covariates and an event history model for the dependent process of interest.

Several existing models, such as Heckman and Singer's non-parametric unobserved heterogeneity model and hazard models with partially observed covariates, are special cases of the general model presented in this chapter. In addition, the general approach makes it possible to extend particular existing approaches by relaxing some of their basic assumptions. Some extensions of the standard methods for dealing with unobserved heterogeneity that were proposed are models in which the unobserved heterogeneity is related to the observed covariates, models with several mutually related latent covariates, and models in which the latent variable capturing the unobserved heterogeneity is time varying. With respect to partially missing covariate values, it was shown that it is possible to relax the assumption that the data are missing at random; in other words, the response mechanism may also be nonignorable.

New missing data applications that were developed on the basis of the general model are models with indirectly measured covariates, event history models which correct for measurement error in the observed states, and models for dealing with general missing data patterns in the dependent variable of interest assuming either an ignorable or nonignorable response mechanism. Event history models with indirectly measured covariates, that is, with covariates which are subject to measurement error, were formulated by defining a latent class model for the latent covariates. In addition, models which correct for measurement error in the states occupied at the different points in time were obtained by using modified path models with latent variables as discrete-time event history models. And finally, models for ignorable and nonignorable 'nonresponse' on the dependent variable were based on the use of a modified path model with partially observed data as a discrete-time event history model together with a log-linear model for the response or censoring mechanism.

On the one hand, the generality and flexibility of the approach that was presented may be problematic since, as was demonstrated by the examples, the results may be rather sensitive to the specification which is used. When correcting for unobserved heterogeneity, the results are strongly influenced by whether the latent variable is related to the observed variables or not. In the latent class models which were used to correct for measurement error in the observed covariates, it was often difficult to decide how many latent classes were needed to sufficiently describe the data. When using latent Markov models with one indicator per occasion to correct for measurement error in the observed states, the results may be influenced by the identifying restrictions which are used and by whether the measurement errors in the observed states are assumed to be correlated. In addition, when using partially observed data, it is difficult to decide whether to assume an ignorable or nonignorable response mechanism, though the examples showed that it is often more important to use the partially observed data in the analysis than to correctly specify the response mechanism.

On the other hand, existing approaches, in which assumptions are often made that are not tested at all, may lead to misspecified models as well. The great advantage of the approach presented in this chapter is that it makes it possible to test the underlying assumptions on which standard missing data approaches are based. It is thus possible to test whether the unobserved heterogeneity is independent of the observed covariates, whether covariates and states are measured without error, whether the measurement errors are uncorrelated between time points, whether covariate values are missing at random, whether the censoring mechanism is ignorable, etc. Consequently, it is possible to use that particular specification which seems to be the most realistic from a substantive point of view, without the necessity of making too strong a priori assumptions. Moreover, it is possible to investigate the sensitivity of the results for the specification of the unobserved heterogeneity, the measurement error, and the response mechanism.

Appendix A
Computation of the Log-Linear Parameters When Using the IPF Algorithm

A.1. Removing parameters from the estimated expected frequencies

The IPF algorithm can be used for obtaining maximum likelihood estimates for the expected cell frequencies according to a particular log-linear model. Since the IPF algorithm does not provide estimates for the log-linear parameters, they must be calculated separately. One of the methods that can be used to obtain the log-linear parameters is calculating a particular set of parameters and subsequently removing them from the estimated expected frequencies.

Suppose the log-linear model for which the estimated expected frequencies $\hat{m}_{abc}$ are computed by means of IPF is of the form $\{AB, BC\}$. Assume, moreover, that we want to obtain effect-coded log-linear parameters, that is, parameters which are identified by ANOVA-like restrictions. To obtain these parameters, first the overall mean has to be calculated by

$$\hat{u} = \sum_{abc} \frac{\log \hat{m}_{abc}}{A^* B^* C^*},$$

and removed from $\hat{m}_{abc}$ by

$$\hat{m}'_{abc} = \hat{m}_{abc} \exp(-\hat{u}) \; .$$

Here, A^*, B^*, and C^* denote the number of categories of the variables A, B, and C, respectively.

The one-variable effects can be computed by means of $\hat{m}'_{abc}$ as follows:

$$\hat{u}^A_a = \sum_{bc} \frac{\log \hat{m}'_{abc}}{B^* C^*} \; ,$$

$$\hat{u}^B_b = \sum_{ac} \frac{\log \hat{m}'_{abc}}{A^* C^*} \; ,$$

$$\hat{u}^C_c = \sum_{ab} \frac{\log \hat{m}'_{abc}}{A^* B^*} \; .$$

These effects have to be removed from $\hat{m}'_{abc}$ to obtain $\hat{m}''_{abc}$ by

$$\hat{m}''_{abc} = \hat{m}'_{abc} \exp\left(-\hat{u}^A_a - \hat{u}^B_b - \hat{u}^C_c\right) \; .$$

And finally, the two-variable effects can be obtained by means of the $\hat{m}''_{abc}$ as follows:

$$\hat{u}^{AB}_{ab} = \sum_c \frac{\log \hat{m}''_{abc}}{C^*} \; ,$$

$$\hat{u}^{BC}_{bc} = \sum_a \frac{\log \hat{m}''_{abc}}{A^*} \; .$$

As can be seen from the above equations, effect-coded log-linear parameters can be simply obtained by calculating the mean of the log of the expected frequencies from which the lower-order effects are removed within the categories of the variables which are not involved in the effect concerned.

When using dummy coding, a similar procedure can be followed. The difference is, however, that in dummy coding, the parameters are obtained in the reference categories of the variables which are not involved in the effect concerned rather than by calculating the mean within the categories of these variables.

A.2. Removing parameters from the cumulated multipliers

An alternative procedure for calculating the log-linear parameters in combination with IPF is based on the use of the cumulated multipliers of the IPF iterations rather than of the estimated expected frequencies. In the LOGLIN program (Olivier and Neff, 1976), the parameters are obtained by using the cumulated multipliers for all cell entries. Removing parameters from the logs of these multipliers proceeds in the same way as was discussed in the previous section. A slightly modified version of this procedure has been implemented in the ℓEM program (Vermunt, 1993). The parameters are computed by means of the cumulated multipliers for the marginal cell entries which have to be reproduced according to the postulated log-linear model. In the case of log-linear model $\{AB, BC\}$, these cumulated multipliers of the IPF cycles, denoted by cm_{ab} and cm_{bc}, are obtained by

$$cm_{ab} = \prod_{\nu} \frac{n_{ab+}}{\hat{m}_{ab+}^{(\nu-1)}},$$

$$cm_{bc} = \prod_{\nu} \frac{n_{+bc}}{\hat{m}_{+bc}^{(\nu)'}},$$

where the product is over all IPF iterations. Moreover, $\hat{m}_{ab+}^{(\nu-1)}$ denotes the estimated expected marginal frequency for $A = a$ and $B = b$ after iteration $\nu - 1$, and $\hat{m}_{+bc}^{(\nu)'}$ the estimated expected marginal frequency for $B = b$ and $C = c$ after adjusting the marginal AB in iteration ν.

When using effect coding, the parameters can be obtained by removing the mean of the logs of cm_{ab} and cm_{bc}. For each log-linear parameter, the multipliers have to be used which contain the indices of the effect concerned as a subset. First, the overall mean is computed using cm_{ab} and cm_{bc},

$$\hat{u}^{(1)} = \sum_{ab} \frac{\log cm_{ab}}{A^* B^*},$$

$$\hat{u}^{(2)} = \sum_{bc} \frac{\log cm_{bc}}{B^* C^*},$$

$$\hat{u} = \hat{u}^{(1)} + \hat{u}^{(2)}.$$

Then, $\hat{u}^{(1)}$ and $\hat{u}^{(2)}$ are removed from cm_{ab} and cm_{bc}, respectively

$$cm'_{ab} = cm_{ab} \exp\left(-\hat{u}^{(1)}\right),$$

$$cm'_{bc} = cm_{bc} \exp\left(-\hat{u}^{(2)}\right).$$

The one-variable effects are obtained by

$$\hat{u}^A_a = \sum_b \frac{\log cm'_{ab}}{B^*},$$

$$\hat{u}^{B(1)}_b = \sum_a \frac{\log cm'_{ab}}{A^*},$$

$$\hat{u}^{B(2)}_b = \sum_c \frac{\log cm'_{bc}}{C^*},$$

$$\hat{u}^B_b = \hat{u}^{B(1)}_b + \hat{u}^{B(2)}_b,$$

$$\hat{u}^C_c = \sum_{ab} \frac{\log cm'_{bc}}{A^*B^*}.$$

Note that $\hat{u}^B_b$ is based on both multipliers because index b appears in both cm_{ab} and cm_{bc}. After removing the components belonging to the one-variable effects, the two-variable effects remain, i.e.,

$$\hat{u}^{AB}_{ab} = \log\left(cm'_{ab} \exp\left(-\hat{u}^A_a - \hat{u}^{B(1)}_b\right)\right),$$

$$\hat{u}^{BC}_{bc} = \log\left(cm'_{bc} \exp\left(-\hat{u}^{B(2)}_b - \hat{u}^C_c\right)\right).$$

This procedure can easily be modified to obtain parameter estimates under other kinds of identifying restrictions. In dummy coding, for instance, the parameters are obtained from the logs of the cumulated multipliers within the reference categories of the variables not involved in the effect concerned. Removing the parameters proceeds in the same manner as discussed above.

Two final remarks have to be made. First, when using the above-mentioned procedure for obtaining the estimates for the log-linear parameters, the starting values for the log-linear parameters must not only be implemented in the estimated expected frequencies, but also in the cumulated multipliers because otherwise the parameters estimates will not be correct. Second, this procedure can also be applied when a model contains structural zeros as long as no zeros (sampling or structural) occur in the minimal sufficient statistics.

Appendix B
The Log-Linear Model as One of the Generalized Linear Models

It can be demonstrated that the log-linear model is a member of the family of generalized linear models (GLMs) (Nelder and Wedderburn, 1972; McCullagh and Nelder, 1983, 1989). GLMs are characterized by three components: a random component, a systematic component, and a link between the random component and the systematic component.

Models belong to the family of generalized linear models when the random component of each of n independent observations y_i, or, in other words, the probability density function of the data, has a distribution in the exponential family taking the form

$$f(y_i; \theta_i, \phi) = \exp\{[y_i\theta_i - b(\theta_i)]/a(\phi) + c(y_i, \phi)\}$$

for some specific functions $a(.)$, $b(.)$, and $c(.)$. The term θ_i is called the natural parameter of the distribution. Assuming a Poisson distribution, the probability density function for an observed cell count n_i is

$$f(n_i; m_i) = \frac{\exp(-m_i) m_i^{n_i}}{n_i!}$$

$$= \exp[n_i \log(m_i) - m_i - \log(n_i!)] .$$

This implies that $\theta_i = \log(m_i)$, $b(\theta_i) = \exp(\theta_i) = m_i$, $a(\phi) = 1$, and $c(y_i, \phi) = -\log(n_i!)$.

The systematic component of a GLM relates the linear predictor η_i to a set of j explanatory variables x_{ij},

$$\eta_i = \sum_j \beta_j x_{ij} \, ,$$

where β_j are the model parameters.

The third component is a link between the random component and the systematic component. The expected values of the observations, $\mu_i = E(y_i)$, are linked to the linear predictor η_i by a function $g(\mu_i)$,

$$\eta_i = g(\mu_i) = \sum_j \beta_j x_{ij} \, .$$

When the link transforms the expected value of an observation to the natural parameter θ_i, it is called a canonical link. Using a canonical link has the advantage that j sufficient statistics exist which equal

$$\sum_i x_{ij} y_i \, .$$

Since the natural parameter of the Poisson distribution is $\log m_i$, the canonical link function is $\eta_i = \log m_i$. So, in its most general form, the log-linear model can be written as

$$\log m_i = \sum_j \beta_j x_{ij} \, ,$$

in which β_j is a log-linear parameter and x_{ij} is an element of the design matrix. It can be formulated shorter in matrix notation as

$$\log \mathbf{m} = \mathbf{X}\boldsymbol{\beta} \, .$$

Moreover, the sufficient statistics are given by

$$\sum_i x_{ij} n_i \, .$$

Appendix C
The Newton-Raphson Algorithm

C.1. Log-linear models

Suppose we want to obtain maximum likelihood estimates for the β_j parameters of log-linear model

$$\log m_i = \sum_j \beta_j x_{ij}.$$

Assuming a Poisson distribution, the kernel of the log-likelihood function to be maximized to find the ML estimates for the β_j parameters of the above log-linear model is

$$\log \mathcal{L} = \sum_i n_i \left(\sum_j \beta_j x_{ij} \right) - \sum_i \exp \left(\sum_j \beta_j x_{ij} \right).$$

Differentiation with respect to β_j yields

$$q_j = \frac{\partial \log \mathcal{L}}{\partial \beta_j} = \sum_i n_i x_{ij} - \sum_i m_i x_{ij} = \sum_i (n_i - m_i) x_{ij}.$$

A particular element of the matrix of second-order partial derivatives used by the Newton-Raphson algorithm can be obtained by

$$H_{jk} = \frac{\partial^2 \log \mathcal{L}}{\partial \beta_j \beta_k} = - \sum_i m_i x_{ij} x_{ik} \, .$$

Let $\boldsymbol{\beta}^{(\nu)}$ denote the vector containing the νth approximation for the parameter estimates and $\mathbf{m}^{(\nu)}$ the νth approximation for the estimated expected frequencies, where $\mathbf{m}^{(\nu)} = \exp\left(\mathbf{X}\boldsymbol{\beta}^{(\nu)}\right)$. Iteration ν of the Newton-Raphson algorithm involves finding improved estimates of the β parameters as follows

$$\boldsymbol{\beta}^{(\nu)} = \boldsymbol{\beta}^{(\nu-1)} - \left(\mathbf{H}^{(\nu)}\right)^{-1} \mathbf{q}^{(\nu)} \, .$$

The vector $\mathbf{q}^{(\nu)}$ denotes the gradient vector containing the partial derivatives of the log-likelihood function with respect to the parameters to be estimated. Matrix $\mathbf{H}^{(\nu)}$ is the matrix of the second partial derivatives, also called the Hessian matrix. Both are evaluated at the parameter estimates from the $(\nu - 1)$th iteration,

$$q_j^{(\nu)} = \sum_i \left(n_i - m_i^{(\nu-1)}\right) x_{ij} \, ,$$

$$H_{jk}^{(\nu)} = - \sum_i m_i^{(\nu-1)} x_{ij} x_{ik} \, .$$

The Newton-Raphson algorithm, which starts with an initial guess of the β parameters, involves calculating the gradient vector and the Hessian matrix every iteration. In addition, the Hessian matrix has to be inverted every iteration, which implies that it must be nonsingular; in other words, there may be no linear dependencies between the parameters. The estimated large-sample covariance matrix of $\hat{\boldsymbol{\beta}}$ is $\left(-\hat{\mathbf{H}}\right)^{-1}$.

C.2. Multinomial response models

According to Haberman (1979), in its most general form, the multinomial response model can be written as

$$\log m_{ik} = \alpha_k + \sum_j \beta_j x_{ijk} \, ,$$

where k is the index for the joint distribution of the independent variables and i is the index for the (joint) response variable. Haberman (1979) developed a special variant of the Newton-Raphson algorithm for estimating the multinomial response model. This is necessary because the number of α_k can become very large. In Haberman's algorithm, the elements of the gradient vector and the Hessian matrix are obtained by

$$q_j^{(v)} = \sum_{ik} \left(n_{ik} - m_{ik}^{(v-1)} \right) \left(x_{ijk} - \theta_{jk} \right) ,$$

$$H_{jh}^{(v)} = -\sum_{ik} m_{ik}^{(v-1)} \left(x_{ijk} - \theta_{jk} \right) \left(x_{ihk} - \theta_{hk} \right) ,$$

where

$$\theta_{jk} = \sum_i x_{ijk} m_{ik}^{(v-1)} / \sum_i m_{ik}^{(v-1)} .$$

The updated parameter estimates $\beta_j^{(v)}$ and $\alpha_k^{(v)}$ are found by

$$\boldsymbol{\beta}^{(v)} = \boldsymbol{\beta}^{(v-1)} - \left(\mathbf{H}^{(v)} \right)^{-1} \mathbf{q}^{(v)} ,$$

$$\alpha_k^{(v)} = \log \left(\frac{\sum_i n_{ik}}{\sum_i \exp \left(\sum_j \beta_j^{(v)} x_{ijk} \right)} \right) .$$

In fact, Haberman's procedure consists of applying a Newton-Raphson cycle to update the β_j parameters, followed by an IPF-like cycle to update the α_k parameters. Note that the calculation of the α_k parameters is such that $\sum_i m_{ik} = \sum_i n_{ik}$, in other words, that the marginals belonging to the joint independent variable are reproduced exactly. The asymptotic variance-covariance matrix of the β parameters is given by $\left(-\hat{\mathbf{H}} \right)^{-1}$.

Appendix D
The Uni-Dimensional
Newton Algorithm

D.1. Log-linear models

An alternative for the Newton-Raphson algorithm is the uni-dimensional Newton algorithm. It differs from the multi-dimensional Newton algorithm discussed in Appendix C in that it adjusts only one parameter at a time instead of adjusting all parameters simultaneously. In that sense, it resembles IPF. Instead of using the complete Hessian matrix, the uni-dimensional Newton algorithm only uses the diagonal element belonging to the parameter to be updated (Andersen, 1990; Jensen, Johansen, and Lauritzen, 1991).

Suppose we want to obtain maximum likelihood estimates for the β_j parameters of log-linear model

$$\log m_i = \sum_j \beta_j x_{ij}.$$

Successive approximations of β_j involve

$$\beta_j^{(v)} = \beta_j^{(v-1)} - \frac{q_j^{(v)}}{H_{jj}^{(v)}} = \beta_j^{(v-1)} - \frac{\sum_i \left(n_i - m_i^{(v-1)} \right) x_{ij}}{-\sum_i m_i^{(v-1)} x_{ij} x_{ij}} . \qquad [D.1]$$

Of course, these adjustments can be performed much faster than an iteration with the Newton-Raphson algorithm because it is not necessary to invert the complete Hessian matrix. This is especially true when a model contains many parameters.

Goodman (1979, 1984) presented a slightly different version of the uni-dimensional Newton algorithm. The main difference with the algorithm given in Equation D.1 is that his formulas involve the adjustment of the multiplicative parameters instead of the log-linear parameters, i.e.,

$$\exp \beta_j^{(v)} = \exp \beta_j^{(v-1)} \left[1 + \frac{\sum_i \left(n_i - m_i^{(v-1)} \right) x_{ij}}{\sum_i m_i^{(v-1)} x_{ij} x_{ij}} \right], \qquad \text{[D.2]}$$

which in terms of the log-linear parameters can also be written as

$$\beta_j^{(v)} = \beta_j^{(v-1)} + \log \left[1 + \frac{\sum_i \left(n_i - m_i^{(v-1)} \right) x_{ij}}{\sum_i m_i^{(v-1)} x_{ij} x_{ij}} \right]. \qquad \text{[D.3]}$$

It can easily be demonstrated that the two versions of the uni-dimensional Newton algorithm described in Equations D.1 and D.3 are almost equivalent. Let $\delta_j^{(v)}$ denote $q_j^{(v)}/H_{jj}^{(v)}$. This term appears at the right-hand side of both Equation D.1 and Equation D.3. In Equation D.1, $\delta_j^{(v)}$ is added to the current trial value of $\hat{\beta}_j$ to obtain a new trial value. On the other hand, Equation D.3 involves adding $\log(1 + \delta_j^{(v)})$ to the old guess to improve the estimated value for β_j. Thus, the main differences between the two versions of the uni-dimensional Newton algorithm occur when $\delta_j^{(v)}$ is large. This will generally be the case in the first iterations, especially if the starting values for the parameters are far from the final solution. In that case, Goodman's algorithm will use smaller approximation steps because $\left| \log(1 + \delta_j^{(v)}) \right| < \left| \delta_j^{(v)} \right|$. However, if $\delta_j^{(v)} \to 0$, the difference between the two algorithms becomes negligible because in that case $\log(1 + \delta_j^{(v)}) \to \delta_j^{(v)}$.

It can be demonstrated that IPF is a special case of Goodman's version of the uni-dimensional Newton algorithm. Suppose the model of interest is a hierarchical log-linear model of the form $\{AB, BC\}$. Fitting this model by means of IPF is equivalent to using a design matrix which contains one parameter for each of the marginal cells of the margins AB and BC, without imposing identifying restrictions on these parameters. More precisely, the design matrix consists of $A^*B^* + B^*C^*$ columns, in which a particular x_{ij} equals 1 if cell i contributes to effect j, in other words, to the minimal sufficient statistic concerned. Otherwise x_{ij} is equal to 0. The adjustment of the jth log-linear parameter by means of Equation D.2 is equivalent to the following adjustment of the estimated expected frequencies:

$$m_i^{(\nu)} = m_i^{(\nu-1)} \left[1 + \frac{\sum_i \left(n_i - m_i^{(\nu-1)} \right) x_{ij}}{\sum_i m_i^{(\nu-1)} x_{ij} x_{ij}} \right]^{x_{ij}}.$$

If, as in this case, the x_{ij} take only the values 0 or 1, this equation is simplified to

$$m_i^{(\nu)} = m_i^{(\nu-1)} \left[1 + \frac{\sum_i n_i x_{ij} - \sum_i m_i^{(\nu-1)} x_{ij}}{\sum_i m_i^{(\nu-1)} x_{ij}} \right]^{x_{ij}}$$

$$= m_i^{(\nu-1)} \left[\frac{\sum_i n_i x_{ij}}{\sum_i m_i^{(\nu-1)} x_{ij}} \right]^{x_{ij}}.$$

This is just an IPF adjustment in which the term $\sum_i n_i x_{ij}$ is an observed marginal cell count, or a minimal sufficient statistic, and $\sum_i m_i^{(\nu-1)} x_{ij}$ is the current estimate for the same marginal cell count. The new estimated expected frequencies $m_i^{(\nu)}$ will satisfy the condition $\sum_i n_i x_{ij} = \sum_i \hat{m}_i^{(\nu)} x_{ij}$.

D.2. Log-multiplicative models

Goodman (1979) proposed estimating the parameters of the log-multiplicative RC association models by means of the uni-dimensional Newton algorithm. As mentioned above, this procedure adjusts only one parameter at a time, treating the other parameters as fixed. Clogg (1982) and Eliason (1995) used the same algorithm for more extended RC association models.

Suppose there is an RC association model of the form

$$\log m_{abc} = u + u_a^A + u_b^B + u_c^C + \mu_a^{AB} \phi^{AB} \mu_b^{AB} + \mu_b^{BC} \phi^{BC} \mu_c^{BC}.$$

The estimation of, for instance, the log-multiplicative parameters of the association between A and B involves solving the following set of likelihood functions:

$$\frac{\partial \log \mathcal{L}}{\partial \phi^{AB}} = \sum_{abc} (n_{abc} - m_{abc}) \mu_a^{AB} \mu_b^{AB} = 0,$$

$$\frac{\partial \log \mathscr{L}}{\partial \mu_a^{AB}} = \sum_{bc} (n_{abc} - m_{abc}) \phi^{AB} \mu_b^{AB} = 0 \,,$$

$$\frac{\partial \log \mathscr{L}}{\partial \mu_b^{AB}} = \sum_{ac} (n_{abc} - m_{abc}) \mu_a^{AB} \phi^{AB} = 0 \,.$$

The second partial derivatives needed by the uni-dimensional Newton algorithm are

$$\frac{\partial \log \mathscr{L}}{\partial \phi^{AB} \partial \phi^{AB}} = -\sum_{abc} m_{abc} \left(\mu_a^{AB} \mu_b^{AB} \right)^2 \,,$$

$$\frac{\partial \log \mathscr{L}}{\partial \mu_a^{AB} \partial \mu_a^{AB}} = -\sum_{bc} m_{abc} \left(\phi^{AB} \mu_b^{AB} \right)^2 \,,$$

$$\frac{\partial \log \mathscr{L}}{\partial \mu_b^{AB} \partial \mu_b^{AB}} = -\sum_{ac} m_{abc} \left(\mu_a^{AB} \phi^{AB} \right)^2 \,.$$

Consequently, the (ν)th uni-dimensional Newton iteration equals

$$\phi^{AB(\nu)} = \phi^{AB(\nu-1)} - \frac{\sum_{abc} \left(n_{abc} - m_{abc}^{(\nu-1)} \right) \mu_a^{AB(\nu-1)} \mu_b^{AB(\nu-1)}}{-\sum_{abc} \hat{m}_{abc} \left(\mu_a^{AB(\nu-1)} \mu_b^{AB(\nu-1)} \right)^2} \,,$$

$$\mu_a^{AB(\nu)} = \mu_a^{AB(\nu-1)} - \frac{\sum_{bc} \left(n_{abc} - m_{abc}^{(\nu)'} \right) \phi^{AB(\nu)} \mu_b^{AB(\nu-1)}}{-\sum_{bc} \hat{m}_{abc} \left(\phi^{AB(\nu)} \mu_b^{AB(\nu-1)} \right)^2} \,,$$

$$\mu_b^{AB(\nu)} = \mu_b^{AB(\nu-1)} - \frac{\sum_{ac} \left(n_{abc} - m_{abc}^{(\nu)''} \right) \mu_a^{AB(\nu)} \phi^{AB(\nu)}}{-\sum_{ac} \hat{m}_{abc} \left(\mu_a^{AB(\nu)} \phi^{AB(\nu)} \right)^2} \,,$$

in which $m_{abc}^{(\nu)'}$ and $m_{abc}^{(\nu)''}$ denote the updated estimated expected frequencies after updating ϕ^{AB} and μ_a^{AB}, respectively. The necessary rescaling to identify the parameters can be performed after every iteration cycle.

As demonstrated by Becker (1990), the same version of the uni-dimensional Newton algorithm can be used for estimating RC(M) models. The only difference is that in that case the parameters of the different dimensions have to be orthogonalized after the last iteration by means of a singular-value decomposition (Goodman, 1991).

Appendix E
Likelihood Equations for Modified
Path Models

Below, it is shown that if the parameters of the various modified path steps are distinct, the parameters of a modified path model can be estimated using the observed frequencies in the separate subtables. Moreover, it is demonstrated that the likelihood equation for a parameter that appears in different modified path steps can be simply obtained by summing the contributions of the modified path steps concerned. Although the derivations concern the likelihood equations for the case of completely observed data, the results can, of course, also be used in the M-step of the EM algorithm if there are missing data. The next three sections derive the likelihood equations for a parameter of an ordinary multinomial logit model, for a parameter of a modified path model, and for a parameter which appears in different steps of a modified path model.

E.1. Multinomial logit model

Consider a multinomial logit model in which C is the dependent variable and A and B are the independent variables:

$$\pi_{c|ab} = \frac{\exp\left(\sum_j x_{abcj}\beta_j\right)}{\sum_c \exp\left(\sum_j x_{abcj}\beta_j\right)} . \qquad [\text{E.1}]$$

Here, β_j denotes a log-linear or logit parameter and x_{abcj} is an element of the design matrix.

Given the kernel of (product) multinomial likelihood

$$\log \mathcal{L} = \sum_{abc} n_{abc} \log \pi_{c|ab} ,$$

the first derivative with respect to β_j is

$$\frac{\partial \log \mathcal{L}}{\partial \beta_j} = \sum_{abc} \frac{n_{abc}}{\pi_{c|ab}} \frac{\partial \pi_{c|ab}}{\partial \beta_j} . \qquad [\text{E.2}]$$

When using ϵ as an abbreviation of $\exp\left(\sum_j x_{abcj}\beta_j\right)$,

$$\frac{\partial \pi_{c|ab}}{\partial \beta_j} = \frac{1}{(\sum_c \epsilon)^2} \left[\left\{ \sum_c \epsilon \right\} \epsilon\, x_{abcj} - \epsilon \left\{ \sum_c \epsilon\, x_{abcj} \right\} \right]$$

$$= \frac{\epsilon}{\sum_c \epsilon} \left[x_{abcj} - \frac{\sum_c \epsilon\, x_{abcj}}{\sum_c \epsilon} \right] = \pi_{c|ab} \left[x_{abcj} - \frac{\sum_c \epsilon\, x_{abcj}}{\sum_c \epsilon} \right]$$

$$= \pi_{c|ab} \left[x_{abcj} - \sum_c x_{abcj}\pi_{c|ab} \right] .$$

Substituting into Equation E.2 and setting the result equal to zero yields the likelihood equation

$$\sum_{abc} \frac{n_{abc}}{\pi_{c|ab}} \pi_{c|ab} \left[x_{abcj} - \sum_c x_{abcj}\pi_{c|ab} \right] = 0 ,$$

or simplified

$$\sum_{abc} n_{abc} \left[x_{abcj} - \sum_c x_{abcj}\pi_{c|ab} \right] = 0 , \qquad [\text{E.3}]$$

which is the well-known likelihood equation for a parameter of a multinomial logit model. Note that

$$\sum_{abc} n_{abc} \sum_c x_{abcj}\pi_{c|ab} = \sum_{ab} n_{ab+} \sum_c x_{abcj}\pi_{c|ab}$$

$$= \sum_{abc} x_{abcj}\pi_{c|ab}n_{ab+}$$

$$= \sum_{abc} x_{abcj}m_{abc} ,$$

of course, given that

$$\sum_c n_{abc} = \sum_c m_{abc},$$ [E.4]

which is always the case in a logit model because of the normalization taking place by the denominator of logit model described in Equation E.1. Substitution into Equation E.3 gives

$$\sum_{abc} x_{abcj}[n_{abc} - m_{abc}] = 0.$$ [E.5]

This expression is equivalent to the likelihood equation derived from the Poisson likelihood function for a parameter of the log-linear model of the form

$$m_{abc} = \exp\left(\alpha_{ab} + \sum_j x_{abcj}\beta_j\right),$$ [E.6]

which demonstrates the well-known equivalence of logit models and log-linear models.

   In the *ℓEM* program (Vermunt, 1993), the log-linear model described in Equation E.6 is estimated rather than the logit model described in Equation E.1. This results from the fact that the likelihood function represented in Equation E.5 is used instead of Equation E.3, of course, under the condition given in Equation E.4. This condition is automatically fulfilled by including the intercept α_{ab} in the model.

E.2. Modified path model

   Suppose that the logit model for $\pi_{c|ab}$ is now a step in a modified path model of the form

$$\pi_{abcd} = \pi_{ab}\pi_{c|ab}\pi_{d|abc},$$ [E.7]

where the other π's may be restricted by a logit parameterization as well. In that case, the kernel of likelihood equation changes into

$$\log \mathcal{L} = \sum_{abcd} n_{abcd} \log \pi_{abcd}.$$

The first derivative with respect to β_j is now

$$\frac{\partial \log \mathcal{L}}{\partial \beta_j} = \sum_{abcd} \frac{n_{abcd}}{\pi_{abcd}} \frac{\partial \pi_{abcd}}{\partial \beta_j} \, ,$$

where

$$\frac{\partial \pi_{abcd}}{\partial \beta_j} = \frac{\partial \pi_{ab} \pi_{c|ab} \pi_{d|abc}}{\partial \beta_j} = \pi_{ab} \pi_{d|abcd} \frac{\partial \pi_{c|ab}}{\partial \beta_j}$$

$$= \pi_{ab} \pi_{d|abcd} \pi_{c|ab} \left[x_{abcj} - \sum_c x_{abcj} \pi_{c|ab} \right]$$

$$= \pi_{abcd} \left[x_{abcj} - \sum_c x_{abcj} \pi_{c|ab} \right] . \qquad [E.8]$$

This yields the following likelihood equation:

$$\sum_{abcd} \frac{n_{abcd}}{\pi_{abcd}} \pi_{abcd} \left[x_{abcj} - \sum_c x_{abcj} \pi_{c|ab} \right] = 0 \, ,$$

or simplified

$$\sum_{abc} n_{abc+} \left[x_{abcj} - \sum_c x_{abcj} \pi_{c|ab} \right] = 0 \, ,$$

which is equivalent to Equation E.3, the likelihood equation for an ordinary multinomial logit model. This shows that the parameters of each modified path step may be estimated separately, with the observed cell counts of the marginal table formed by the dependent and independent variables appearing in the modified path step concerned serving as data.

E.3. Restricted modified path model

Suppose there is a model of the form given in Equation E.7 in which two log-linear parameters appearing in two different modified path steps are postulated to be equal. Suppose that the β_j parameter concerned appears in both $\pi_{c|ab}$ and $\pi_{d|abc}$. In that case,

$$
\frac{\partial \pi_{abcd}}{\partial \beta_j} = \frac{\partial \pi_{ab} \pi_{c|ab} \pi_{d|abc}}{\partial \beta_j}
$$

$$
= \pi_{ab} \pi_{d|abc} \frac{\partial \pi_{c|ab}}{\partial \beta_j} + \pi_{ab} \pi_{c|ab} \frac{\partial \pi_{d|abc}}{\partial \beta_j}
$$

$$
= \pi_{abcd} \left\{ \left[x_{abcj} - \sum_c x_{abcj} \pi_{c|ab} \right] \right.
$$

$$
\left. + \left[x_{abcdj} - \sum_d x_{abcdj} \pi_{d|abc} \right] \right\} .
$$

This yields the following likelihood equation for β_j:

$$
\sum_{abcd} \frac{n_{abcd}}{\pi_{abcd}} \pi_{abcd} \left\{ \left[x_{abcj} - \sum_c x_{abcj} \pi_{c|ab} \right] \right.
$$

$$
\left. + \left[x_{abcdj} - \sum_d x_{abcdj} \pi_{d|abc} \right] \right\} = 0 ,
$$

or simplified

$$
\sum_{abc} n_{abc+} \left[x_{abcj} - \sum_c x_{abcj} \pi_{c|ab} \right]
$$

$$
+ \sum_{abcd} n_{abcd} \left[x_{abcdj} - \sum_d x_{abcdj} \pi_{d|abc} \right] = 0 .
$$

Note that the first part of this equation is identical to the left-hand side of Equation E.3. Moreover, the second part is the derivative with respect to β_j that would have been obtained if β_j would have appeared only in $\pi_{d|abc}$. This implies that the likelihood equation for a parameter that appears in different modified path steps can easily be obtained by summing the contributions of the modified path steps in which the parameter concerned appears.

As mentioned in section E.1, the ℓEM program (Vermunt, 1993) uses the log-linear equivalent of the likelihood equations, which in this case is

$$
\sum_{abc} x_{abcj} [n_{abc+} - m_{abc}] + \sum_{abcd} x_{abcdj} [n_{abcd} - m_{abcd}] = 0 ,
$$

with the additional restrictions that

$$\sum_c n_{abc} = \sum_c m_{abc},$$

$$\sum_d n_{abcd} = \sum_d m_{abcd},$$

to reproduce the marginal distributions of the independent variables. Here, m_{abc} and m_{abcd} denote the expected cell frequencies in the marginal tables ABC and $ABCD$, respectively.

Appendix F
The Estimation of Conditional Probabilities Under Restrictions

Suppose there is modified path model of the form

$$\pi_{abcd} = \pi_{ab}\,\pi_{c|ab}\,\pi_{d|abc}\,.$$

In contrast to the models presented in the previous appendices, the (conditional) probabilities of this model are not restricted by a log-linear parameterization. Unrestricted estimates for π_{ab}, $\pi_{c|ab}$, and $\pi_{d|abc}$, denoted by $\hat{\pi}_{ab}$ $\hat{\pi}_{c|ab}$, and $\hat{\pi}_{d|abc}$, can be obtained by

$$\hat{\pi}_{ab} = \frac{n_{ab++}}{n_{++++}}\,,$$

$$\hat{\pi}_{c|ab} = \frac{n_{abc+}}{n_{ab++}}\,,$$

$$\hat{\pi}_{d|abc} = \frac{n_{abcd}}{n_{abc+}}\,,$$

respectively. However, it is sometimes necessary to restrict some (conditional) probabilities to be equal to one another or to be equal to some fixed value. Suppose we want to restrict three arbitrary conditional probabilities, $\pi_{1|22}$, $\pi_{2|13}$, and $\pi_{3|213}$, to have the same value. According to

Goodman (1974b), maximum likelihood estimates for these restricted probabilities, denoted by $\hat{\pi}^r_{1|22}$, $\hat{\pi}^r_{2|13}$, and $\hat{\pi}^r_{3|213}$, can be obtained by

$$\hat{\pi}^r_{1|22} = \hat{\pi}^r_{2|13} = \hat{\pi}^r_{3|213} = \frac{n_{22++}\hat{\pi}_{1|22} + n_{13++}\hat{\pi}_{2|13} + n_{213+}\hat{\pi}_{3|213}}{n_{22++} + n_{13++} + n_{213+}},$$

in other words, by calculating the weighted average of the unrestricted probabilities, where the weights are the observed cell counts of the marginal distributions of the independent variables concerned.

After imposing these equality restrictions, the estimated probabilities for $\pi_{c|22}$, $\pi_{c|13}$, and $\pi_{d|213}$ will generally no longer sum to 1 within each level of the joint independent variable. Therefore, the unrestricted probabilities must be rescaled to again fulfill the requirement that the probabilities sum to unity. The rescaling of, for instance, the unrestricted probability that $C = c$ given $A = 2$ and $B = 2$, $\hat{\pi}^u_{c|22}$, is accomplished by

$$\hat{\pi}^{u'}_{c|22} = \hat{\pi}^u_{c|22} \frac{1 - \sum_c \hat{\pi}^r_{c|22}}{\sum_c \hat{\pi}^u_{c|22}},$$

where $\hat{\pi}^{u'}_{c|ab}$ denotes the value of a particular unrestricted probability after rescaling it. Note that in this case, $\sum_c \hat{\pi}^r_{c|22} = \hat{\pi}^r_{1|22}$ because only one probability was restricted for $A = 2$ and $B = 2$. The unrestricted probabilities $\hat{\pi}^u_{c|13}$ and $\hat{\pi}^u_{d|213}$ have to be rescaled in a similar manner.

Any set of conditional probabilities can be restricted in this way, irrespective of whether they belong to the same or to different modified path steps. Moreover, fixed-value restrictions can be imposed by replacing the unrestricted probabilities concerned by the values to which they have to be fixed and subsequently rescaling the other probabilities belonging to the same value of the independent variable (Van de Pol and Langeheine, 1990). The above algorithm is implemented in several programs for latent class analysis, such as MLLSA (Clogg, 1977), LCAG (Hagenaars and Luijkx, 1990), PANMARK (Van der Pol, Langeheine, and De Jong, 1989), and ℓEM (Vermunt, 1993).

Mooijaart and Van der Heijden (1992) demonstrated, however, that Goodman's algorithm does only work properly in specific situations, which fortunately are not the most common ones. The algorithm does not yield maximum likelihood estimates when there is no closed formula for the rescaling of the probabilities to let them sum to unity.[1] They proposed computing ML estimates of the parameters of restricted latent

---

[1] It should be noted that MLLSA and LCAG not only give incorrect estimates in the situations mentioned by Mooijaart and Van der Heijden (which they refer to as case 4),

class models by adding a set of Lagrange multipliers to the complete data log-likelihood function which is maximized in the M step of the EM algorithm. They also gave the corresponding likelihood equations for the restricted and unrestricted probabilities and the Lagrange multipliers. Below, their formulation is generalized to any type of modified path model with or without latent variables. In addition, it is demonstrated how to solve the obtained likelihood equations by means of unidimensional Newton.

Let $\pi_{i|k}^{F}$ denote a probability which is fixed to be equal to a specific value c_{ik}. Probabilities which belong to the lth equality restriction are denoted by $\pi_{i|k}^{E_l}$ and unrestricted probabilities by $\pi_{i|k}^{U}$. It should be noted that k indicates a level of the variable which is obtained by stacking the independent variables of the various modified path steps. So, $\pi_{i|k}^{F}$, $\pi_{i|k}^{E_l}$, and $\pi_{i|k}^{U}$ may be any of the probabilities in the modified path model concerned. The likelihood equations for the above probabilities are

$$\pi_{i|k}^{F} = c_{ik}$$

$$\pi_{i|k}^{E_l} = \frac{n_{++}^{E_l}}{\sum_k d_{lk}\, \alpha_k} \qquad [\text{F.1}]$$

$$\pi_{i|k}^{U} = \frac{n_{ik}^{U}}{\alpha_k}. \qquad [\text{F.2}]$$

Here, n_{ik}^{U} is an observed cell entry belonging to an unrestricted probability, $n_{++}^{E_l}$ is the sum of the observed cell entries belonging to the lth equality restriction, α_k is the Lagrange multiplier belonging to level k of the independent variable, and d_{lk} is the number of equality restrictions of type l in level k of the independent variable. The likelihood equations for the Lagrange multipliers are of the form

$$\sum_l \frac{d_{lk}\, n_{++}^{E_l}}{\sum_j d_{lj}\, \alpha_j} + \frac{n_{+k}^{U}}{\alpha_k} = c_{+k}, \qquad [\text{F.3}]$$

where n_{+k}^{U} is the sum of the observed frequencies belonging to the unrestricted probabilities and c_{+k} the sum of the probabilities with a fixed value within level k of the independent variable.

---

but also when equality and fixed-value constraints are combined within a set of conditional probabilities that must sum to one.

First, we have to solve the likelihood equations for the α_k parameters described in F.3. In the ℓEM program (Vermunt, 1993), this is accomplished by means of the uni-dimensional Newton algorithm. Element k of the gradient vector and diagonal element kk of the Hessian matrix equal

$$q_k^{(\nu)} = \sum_l \frac{d_{lk}\, n_{++}^{E_l}}{\sum_j d_{lj}\, \alpha_j^{(\nu-1)}} + \frac{n_{+k}^{U}}{\alpha_k^{(\nu-1)})} - c_{+k}$$

$$H_{kk}^{(\nu)} = \sum_l \frac{(d_{lk})^2\, n_{++}^{E_l}}{\left(\sum_j d_{lj}\, \alpha_j^{(\nu-1)}\right)^2} + \frac{n_{+k}^{U}}{(\alpha_k^{(\nu-1)})^2}\,,$$

respectively. This leads to the following adjustment of the Lagrange multipliers in the νth iteration:

$$\alpha_k^{(\nu)} = \alpha_k^{(\nu-1)} - \frac{q_k^{(\nu)}}{H_{kk}^{(\nu)}}\,.$$

Ones we have estimates for the α_k parameters, we can use them to obtain estimates for the restricted and unrestricted probabilities by means of Equations F.1 and F.2. Of course, if there are missing data, the same procedure can be used in the M step of the EM algorithm.

Appendix G
The Information Matrix in Modified Path Models With Missing Data

This appendix shows how to calculate the information matrix in modified path models with missing data. When using the EM algorithm, this matrix can be used to compute the standard deviations and check the identifiability of the parameters. In Fisher's scoring algorithm, the inverse of expected information matrix is used to determine the optimal size of the adjustments of the parameters.

Suppose there is a modified path model consisting of S^* steps, where index s denotes a particular step. In its most general form, the logit model for step s is given by

$$\pi_{i_s|k_s} = \frac{\exp\left(\sum_{j_s} \beta_{j_s} x_{i_s j_s k_s}\right)}{\sum_{i_s} \exp\left(\sum_{j_s} \beta_{j_s} x_{i_s j_s k_s}\right)}.$$

Here, i_s denotes the value of the joint dependent variable; k_s is the value of the joint independent variable; and j_s is the jth parameter of modified path step s.

Let l be the index for the joint distribution of the latent variables and o the index for the joint distribution of the observed variables. This means that an observed cell count can be denoted by n_o, an expected probability in the incomplete table by π_o, and a probability in the complete table by

316

π_{lo}. In its most general form, a modified path model with latent variables can be written as

$$\pi_{lo} = \prod_s \pi_{i_s | k_s}$$

Assuming a multinomial sampling scheme, obtaining maximum likelihood estimates for parameters β_{j_s} involves maximizing

$$\log \mathcal{L} = \sum_o n_o \log \pi_o .$$

The first-order derivative with respect to β_{j_s} is

$$\frac{\partial \log \mathcal{L}}{\partial \beta_{j_s}} = \sum_o \frac{n_o}{\pi_o} \frac{\partial \pi_o}{\partial \beta_{j_s}} ,$$

and the expected value of the second-order derivative with respect to β_{j_s} and β_{h_t} equals

$$E\left(\frac{\partial^2 \log \mathcal{L}}{\partial \beta_{j_s} \partial \beta_{h_t}} \right) = -N \sum_o \frac{1}{\pi_o} \frac{\partial \pi_o}{\partial \beta_{j_s}} \frac{\partial \pi_o}{\partial \beta_{h_t}} .$$

To solve these derivatives, it is necessary to calculate

$$\frac{\partial \pi_o}{\partial \beta_{j_s}} = \frac{\partial \sum_l \pi_{lo}}{\partial \beta_{j_s}} = \sum_l \frac{\partial \pi_{lo}}{\partial \beta_{j_s}} = \sum_l \pi_{lo} \left[x_{i_s j_s k_s} - \sum_{i_s} x_{i_s j_s k_s} \pi_{i_s | k_s} \right] .$$

Except for the summation over the joint latent dimension, this expression is the same as the expression for modified path models without latent variables, which is given in Equation E.8.

Iteration ν of Fisher's scoring algorithm involves finding improved estimates of the β parameters as follows:

$$\boldsymbol{\beta}^{(\nu)} = \boldsymbol{\beta}^{(\nu-1)} + \left(\mathbf{Inf}^{(\nu)} \right)^{-1} \mathbf{q}^{(\nu)} ,$$

in which

$$\mathbf{q}^{(\nu)} = \frac{\partial \log \mathcal{L}}{\partial \boldsymbol{\beta}^{(\nu-1)}} ,$$

$$\mathbf{Inf}^{(\nu)} = -E\left(\frac{\partial^2 \log \mathcal{L}}{\partial \boldsymbol{\beta}^{(\nu-1)} \partial \boldsymbol{\beta}'^{(\nu-1)}} \right) .$$

At the last iteration ν^*, the inverse of the expected information matrix, $\left(\mathbf{Inf}^{(\nu^*)}\right)^{-1}$, contains estimates of the variances and covariances of the parameters. Moreover, if matrix $\mathbf{Inf}^{(\nu^*)}$ is positive definite, all model parameters can be identified.

There are several alternative methods for obtaining standard errors and checking identifiability of the parameters when using the EM algorithm. One method, which was first proposed by Louis (1982), involves computing the observed information from the complete information and the missing information (see also Tanner, 1993: Chapter 4). The complete information is the information obtained from the complete data likelihood, that is, the likelihood which is maximized in the M step of the EM algorithm. The missing information is the difference between the observed information and the complete information. Louis gave formulas for calculating this missing information.

Another quite simple but computationally intensive approach is the numeric approximation of the observed information matrix. Van de Pol and De Leeuw (1986) applied this method for obtaining standard errors of the parameters of latent Markov models. In the most recent version of the ℓEM program (Vermunt, 1993), this procedure is implemented to estimate the standard errors and check the identifiability of the parameters of modified path models and event history models with missing data. Numerical approximation of the second-order derivatives of the log-likelihood function involves

$$\frac{\partial^2 \log \mathcal{L}}{\partial \beta_{j_s} \partial \beta_{h_t}} = \frac{\log \mathcal{L}_{(\beta_{j_s}+\epsilon;\, \beta_{h_t}+\epsilon)} - \log \mathcal{L}_{(\beta_{j_s}+\epsilon)} - \log \mathcal{L}_{(\beta_{h_t}+\epsilon)} + \log \mathcal{L}}{\epsilon^2}.$$

Here, ϵ denotes a small number that is added to the parameter concerned, and $\log \mathcal{L}_{(\beta_{j_s}+\epsilon;\, \beta_{h_t}+\epsilon)}$, $\log \mathcal{L}_{(\beta_{j_s}+\epsilon)}$, and $\log \mathcal{L}_{(\beta_{h_t}+\epsilon)}$ denote the values of the log-likelihood function after adding ϵ to both β_{j_s} and β_{h_t}, β_{j_s}, and β_{h_t}, respectively. The matrix with elements $-\frac{\partial^2 \log \mathcal{L}}{\partial \beta_{j_s} \partial \beta_{h_t}}$ is the observed information matrix. As the expected information matrix, the observed information matrix will only be positive definite if all parameters are identified. Moreover, its inverse supplies asymptotic variances and covariances of the model parameters. It should be noted that the numerical second-order derivatives can also be used to switch from EM to Newton-Raphson after some iterations.

References

Agresti, A. (1984). *Analysis of ordinal categorical data*. New York: John Wiley.

Agresti, A. (1990). *Categorical data analysis*. New York: John Wiley.

Agresti, A. (1993). Computing conditional maximum likelihood estimates for generalized Rasch models using simple loglinear models with diagonal parameters. *Scandinavian Journal of Statistics*, 20, 63-71.

Aitkin, M., and Clayton, D. (1980). The fitting of exponential, Weibull and extreme value distributions to complex survival data using GLIM. *Applied Statistics*, 29, 156-163.

Akaike, H. (1987). Factor analysis and AIC. *Psychometrika*, 52, 317-332.

Alba, R.D. (1988). Interpreting the parameters of log-linear models. S. Long (ed.), *Common problems/proper solutions*, 258-287.

Allison, P.D. (1982). Discrete-time methods for the analysis of event histories. S. Leinhardt (ed.), *Sociological Methodology 1982*, 61-98. San Francisco: Jossey-Bass.

Allison, P.D. (1984). *Event history analysis: regression for longitudinal event data*. Beverly Hills, CA: Sage.

Allison, P.D. (1987). Estimation of linear models with missing data. C.C. Clogg (ed.), *Sociological Methodology 1987*, 17, 71-104. Washington DC: American Sociological Association.

Allison, P.D. (1990). Change scores as dependent variables in regression analysis. C. Clogg (ed.), *Sociological Methodology 1990*, 93-114.

Allison, P.D. (1994). Using panel data to estimate the effects of events. *Sociological Methods and Research*, 23, 174-199.

Andersen, E.B. (1990). *The statistical analysis of categorical data*. Berlin: Springer-Verlag.

Andersen, P.K., and Gill, R.D. (1982). Cox's regression model for counting processes: A large sample study. *Annals of Statistics*, 10, 1100-1120.

Anderson, T.W., and Goodman, L.A. (1957). Statistical inference about Markov chains. *Annals of Mathematical Statistics*, 28, 89-110.

Arminger, G. (1996). The analysis of panel data with nonmetric variables: probit models and a Heckman correction for selectivity bias. U. Engel and J. Reinecke (eds.), *Analysis of change: advanced techniques in panel data analysis*, 61-85. Berlin/New York: Walter de Gruyter.

Baker, R.J., and Nelder, J.A. (1978). *The GLIM sytem*. Oxford: NAG.

Baker, S.G. (1994). Regression analysis of grouped survival data with incomplete covariates: nonignorable missing-data and censoring mechanisms. *Biometrics*, 50, 821-826.

Baker, S.G., and Laird, N.M. (1988). Regression analysis for categorical variables with outcome subject to nonignorable nonresponse. *Journal of the American Statistical Association*, 83, 62-69.

Baker, S.G., Wax, Y., and Patterson, B.H. (1993). Regression analysis of grouped survival data: informative censoring and double sampling. *Biometrics*, 49, 379-389.

Bartholomew, D.J. (1987). *Latent variables models and factor analysis*. London: Griffin.

Bassi, F., Croon, M., Hagenaars, J., and Vermunt, J. (1995). *Estimating latent turnover tables when data are affected by classification errors*. WORC Paper 95.12.25/7, Tilburg University.

Becker, G.S. (1981). *A treatise on the family*. Cambridge, MA: Harvard University Press.

Becker, M.P. (1989). Models for the analysis of association in multivariate contingency tables. *Journal of the American Statistical Association*, 84, 1014-1019.

Becker, M.P. (1990). Algorithm AS253: Maximum likelihood estimation of the RC(M) association model. *Applied Statistics*, 39, 152-167.

Becker, M.P., and Clogg, C.C. (1989). Analysis of sets of two-way contingency tables using association models. *Journal of the American Statistical Association*, 84, 142-151.

Bergsma, W. (1997). *Modeling the joint and marginal distribution of categorical variables*. Tilburg University: PhD dissertation.

Berkson, J. (1968). Application of minimum logit χ^2 estimate to a problem of Grizzle with a notation on the problem of 'no interaction'. *Biometrics*, 24, 75-95.

Berkson, J. (1972). Minimum discrimination information, the 'no interaction' problem and the logistic function. *Biometrics*, 28, 443-468.

Bernhardt, E. (1986). Women's home attachment at first birth: The case of Sweden. *European Journal of Population*, 2, 5-29.

Bishop, R.J., Fienberg, S.E., and Holland, P.W. (1975). *Discrete multivariate analysis: Theory and practice*. Cambridge, Mass.: MIT Press.

Blair, N., Goodyear, N.N., Gibbons, L.W., and Cooper, K.H. (1984). Physical fitness and incidence of hypertension in healthy normotensive men and women. *Journal of the American Medical Association*, 252, 487-490.

Blossfeld, H., Hamerle, A., and Mayer, K.U. (1988). *Event history analysis: Statistical theory and application in economics and social sciences*. Hillsdale, N.J.: Erlbaum.

Blossfeld, H.P., and Rohwer, G. (1995). *Techniques of event history modeling*. Mahwah, New Jersey: Lawrence Erlbaum Associates, Publishers.

Breslow, N. (1972). Contribution to the discussion on paper of Cox (1972). *Journal of the Royal Statistical Society*, 34, 187-220.

Breslow, N. (1974). Covariance analysis of censored survival data. *Biometrics*, 30, 89-100.

Brown, C.C. (1975). On the use of indicator variables for studying the time dependence of parameters in a response-time model. *Biometrics*, 31, 863-972.

Bryk, A.S., and Raudenbush, S.W. (1992). *Hierarchical linear models: applications and data analysis methods*. Newbury Park, CA: Sage.

Brüderl, J., and Diekman, A. (1995). The log-logistic rate model: two generalizations with an application to demographic data. *Sociological Methods and Research*, 24, 158-186.

Butler, J.S., Anderson, K.H., and Burkhauser, R.V. (1988). Work and health after retirement: A competing risks model with semi-parametric unobserved heterogeneity. *Review of Economics and Statistics*, 71, 46-53.

Böckenholt, U. (1993). A latent class regression approach for the analysis of recurrent choice data. *British Journal of Mathematical and Statistical Psychology*, 46, 95-118.

Böckenholt, U (1996). Analyzing multi-attribute ranking data: Joint and conjoint approaches. *British Journal of Mathematical and Statistical Psychology*, 49, 57-78.

Böckenholt, U., and Langeheine, R. (1996). Latent change in recurrent choice data. *Psychometrika*, 61, 285-302.

Chamberlain, G. (1985). Heterogeneity, omitted variable bias, duration dependence. J.J. Heckman and B. Singer (eds.), *Logitudinal analysis of labor market data*. Cambridge, UK: Cambridge University Press.

Chen, T.T. (1979). Log-linear models for categorical data with misclassification and double sampling. *Journal of the American Statistical Association*, 74, 481-488.

Chen, T., and Fienberg, S.E. (1974). Two-dimensional contingency tables with both completely and partially cross-classified data. *Biometrics*, 30, 629-642.

Chiang, C.L. (1984). *The life table and its applications*. Malabar, Florida: Krieger Publ. Co..

Clayton, D. (1983). Fitting a general family of failure-time distributions using GLIM. *Applied Statistics*, 32, 102-109.

Clayton, D., and Cuzick, J. (1985). The EM algorithm for Cox's regression model using GLIM. *Applied Statistics*, 34, 148-156.

Clayton, D., and Cuzick, J. (1985). Multivariate generalizations of the proportional hazards models. *Journal of the Royal Statistical Society A*, 148, 82-117.

Clogg, C.C. (1977). *Unrestricted and restricted maximum likelihood latent structure analysis: A manual for users*. University Park: PA: Working Paper 1977, Populations Issues Research Center.

Clogg, C.C. (1979). Some latent structure models for the analysis of Likert-type data. *Social Sciences Research*, 8, 287-301.

Clogg, C.C. (1981). New developments in latent structure analysis. D.J. Jackson and E.F. Borgotta (eds.), *Factor analysis and measurement in sociological research*, 215-246. Beverly Hills, CA: Sage.

Clogg, C.C. (1982). Some models for the analysis of association in multiway cross-classifications having ordered categories. *Journal of the American Statistical Association*, 77, 803-815.

Clogg, C.C., and Eliason, S.R. (1987). Some common problems in log-linear analysis. *Sociological Methods and Research*, 16, 8-14.

Clogg, C.C., and Goodman, L.A. (1984). Latent structure analysis of a set of multidimensional contingency tables. *Journal of the American Statistical Association*, 79, 762-771.

Clogg, C.C., and Goodman, L.A. (1985). Simultaneous latent structure analysis in several groups. N.B. Tuma (ed.), *Sociological Methodology 1985*, 81-110. San Francisco: Jossey-Bass.

Clogg, C.C., and Goodman, L.A. (1986). On scaling models applied to data from several groups. *Psychometrika*, 51, 123-135.

Clogg, C.C., and Sawyer, D.O. (1981). A comparison of alternative models for analysing scalability of response patterns. S. Leinhard (ed.), *Sociological Methodology 1981*, 240-280. San Francisco: Jossey-Bass.

Clogg, C.C., and Shihadeh, E.S. (1994). *Statistical models for ordinal data*. Thousand Oaks, CA: Sage.

Coleman, J.S. (1964). *Models of change and response uncertainty*. Englewood Cliffs, NJ: Prentice Hall, Inc..

Coleman, J.S. (1981). *Longitudinal data analysis*. New York: Basic Books.

Collins, L.M., Fidler, P.F., Wugalter, S.E., and Long, L.D. (1993). Goodness-of-fit testing for latent class models. *Multivariate Behavioral Research*, 28, 375-389.

Collins, L.M., and Wugalter, S.E. (1992). Latent class models for stage-sequential dynamic latent variables. *Multivariate Behavioral Research*, 27, 131-157.

Conaway, M.R. (1989). Analysis of repeated categorical measurements with conditional likelihood measures. *Journal of the American Statistical Association*, 84, 53-62.

Conaway, M.R. (1992). The analysis of repeated categorical measurements subject to non-ignorable nonresponse. *Journal of the American Statistical Association*, 87, 817-824.

Conaway, M.R. (1993). Nonignorable nonresponse models for time-ordered categorical variables. *Applied Statistics*, 42, 105-115.

Courgeau, D., and Lelièvre, E. (1992). *Event history analysis in demography*. Oxford: Clarendon Press.

Cox, D.R. (1962). *Renewal theory*. London: Methuen.

Cox, D.R. (1972). Regression models and life tables. *Journal of the Royal Statistical Society B*, 34, 187-203.

Cox, D.R. (1975). Partial likelihood. *Biometrika*, 62, 269-276.

Cox, D.R., and Lewis, P.A.W. (1966). *The statistical analysis of events*. London: Chapman and Hall.

Cox, D.R., and Oakes, D. (1984). *Analysis of survival data*. London: Chapman and Hall.

Croon, M.A. (1989). Latent class models for the analysis of rankings. G. De Soete, H. Feger, and K.C. Klauer (eds.), *New developments in psychological choice modeling*, 99-121. Elsevier Science Publishers B.V. (North-Holland).

Croon, M. (1990). Latent class analysis with ordered latent classes. *British Journal of Mathematical and Statistical Psychology*, 43, 171-192.

Croon, M.A., and Luijkx, R. (1993). Latent structure models for ranking data. M.A. Fligner and J.S. Verducci (eds.), *Probability models and statistical analysis of ranking data*, 53-74. New York: Springer-Verlag.

Crouchley, R., and Pickles, A. (1989). An empirical comparison of conditional and marginal likelihood methods in a longitudinal study. C.C. Clogg (ed.), *Sociological Methodology 1989*, 161-181. Oxford: Basil Blackwell.

Darroch, J.N., and Ratcliff, D. (1972). Generalized iterative scaling for log-linear models. *The Annals of Mathematical Statistics*, 43, 1470-1480.

Davies, R.B. (1987). Mass point methods for dealing with nuisance parameters in longitudinal studies. R. Crouchley (ed.), *Longitudinal data analysis*, 88-109. Aldershot: Gower.

Dayton, C.M., and Macready, G.B. (1988). Concomitant-variable latent-class models. *Journal of the American Statistical Assocaition*, 83, 173-178.

Deming, W.E., and Stephan, F.F. (1940). On the least squares adjustment of a sampled frequency table when the expected marginal totals are known. *Annals of Mathematical Statistics*, 11, 427-444.

Dempster, A.P., Laird, N.M., and Rubin, D.B. (1977). Maximum likelihood estimation from incomplete data via the EM algorithm (with discussion). *Journal of the Royal Statistical Society, Ser. B.*, 39, 1-38.

Diggle, P.J., Liang, K.Y., and Zeger, S.L. (1994). *Analysis of longitudinal data*. Oxford: Clarendon Press.

Elandt-Johnson, R.C., and Johnson, N.L. (1980). *Survival models and data analysis*. New York: John Wiley.

Elbers, C., and Ridder, G. (1982). True and spurious duration dependence: The identifiability of the proportional hazard model. *Review of Economic Studies*, 49, 403-409.

Eliason, S.R. (1995). Modeling manifest and latent dimensions of association in two-way cross-classifications. *Sociological Methods and Research*, 24, 30-67.

Everitt, B.S. (1980). *Cluster analysis*. London: Heinemann.

Everitt, B.S. (1988). A monte carlo investigation of the likelihood ratio test for number of classes in latent class analysis. *Multivariate Behavioral Research*, 23, 531-538.

Everitt, B.S., and Hand, D.J. (1981). *Finite mixture distributions*. London: Chapman and Hall.

Evers, M., and Namboodiri, N.K. (1978). On the design matrix strategy in the analysis of categorical data. K.F. Schuessler (ed.), *Sociological Methodology 1979*, 86-111. San Fransisco: Jossey Bass.

Farewell, V.T. (1982). The use of mixture models for the analysis of survival data with long-term survivors. *Biometrics*, 38, 1041-1046.

Fay, R.E. (1986). Causal models for patterns of nonresponse. *Journal of the American Statistical Association*, 81, 354-365.

Fay, R.E. (1989). Estimating nonignorable nonresponse in longitudinal surveys through causal modeling. D. Kasprzyk, G.J. Duncan, G. Kalton and M.P. Singh (eds.), *Panel Surveys*, 375-399. New York: John Wiley.

Fay, R.E., and Goodman, L.A. (1975). *ECTA program: Description for users*. Chicago: Department of Statistics, University of Chicago.

Featherman, D.L., and Hauser, R.M. (1975). Design for a replicate study of social mobility in the United States. K. Land and S.Spilerman (eds.), *Social indicator models*, 219-251.

Fienberg, S.E. (1970). An iterative procedure for estimating contingency tables. *Annals of Mathematical Statistics*, 41, 907-917.

Fienberg, S.E. (1972). The analysis of incomplete multi-way contingency tables. *Biometrics*, 28, 177-202.

Fienberg, S.E. (1980). *The analysis of cross-classified categorical data*. Cambridge, MA: MIT Press.

Fleiss, J.L. (1981). *Statistical models for rates and proportions*. New York: John Wiley.

Flinn, C.J., and Heckman, J.J. (1982). New methods for analysing individual event histories. S. Leinhardt (ed.), *Sociological Methodology 1982*, 99-140.

Follman, D.A., and Lambert, D. (1989). Generalizing logistic regression by nonparametric mixing. *Journal of the American Statitical Association*, 84, 295-300.

Formann, A.K. (1982). Linear logistic latent class analysis. *Biometrical Journal*, 24, 171-190.

Formann, A.K. (1992). Linear logistic latent class analysis for polytomous data. *Journal of the American Statistical Association*, 87, 476-486.

Freedman, D., Camburn, A., Thornton, D., Alwin, D., and Young-Marco, L. (1988). The life history calendar: a technique for collecting retrospective data. C.C. Clogg (ed.), *Sociological Methodology 1988*, 37-68. Washington, DC: American Sociological Association.

Fuchs, C. (1982). Maximum likelihood estimation and model selection in contingency tables with missing data. *Journal of the American Statistical Association*, 77, 270-278.

Gilula, Z., and Haberman, S.J. (1988). The analysis of contingency tables by restricted canonical and restricted association models. *Journal of the American Statistical Association*, 83, 760-771.

Gilula, Z., and Haberman, S.J. (1994). Conditional log-linear models for analyzing panel data. *Journal of the American Statistical Association*, 89, 645-656.

Goldstein, H. (1987). *Multilevel models in educational and social research*. London: Charles Griffin & Compagny Ltd..

Gong, G., Whittemore, A.S., and Grosser, S. (1990). Censored survival data with misclassified covariates: a case study of breast-cancer mortality. *Journal of the American Statistiical Association*, 85, 20-28.

Goodman, L.A. (1961). Statistical methods for the mover-stayer model. *Journal of the American Statistical Association*, 56, 841-868.

Goodman, L.A. (1972). A modified multiple regression approach for the analysis of dichotomous variables. *American Sociological Review*, 37, 28-46.

Goodman, L.A. (1973). The analysis of multidimensional contingency tables when some variables are posterior to others: A modified path analysis approach. *Biometrika*, 60, 179-192.

Goodman, L.A. (1974a). The analysis of systems of qualitative variables when some of the variables are unobservable: Part I - A modified latent structure approach. *American Journal of Sociology*, 79, 1179-1259.

Goodman, L.A. (1974b). Exploratory latent structure analysis using both indentifiable and unidentifiable models. *Biometrika*, 61, 215-231.

Goodman, L.A. (1978). *Analysing qualitative/categorical variables: Loglinear models and latent structure analysis*. Cambridge: Abt.

Goodman, L.A. (1979). Simple models for the analysis of association in cross-classifications having ordered categories. *Journal of the American Statistical Association*, 74, 537-552.

Goodman, L.A. (1984). *The analysis of cross-classified data having ordered categories*. Cambridge, MA: Harvard University Press.

Goodman, L.A. (1986). Some useful extensions of the usual correspondence analysis approach and the usual log-linear approach in the analysis of contingency tables. *International Statistical Review*, 54, 243-309.

Goodman, L.A. (1991). Measures, models, and graphical displays in the analysis of cross-classified data. *Journal of the American Statistical Association*, 86, 1085-1111.

Grizzle, J.E., Starmer, C.F., and Koch, G.G. (1969). Analysis of categorical data by linear models. *Biometrics*, 25, 489-504.

Guo, G. (1993). Event-history analysis for left-truncated data. P.V. Marsden (ed.), *Sociological Methodology 1993*, 217-243. Oxford: Basil Blackwell.

Guo, G., and Rodriguez, G. (1994). Estimating a multivariate proportional hazards model for clustered data using the EM algorithm, with an application to child survival in Guatemala. *Journal of the American Statistical Association*, 87, 969-976.

Haber, M., and Brown, M.B. (1986). Maximum likelihood methods for log-linear models when expected frequencies are subject to linear contraints. *Journal of the American Statistical Association*, 81, 477-482.

Haberman, S.J. (1974). *The analysis of frequency data*. Chicago: University of Chicago Press.

Haberman, S.J. (1977). Log-linear models and frequency tables with small expected cell counts. *Annals of Statistics*, 5, 1148-1169.

Haberman, S.J. (1978). *Analysis of qualitative data, Vol. 1, Introduction topics*. New York, San Francisco, London: Academic Press.

Haberman, S.J. (1979). *Analysis of qualitative data, Vol 2, New developments*. New York: Academic Press.

Haberman, S.J. (1988). A stabilized Newton-Raphson algorithm for log-linear models for frequency tables derived by indirect observations. C.Clogg (ed.), *Sociological Methodology 1988*, 193-211. San Francisco: Jossey-Bass.

Haberman, S.J. (1995). Computation of maximum likelihood estimates in association models. *Journal of the American Statistical Association*, 90, 1438-1446.

Hachen, D.S. (1988). The competing risk model: a method for analysing processes with multiple types of events. *Sociological Methods and Research*, 17, 21-54.

Hagenaars, J.A. (1985). *Loglineaire analyse van herhaalde surveys: panel-, trend- en co-hortonderzoek, proefschrift, Tilburg*. Unpublished doctoral dissertation. Tilburg, The Netherlands.

Hagenaars, J.A. (1986). Symmetry, quasi-symmetry and marginal homogeneity on the latent level. *Social Science Research*, 15, 241-255.

Hagenaars, J.A. (1988). Latent structure models with direct effects between indicators: local dependence models. *Sociological Methods and Research*, 16, 379-405.

Hagenaars, J.A. (1990). *Categorical longitudinal data - loglinear analysis of panel, trend and cohort data.*. Newbury Park: Sage.

Hagenaars, J.A. (1992). Exemplifying longitudinal loglinear analysis with latent variables. P.G.M. Van der Heijden, W. Jansen, B. Francis and G.U.H. Seeber (eds.), *Statistical modelling*, 105-120. Amsterdam: Elsevier Science Publishers B.V..

Hagenaars, J.A. (1993). *Loglinear models with latent variables*. Newbury Park: CA: Sage.

Hagenaars, J., and Luijkx, R. (1990). *LCAG: A program to estimate latent class models and other loglinear models with latent variables with and without missing data*. Tilburg: Working Paper #17, Tilburg University, Dept. of Sociology.

Hamerle, A. (1989). Multiple-spell regression models for duration data. *Applied Statistics*, 38, 127-138.

Hamerle, A. (1991). On the treatment of interrupted spells and initial conditions in event history analysis. *Sociological Methods and Research*, 19, 388-414.

Hanushek, E.A., and Jackson, J.E. (1977). *Statistical methods for social scientists*. New York: Academic Press.

Heckman, J.J. (1979). Sample selection bias as a specification error. *Econometrica*, 47, 153-161.

Heckman, J.J., and Honore, B.E. (1989). The identifiability of the competing risks models. *Biometrika*, 76, 325-330.

Heckman, J.J., and Singer, B. (1982). Population heterogeneity in demographic models. K. Land and A. Rogers (eds.), *Multidimensional mathematical demography*. New York: Academic Press.

Heckman, J.J., and Singer, B. (1982). The identification problem in econometric model for duration data. W. Hildebrand (ed.), *Advances in econometrics*, 39-77. Cambridge, UK: Cambridge University Press.

Heckman, J.J., and Singer, B. (1984). The identifiability of the proportional hazard model. *Review of Economic Studies*, 51, 231-241.

Heckman, J.J., and Singer, B. (1985). Social sciences duration analysis. J.J. Heckman and B. Singer (eds.), *Longitudinal analysis of labour market data*, 39-110. Cambridge, UK: Cambridge University Press.

Heckman, J.J., and Singer, B. (1986). Econometric analysis of longitudinal data. Z. Griliches and M.D. Intriligator (eds.), *Handbook of Econometrics, Vol. 3*, 1689-1763. Amsterdam: North-Holland.

Heckman, J.J., and Willis, R. (1977). A beta-logistic model for the analysis of sequential labour force participation of married woman. *Journal of Political Economy*, 85, 27-58.

Heinen, A. (1993). *Discrete latent variables models*. Tilburg, The Netherlands: Tilburg University Press.

Heinen, T. (1996). *Latent class and discrete latent trait models: similarities and differences*. Thousand Oakes: Sage Publications.

Heinen, A., and Vermaseren, P. (1992). *Diltran user's guide*. Tilburg University, The Netherlands, Department of Social Sciences.

Hill, D.H., Axinn, W.G., and Thornton, A. (1993). Competing hazards with shared unmeasured risk factors. P.V. Marsden (ed.), *Sociological Methodology 1993*, 245-277. Oxford: Basil Blackwell.

Hocking, R.R., and Oxspring, H.H. (1971). Maximum likelihood estimation with incomplete multinomial data. *Journal of the American Statistical Association*, 66, 65-70.

Hocking, R.R., and Oxspring, H.H. (1974). The analysis of partially categorized contingency data. *Biometrics*, 30, 469-483.

Hoem, J.M., and Jensen, U.F. (1982). Multistate life table methodology: A probabilitic critique. K. Land and A. Rogers (eds.), *Multidimensional mathematical demography*, 155-177. New York: Academic Press.

Holford, T.R. (1976). Life tables with concomitant variables. *Boimetrics*, 32, 387-387.

Holford, T.R. (1980). The analysis of rates and survivorship using log-linear models. *Biometrics*, 32, 299-306.

Hougaard, P. (1984). Life table methods for heterogeneous populations: distributions describing heterogeneity. *Biometrika*, 71, 75-83.

Jensen, S.T., Johansen, S., and Lauritzen, S.L. (1991). Globally convergent algorithms for maxizing a likelihood function. *Biometrika*, 78, 867-877.

Jöreskog, K.G. (1971). Statistical analysis of sets of congeneric tests. *Psychometrika*, 36, 109-133.

Jöreskog, K.G. (1971). Simultaneous factor analysis in several populations. *Psychometrica*, 36, 409-426.

Jöreskog, K.G., and Goldberger, A.S. (1975). Estimation of a model with multiple indicators and multiple causes of a single latent variables. *Journal of the American Statistical Association*, 10, 631-639.

Jöreskog, K.G., and Sörbom, D. (1988). *Lisrel 7: A guide to the programm and applications*.

Kalbfleisch, J.D., and Prentice, R.L. (1980). *The statistical analysis of failure time data*. New York: John Wiley.

Kamakura, W.A., Wedel, M., and Agrawal, J. (1992). *Concomitant variable latent class models for the external analysis of choice data*. University of Groningen, The Netherlands: Research Memorandum nr 486, Institute of Economic Research.

Kaplan, E.L., and Meier, P. (1958). Nonparametric estimation from incomplete observations. *Journal of the American Statistical Association*, 53, 457-481.

Kelderman, H. (1984). Log-linear Rasch model tests. *Psychometrika*, 49, 223-245.

Klein, J.P. (1992). Semiparametric estimation of random effects using the Cox model based on the EM algorithm. *Boimetrics*, 48, 795-806.

Koehler, K.J. (1986). Goodness-of-fit statistics for log-linear models in sparse contingency tables. *Journal of the American Statistical Association*, 81, 483-493.

Koehler, K.J., and Larntz, K. (1980). An empirical investigation of goodness-of-fit statistics for sparse multinomials. *Journal of the American Statistical Association*, 75, 336-344.

Kortram, R.A., Van Rooij, A.C.M., Lenstra, A.J., and Ridder, G. (1995). Constructive identification of the mixed proportional hazards model. *Statistica Neerlandica*, 49, 269-281.

Kuk, A.Y.C., and Chen, C.H. (1992). A mixture model combining logistic regression with proportional hazards regression. *Biometrika*, 79, 531-541.

Lagakos, S.W. (1979). General right censoring and its impact on the analysis of survival data. *Biometrics*, 35, 139-156.

Laird, N. (1978). Nonparametric maximum likelihood estimation of a mixture distribution. *Journal of the American Statistial Association*, 73, 805-811.

Laird, N., and Oliver, D. (1981). Covariance analysis of censored survival data using log-linear analysis techniques. *Journal of the American Statistical Association*, 76, 231-240.

Lancaster, T. (1979). Econometric methods for the duration of unemployment. *Econometrica*, 47, 939-956.

Lancaster, T. (1990). *The economic analysis of transition data*. Cambridge, UK: Cambridge University Press.

Land, C.K., McCall, P.L., and Nagin, D.S. (1996). A comparison of Poisson, negative binomial, and semiparametric mixed Poisson regression models. *Sociological Methods and Research*, 24, 387-442.

Lang, J.B., and Agresti, A. (1994). Simultaneously modeling joint and marginal distributions of multivariate categorical responses. *Journal of the American Statistical Association*, 89, 625-632.

Langeheine, R., Pannekoek, J., and Van de Pol, F. (1996). Bootstrapping goodness-of-fit measures in categorical data analysis. *Sociological Methods and Research*, 24, 492-516.

Langeheine, R., and Van de Pol, F. (1990). A unifying framework for Markov modeling in discrete space and discrete time. *Sociological Methods and Research*, 18, 416-441.

Langeheine, R., and Van de Pol, F. (1994). Discrete-time mixed Markov latent class models. A. Dale and R.B. Davies (eds.), *Analyzing social and political change: A casebook of methods*, 171-197.

Larson, M.G. (1984). Covariate analysis of competing-risk data with log-linear models. *Biometrics*, 40, 459-469.

Lawless, J.F. (1982). *Statistical models and methods for lifetime data*. New York: John Wiley.

Lazarsfeld, P.F. (1950a). The logical and mathematical foundation of latent structure analysis. S.A. Stouffer et al. (eds.), *Measurement and Prediction*, 362-412. Princeton, NJ: Princeton University Press.

Lazarsfeld, P.F. (1950b). The interpretation and mathematical foundation of latent structure analysis. S.A. Stoufer et al. (eds.), *Measurement and Prediction*, 413-472. Princeton, NJ: Princeton University Press.

Lazarsfeld, P.F., and Henry, N.W. (1968). *Latent structure analysis*. Boston: Houghton Mifflin.

Lesthaege, R., and Meekers, D. (1986). Value changes and the dimensions of familism. *European Journal of Population*, 2, 225-268.

Liang, K.Y., and Zeger, S.L. (1986). Longitudinal data analysis using generalized linear models. *Biometrika*, 73, 673-687.

Lindsay, B., Clogg, C.C., and Grego, J. (1991). Semiparametric estimation in the Rasch model and related models, including a simple latent class model for item analysis. *Journal of the American Statistical Association*, 86, 96-107.

Lipsitz, S., Laird, N., and Harrington, D. (1991). Generalized estimating equations for correlated binary data: Using odds ratios as a measure of association. *Biometrika*, 78, 153-160.

Little, R.J.A. (1982). Models for nonresponse in sample surveys. *Journal of the American Statistical Association*, 77, 237-250.

Little, R.J. (1985). Nonresponse adjustment in longitudinal surveys: models for categorical data. *Bulletin of the International Statistical Association*, 15, 1-15.

Little, R.J., and Rubin, D.B. (1987). *Statistical analysis with missing data*. New York: Wiley.

Long, J.S. (1984). Estimable functions in loglinear models. *Sociological Methods and Research*, 12, 399-432.

Louis, T.A. (1982). Finding the observed information matrix when using the EM algorithm. *Journal of the Royal Statistical Society, series B*, 51, 127-138.

Luijkx, R. (1994). *Comparative loglinear analyses of social mobility and heterogamy*. Tilburg, The Netherlands: Tilburg University Press.

Magidson, J. (1981). Qualitative variance, entropy, and correlation ratios for nominal dependent variables. *Social Science Research*, 10, 177-194.

Manting, D. (1994). *Dynamics in marriage and cohabitation: an inter-temporal, life course analysis of firtst union formation and dissolution*. Amsterdam: Thesis Publishers.

Manton, K.G., and Stallard, E. (1987). *Chronic desease modelling*. London: Charles Griffin.

Manton, K.G., Stallard, E., and Vaupel, J.W. (1986). Alternative models for the heterogoneity of mortality risks among the aged. *Journal of the American Statistical Association*, 81, 635-644.

Manton, K.G., and Woodbury, M.A. (1985). A continuous-time multivariate Gaussian stochastic model of change in discrete and continuous variables. N.B. Tuma (ed.), *Sociological Methodology 1985*, 277-315. San Francisco: Jossey-Bass.

Manton, K.G., Woodbury, M.A., and Stallard, E. (1988). Models of the interaction of mortality and the evoluton of risk factor distribution: a general stochastic process approach. T. Colton, L.S. Freedman, A.L. Johnson, and D.Machin (eds.), *Statistics in medicine (vol. 7)*. Chichester: Wiley.

Mare, R.D. (1994). Discrete-time bivariate hazards with unobserved heterogeneity: A partially observed contingency table approach. P.V. Marsden (ed.), *Sociological Methodology 1994*, 341-385. Oxford: Basil Blackwell.

Mare, R.D., and Winship, C. (1991). Loglinear models for reciprocal and other simultaneous effects. C.C. Clogg (ed.), *Sociological Methodology 1991*, 199-234. Oxford: Basil Blackwell.

Marini, M., Olsen, A., and Rubin, D. (1979). Maximum-likelihood estimation in panel studies with missing data. K. Schuessler (ed.), *Sociological Methodoly 1980*, 314-357. San Fransisco: Jossey Bass.

Marini, M.M., and Singer, B. (1988). Causality in social sciences. C.C. Clogg (ed.), *Sociological Methodology 1988*, 18, 347-409. San Francisco: Jossey-Bass.

Markus, G.B. (1979). *Analyzing panel data*. Beverly Hills, CA: Sage.

Mason, W.M., and Fienberg, S.E. (1985). *Cohort analysis in social research: beyond the identification problem*. New York: Springer Verslag.

McCullagh, P., and Nelder, J.A. (1983). *Generalized linear models*. London: Chapman & Hall, second edition 1989.

McCutcheon, A.L. (1988). Sexual morality, pro-life values and attitudes toward abortion. *Sociological Methods and Research*, 16, 256-275.

McFadden, D. (1974). Conditional logit analysis of qualitative choice behavior. P. Zarembka (ed.), *Frontiers in Econometrics*, 105-142. New York: Academic Press.

McFadden, D. (1981). Econometric models of probabilistic choice. C. Manski and D. McFadden (eds.), *Structural analysis of discrete data: with econometric applications*, 198-272. Cambridge: MIT Press.

Mellenbergh, G.J. (1994). A unidimensional latent trait model for continuous item responses. *Multivariate Behavioral Research*, 29, 223-236.

Mellenbergh, G.J., and Vijn, P. (1981). The Rasch model as a log-linear. *Applied Psychological Measurement*, 5, 369-376.

Meng, X.L., and Rubin, D.B. (1993). Maximum likelihood estimation via the ECM algorithm: A general framework. *Biometrika*, 80, 267-278.

Mooijaart, A., and Van der Heijden, P.G.M. (1992). The EM algorithm for latent class models with constraints. *Psychometrica*, 57, 261-271.

Moon, C.G. (1991). A grouped data semiparametric competing risks model with nonparametric unobserved heteogeneity and mover-stayer structure. *Economics Letters*, 37, 279-285.

Mulder, C.H. (1993). *Migration dynamics: a life course approach*. Amsterdam: Thesis Publishers.

Muthén, B. (1984). A general structural equation model with dichotomous, ordered categorical and continuous latent variable indicators. *Psychometrika*, 49, 115-132.

Muthén, B., Kaplan, D., and Hollis, M. (1987). On structural equation modeling with data that are not missing completely at random. *Psychometrika*, 52, 431-462.

Myers, M.H., Hankey, B.F., and Mantel, N. (1973). A logistic-exponential model for use with response-time data involving regressor variables. *Biometrics*, 29, 257-269.

Namboodiri, K., and Suchindran, C.M. (1987). *Life table techniques and their applications*. New York: Academic Press.

Nelder, J.A., and Wedderburn, R.W.M. (1972). Generalized linear models. *Journal of the Royal Statistical Society A*, 135, 370-384.

Newman, J.L., and McCulloch, C.E. (1984). A hazard rate approach to timing of births. *Econometrica*, 52, 939-961.

NIDI (1989). *Relatievorming in Nederland: Resultaten van een surveyonderzoek*. Den Haag, The Netherlands: NIDI.

Nielsen, G.G., Gill, R.D., Andersen, P.K., and Sorensen, T.I.A. (1992). A counting process approach to maximum likelihood estimation in frailty models. *Scandinavian Journal of Statistics*, 19, 25-43.

Nordheim, E.V. (1984). Inference from nonrandomly missing categorical data: an example from a genetic study on Turner's syndrome. *Journal of the American Statistical Association*, 79, 772-780.

Olivier, D.C., and Neff, R.K. (1976). *LOGLIN 1.0 User's guide*. Harvard, MA: Harvard School of Public Health.

Petersen, T. (1986). Estimating fully parametric hazard rate models with time dependent covariates: use of maximum likelihood. *Sociological Methods and Research*, 14, 219-246.

Petersen, T. (1991). Time-aggregation bias in continuous-time hazard-rate models. P.V. Marsden (ed.), *Sociological Methodology 1991*, 263-290. Washington, DC: American Sociological Association.

Petersen, T. (1995). Models for interdependent event-history data: specification and estimation. P.V. Marsden (ed.), *Sociological Methodology 1995*, 317-375. Oxford: Basil Blackwell.

Petersen, J.H., Andersen, P.K., and Gill, R.D. (1996). Variance components models for survival data. *Statistica Neerlandica*, 50, 193-211.

Peto, R. (1972). Contribution to the discussion of paper by D.R. Cox. *Journal of the Royal Statistical Society*, 34, 205-207.

Poulsen, C.A. (1982). *Latent structure analysis with choice modelling*. Aarhus, Denmark: Aarhus School of Business Administratioon and Economics.

Prentice, R.L., and Kalbfleisch, J.D. (1979). Hazard rate model with covariates. *Biometrics*, 35, 25-39.

Press, W.H., Flannery, B.P., Teukolsky, S.A., and Vetterling, W.T. (1986). *Numerical recipes: The art of scientific computing*. Cambridge: Cambridge University Press.

Raftery, A.E. (1986). Choosing models for cross-classifications. *American Sociological Review*, 51, 145-146.

Raftery, A.E. (1993). Bayesian model selection in structural equation models. K.A. Bollen and J.S. Long (eds.), *Testing structural equation models*, 163-180. Newbury Park: CA: Sage.

Rai, S.N., and Matthews, D.E. (1993). Improving the EM algorithm. *Biometrics*, 49, 587-591.

Read, T.R.C., and Cressie, N.A.C. (1988). *Goodness-of-fit-statistics for discrete multivariate data*. New York: Springer.

Ridder, G. (1984). The distribution of single spell data duration data. G.R. Neumann and N.C. Westergard-Nielsen (eds.), *Studies in labour market dynamics*, 45-73. New York: Springer.

Ridder, G., and Verbakel, W. (1983). *On the estimation of the proportional hazard model in the presence of unobserved heterogeneity*. Faculty of Actuarial Science and Econometrics: Report AE 22/83, University of Amsterdam, The Netherlands.

Rindskopf, D. (1990). Nonstandard loglinear models. *Psychological Bulletin*, 108, 150-162.

Rohwer, G. (1993). *TDA Working Papers*.

Rost, J. (1985). A latent class model for rating data. *Psychometrika*, 50, 37-49.

Rost, J. (1990). Rasch models in latent classes: an integration of two approaches to item analysis. *Journal of Applied Psychological Measurement*, 14, 271-282.

Rubin, D.B. (1976). Inference and missing data. *Biometrika*, 63, 581-592.

Santner, T.J., and Duffy, D.E. (1989). *The statistical analysis of discrete data*. New York: Springer.

Schluchter, M.D., and Jackson, K.L. (1989). Log-linear analysis of censored survival data with partially observed covariates. *Journal of the American Statistical Association*, 84, 42-52.

Schwarz, G. (1978). Estimating the dimensions of a model. *Annals of Statistics*, 6, 461-464.

Sörbom, D. (1974). A general method for studying differences in factor means and factor structures between groups. *British Journal of Mathematical and Statistical Psychology*, 27, 229-239.

Sörbom, D. (1975). Detection of correlated errors in longitudinal data. *British Journal of Mathematical and Statistical Psychology*, 28, 138-151.

Tanner, M.A. (1993). *Tools for statistical inference: Methods for the exploration of posterior distributions and likelihood functions*. New York: Springer.

Thompson, W.A. (1977). On the treatment of grouped observations in life studies. *Biometrics*, 33, 463-470.

Titterington, D.M., Smith, A.F., and Makov, U.E. (1985). *Statistical analysis of finite mixture dsitributions*. Chichester, UK: John Wiley.

Trussell, J., and Hammerslough, C. (1983). A hazard-model analysis of the covariates of infant and child mortality in Sri Lanka. *Demography*, 20, 1-26.

Trussell, J., and Richards, T. (1985). Correcting for unobserved heterogeneity in hazard models using the Heckman-Singer procedure. N. Tuma (ed.), *Sociological Methodology 1985*, 242-276. San Francisco: Jossey-Bass.

Tsiatis, A.A. (1981). A large sample study of Cox's regression model. *Annals of Statistics*, 9, 93-108.

Tuma, N.B. (1979). *Invoking RATE*. Menlo Park, CA: SRI International.

Tuma, N.B. (1985). Effects of labor market structure on job shift patterns. J.J. Heckman and B. Singer (eds.), *Longitudinal analysis of labor market data*, 327-363.

Tuma, N.B., and Hannan, M.T. (1984). *Social dynamics: models and methods*. New York: Academic Press.

Tutz, G. (1995). Competing risks models in discrete time with nominal or ordinal categories of response. *Quality and Quantity*, 29, 405-420.

Van de Geer, J.P. (1993). *Multivariate analysis of categorical data: theory/applications*. Thousand Oaks: Sage.

Van de Pol, F., and De Leeuw, J. (1986). A latent Markov model to correct for measurement error. *Sociological Methods and Research*, 15, 118-141.

Van de Pol, F., and Langeheine, R. (1990). Mixed Markov latent class models. C.C. Clogg (ed.), *Sociological Methodology 1990*. Oxford: Basil Blackwell.

Van de Pol, F., Langeheine, R., and De Jong, W. (1989). *PANMARK user manual: PAnel analysis using MARKov chains*. Voorburg: Netherlands Central Bureau of Statistics.

Van der Heijden, P.G.M., and Dessens, J. (1994). *Incorporating continuous explanatory variables in latent class analysis*. Utrecht: Methods Series MS-94-5, Utrecht University.

Van der Heijden, P.G.M., De Falguerolles, A., and De Leeuw, J. (1989). A combined approach to contingency table analysis using correspondence analysis and log-linear analysis. *Applied Statistics*, 38, 249-292.

Van der Heijden, P.G.M., Mooijaart, A., and De Leeuw, J. (1992). Constraint latent budget analysis. *Sociological Methodology 1992*.

Van Rees, K., and Vermunt, J.K. (1996). Event history analysis of authors' reputation: effects of critics' attention on debutants' careers. *Poetics*, 23, 317-333.

Vaupel, J.W., Manton, K.G., and Stallard, E. (1979). The impact of heterogeneity in individual frailty on the dynamics of mortality. *Demography*, 16, 439-454.

Vaupel, J.W., and Yashin, A.I. (1985). The deviant dynamics of death in heterogeneous populations. N.B. Tuma (ed.), *Sociological Methodology 1985*, 179-211. San Francisco: Jossey Bass.

Vermunt, J.K. (1988). *Loglineaire modellen met latente variabelen en missing data*. Tilburg, The Netherlands: Doctoraalscriptie.

Vermunt, J.K. (1991a). Een multivariaat model voor de geboorte van het eerste kind. *Maandstatistiek van de Bevolking 91/5*, 22-33. Voorburg: CBS.

Vermunt, J.K. (1991b). Leefstijl en demografisch gedrag: Een toepassing van latente-klasse-analyse. *Maandstatistiek van de Bevolking 91/11*, 13-25. Voorburg: CBS.

Vermunt, J.K. (1993). *LEM: log-linear and event history analysis with missing data using the EM algorithm*. WORC PAPER 93.09.015/7, Tilburg University, Tilburg, The Netherlands.

Vermunt, J.K. (1994). *Causal log-linear modeling with missing data*. WORC PAPER 94.05.021/7, Tilburg University.

Vermunt, J.K. (1996). *Log-linear event history analysis: a general approach with missing data, unobserved heterogeneity, and latent variables*. Tilburg, The Netherlands: Tilburg University Press.

Vermunt, J.K. (1996). Causal log-linear modeling with latent variables and missing data. U.Engel and J. Reinecke (eds.), *Analisis of change: advanced techniques in panel data analysis*, 35-60. Berlin/New York: Walter de Gruyter.

Vermunt, J.K., and Georg, W. (1995). Die Analyse kategorialer Panel-Daten mit Hilfe von log-linearen Kausalmodellen mit latenten Variablen: Eine Anwendung am Beispiel der Skala 'Jugendzen. *ZA-Information*, 36, 61-90.

Vermunt, J.K., and Georg, W. (1995). *Analyzing categorical panel data by means of causal log-linear models with latent variables: An application to the change in yougth-centrism*. WORC Paper 95.06.012/7.

Vermunt, J.K., Langeheine, R., and Böckenholt, U. (1995). *Discrete-time discrete-state latent Markov models with time-constant and time-varying covariates*. WORC Paper 95.06.013/7, Tilburg University, The Netherlands.

Vossen, A.P. (1989). Naar een referentiekader voor vruchtbaarheidsscenario's: De introductie van het concept leefstijl. *Bevolking en Gezin*, 135-156.

Wedel, M., and DeSarbo, W.S (1994). A review of recent developments in latent class regression models. R.P. Bagozzi (ed.), *Advanced methods of Marketing Research*, 352-388.

Wedel, M., and DeSarbo, W.S. (1995). A mixture likelihood approach for generalized linear model. *Journal of Classification*, 12, 21-55.

Wedel, M., DeSarbo, W.S., Bult, J.R., and Ramaswamy, V. (1993). A latent class Poisson regression model for heterogeneous count data with an application to direct mail. *Journal of Applied Econometrics*, 8, 397-411.

Wedel, M., Kamakura, W.A., DeSarbo, W.S., and Ter Hofstede, F. (1995). Implications of asymmetry, nonproportionality, and heterogeneity in brand switching from piece-wise exponential mixture hazard models. *Journal of Marketing Research*, 32, 457-462.

Wermuth, N., and Lauritzen, S.L. (1983). Graphical and recursive models for contingency tables. *Biometrika*, 70, 537-552.

Wermuth, N., and Lauritzen, S.L. (1990). On substantive research hyphotheses, conditional independence graphs and graphical chain models. *Journal of the Royal Statistical Association B*, 52, 21-50.

Whitehead, J. (1980). Fitting Cox's regression model to survival data using GLIM. *Applied Statistics*, 29, 268-275.

Whittaker, J. (1990). *Graphical models in applied multivariate statistics*. Chichester, UK: John Wiley.

Wiggins, L.M. (1955). *Mathematical models for the interpretation of attitude and behavior change: The analysis of multi-wave panels*. unpublished PhD dissertation, New York: Columbia University.

Wiggins, L.M. (1973). *Panel analysis*. Amsterdam: Elsevier.

Willekens, F.J. (1990). *Life course analysis: Stochastic process models*.

Willekens, F.J. (1991). Understanding the interdependence between parallel careers. J.J. Siegers, J. De Jong-Gierveld and E. Van Imhoff (eds.), *Female labour market behavior and fertility, a rational choice approach*, 2-31.

Willekens, F. (1994). *Binary data analysis for social scientists*. DRAFT. Groningen: Population Research Centre, University of Groningen.

Willekens, F., and Shah, M.R. (1983). *A note on log-linear modelling of rates and proportions*. Voorburg: Working paper no. 36, NIDI.

Winship, C. (1986). Heterogeneity and interdependence: a test using survival models. N.B. Tuma (ed.), *Sociological Methodology 1986*, 250-282. Washington, DC.: American Sociological Association.

Winship, C., and Mare, R.D. (1989). Loglinear models with missing data: A latent class approach. C.C. Clogg (ed.), *Sociological Methodology 1989*, 331-367. San Francisco: Jossey-Bass.

Wong, R.S.K. (1995). Extensions in the use of log-multiplicative scaled association models in multiway contingency tables. *Sociological Methods and Research*, 23, 507-538.

Wrigley, N. (1990). Unobserved heterogeneity and the analysis of longitudinal spatial choice data. *European Journal of Population*, 6, 327-358.

Wu, C.F.J. (1983). On the convergence properties of the EM algorithm. *Annals of Statistics*, 11, 95-103.

Xie, Yu (1992). The log-multiplicative layer effects model for comparing mobility tables. *American Sociological Review*, 57, 380-395.

Xie, Yu (1994). Log-multiplicative models for discrete-time, discrete-covariate event history data. P.V. Marsden (ed.), *Sociological Methodology 1994*, 301-340. Oxford: Basil Blackwell.

Yamaguchi, K. (1986). Alternative approaches to unobserved heterogeneity in the analysis of repeatable events. N.B. Tuma (ed.), *Sociological Methodology 1986*, 213-249. Washington, DC.: American Sociological Association.

Yamaguchi, K. (1990). Logit and multinomial logit models for discrete-time event-history analysis: a causal analysis of interdependent discrete-state processes. *Quality and Quantity*, 24, 323-341.

Yamaguchi, K. (1991). Event history analysis. *Applied Social Research Methods, Volume 28*. Newbury Park, CA: Sage.

Yamaguchi, K. (1992). Accelerated failure-time regression models with a regression model of surviving fraction: An application to "permanent employment" in Japan. *Journal of the American Statistical Association*, 87, 284-292.

Yamaguchi, K., and Ferguson, L.R. (1995). The stopping and spacing of childbirths and their birth-history predictors: Rational-choice theory and event history analysis. *American Sociological Review*, 60, 272-298.

Yang, M., and Goldstein, H. (1996). Multilevel models for longitudinal data. U. Engel and J. Reinecke (eds.), *Analysis of change: advanced techniques in panel data analysis*, 191-220. Berlin/New York: Walter de Gruyter.

Yashin, A.I., Manton, K.G., and Stallard, E. (1986). Dependent competing risks: A stochastic process model. *Journal of Mathematical Biology*, 24, 119-140.

Author Index

Subject Index

About the Author

Jeroen K. Vermunt is Assistant Professor in the Methodology Department of the Faculty of Social Sciences and Research, and Research Associate at the Work and Organization Research Center at Tilburg University in The Netherlands.